W9-CAZ-266

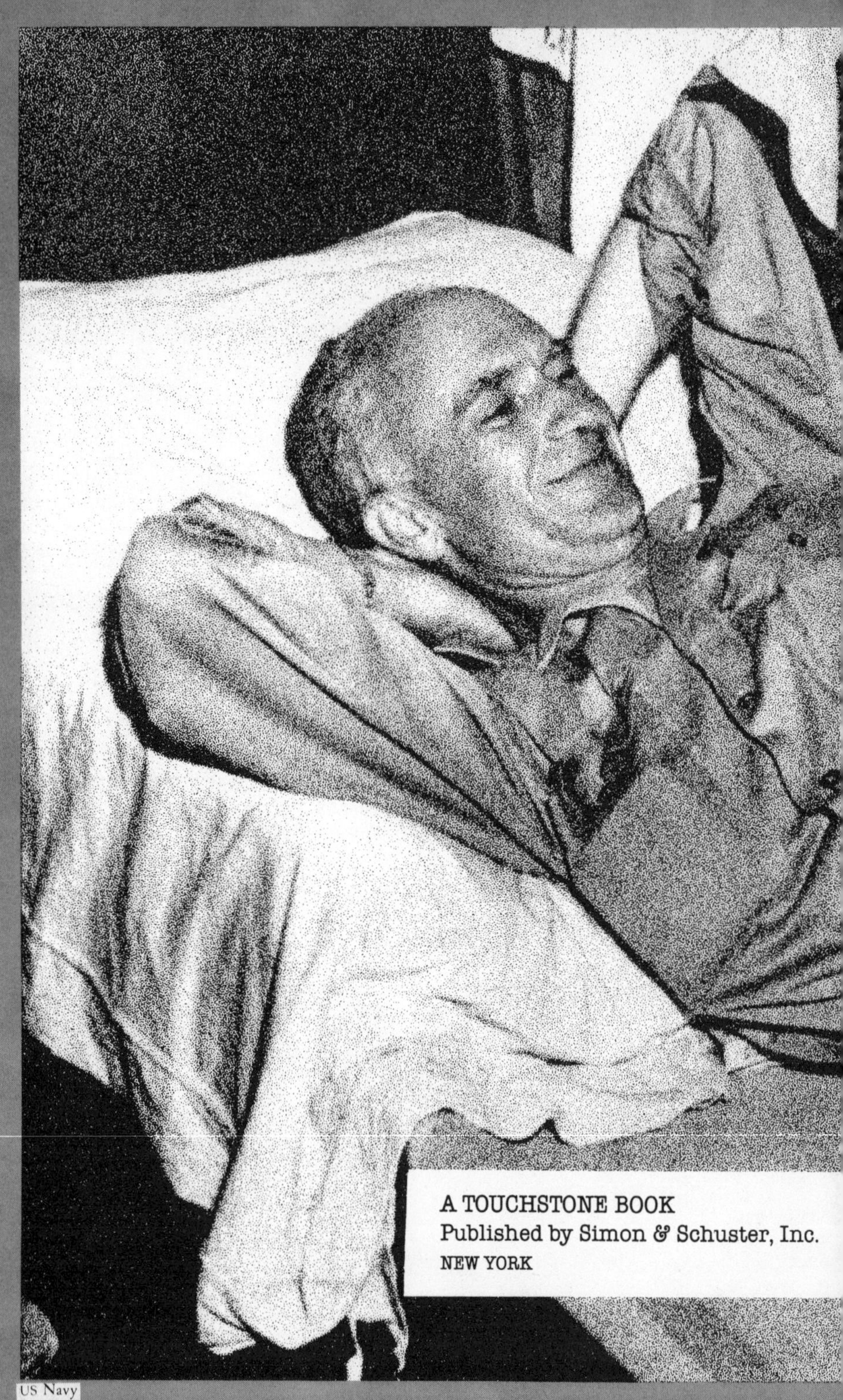

US Navy

A TOUCHSTONE BOOK
Published by Simon & Schuster, Inc.
NEW YORK

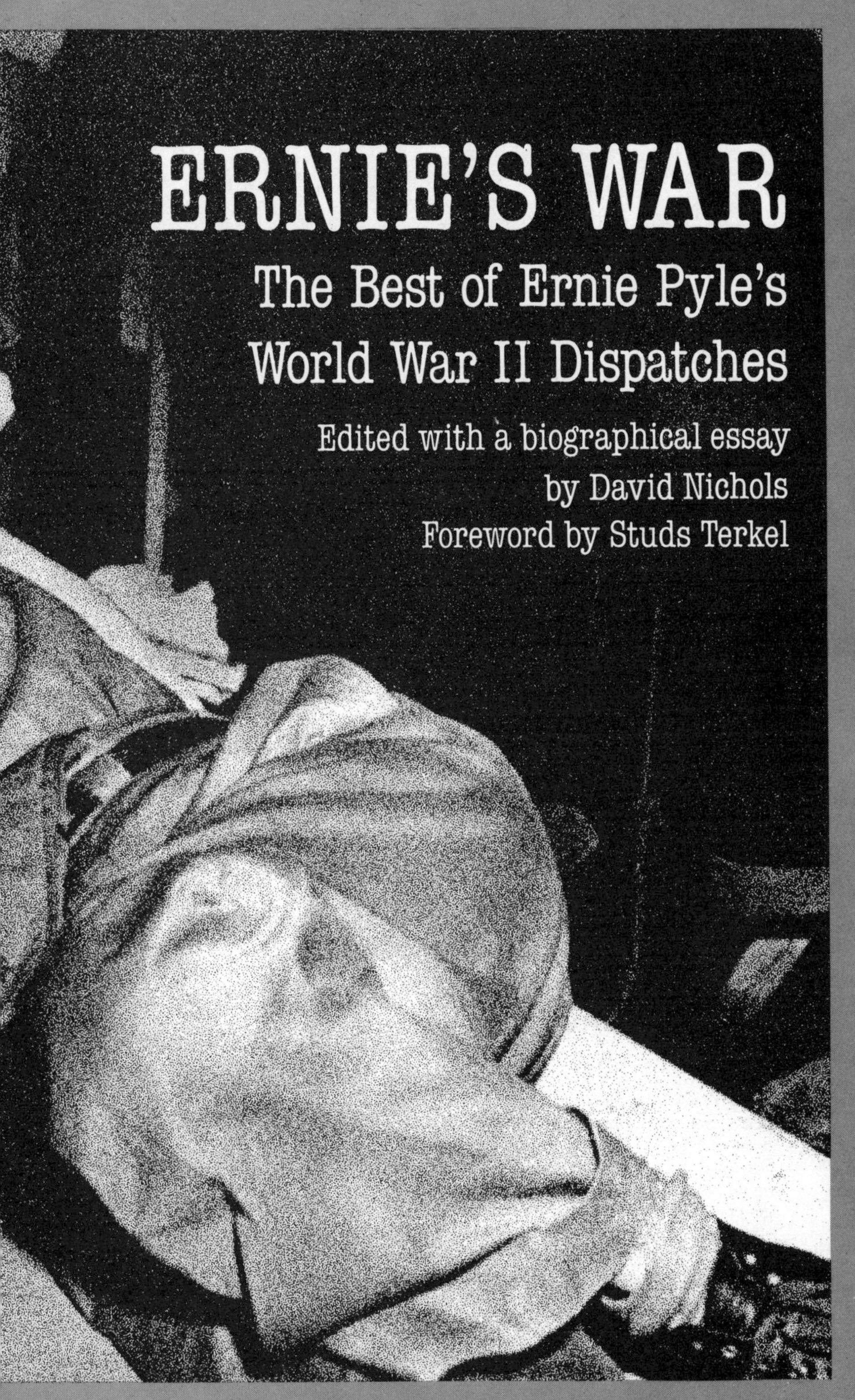
ERNIE'S WAR
The Best of Ernie Pyle's
World War II Dispatches
Edited with a biographical essay
by David Nichols
Foreword by Studs Terkel

First Touchstone Edition, 1987
Published by Simon & Schuster, Inc.
Simon & Schuster Building
Rockefeller Center
1230 Avenue of the Americas
New York NY 10020

Published by arrangement with Random House, Inc.

TOUCHSTONE and colophon is a registered trademark
of Simon & Schuster, Inc.

Designed by Bernard Klein

Manufactured in the United States of America

10 9 8 7 6 5 4 3 Pbk.

Library of Congress Cataloging-in-Publication Data

Pyle, Ernie, 1900–1945.
Ernie's war.
(A Touchstone book)
Bibliography: p.
Includes index.
1. Pyle, Ernie, 1900–1945. 2. World War. 1939–1945.
3. World War, 1939–1945—Personal narratives, American.
4. Journalists—United States—Biography. I. Nichols,
David, date. II. Title.
D743.P95 1987 940.53 87-16316

ISBN 0-671-64452-1 Pbk.

Grateful acknowledgment is made to the Scripps-Howard Foundation for permission to reprint columns written by Ernie Pyle as a correspondent for Scripps-Howard Newspaper Alliance and published originally by various Scripps-Howard newspapers. The columns are subject to certain copyrights© owned by the Scripps-Howard Foundation. All rights reserved. Certain revenue generated by sales of this work will be donated to the Foundation, which sponsors an annual newspaper-feature-writing competition in Ernie Pyle's name and scholarships for journalists. Also, grateful acknowledgment is made to Paige Cavanaugh for permission to quote from Ernie Pyle letters he donated to the Lilly Library at Indiana University, Bloomington.

We have to remember that in the future we will want to keep before our children what this war was really like. It is so easy to forget; and then, for the younger generation, the heroism and the glamour remain, while the dirt, the hardships, the horror of death and the sorrow fade somewhat from their consciousness.

—Eleanor Roosevelt

We felt most the moral qualities of [Ernie Pyle's] work and life; but we could not help realizing that his work was, in our time, an unprecedented aesthetic triumph: because of it most of the people of a country *felt,* in the fullest moral and emotional sense, something that had never happened to them, that they could never have imagined without it—a war.

—Randall Jarrell

CONTENTS

ACKNOWLEDGMENTS

It is to my wife, Mary Pat, that my labors on this volume are lovingly dedicated. Not only did she repeatedly read various drafts of the manuscript, she offered untold moral support during my after-hours work sessions.

My parents, George and Pauline Nichols, helped me in many ways, too. It was my father, a veteran of Army Air Corps service in World War II, who first introduced me to Ernie Pyle's writing. Later, as I worked on this project, he helped me assemble material on the various campaigns Pyle wrote about.

Paige and Edna Cavanaugh shared their memories of Ernie Pyle with me over a long weekend memorable for its good food, good drink, good humor, and pleasant Southern California weather. Matt Sarad, also of Southern California, repeatedly refueled my enthusiasm for Pyle's work by writing me letters, sending me books, and twice visiting me on his annual trips to the Midwest.

David Stolberg, assistant general editorial manager of Scripps-Howard Newspapers and vice president of the Scripps-Howard Foundation, was encouraging from the start, and later helped with the permissions.

I owe much to several librarians, particularly Frances Wilhoit, head librarian at the Weil Journalism Library at Indiana University, Bloomington, which houses much Pyle material. Mrs. Wilhoit was flexible and resourceful beyond the call of duty, as were her associates Michael Main, Martha Beaty, and Renee Risk. Also at Indiana University, Sondra Taylor and Becky Gibson of the Lilly Library were extremely helpful.

At the Allen County Public Library in Fort Wayne, librarians Rick Ashton, John Hall, Laura McCaffery, Susan Pallone, Becky Brooks, and Margaret Braden were accommodating and patient with my repeated requests for information and extensions on long-term borrowings.

Phyllis Gunderson of Valentine-Gunderson Enterprises and her good-humored associates Valerie Gunderson, Lori Griggs, Heather Blickendorf, Irene Couch, and Judy Lyte typed the manuscript.

Phyllis extracted me from many messes with her low-key maternalism, and lent no little order to my chaotic work patterns.

John Jordan read (and re-read) the biography and preface, often on short notice, making useful comments all along. He also pointed the way to many a useful background source, lent me many a good book, and later prepared the index. Cindi Deitering, Diane Nielsen, and Bob Floyd also read and commented on the biography—all made good suggestions. Cindi Deitering helped me standardize usage and spelling throughout the manuscript and advised me on the preparation of the end notes. Syd Smith arranged for (speedy) photocopying.

Evelyn Hobson and her associate Esther Campbell at the Ernie Pyle State Memorial at Dana, Indiana, work hard to keep Pyle's name and work before the public. Both helped me in my search for information, which Marty Shank later helped me organize.

My employer generously granted me a ten-week leave of absence in which to finish the book. My thanks to Wayne Hasty, Roger Dyer, and Vanette Dylan for arranging the leave, and to my associates Mike Brian, Kim Sabrosky, and Mark Dollins for picking up the slack in my absence.

Bob Loomis, executive editor at Random House, was a gentleman from start to finish, good-natured and infinitely patient. His careful reading and subsequent suggestions made this a better book. His assistants Jodie Klavans and John Christel saw to many details I would otherwise have overlooked. Sam Flores copy-edited the manuscript in New York and offered many fine suggestions.

My agent, Eric Ashworth of Candida Donadio & Associates, steered me through myriad detail and always kept his cool.

Thanks, too, to Dan Nichols, Studs Terkel, Joan Catapano, William Allen, Richard Hollander, Skip Carsten, Herb Weber, and Acme Bar's Edna Heckber, who repeatedly loans me her pen and who always takes a check.

FOREWORD
by Studs Terkel

> There was nothing macho about the war at all. We were a bunch of scared kids who had a job to do. People tell me I don't act like an ex-marine. How is an ex-marine supposed to act? They have some Hollywood stereotype in mind. No, I don't look like John Wayne.* We were in it to get it over with, so we could go back home and do what we wanted to do with our lives.

E. B. Sledge, a small-boned, gentle professor of biology—ornithology, to be specific; he loves watching birds—is reflecting on a nineteen-year-old's "job" experience in Okinawa some forty-odd years ago. An elderly man's retrospection.

Well, Ernie Pyle knew all that, and so reported it to the home front, some forty-odd years ago. It's not that he was prescient; he was simply there, listening. Whether he was in retreat with these kids at Kasserine Pass or landing with them in Sicily or wading ashore on D-Day 2 of the Normandy invasion or dying with them on some godforsaken island in the Pacific, something called Ie Shima, he was one of them.

Dave Nichols says it—Dave, a fellow Hoosier: Pyle "would not be on a balcony looking down; he would be in a foxhole, looking up. And what he would see then would forever dispel his adolescent view of the romance of war." Even The Good War.

It seems crazy to bracket Ernie Pyle with Bertolt Brecht, yet in this instance the gentle Indiana bantam and the acerbic Bavarian observed the same thing. When the Armada sank, Brecht writes, we read that King Philip wept. He goes on to ask: Were there no other tears? That was Ernie's question, too. He replied in dispatches that touched millions of readers.

It is exquisite irony that this journalist became celebrated for celebrating the non-celebrated. It is further irony that his deeply

*And certainly not like a muscular Rambo.

moving pieces became so disremembered at war's end. So did the war, for that matter. We may be the richest country in material things and possibly the poorest in memory.

Ernie Pyle was painfully aware of this. In writing of the footsloggers, the grunts, Bill Mauldin's Willie and Joe, he let us know it: "All the war of the world has seemed to be borne by the few thousand front-line soldiers here, destined merely by chance to suffer and die for the rest of us." He sensed immediately what Wilfred Owen, who died in some other war, called Chance's strange arithmetic.

He knew, too, that it was neither God nor Flag nor Mother that impelled a pimply faced kid to risk, to lose his life in an obscene adventure. He did it for the kid next to him; he couldn't let him down. They needed one another so bad. "I lay there in the darkness . . . thinking of the millions far away at home who must remain forever unaware of the powerful fraternalism in the ghastly brotherhood of war."

When they found Ernie's body on Ie, they came across a rough draft of a column. Fragments: "Dead men in such familiar promiscuity that they become monotonous. Dead men in such monstrous infinity that you come almost to hate them. These are the things that you at home need not even try to understand. To you at home they are columns of figures. . . ."

In his most memorable piece, during the Italian campaign, he recounted the death of a beloved captain. Waskow had been brought down the mountain, lashed to the back of a mule. A soldier looked at the corpse and said, "God damn it to hell anyway." That's all the boy said. That's pretty much what Ernie Pyle had been saying all along. God damn war, even the good one.

INTRODUCTION

Ernie Pyle covered World War II the way the infantry soldier fought it: on the ground and on the move, subject to fear, filth and the capricious fates that dealt death to one man, life to another. Pyle was a novelty as a war correspondent. Only rarely did he write about the so-called "big picture." Rather, Pyle focused on the individual combatant—how he lived, endured by turns battle and boredom, and sometimes how he died, far from home in a war whose origins he only vaguely understood.

In North Africa, Sicily, Italy, France, and the Pacific, Ernie Pyle lived with the men he wrote about, six times weekly offering thirteen million stateside readers his view of life at the front in prose substantial beyond the call of daily journalism. When he was killed in the Okinawan campaign during the spring of 1945, Pyle was the most-read war correspondent in U.S. newspapers, and one of the most popular men in America at a time when Americans were hungry for heroes and creating them at every turn.

To those who fought in World War II, or who waited at home for loved ones, his name still musters an uncanny amount of familiarity and affection. His family home at Dana, Indiana, which contains a small museum, yearly draws thousands of visitors, most of whom are in their fifties, sixties, and seventies, and most of whom have traveled considerably out of their way to get there.

Younger Americans, seeking information about the war that shaped their world, are discovering Pyle. The actor William Windom has performed his one-man show based on Pyle's life and writings to enthusiastic audiences nationwide, including those on university campuses. Film-rental companies report the 1945 movie *The Story of G.I. Joe*—based on Pyle's coverage of the infantry and considered one of Hollywood's best World War II films—is particularly popular among college students.

Numerous posthumous honors have been conferred upon Pyle in recent years, including a Purple Heart, the dedication of an Army Reserve center bearing his name, and, on the fortieth anniversary of his death, the sort of outpouring of affection accorded only those who have made a lasting contribution to their times. On April 18, 1985, newspapers from New York to California ran articles and editorials celebrating Pyle. At the Pentagon, Army brass and former war correspondents gathered to commemorate Pyle at a brief ceremony. Underlying the ceremony was the tension between the press and the military brought on by exclusion of reporters from the 1983 invasion of Grenada. Pyle's name and reputation have frequently been invoked by both sides in the debate over how (if at all) the press can be included in future military operations without jeopardizing the safety of American forces or the success of their missions.

After the bitterness of Vietnam, it's hard to conceive of a war correspondent's finding such widespread favor with both his subjects and his audience, of the reporter as both observer and proponent. But as a feature columnist at liberty to write about whatever or whoever engaged his attention, Pyle had a unique forum, and his writing both reflected and fueled the extraordinary unity of the American people in an extraordinary time.

For the second time in as many generations, American boys were leaving home by the millions, off to foreign lands to fight in a war not of their making. Conscious now of the horrors of modern warfare, Americans had entered this war reluctantly; and while they were confident enough of victory, they were ever mindful of its price. As a non-combatant, Pyle was less at war with the Axis than with geography. He knew it was easy for the American public to become emotionally detached from young men whose identities were obscured by distance.

Thus Pyle's obsession with soldiers' names and addresses, with their pre-war lives and post-war dreams, was an attempt to counter with specificity the all-too-anonymous tone of much war correspondence. Those soldiers who looked so generic in black-and-white press photographs were real young men with real families who daily worried after their safety and who grieved when they died. *Look*, Pyle seemed to say, *these men are over here, living this way, doing these things, on your behalf. They are of you, and don't forget it.*

No other World War II writer so routinely served up for his readers such sensory descriptions of soldier life. But there was more than documentary detail in Pyle's columns: there was a strong moral sensibility at work, too. Pyle described, and bemoaned, the unsavory moral changes war thrusts upon young men. The boy next door, he reminded his readers, was now a killer; he had made "the psychological transition from the normal belief that taking human life is sinful, over to a new professional outlook where killing is a craft." Pyle didn't judge the soldiers for doing what they had to do, but to him killing was murder and war the institutionalization of such. Repeatedly he warned readers their sons and husbands were changed men, that what they had endured was inconceivable to an outsider, and that patience and understanding must be the hallmarks of their homecoming.

Though he made his reputation writing about the American men who fought the war that changed the world forever, Pyle died unaware of the spectacular evils that attended the war's end. He had been dead several weeks when the Allies liberated the Nazi death camps, several months when the Americans opened the atomic age by bombing Hiroshima and Nagasaki. That he died innocent of both might separate him from the modern age in the minds of younger readers, for whom the threat of nuclear war is an unrealized inheritance and the death camps a tangible reminder of the presence of evil in the world. While Pyle's war writing is more benign than it would have been had he lived a little longer, it can still be a rich source of revelation for anyone seeking to understand the central experience (and sacrifice) of the World War II generation's lives—the "sense of surging accomplishment" induced by participation in a collective enterprise the likes of which the world had never seen.

For veterans of that war, Pyle's writing can be an evocative means of recalling, some forty years hence, things experienced in youth. The French soldier-turned-journalist Jean Larteguy has written: "That which is most unendurable in war, the awful, ordinary daily routine of war, is relegated to those dim regions where men hide all bad memories. But those memories survive, no matter how deeply buried, and sometimes they emerge."

Perhaps the Pyle pieces herein will help the process along.

* * *

I have selected for inclusion in this volume what I considered to be the best of the pieces Pyle wrote in his two-and-a-half years of war reporting.

While personal preference colored my selection, the greater criteria were less subjective. Pyle's work, like that of any newspaper columnist, was understandably uneven, and weeding out the filler from the pieces that illuminate over time was easy enough.

More difficult was choosing between the remaining columns, and this I did with an eye to three things: descriptions of the terrain and people of the countries in which the soldiers fought, any and all details about infantry life (Pyle was most fond of the infantry), and comments about the character and proclivities of the soldiers Pyle encountered.

My source for the Pyle columns was the wire copy distributed by United Feature Syndicate (then and now a subsidiary of Scripps-Howard) to subscribing papers outside the Scripps-Howard chain. Thus the pieces bear editorial changes of military field censors and Scripps-Howard editors in Washington, but not those made by local editors. (The wire copy is housed at the Weil Journalism Library at Indiana University in Bloomington.)

I have made few changes in the copy. I did standardize abbreviations for military titles, and, because street addresses would be meaningless today, I eliminated them while retaining soldiers' hometowns.

Ten days to two weeks usually passed between Pyle's writing a column and the piece's publication in stateside papers. Thus the reader may notice that column datelines often don't jibe with historical dates. As a practical matter, there's no way to know when Pyle wrote a given column, and in most cases it doesn't matter: readers turned to Pyle for a different sort of news. The dates I've used here are the release dates assigned by United Feature. For clarity's sake, I've occasionally positioned a piece out of chronological order. Mostly, though, the columns are in the order in which they were published.

Pyle's pieces appear here in two forms: full columns, bearing datelines and headlines (except those in a series on the same subject), and column fragments, bearing datelines and with ellipses indicating my deletions. All textual space breaks are Pyle's.

My source for Pyle's famous account of the death of Captain Waskow is Lee Miller's *The Story of Ernie Pyle.* Miller quoted Pyle's original manuscript, which, because of transmission difficulties from overseas, differed slightly from versions published in newspapers.

David Nichols
Fort Wayne, Indiana

ERNIE'S WAR

BIOGRAPHY

So many photographs of leave-takings, but two in particular stand out.

One is of Ernie and Jerry in June of 1926, a year after their marriage. Both look happy and confident. They are standing side by side, she slightly in front of him, her arm and shoulder touching his. Jerry's expression is demure, almost girlish; his is shy and boyish. Already his hairline has receded, leaving the impression that he is several years older than she, though they are both twenty-five, nearly as old as the century but hardly privy to its discontents.

The picture was taken just before they set off from Washington to drive around the United States. They had quit their jobs, pooled their savings, bought a car, a tent, a small camp stove, an enormous canteen, the white coveralls. It was Ernie's idea, this trip, but she was going along.

FROM *AN ERNIE PYLE ALBUM*

Having once indulged his passion for travel, he would take to the road time and again, at first with her and later alone. But this picture contains no hint of the estrangement to come: they are inseparable, set for their big adventure. They are young and in love in the summer of their twenty-fifth year, and the world seems very manageable indeed.

Another photograph, another leave-taking: eighteen years have passed. Ernie and Jerry are standing side by side at the railroad depot in Albuquerque in late December of 1944. Gone is the youthful expectation; gone, too, is even a trace of youth. Both look much older than their forty-four years. Neither looks at the camera. Jerry, who had tried to kill herself a month before, glances down, her face lined and her mouth drawn. Ernie stares off into the distance, lips thinly set, eyes squinting. In the foreground is their luggage. It is mostly his—duffel bag, mussette bag, a combat helmet, two suitcases, a trench coat with wide belt.

They were on their way to Los Angeles, where they would visit their friends the Cavanaughs and watch the filming of a movie in which Burgess Meredith was playing Ernie. Jerry was desperate about Ernie's returning to war again, this time in the Pacific.

This would be their last trip together. In a week, they would dine at a Hollywood nightclub and dance together for the first time in years and

FROM AN ERNIE PYLE ALBUM

the last time ever. Ernie would take Jerry to the train station for a tearful goodbye. In eleven months, both would be dead.

Ernie Pyle was born August 3, 1900, on a farm a few miles outside Dana, Indiana, the first and only child of Will and Maria Pyle. He was a senior in high school when a neighbor boy went off to World War I. Pyle wanted to go, too. Bored with the steady rhythms of farm life and enamored of men of action, he found the prospect of marching off to war in storied Europe irresistible. He shared with countless other Americans a love of parades and boisterous song. His parents, however, insisted that he finish high school, a big disappointment for a young romantic. Upon graduation he enrolled in the Naval Reserve, but the Armistice was signed before he made it to advanced training.

He entered Indiana University at Bloomington in the fall of 1919. Shortly after he arrived, he met Paige Cavanaugh, a war veteran several months his senior. Both were Indiana farm boys anxious to make as solid a break with the farm as possible. Soon they became good friends, Cavanaugh telling of his wartime experiences in France and Pyle wishing he had been so blessed. "He thought the war was a great experience for me," Cavanaugh has said, "and he regretted that he'd not been able to be a part of it—the risk, the romance, the adventure of it, perhaps." Cavanaugh, both in his urge to travel and in his contempt for the conventional, was to deeply influence Pyle.

In January 1923, just short of completing his journalism degree, Pyle left the university to take a general-reporting job on the *La Porte Herald* in La Porte, Indiana. His parents were strongly opposed to it (the graduation issue again), but Pyle had deferred to their wishes once and missed a war for it. He was not about to pass up a real newspaper job.

Pyle left La Porte after a few months to become a reporter for the Scripps-Howard *Washington Daily News,* a one-cent tabloid of generally twelve pages, competing against three more established publications, including the *Washington Post.* Pyle, his bosses discovered, had a knack for writing punchy headlines, and soon they made him a copy editor. Only a few months short of twenty-three when he arrived in Washington, Pyle began what would be a long association with Scripps-Howard, the only employer of any duration he would ever have. He met Lee Miller, also an Indiana native, who would steadily promote his career, encourage him when depression overcame him, edit his copy (leniently, for the most part), and, when fame arrived, handle his business matters. Miller would also write a posthumous Pyle biography.

In college, Pyle had written a windy editorial entitled "The Ideal Girl," in which he described the kind of young woman a young man ought to marry. She would be "the type who is willing to share your troubles, sympathize with you in your periods of adverses, and makes your interests her interests." Ernie believed he had found such a woman in Geraldine Siebolds, to whom he was married on July 7, 1925, by a justice of the peace in Alexandria, Virginia. Jerry, twenty days her husband's junior, was a civil-service worker who had moved to Washington from her native Minnesota shortly after graduating from high school. She was an extremely bright, attractive woman, willing to share Ernie's troubles and sympathize with him in his "periods of adverses." For the most part, she was also willing to make his interests her interests. But she had little use for marriage. Jerry was stubbornly nonconformist and agreed to marriage only if the deed were kept hidden from their Washington friends. Ernie, whose only concern in the matter was his parents' feelings, agreed, and "for years," Miller wrote, "they made a fetish of insisting they weren't really married."

They fancied themselves bohemians and were not model housekeepers. When they socialized, it was with the newspaper crowd, including Lee Miller, who described the floor of their downtown apartment as tobacco covered, the window sills stained by party drinks, the furnishings limited to army cots, wicker chairs, and a breakfast grill.

In the summer of 1926, the Pyles quit their jobs and left Washington to drive around the United States. They traveled nine thousand miles in ten weeks. The trip ended in New York, where Ernie got a job on the copy desk of the *Evening World* and later the *Post.* In December of 1927, the *Washington Daily News* invited him to return as its telegraph editor, and Pyle, never fond of New York, readily accepted. Although it was another desk job, he was soon able to compensate for the long, hectic hours of editing wire-service stories and writing headlines by carving out a beat all his own, the first daily aviation column in American journalism.

Pyle undertook the aviation column about a year after Charles Lindbergh's celebrated transatlantic flight. Lindbergh's feat and the attendant hero worship in the press must have profoundly touched him: even as an adult he was fascinated with men of action, much as he had marveled at Indianapolis 500 drivers as a student. His work on the copy desk completed by early afternoon, Pyle would hunt for material at the several airports in and around Washington. The writing he did on his own time, in the evenings at home. Soon his apartment became a gathering place for flyers and assorted hangers-on.

Two things germane to Pyle's later success emerged from his dealings with aviators. He found that total immersion in his subject matter yielded the best results, that he had a gift for becoming a member of a group while retaining his ability to explain it to outsiders. Just as important, Pyle discovered that he could mix with all kinds of people. Inherently shy, he was a democratizer in a group. Meeting him, even reading his column, people felt at ease and were inclined to open up.

Scripps-Howard eventually made Pyle aviation editor for the entire chain. Aviators were the heroes of the hour, and he was their scribe. Yet Pyle was not an altogether happy man. Paige Cavanaugh was routinely indulging his wanderlust by traveling to Europe, and it's likely that Pyle wanted some of that for himself. Cavanaugh, however, was single and perfectly content to drift from job to job, abandoning any pursuit he found even marginally dull. Pyle cared about financial security. It was one thing to live a pared-down existence, mock middle-class aspirations, drink bootleg liquor, and listen to Jerry read poetry aloud, but it was quite another to be unemployed, and Pyle feared being out of work. Even so, what others might have taken for ambition—working on his own time at the aviation writing, for example—was mostly a flight from boredom, a lifelong affliction for Pyle.

Much to the disappointment of aviators and readers alike, Pyle quit the aviation column in 1932 to become managing editor of the *Washington Daily News.* He didn't want the position, but he didn't think he could turn it down, either. While Pyle did a good job in his three years as managing editor, neither inside work nor politics appealed to him. In one picture taken near the end of his managing-editor term, Pyle looks fifty years old. He was only thirty-four, just beginning the hectic period of his life.

In the winter of 1934, Pyle developed a severe and lingering case of influenza. His doctor ordered him to seek a warmer climate, and the *News* granted him a leave of absence. With Jerry, he traveled by car to Los Angeles, where they boarded a freighter and sailed six thousand miles to Philadelphia in three weeks. It was an arduous convalescence that suggested a new career. Back in Washington, he wrote a series of articles about his vacation. The pieces were well received, and soon Pyle talked his bosses into giving him a try as a roving columnist. Now officially employed by Scripps-Howard Alliance, he was to write six columns a week for distribution to the twenty-four Scripps-Howard papers, including the *Washington Daily News.*

". . . I will go where I please and write what I please," he told a friend, and for the next six years he did just that. Thirty-five times he crossed the American continent, dipping into each state at least three times. He reported from Alaska, Hawaii, and Central and South America, moving by car, truck, plane, boat, horse and muleback.

It was Pyle's habit to travel for a week or so, collecting material as he went, then hole up in a hotel room to write. If the week had gone well, he might have, say, four interviews with which to work. These he would write as reports, almost always including himself. They revealed a man who enjoyed a tall tale and the company of rugged individualists—Alaskan gold miners or a squatter who painted pictures in his shack behind the Memphis city dump. Thus readers met a variety of interesting characters whose personalities were revealed in apposition to Pyle's. The balance of the week's pieces would be personal essays on his own foibles and illnesses (which were legion), or on curious things that happened to him as he puttered across country at speeds rarely exceeding forty-five miles per hour.

The latitude the job offered was far from liberating, however. Ernie and Jerry were free enough to follow their own inclinations, but there was a purpose to it all, and that weighed heavily. Both were often discontent with their traveling life. Paige Cavanaugh had married and settled in Inglewood, California, and though he still regularly changed jobs, Cavanaugh was becoming more rooted. "Many times on this trip, Mr. Cavanaugh," Pyle wrote from Guatemala, "I've envied you—just thinking of you sitting there . . . with every comfort in the world. . . ." Pyle had in Cavanaugh a friend whose light-hearted approach to life offered respite from the wearisome routine of travel and from his concern for Jerry, who, early in their travel days, had begun to show signs of the depression that would later twice cause her to attempt suicide.

It's impossible almost forty years after her death to offer anything but conjecture about Jerry's unhappiness. A mystery to Ernie, as well as to his friends and associates, it was likely a mystery to Jerry herself. She was an emotional chameleon, capable of change at a moment's notice. Column readers knew her as "that Girl who rides with me," though she was a vague figure, never well developed. She lived out of suitcases, retyped his copy, offered praise and criticism of his work, her life revolving around Ernie and his restive disposition. Life on the road held very little for Jerry, whose pleasures—reading, playing the piano, working crossword puzzles—were largely sedentary. More than ever before, Pyle's college description of the "ideal girl" applied to her: she shared in his troubles and sympathized with him in his "periods of adverses." Even sex was denied her.

Ernie and Jerry probably never wanted children early in their married lives, but later on—just when is unclear—the question was moot. Ernie had become impotent. He often joked about the problem in letters to Cavanaugh and eventually sought treatment for the condition in San Diego, but he apparently never recovered. Later, in desperation, Jerry would want a child.

Beginning with Ernie's extended trip to Alaska in April of 1937, they began spending more time apart, carrying on their marriage by correspondence. Their letters were full of the superlatives of endearment, but something was amiss. Jerry's depression, slowly building for two years, was now virtually unchecked; she drank heavily and used sedatives and Benzedrine. While Pyle toured Alaska and the Aleutian Islands, Jerry closed their Washington apartment for good. For three years, until they built a house in Albuquerque, she was a woman without a home, living variously with her mother in Minnesota or with friends around the country.

Ernie, meanwhile, was in demand and carried along by the pleasure he took in his new-found popularity, but in these years, he surrendered the only intimate relationship he had ever had—that with Jerry—to the pressures of a largely unseen audience. He was aware of this—aware, too, that the more successful the column became the harder it would be to quit. Still, he pushed ahead toward syndication outside the Scripps-Howard chain, often chafing when the results were meager.

In September 1938, the Pyles began a tour of Central and South America. They parted in French Guiana so that Ernie could visit the penal colony at Devil's Island; Jerry ended up in Miami, alone in a hotel and drinking heavily. Ernie later found her incoherent, emaciated, and unable to eat. Outwardly, she recovered quickly, and they resumed their travels.

When the war that would make him a national hero was breaking out overseas, Pyle was mostly uninterested. Not until September 3,

1939, when Great Britain and France declared war on Germany, did he take serious notice. Eight days after the declaration, he wrote to Cavanaugh: "Personally, I'm just about to bust I want to get over there as a war correspondent or something so bad. However, there is an unspoken stalemate on between Miss Geraldine and me as regards that subject. The matter has never been discussed openly, but we know how each other stands. I'll probably win in the end, however. Pacifism is fine as long as there ain't no war around. But when they start shooting I want to get close enough just a couple of times to get good and scared."

At the age of thirty-nine, Pyle still had a schoolboy's vision of battle, an untutored conception of war that recalled his disappointment over not accompanying his neighbor friend to World War I twenty-two years before. He was restless. He had avoided doing pieces on serious topics for so long that now, in the face of world crisis, his work seemed trivial. "For the last two weeks I've been so goddam bored writing silly dull columns about Mt. Hood and hop ranches that I think I'm going nuts," he wrote Cavanaugh. But relief was slow in coming.

It was a little over a year later, in mid-November 1940, that Ernie sailed to England to report on the Battle of Britain. He left Jerry in Albuquerque to oversee the construction of their new house, the first and only house they would ever own. Though Jerry eventually came to love the little house, she hardly found it compensation for her husband's decision to go to war. She wrote to friends of her fears for Ernie's safety, which, she said, she was learning to live with. She added: "But to pretend that I give one single solitary good goddamn about a shack or a palace or any other material consideration in this world would be to foist upon everybody at all interested the greatest gold-brick insult a low mind could conceive."

Frightened but animated after waiting twenty-three years for his first taste of war, Pyle arrived in England in mid-December for a three-month stay. Shortly thereafter, London received a particularly brutal pounding by Luftwaffe fire bombs, which Pyle watched from a balcony. He described the city as "stabbed with great fires, shaken by explosions, its dark regions along the Thames sparkling with the pinpoints of white-hot bombs. . . ."

Pyle soon found that he liked England and the English. His columns, flavored by their persistence and understated humor, the copy chatty and somewhat glib, were well received in the States. He wrote about life in the subway shelters, about the firemen who worked through the night and the spotters who enforced blackout provisions and watched for roof fires. He took a long tour of England's industrial midlands and stood in the ruins of Coventry. Now marginally familiar with one aspect of war, Pyle had yet to shed his dilettante's view of it. He was a tourist, a visitor sharing his hosts' misery in a cursory way. When Pyle next went to war—almost two years later—he would not be on a balcony looking down; he would be in a foxhole, looking up. And what he would see then would dispel forever his adolescent view of the romance of war.

Since he had begun his travel work five years before, it had been cruelly true that for every gain Pyle made professionally, he had suffered a personal setback. As his popularity increased, his marital happiness declined. Privacy was a thing of the past: in the spring of 1941, tourists began driving past his house in Albuquerque at all hours, hoping to get a glimpse of him. Even his stay in England had been marred by word of his mother's death in Indiana.

Much as the new house delighted him, Pyle had little time to enjoy it because he had to travel frantically to keep the column going. Jerry's unhappiness had deepened during his months abroad, partly out of concern for Ernie's well-being, and now her troubles took a new turn: she tried to take her life, apparently by closing herself off in the kitchen and turning on the gas jets. Ernie took her to Denver for a thorough physical, but the doctors found nothing wrong.

He was on a tour of Canadian air bases in late August when friends summoned him back to Albuquerque. A friend had found Jerry near death, hemorrhaging at the mouth. An ulcer had eaten through a blood vessel in her stomach. Her doctors predicted a slow recovery. Jerry had been "drinking colossally for days," Ernie wrote Cavanaugh. "Will stay here until she gets completely back to normal, and may have to completely reshape our lives to prevent her ever doing this again." He offered Scripps-Howard his resignation, but the company flatly refused it. They settled on a three-month leave of absence—with no pay, at Pyle's insistence.

Calling Jerry a "psychopathic case," he explained her condition to his bosses: "Because of her futility complex (I suppose) she is not permanently interested in anything. And without any interest, she frequently gets to wallowing in boredom and melancholy and hopelessness, and that leads her to progress from normal drinking to colossal drinking. . . ."

Jerry made a remarkable recovery. By mid-fall, Ernie was proposing a three-month trip to the Orient, but when his plans fell through, he had to make do with resuming the column stateside. Jerry, meanwhile, turned again to heavy drinking. That December the Japanese attacked Pearl Harbor, and the United States declared war on Japan and the other Axis powers.

The year 1942 was the low point of Pyle's life. In the year's first six months, he began and ended a love relationship, apparently platonic, with a woman in San Francisco. He traveled relentlessly to rebuild circulation lost during his three months of leave, concentrating mainly on the West Coast so that he could undergo a series of painful (and nonproductive) treatments for impotence in San Diego. All the while, Jerry's condition steadily worsened. She was in and out of the hospital, "doping and drinking to excess again," eventually coming to believe that having a baby would help her right her life. " . . . I *can't* give you a child, as you know," Ernie told her. "I haven't been lying when I've told you that the power of sex had gone from me."

Finally, with the concurrence of Jerry's doctors and family, Ernie reluctantly divorced her on April 14, 1942, hoping the shock would force her "into a realization that she [has] to face life like other people." He left open the possibility of remarriage, assuming that Jerry would "get to work and cure herself. . . ." Ernie signed the house over to her, divided their savings equally between them, and provided her with a weekly income.

Scripps-Howard, meanwhile, wanted Pyle to prepare for a foreign trip, something interesting to give the column the impetus it lacked after his frequent absences over the last year. He flew to Washington and quickly concluded that Great Britain was his best bet. The law required that he register for the draft, and he did so, discovering in the process that his classification was 1-A. He requested and was granted a six-month draft extension.

Shortly before he left the United States for Britain, Jerry's mental health slipped sufficiently that Ernie found the courage to do what he said he should have done long before. He committed her to a sanitarium at Pueblo, Colorado, for six months. When she pleaded to be released and remarried to him, Ernie refused, admitting that his comments seemed cold. " . . . I'm coming back (permanently I mean) when you are so far along the road of cheerfulness and normal outlook and usefulness to yourself and other people, that there can be no doubt about our future, and not until then. . . ." Emotionally unstable himself, Ernie in his dealings with Jerry had assumed more the outlook of a foster parent than that of an ex-husband. That he urged her to make herself useful to others is significant. For years, Ernie and Jerry had dismissed middle-class American life as unworthy of their aspirations. They had lived a rootless existence, clung to the bohemian pretensions of their Washington days, and traveled at Scripps-Howard's expense, liberally dispensing tips at a time when most Americans their age were struggling to raise families in the Depression.

"Stability cloaks you with a thousand little personal responsibilities, and we have been able to flee from them," Ernie had written of their traveling life. Blind as he was to the fact Jerry desperately needed his steady company to overcome her problems, Ernie was quicker than she to apprehend that service to others in a time of national need was a potential antidote to their troubles. With the country mobilized for war and the government enjoining everyone to do his part, Pyle felt the tug of usefulness. He was not certain how to act upon those sentiments, but he closed the travel-writing phase of his career on a note of chagrin, sure only that what lay ahead would be preferable to the strain of the preceding twelve months.

Before Pyle flew from New York to Ireland during mid-June 1942, he wrote his ex-wife, "I am all alone. Be my old Jerry when I come back. I love you."

Americans were already at war in the Pacific as Pyle began writing about the training of American troops in Ireland and England. By studying the men he wrote about, he picked up on their longings and away-from-home habits and sent back the kind of detail no other reporter bothered with. His circulation figures steadily improved, and slowly his frame of mind did, too, though mail from Jerry was infrequent, and this bothered him. In late summer, he received word from her that she had left the Colorado sanitarium and was living in Albuquerque, in a house on the grounds of a Catholic hospital. (She had prevailed upon her sister to authorize her release.) Perplexed, Ernie urged her to find a job, something congenial to get her mind off her problems.

Living close to his subjects worked an insidious change in Pyle, the one-time bohemian outsider. He found himself in the unlikely position of chronicling the daily lives of the conscripted soldiers of what was becoming a very middle-class nation. Pyle's subjects were men whose backgrounds were often strikingly "normal," even boring, and whose postwar dreams called for more of the same. Many a Pyle subject wanted nothing so much as a little white house with a yard bordered by a white picket fence—precisely the sort of house

Pyle and Jerry had built in Albuquerque, which he had sardonically described to Cavanaugh as a "regular little boxed-up mass production shack in a cheap new suburb."

Though some days he believed induction into the Army would be a relief, by late September Pyle had guardedly decided to stay with column writing. Homefront reaction to his pieces was favorable, so he asked Lee Miller to file with the draft board for another six-month extension. The board promptly granted it, but soon thereafter the government stopped drafting men thirty-eight and older. By month's end he had come to equate writing with service. He told Jerry, "As much as I would like to come home, I don't see any point in getting home for a few days and then spending the rest of the war as a private when I can do more good—if any at all—by sticking to what I'm doing."

Visiting Air Corps bases consumed most of his time in October. There were rumors that a second front would be opened soon, and Pyle concluded that he would go along, not with the forces actually making the landings, but a little later. From London, in late October, he wrote Jerry a long, introspective letter. "My future without you is unthinkable," he said, "and I hope you feel the same way. We have both suffered so much that surely there is peace waiting for us ahead. . . . I too look at things much differently than I did; I have sobered a great deal, and I see now that I was bad in so many ways. I've finally realized that I unconsciously had the German attitude—that everything I did was right just because I did it. . . . I don't waste any time reproaching myself for the past, but somehow I feel that my character and my mind have deteriorated so terribly; I don't have any spiritual stability within myself at all. . . . all purpose seems to have gone out of life for me (except the one of hope) and I've no interest in anything."

His spirits continued to sag. The column had become "something I don't love anymore," he wrote Jerry on November 3, 1942. "I would do almost anything to abandon it forever. I have no interest in it, and I'm weary almost unto illness of thinking for a living."

Shortly after that, he boarded the *Rangiticki*, a British transport ship carrying troops to replace those wounded or killed in the Allied invasion of North Africa. He had shared several months of agreeable companionship in Ireland and England with the American men quartered in the ship's hold. By traveling with them through hostile waters to a foreign place, he was beginning to share their future in a serious way. Yet he had no intention of becoming their spokesman in this war; he planned, rather, to take a quick look at Africa, then travel to India or China. Had he been in a better frame of mind, he might have seen that he had already found a new outlet for his ability to capture the human side of events great and small, a talent previously diluted for want of focus.

Pyle went ashore in Algeria on November 22, 1942, and spent the balance of the year in and around Oran. From his column, readers got a sense of how massive an effort the war was, of how diverse were the duties of its participants.

A few days after he landed in North Africa, Ernie, depressed and lonely, wrote Jerry a letter asking her to be remarried to him by proxy. He got an Army judge to draw up the papers, which he forwarded to Albuquerque. Bedridden with influenza over the Christmas holidays, he was horrified by a dream in which Jerry had married someone else. It was their third straight Christmas apart.

Shortly after the holidays, Pyle was ready for a look at the front. In January 1943, he flew from Oran to a desert airfield called the Garden of Allah. He planned to write a series of columns on the bomber crews and fighter pilots stationed there, take a look at how the infantry was faring, then resume the travel column. Thus far, his portrait of the American soldiers in North Africa was instructive but incomplete. In this next phase of his introduction to war, Pyle would come face to face with what most people understand intellectually but that only the combatant or his astute observer comes to know emotionally—that battle demands of its participants a suspension of the peacetime moral sense that killing is wrong. Pyle would see nothing of the sublime in this moral transformation, necessary as it was.

He spent a week with a group of P-38 Lightning pilots who generally flew escort for the bombers but who delighted in an occasional strafing mission. After one such mission, during which they had blown a German truck convoy to pieces, the pilots laughed as they told their story of Germans flying out of the trucks "like firecrackers." It bothered Pyle to see men so young kill so readily—and with such relish. He "couldn't help having a funny feeling about them. . . . they were so casual about everything. . . . they talked about their flights and killing and being killed exactly as they would discuss girls or their school lessons."

The column on the fighter pilots and their strafing marked the emergence of a more serious Pyle voice, at the core of which was an engaging tension: the enormous moral difference between life at home and life at war. Pyle was well acquainted with offbeat behavior from offbeat people; he had spent years tracking down such characters and writing their stories. Now he found so-called normal men doing bestial things, and he was both intrigued and repelled.

Pyle left the relative comfort of the Garden of Allah in late January 1943 and joined the infantry of General Fredendall's (later General Patton's) II Corps, headquartered at Tébessa in Algeria, near the Tunisian border. By jeep he traveled to the Tunisian front lines, getting to know the commanders and their men. His unobtrusive style of reporting—mingling, listening, rarely taking notes—ingratiated him with nearly everyone he encountered. He shared in the soldiers' tight-knit company, endured the same privations, subjected himself to the same dangers, and thus began his most significant body of work—describing for those at home the daily lives of the infantrymen who fought the war at its dirtiest level. Reporting the actual news of the war—"the big picture," in the parlance of the time—was the job of numerous other reporters; Pyle was free to seek his own line of inquiry. He could spend a week or two living at the front before withdrawing to write his pieces.

Pyle soon rejected the notion of resuming his travel work, preferring to cover the story unfolding before him. For the first time in his life, he had become morally connected to an undertaking of great moment. His nerves were smoothing out; he had virtually stopped drinking—admittedly for lack of supply—and the combination of the tan he had picked up at the Garden of Allah and the windburn from the front gave him a ruddy look of health and well-being.

Ernie's pleasure in his work was diminished in early February 1943 by a letter from Albuquerque: Jerry had refused his offer of remarriage, perhaps because she still resented him for having committed her to a sanitarium. "It was just dusk when I got the letter," he wrote her, "and I sat on a stump all bundled up against the cold, and read it. I was so disappointed I almost felt like crying."

On February 14, German tanks and infantry under the command of General Erwin Rommel startled the inexperienced Americans by driving fifty miles through their positions at Kasserine Pass in Tunisia. The Americans retreated, Pyle with them. The retreat was for the Army what Pearl Harbor had been for the Navy, and Pyle's front-line description of it was radioed back to the United States for immediate distribution to subscribing papers.

"I've been at the front for seven solid weeks, and although you may not believe it, I like it up there because life becomes so wonderfully simple—even a lot simpler than you've got yours arranged," he wrote Cavanaugh from Algiers, to which he had fled after the retreat. "There are only four essentials—clothes, food, cigarets, and whatever portion of safety you can manage to arrange for yourself."

For the first time in over a year, Pyle was optimistic. Life at the front was invigorating. A letter to Jerry was confident, good-humored, and full of pride in his own capacity. "If anybody had ever told me I could stand to sleep right out on the ground and wake up with snow on my bedroll I'd have called him nuts; but I have and you find you can stand almost anything." While Pyle spent ten days in Algiers writing about what he had seen in the last seven weeks, Jerry sent a cable informing him that she was working as a civil-service clerk at Kirtland Field in Albuquerque and that she was moving back into the house. This pleased him. He was elated when, on March 12, during a few weeks' break from the front lines, he received notice that Jerry had reconsidered his offer of remarriage and exercised the proxy on her lunch hour. This made him feel "some peace with the world again. . . ."

There was also evidence of his quickening stateside popularity. More papers now ran the column, which increased his earnings. Accepting an offer from Henry Holt & Company to reprint his North Africa work in book form was the happy coincidence of two good fortunes—an upswing professionally and personally.

What's more, Pyle had finally resolved the question of what to do with himself. He was committed to staying with the men whose blooding he had only begun to describe. His dilettante's sense of war had evolved into a more mature outlook. He hated the "tragedy and insanity" of war, but "I know I can't escape and I truly believe the only thing left to do is be in it to the hilt."

When Pyle returned to the front lines in early April 1943, he found he had become inured to carnage—"somehow I can look upon mutilated bodies without flinching or feeling deeply"—but not to fitful sleep after a day of watching men kill and be killed; then "at last the enormity of all these newly dead strikes me like a living nightmare. And there are times when I feel that I can't stand it all and will have to leave."

As the Tunisian war wound its way northward toward the Mediterranean port cities of Bizerte and Tunis, Pyle lived and traveled with the 1st Division. It was here that he wrote his most memorable columns of the North Africa campaign, reflecting his new maturity and, as always, his keen eye for detail. What was most engaging was the fusion of Pyle's documentary impulse with his heightened moral sense. He now celebrated true character traits versus absurd ones;

gone was the juvenile admiration of race-car drivers and Air Mail pilots who brazened it out in the face of quick and violent death. The infantrymen with whom he now spent his time lived decidedly unromantic lives. They fought, they waited, they endured dive bombings and heavy-artillery shellings—they were the ultimate victims. To Pyle, they were heroes, not dashing or even particularly brave, but men who persisted in the face of great fear and discomfort because they had to. By sharing their lives, Pyle was becoming one of them in spirit if not in age, in practice if not by force of conscription.

By mid-May, the Tunisian war was over. While the troops practiced for the invasion of Sicily, Pyle and the other correspondents retreated to a press camp on the shore of the Mediterranean near Algiers. Lee Miller suggested that he return home for several weeks, but Pyle declined, fearing guilt pangs. Perhaps by fall he could take a leave "with a clear conscience." Meanwhile, he turned his attention to the long essay that would be the last chapter of his book *Here Is Your War.*

It was a remarkable piece. The war in North Africa had been a testing ground for American men and equipment, Pyle wrote. The men had been well cared for, their food and medical care were good, their equipment less so but getting better. Because Pyle was "older and a little apart," he could see the changes in the soldiers, and he emphasized that no one could undergo what these men had without being permanently affected. War had made them rougher, more profane, and prone to taking what they needed when and where they could find it. "The stress of war puts old virtues in a changed light," he wrote. "We shall have to relearn a simple fundamental or two when things get back to normal. But what's wrong with a small case of 'requisitioning' when murder is the classic goal?"

Six months after Pyle had arrived in North Africa—confused, sickly, and depressed—his fortunes had reversed themselves. He had proved to himself that he could endure. He had found pleasure and purpose in his renewed union with Jerry, and he had forgotten about the woman in San Francisco with whom he had fallen in love. His indecision of six months before had given way to commitment, his lack of interest to singularity of purpose. Battle had brought a terrifying focus to his life, and the clarity that attached to front-line existence was exhilarating, drawing him back whenever he was away. He had yet to prove himself over the long haul, but he was prepared to do so.

On June 29, 1943, a year and ten days after he had arrived in

Ireland, Pyle flew to Bizerte in Tunisia. There he boarded an American ship, the USS *Biscayne*, and settled in for his second invasion voyage in eight months.

The invasion of Sicily marked for Americans and their allies the beginning of the long assault on Axis Europe, and it was with the war in Europe that Pyle would come to be most identified. Even so, his beginning there was slow and unhappy, his work disconnected.

The Sicilian campaign was a short one, lasting only five weeks, from July 10 to August 17. During it Pyle displayed none of the exuberance that had marked his months in Africa. He was tired, sick, and fearful that redundancy would rob his copy of the vitality it had had in North Africa. "I'm getting awfully tired of war and writing about it," he told Jerry. "It seems like I can't think of anything new to say—each time it's like going to the same movie again."

After General George Patton's victory at Palermo two weeks after the invasion, Pyle drove to 45th Division headquarters at Cefalù, where he settled in with the 120th Engineers Battalion. He became ill and spent five days in a tent hospital amidst the "death rattle" of dying men. In the campaign's closing days, Pyle rejoined the 120th Engineers, then the 10th Engineers.

He wrote Jerry, "I find myself more and more reluctant to repeat and repeat the same old process of getting shot at." He added that "the war gets so complicated and confused in my mind; on especially sad days it's almost impossible to believe that anything is worth such mass slaughter and misery; and the after-war outlook seems to me so gloomy and pathetic for everybody."

Ten days after his forty-third birthday, the campaign ended, and Pyle decided to go home for a break. In a wrap-up piece on the Sicilian campaign, he explained:

> I had come to despise and be revolted by war clear out of any logical proportion. . . . Through repetition, I had worn down to the nub my ability to weigh and describe.

Pyle arrived exhausted in New York at four A.M. on September 7, 1943, four days after the Allies had invaded Italy. Within twenty-four hours, he endured several newspaper interviews, countless phone calls from wives and friends of soldiers, requests from the Office of War Information and the WAC recruiting office for radio recordings, and one from Treasury Secretary Henry Morgenthau to appear on the war-bond radio program *We the People.* Two radio networks engaged in a bidding war for Pyle's services. He turned both down.

Washington wasn't any better. Pyle had to see the dentist, his lawyer, his tax accountant, and there were more interviews with reporters, more picture-taking. A Pentagon panel of fifty officers questioned him. He had a private talk with Secretary of War Henry Stimson. For a thousand-dollar fee, Pyle agreed to be photographed for a Chesterfield cigarett advertisement. A movie producer, Lester Cowan, came down from New York to talk about basing a movie on Pyle's forthcoming book.

After a short visit with his father and Aunt Mary (his mother's sister) on the family farm in Indiana, Ernie flew to Albuquerque, where Jerry met him at the airport. But his stay there was chaotic, too. Cavanaugh flew over from Los Angeles for a visit, and Lester Cowan arrived for more movie discussions. Mail from all over the country arrived by the bagful. The telephone rang constantly. Everyone, it seemed, wanted something from him, including Jerry, who by this time was hardly able to articulate anything of her tortured inner life.

Jerry's condition was tentative, Pyle told friends. Even as she slept, there was "horrible anguish in her face." He knew she loved him, but he was ambivalent toward her: on the one hand, "my normal feeling of love for her has been sort of smothered in an academic viewpoint," and on the other, "she is the only thing in the world that means anything to me. . . ." In his months of leave from war, Pyle avoided spending much time alone with Jerry—perhaps out of guilt over their prolonged separations (which she abhorred), perhaps because his sexual dysfunction troubled him, perhaps because he had little need of true intimacy, preferring his associations light and cursory.

Jerry broke down shortly before his stay ended, and Pyle admitted her to the hospital. He told Lee Miller that Jerry was depressed about his forthcoming departure and under a great deal of pressure on her job. Pyle feared that his leaving would be too much for her to bear. "But," as he explained in the column a few weeks later,

> what can a guy do? I know millions of others who are reluctant too, and they can't even get home. . . . [At home] you feel like a deserter and a heel—not so much to the war effort, but to your friends who are still over there freezing and getting shot at.

Pyle spent three weeks in Washington before traveling to Italy. *Here Is Your War* had been published to laudatory notices. He autographed books, went to tea with Eleanor Roosevelt and to film conferences with Lester Cowan. He commented in the column on his own popularity. If, as Lee Miller wrote, Pyle had a "boyish curiosity" about his fame when he had arrived in New York, he now saw celebrity for what it was: an all-consuming claim on his time and a diversion from the things and people who really mattered.

Before he left Washington for Italy in late November, Pyle completed his income-tax return for 1943: he had made about sixty-nine thousand dollars, twenty-nine thousand of which he paid in taxes.

Unlike their German and Italian opponents, who were fighting on or close to native soil, the American soldiers Pyle wrote about saw home as a continuum, a place fixed in the imagination that would stay the same, possibly even improve, in their time away. Before his vacation, Pyle, too, had sustained himself with mildly idealized thoughts of Jerry and the house in Albuquerque. As he began to cover the war in Italy, however, any sense of home as an emotional buffer was gone. What remained was Pyle's ever-growing compulsion to tell the story of the American fighting man from firsthand experience. But that compulsion was now largely a reflex action, a commitment bereft of pleasure.

The winter of 1943–1944 was the worst Italy had seen in years. For soldiers the misery of the cold and mud compounded the confusion of fighting in mountainous terrain. The distant objective was the conquest of Rome, the immediate goal to survive what Pyle called "this semi-barbarian life."

What had been exciting in North Africa, and to a much lesser extent in Sicily, was now debilitating. But even with the chaos of battle and its awful cost wearing on him as never before, his "ability to weigh and describe"—the faculty he said he had lost by the end of the Sicilian campaign—was unimpaired. And the columns he produced in Italy served to further boost his stateside circulation and consolidate his popularity among the troops. Pyle still feared redundancy in his copy, still was reluctant to subject himself to battle, but by Christmas he had already made two extended trips to the front and had written his best piece ever.

The column was an account of the affection an infantry company felt for its commander, young Captain Henry Waskow, who had been killed in the mountain fighting near San Pietro, and whose body had been brought down a mountain on the back of a mule. The column's emotional content was implicit, revealing both the intimate personal waste of war and the depth of Pyle's growth as a writer and observer.

Pyle failed to see the achievement for what it was, but few stateside were so obtuse. The column was a coast-to-coast sensation. The *Washington Daily News* gave over its entire front page to the Waskow piece and sold out the day's paper. If there were any doubts about who was in the ascendant as America's premier war correspondent, the Waskow column laid them to rest. Pyle was on his way to becoming a central figure of the era, a living, high-profile symbol of the fighting man's displacement from ordinary life and of his sacrifice. He had become the focus of his audience's good will toward the soldiers; assigned to him were many of the same idealized sentiments the public assigned to them. The *Saturday Evening Post* noted that Pyle "was probably the most prayed-for man with the American troops. . . ."

At home, just eight weeks before, Pyle had complained that Americans stateside "haven't had anything yet, on a national scale, to burn and crucify [them] into anything greater than [they] were to begin with." His heroes were different because they had suffered and endured and found strength in adversity. Just as Pyle had been drawn away from self-involvement by what he had seen at war, so, too, had the infantrymen. Pyle saw redemption in this collective action, a redemption unavailable to some statesiders who were concerned with the war only insofar as it affected their personal comfort.

After seeing on his vacation how untouched Americans at home were by events overseas, Pyle had arrived in Italy all the more intent upon getting across to his readers the magnitude of the infantryman's sacrifice. While his work in North Africa and Sicily had been largely descriptive reporting, in Italy it became more essay-like. Pyle was not a religious man, but he had been raised in a conservative Christian community, and increasingly he called on the Christian themes and language of his childhood to confer upon his subjects a peculiar brand of secular beatification. He admitted that his admiration for the infantry was obsessive and that to him "all the war of the world has seemed to be borne by the few thousand front-line soldiers here, destined merely by chance to suffer and die for the rest of us." He had found in his heroes an unusual degree of selflessness, of duty perceived and performed, and was deeply moved.

Having acquired a more sophisticated, more fluid, sense of good and evil, Pyle realized the men he wrote about were battling an evil enemy by engaging in murderous behavior themselves—and that, ironically, this often brought out noble characteristics in them. Living with an infantry company of the 34th Division, Pyle encountered Sergeant Buck Eversole, a platoon leader who had been at the front for over a year and who was now "a senior partner in the institution of death." Pyle's pieces on Eversole were the best expression of those characteristics he most admired in the fighting men: Eversole was a killer by necessity, but at core he was a moral man, thoughtful and capable of great feeling in the midst of moral contradictions. "I know it ain't my fault [green replacement soldiers] get killed," Eversole told Pyle.

> And I do the best I can for them, but I've got so I feel like it's me killin' 'em instead of a German. I've got so I feel like a murderer. I hate to look at them when the new ones come in.

Pyle filed his last reports of the Italian campaign in March 1944 from the Anzio-Nettuno beachhead, which was subject to constant shelling and bombing. He was nearly killed when a five-hundred-pound bomb landed near the building in which he lived, blowing a wall into his room, shattering windows, and ripping doors off their hinges. Other correspondents assumed Pyle was dead, but he emerged from the rubble with only a slight cut on his cheek. Despite the constant danger, Pyle told Jerry he was glad he had visited the beachhead; it wouldn't have been "right" for him to have avoided it.

He left Anzio on April 5 "in the clasp of a strange new safety" aboard a hospital ship bound for Naples. From Naples Pyle flew to North Africa, and thence to London. Something big was afoot—he was sure of that—but only later would he learn that the long-awaited invasion of France was imminent.

Shortly after Pyle arrived in London during mid-April 1944, word came that he had won a Pulitzer Prize for "distinguished war correspondence" in 1943, an unexpected but relished honor.

Ernie had received only a few letters from Jerry during his time in Italy and France, but now mail from her was more frequent. He was glad to learn that she was set to undergo a series of hospital treatments. She asked him if he was tired of war, and he replied, "Of course I am very sick of the war, and would like to leave it, and yet

I know I can't. I've been a part of the misery and tragedy of it for so long that I've come to feel a responsibility to it or something. I don't quite know how to put it into words, but I feel if I left it, it would be like a soldier deserting."

Later, when Jerry returned home from the hospital in the company of two nurses and reported that she was abstaining from alcohol, Ernie's mood was still somber, and he explained to her his fear that "I'm going to be so torn up inside and maladjusted by the time [the war] is over that I'll take a lot of 'doin' with, so your mission in life is to get well and ready to take care of me when I get back!"

While Pyle fed Scripps-Howard and United Feature copy on invasion preparations and Air Corps crews, Lee Miller saw to plans for a second compilation of Pyle's columns, *Brave Men.*

Pyle set foot on French soil on June 7, 1944, the day after the Normandy invasion began, at Omaha Beach, one hundred twenty miles to the southwest of Brest, where Paige Cavanaugh had landed with the 36th Division twenty-seven years before. By now, Pyle's post-adolescent fascination with Cavanaugh's war tales was an attitude so remote that a reminder of it would surely have embarrassed him. Intense weariness and a spooky sense of the fragility of life would thread throughout his columns from France. A week after the landings, he told Lee Miller he was "beginning to feel that I've run my last race in this war and can't keep going much longer."

Pyle resumed the advocate's role he had taken on in Italy, writing from the beachhead a description of the effort it took to open a second front so that his audience could "know and appreciate and forever be humbly grateful to those both dead and alive who did it for you." After writing a series on the ack-ack gunners on the beachhead who provided ground troops protection from enemy planes, he spent time with the 1st Division and the 29th Division, then accompanied the 9th Infantry Division in its assault on Cherbourg.

Pyle had gone far toward making what A. J. Liebling of *The New Yorker* later called "a large personal impress on the nation" during the biggest war in its history, and now the inevitable American myth-making apparatus, keyed to perfection in this war, took over. As Pyle became ever more weary, the press increasingly lionized him, often turning the facts of his life to its own ends and casting him in the mold of greatest social utility. Pyle was pleased to learn that *Time* magazine was preparing a cover story on him, but when the article appeared in the July 17, 1944, issue, he was disappointed, then angry. "Some of it of course was swell," he wrote Jerry, "but some was so completely distorted."

Time portrayed Pyle as an anemic Everyman, stumbling willy-nilly into war, all the while suffering silently his sense of inferiority among his fellow correspondents. Moreover, *Time* said, Pyle had early on been the object of many practical jokes and other indignities perpetrated by the soldiers whose stories he sought. Later, the magazine reported, they had let up on him because he shared their miserable lives and wrote such fine things about them. The forthcoming movie based on Pyle's book *Here Is Your War*, from whose scriptwriters *Time* reporters got much of this fictional nonsense, would, the magazine said, "admit his fear of battle, his apprehension about his work, his latest quirk—the conviction that now he is in France, he is going to be killed."

Pyle told Jerry that he had never been the victim of soldiers' scorn or practical jokes, that the article left him "without any dignity, and I believe I do have a little," and that he didn't "have any premonition of death, as they claim." He added, "In fact I certainly plan and dream way ahead all the time about what we'll do after the war." He told Lee Miller the *Time* story "created a legend that makes me a combination of half-wit and coward, and it'll grow and be perpetuated."

Three days after his invective against *Time*, Pyle underwent his most horrifying experience of the war, the climax of his combat reporting from the European Theater.

On July 25, 1944, the American First Army began its breakout from the beachhead toward Saint-Lô. Two hours' worth of heavy bombing and shelling were to precede tank and infantry attacks. But before the ground forces could move forward, a bombing error killed hundreds of Americans. Pyle, who had been assigned to an infantry division, was standing in a farmyard when "all of an instant the universe became filled with a gigantic rattling," and bombs began falling all around him. He and an officer scrambled under a farm wagon for shelter, Pyle remembering afterward "an inhuman tenseness of muscle and nerves." He was "grateful in a chastened way I had never experienced before, for just being alive." In the column, he forgave the flyers their mistake on behalf of the infantry, telling them the "chaos and bitterness" of that afternoon had passed. This equanimity in the aftermath of the bombing was great public relations between service branches, but privately Pyle said he would go crazy if he had to endure anything like it again.

Pyle entered Paris with French troops on August 25, 1944. The pleasure of the newly liberated Parisians and the rich symbolism of the event momentarily eased his fatigue, but within two days he was making preparations for a stateside leave. He was proud of not having taken a break for so long, but now he had to go home. "I have had all I can take for a while," he told his readers.

> I've been immersed in it too long. My spirit is wobbly and my mind is confused. The hurt has finally become too great. All of a sudden it seemed to me that if I heard one more shot or saw one more dead man, I would go off my nut. . . .

When Lee Miller met Pyle's ship in New York on September 18, 1944, he handed Pyle a letter from Jerry. She wrote that she was "humbly—and numbly, thankful" he was back, hastening to add that she was eager to see him, and, knowing his propensity for dawdling, jocularly adding that she would try to be patient. But, "if you linger in the East until frost takes the flowers—and nips the lawn—well! Love, darling." The letter's disjointed syntax held a clue to the instability of Jerry's condition. Like thirteen million other Americans, she read Ernie's column, and if she had experienced "real terror—simply stark terror" while he covered the London blitz four years before, it requires little imagination to sense what she had felt when she read of his narrowly escaping death at the Anzio beachhead and at Saint-Lô.

Jerry understood Ernie's devotion to the American troops he wrote about, but she had argued against his going to war from the start, and she suffered each time he ventured out. He was, after all, her only link to a happier past. Childless, living at great distance from her family in Minnesota, alone save for the impersonal attentions of doctors and private nurses, Jerry needed to be engaged emotionally. Sexual intimacy was out of the question, but the emotional intimacy she had enjoyed with Ernie in their youth wasn't—or so her plaintive letter hopefully implied.

As it turned out, it was. Ernie's capacity for intimacy, never highly developed in the first place, was now severely strained. (After the liberation of Paris, he had written that war had so "wrung and drained" his emotions that they "cringe from the effort of coming alive again.") As Jerry doubtless sensed in her more lucid moments, Ernie had abandoned her years before to marry his audience, with which he had a stylized intimacy that neatly suited his emotional needs. He phoned Jerry and told her he intended to remain in New York for several days so that the sculptor Jo Davidson could make a bust of his head. After that, he would spend a few days on the farm in Indiana, then fly to Albuquerque.

With millions of appreciative readers anxious for his every utterance, the pressures on Pyle had redoubled from those of a year before. So many people wanted so many things! *Editor & Publisher* wanted an interview. People on the street wanted his autograph. Helen Keller wanted to run her hands over his face; John Steinbeck wanted to talk. The mayor of Albuquerque wanted to throw a welcome-home dinner with five hundred guests. Wives and mothers wanted information about their husbands and sons. Roy Howard of Scripps-Howard wanted to have dinner. Lester Cowan wanted to confer about problems with his movie, *The Story of G.I. Joe.* Photographers wanted to take his picture. Scripps-Howard competitors wanted him to work for them.

Jerry, Paige Cavanaugh, and Jerry's private nurse met Pyle's plane at Albuquerque in late September, and within the week Lester Cowan and his director William Wellman arrived to discuss the movie. Shortly thereafter Pyle flew to Hollywood for more film conferences. Back in Albuquerque he spent mornings at the dentist's, while at home two secretaries worked to keep up with the mail and the constantly ringing telephone.

One day Ernie returned home and found Jerry's nurse in hysterics in the front yard. Jerry had locked herself in the bathroom after repeatedly stabbing herself in and about the throat with a pair of scissors. When Ernie broke open the bathroom door, he found Jerry standing expressionless before the wash basin, bleeding profusely. He held her until a surgeon arrived. Jerry neither spoke nor flinched while the doctor stitched her wounds. Luckily, she had not done mortal damage, but her wounds were severe. Ernie wrote to Cavanaugh: "On the right side of her neck, just below the jaw and just ahead of the ear, she had gouged a hole an inch and a half deep. There was a similar hole, though a little smaller, in the same place on the other side. Right square in front, just above the collar bone, she pounded the scissors straight into her neck nearly two inches, and got her windpipe. Then hacked her left wrist. She cut her left breast about 15 times with the razor blade, apparently stabbed with the corner of it."

He sent a long account of Jerry's suicide attempt and her subsequent confinement in an Albuquerque sanitarium to Lee Miller. It was a narrative remarkable chiefly for its documentary coolness and gross insensitivity. The moral sensibility so sharply present in Pyle's war reporting was absent here. Pyle told Miller he had feared for ten years that Jerry might try to kill herself but had decided "that her indirect threats were all part of her act. She had tried it a couple of times in the past but botched them up so badly they were almost laughable and convinced us she was acting. . . . But brother this one was no act. . . ."

While Jerry underwent thirty days of shock-therapy treatments, Ernie accepted honorary doctorates from the University of New Mexico and Indiana University and traveled to Washington to plan his trip to the Pacific Theater and to have his income taxes figured. (His tax bill for 1944 totaled one hundred five thousand dollars.) He had returned to Albuquerque by the time Jerry came home from the hospital, her memory fractured and her behavior erratic. She had learned of Ernie's plans to go to the Pacific and was depressed.

The procession of houseguests resumed. A writer came to prepare a profile of Pyle for *Life*, and Cavanaugh flew in from Los Angeles to sit in on the interviews. A photographer arrived to take pictures. One was of Pyle, Jerry, and their dog Cheetah in the living room of their house. Jerry sat semi-reclined in a dayseat, half smiling as she read a biography of Samuel Johnson. Pyle sat on a hassock, his hands pensively clasped, his jaw set, his eyes fixed on the wall opposite. Between them was the needle-nosed dog, staring in yet another direction. It's a lonely photograph; one can't avoid the sensation that all three were caught in the midst of supreme discomfort.

Pyle and Jerry saw each other for the last time at the railroad station in Los Angeles on or about Christmas Day 1944. They had spent a week or so with the Cavanaughs while Pyle visited the set of *The Story of G.I. Joe.* On their last night together, Lester Cowan took them to Ciro's, the Hollywood nightclub, where they danced together, after which Jerry and her nurse took the train back to Albuquerque. On the evening of New Year's Day, Pyle left Los Angeles for Camp Roberts, near San Francisco, on the first leg of his long journey to the Pacific. He resumed the column in San Francisco by dissembling about his vacation. "Despite all the frenzy, I've felt almost pathetic in my happiness at being home," he told his readers. "I've had a wonderful time." He spoke of Jerry, emphasizing her devotion to him, and ending on a rueful note:

> That Girl has been burdened by recurring illnesses, and has had to revolve between home and hospital. But she has succeeded in keeping

> the little white house just as it always was, which she knew is what I would want. . . .
>
> She lives only for the day when war is over and we can have a life together again. And that's what I live for too. . . . I hope we both last through until the sun shines in the world again.

Pyle had doubts about his surviving the war, despite his protests to Jerry after *Time* magazine had reported that he feared he would die in France. He had recently drawn up a will, laughingly telling Cavanaugh and Lee Miller, "I want you bastards to know that if I'm knocked off in the Pacific, you share in ten percent of my estate." He had arranged with an Albuquerque banker to handle Jerry's immediate financial needs, while his will provided her an income for life. And he told a reporter: "Well, you begin to feel that you can't go on forever without being hit. I feel that I've used up all my chances. And I hate it. . . . I don't want to be killed."

Jerry continued to plead with him to stay home. "I'm sorry darling," he wrote her, "but it's too late now to back out on this trip. You know that I don't want to go any more than you want me to, but the way I look at it it's almost beyond my control. If I stayed I'm afraid that would defeat both of us, for I'd probably gradually work up a guilty feeling that would haunt me. I hate it, but there's just nothing else I can do." Ernie told her, as he had countless times before, that he wanted her to be her old self again. This was not only a futile wish, it utterly ignored the changes Jerry had undergone. He failed to see that Jerry's old self was in part a product of his steady companionship, a commodity she had gone without for ten years.

In her loneliness, Jerry had begun to approach a spiritual understanding of herself and her condition. She wrote Ernie, "I'm a long way from reaching the honest humility I should have—but I see it clearly enough in moments to long for it. . . . I don't know the way—but hope and believe I may find it, dear. . . ." Jerry wanted to learn to pray, but Ernie frowned on the notion. "That has to be up to you, of course," he wrote her, "but it is so different from anything you or I have ever felt. I want you to get better but I wouldn't want you to become pious—for then you wouldn't be *you.*" No, Ernie told her, the solution to her troubles didn't reside in any "mystic device," nor was there any value in what he considered undue contrition. Calmness and a full routine would be her salvation—that and accepting things that made her unhappy, by which he surely meant his again subjecting himself to dangers he publicly admitted frightened him.

Shortly before he left San Francisco, Ernie mailed Jerry a wedding ring. She had never worn one before because she considered such overt symbols of union too conventional for her. Of late, though, she had changed her mind.

Hawaii was to be Pyle's first stop on his way to the Pacific Theater. Shortly before he left San Francisco, he told Jerry, "I think it's the lack of opportunity for calmness in America that has whipped me as much as anything; aboard a ship or in the islands I won't be such a public figure and can get back to normal routine."

It's hard to conceive of covering a war as "normal routine," but for Pyle it was, and he knew that re-establishing his work rhythm was his one hope of regaining peace of mind. But just as he had begun his vacation weary from war, he returned to war weary from home. He never overcame that emotional fatigue, even though Jerry wrote him frequently and at length, and even though her condition seemed improved. Nor did he ever recapture the pleasure work had represented for him. His coverage of the Pacific would be interesting enough, but missing would be the emotional and moral engagement so readily apparent in his European work. Pyle got a bad start in the Pacific, partly because his unyielding loyalty to the European Theater impaired his judgment, and partly because his celebrity forever got in the way.

At San Francisco, the Navy, delighted to have him, presented Pyle his naval insignia—a gold anchor and a gold-braided war correspondent's badge. On a tour of the Port of Embarkation, Pyle was greeted by a thousand cheering soldiers and a fifty-piece band. Newspapers reported that Pyle's presence in the Pacific would be a boost to servicemen's morale, but his comments in San Francisco hardly set the stage. "Ernie is a bit dubious about the prospects of doing a good job covering the Navy," one reporter wrote. "He says it's tougher to dramatize the life of a sailor." In this account, as in many others, Pyle was quoted as saying his time with the Navy would be short and that he would rejoin the infantry as soon as possible.

In Hawaii he told a reporter for a service newspaper that he couldn't "go overboard on sympathy" for men suffering so-called "island complex in the Pacific—not after I've seen the misery and cold and mud and death in Europe." From the Marianas he wrote, "Now we are far, far away from everything that was home or seemed like home. Five thousand miles from America, and twelve thousand miles from my friends fighting on the German border."

Pyle boarded an aircraft carrier, the USS *Cabot,* in a convoy carrying planes that would bomb the Japanese mainland and heavy artillery that would support landings on Iwo Jima. The *Cabot*'s sailors were an amicable bunch, "just as friendly as the soldiers I'd known on the other side," but Pyle believed they talked "more about wanting to go home than even the soldiers in Europe [did]." The sailors lived well—good food, daily baths, clean clothes, a bunk to sleep in, a locker to store things in. Their work was hard but the hours were regular. "The boys ask you a thousand times how this compares with the other side. I can only answer that this is much better. . . ." Most could see his point, but

> others yell their heads off about their lot, and feel they're being persecuted by being kept out of America a year. I've heard some boys say "I'd trade this for a foxhole any day." You just have to keep your mouth shut to a remark like that.

This was not sterling public relations; Pyle knew better than anyone how intensely service branches competed for attention. Moreover, he had lost sight of the fact that his audience comprised not only stateside readers but also servicemen overseas, many of whom received Pyle clippings from home. Pyle's comments did not go unanswered. In Honolulu, the editors of an Air Corps magazine severely rebuked him for his ignorance of the Pacific war and for his generally dismissive attitude.

Part of Pyle's irritation lay in his trouble with Navy censors, who wouldn't allow him to use sailors' names in his copy. Frustrated, Pyle threatened to clear out for the Philippines, where he might have a better chance of writing his sort of material. (The censorship restrictions were eventually lifted.) Here, too, the remoteness of one Pacific outpost from another injected a note of discontinuity into Pyle's writing. His erratic movement was reminiscent of his travel days in the 1930s. It wasn't until the invasion of Okinawa that Pyle returned to his "normal routine"—and that was only seventeen days before his death.

Traveling from Ulithi, near Guam, to Okinawa with units of the 1st Marine Division, Pyle was sure that this time he would be killed. "There's nothing romantic whatever in knowing that an hour from now you may be dead," he wrote of the landings. Ninety minutes after the invasion began, Pyle went ashore with the 5th Marine Regiment and was relieved at the lack of resistance in his sector. He spent two days with the Marines, then returned to the ship to write.

Pyle had always been squeamish about foreign cultures, particularly in matters of personal hygiene, but his comments on the Okinawan civilians were scathing, out of character for him and an indication of his fatigue. The Okinawans were "pitiful" in their poverty, "not very clean"; their houses were "utterly filthy." Certainly their standard of living was low, but Pyle couldn't understand "why poverty and filth need to be synonymous." The Okinawans "were all shocked from the bombardment and yet I think rather stupid too, so that when they talked they didn't make much sense."

Ironically, Pyle had found peace in the chaotic sounds and sights that filled his first night on Okinawa; they constituted the "old familiar pattern, unchanged by distance or time from war on the other side of the world." These were soldier verities, and with them he was comfortable. They were "so imbedded in my soul that, coming back . . . again, it seemed to me as I lay there that I'd never known anything else in my life. And there are millions of us."

Pyle returned to shore and spent a few days with the Marines, then boarded the command ship *Panamint.* So relieved was he to be alive that he promised Jerry this would be his last landing. Short of an accident, he wrote his father, he believed he would survive the war. There was another cause for optimism, too: Jerry's recent letters pointed toward some of the normalcy he had hoped for.

Ernie was pleased with the abundance of mail from her, and he vowed that his next trip home would be for good. She wrote him asking not just for reports on what he was doing, but for an indication of what he was thinking and feeling as well. This was an extraordinary departure from the desperately closed tone of the few letters he had received from her in Europe. When Ernie wrote her about his postwar vision of sitting quietly with no demands on him, she took pleasure in it. She wasn't beyond her troubles, she wrote, but things *were* better. She now saw as "faulty" her contempt for convention; she had revised her youthful notion that appearances were meaningless, and she regretted she had been remiss in keeping up the house and yard. Now she wanted the looks of the place "to fit in with the honor" bestowed on him when New Mexico had designated his birthday Ernie Pyle Day. She wanted to be worthy of being his wife, and she promised she would be useful to him when he came home to stay. "My love reaches out to you—strongly—and wants so much for you—Bless you my Ernie."

Pyle was killed by a Japanese sniper's machine-gun bullet on April 18, 1945, two days after American Marines landed on Ie Shima, a ten-square-mile island west of Okinawa. He had honored his commitment to make no more landings and had gone ashore a day later.

Spending the night in what had been a Japanese soldier's dugout, Pyle was affable and relaxed, glad to be with the infantry again. Shortly after ten the next morning, Pyle set off by jeep with four soldiers to find a command-post site for the 305th Regiment of the 77th Division. When the jeep was fired upon near the village of Ie, Pyle and the others took cover in ditches on either side of the road. Pyle raised his head to look for a companion and died instantly when a bullet pierced his left temple.

Several infantrymen who recovered his body under fire found in his pocket a draft of a column intended for release upon the end of the war in Europe, which Pyle had known was imminent. In it, Pyle urged the living, in their joy, not to forget that the price of victory had been paid by the dead. For his part, Pyle would never forget

> the unnatural sight of cold dead men scattered over the hillsides and in the ditches along the high rows of hedge throughout the world.
>
> Dead men by mass production—in one country after another—month after month and year after year. Dead men in winter and dead men in summer.
>
> Dead men in such familiar promiscuity that they become monotonous.
>
> Dead men in such monstrous infinity that you come almost to hate them. . . .

Pyle was buried on Ie Shima in a crude wooden coffin a soldier constructed.

In death as in life, Pyle was a democratizer. Reaction to his death was swift and effusive. The news followed by six days that of President Roosevelt's death, and everyone responded to it, from the newly sworn-in President of the United States to GIs all over the world, from General Eisenhower to a blacksmith in La Porte, Indiana. The tone of the comments was unanimous: Pyle's death was a personal loss for everyone. Official comments were no less sincere for their being steeped in press-release sentiment.

"The nation," said President Harry Truman, "is saddened again by the death of Ernie Pyle." War Secretary Henry Stimson felt "great distress," and Navy Secretary James Forrestal said America owed Pyle its "unending gratitude." "I have known no finer man, no finer soldier than he," said General Omar Bradley. Cartoonist Bill Mauldin, for whom Pyle had helped arrange stateside syndication, said, "The only difference between Ernie's death and the death of any other good guy is that the other guy is mourned by his company. Ernie is mourned by his army."

At Albuquerque, Jerry's doctor brought her the news, and newspaper headlines told the public " 'That Girl' Takes News Bravely." Paige Cavanaugh was at home in Inglewood, California, when a friend called with the sad message. (He immediately flew to Albuquerque to be with Jerry.) Lee Miller was shaving in the Philippines when he heard a bulletin on Armed Forces Radio. At Dana, a neighbor told Pyle's father and Aunt Mary.

It soon became clear that Pyle's demise meant more than the loss of a personal friend; it also represented the loss of a potent symbol. Because, as one newspaper noted, there was "no vice president to take Ernie Pyle's place," in the weeks following his death Americans sought to reclaim his symbolic value as the perfect embodiment of a democracy at war; and the expression of this reclamation, like the immediate reaction to the loss of him, ran from the eloquent to the bombastic. The poet Randall Jarrell wrote in *The Nation:*

> There are many men whose profession it is to speak for us—political and military and literary representatives . . . ; [Pyle] wrote what he had seen and heard and felt himself, and truly represented us.

Others sought to canonize him. In their eyes, Pyle was a martyr, and the popular conception of a martyred saint admits no moral ambivalence, much less moral failing. These comments were published in the *Congressional Record:*

> A brave man, a courageous man, a modest man, with the whole world as his assignment, Ernie Pyle looked out on the field of light and life with eyes that were kind and charitable and understanding. . . . It has been said that the dead take with them clutched tightly in their hands only the things they have given away. . . . Ernie Pyle took much with him in death, because he had given . . . [of] the best that was in him every day of his adult life.

Meanwhile, news items appeared in papers nationwide detailing the provisions of Pyle's will, President Truman's wish that Pyle be honored with a special Congressional medal, and the christening of a new troop transport with Pyle's name.

The Story of G.I. Joe was approaching release when Lester Cowan hit a snag with the Hays Office of the Motion Picture Producers and Distributors of America. This was to be the movie that faithfully portrayed the roughness of infantry life, including the coarseness of soldier talk. Nonetheless, the Hays Seal of Approval could not be granted the film because "certain lines of dialogue . . . are regarded as profanity under the Production Code. . . ." Cowan protested that the dialogue was spoken with "such deep feeling and conviction that it could not be construed as blasphemy," but eventually he changed the lines, and the Hays Office passed on the picture.*

On July 4, Jerry and her sister flew to Washington for an advance showing of the film at a meeting of the National Press Club, after which an Army general and a Navy admiral jointly presented her a posthumous Medal For Merit for Pyle on behalf of their service branches and the State Department. Present were the British ambassador, war correspondents, members of Congress, and several Supreme Court justices.

The Scripps-Howard *Indianapolis Times* had engineered an auction of Pyle's last manuscript ("bearing his own pencilled corrections"), with the proceeds going to war bonds. The bidding had lasted several weeks, with each bid duly reported in the paper. Finally, American United Life Insurance Company had come through with the fantastic sum of ten million five hundred twenty-five thousand dollars, and the company's treasurer accepted the manuscript at the world premiere of *The Story of G.I. Joe* on July 6. That evening, two thousand people viewed the film, including three hundred wounded veterans whose ten-dollar tickets had been paid for by civilians.

The citizens of Dana, meantime, had decided that a thirty-five-thousand-dollar library named for Pyle would be a suitable way to honor a celebrated native son. A New York public-relations firm got wind of the idea and formed a company, Ernie Pyle Memorial, Inc., through which to promote a grander scheme: a multi-million-dollar, one-hundred-acre, "landscaped, lake-studded park and cemetery, to which [Pyle's body] could be moved from Ie Shima. . . ." Pyle's tomb was to be surrounded by "honored dead of all states, [and] symbolic scenes of allied nations. . . ."

The proposal enraged Jerry, who told reporters her late husband

*Pyle had anticipated this problem and had urged Paige Cavanaugh, then in Cowan's employ, to intercede. Pyle wrote to Cavanaugh in June 1944: "I hope to God you succeed in keeping out of the dialogue the 'oh heck' shit you wrote me about."

would have been "horrified and indignant" at such an ostentatious undertaking. It was "entirely out of keeping with everything that Ernie ever did, or said, or thought, or was," she said. Moreover, she would never "consent to having his body moved," because "Ernie is lying where he would wish to be, with the men he loved." Editorial writers applauded Jerry's comments; Chicago columnist Sydney Harris thought she should be awarded a prize equivalent to the Pulitzer for her "magnificent blast at the press agents and promoters who have attached themselves like body lice to Ernie's well-deserved fame." Harris aptly dismissed the memorial park as "vulgar" and, with Jerry, endorsed "living memorials," like the Dana town library, in honor of Pyle and the other war dead.

Jerry's health steadily declined in the months following Pyle's death. In mid-November, she contracted influenza. Her weight dangerously low, she checked into St. Joseph's Hospital in Albuquerque, where she died of uremic poisoning the morning of November 23, 1945. One of her sisters told reporters Jerry had lost all interest in living in the seven months since Pyle's death. Paige Cavanaugh flew to Albuquerque to close out the Pyles' house. He retrieved bundles of letters Pyle had written Jerry over the years—"reams and reams of lovely lovemaking by mail," he called them.

Jerry was buried November 27 on a snow-covered hill near Afton, Minnesota. Pyle's body was later moved to Hawaii and buried in the National Memorial Cemetery of the Pacific in Punchbowl Crater. That they are buried forty-five hundred miles apart befits the physical and emotional distance at which they lived in the last decade of their lives. But the burial place of each is ironic in its own right.

Jerry had sung in the church choir and been active in the Christian Endeavor Society in her native Minnesota; but she had departed from the conservatism of her upbringing in 1918, when she moved to Washington, hopeful, in a girlish way, of finding excitement and freedom in the nation's capital. She found some of both, but she had spent the better part of her short life rebelling against what she had left behind.

Pyle had accepted the possibility that he would die in a war zone, but he would certainly have preferred to have been buried in Europe, where, after so many years of rootlessness, he had found a home and a sense of purpose with the infantry. Still, there is a curious bit of circularity about his having been buried in the Hawaiian Islands.

On a 1937 trip there, Pyle had visited the Kalaupapa leper colony on Molokai made famous by the Belgian priest Father Damien. His walk into "the foothills of martyrdom" bordered on the spiritual, and he told his readers he felt "a kind of unrighteousness at being whole and 'clean'; I experienced an acute feeling of spiritual need to be no better off than the leper."

Quite accurately, he knew that "in real life I am a 'sprint' martyr; the long steady pull is not for me. I tire of too much goodness, and wish to dart off and chase a rabbit." He abandoned his rabbit-chasing days five years later, when he landed with American soldiers in North Africa. That he was later killed was a direct result of his having taken up the long, steady pull.

GREAT BRITAIN:

December 1940—March 1941

FROM *AN ERNIE PYLE ALBUM*

When Ernie Pyle arrived in London in December 1940, German armies occupied much of central Europe, Holland, Belgium, Luxembourg, northern France and its western seacoast. Paris was also under Nazi control.

Japan had annexed part of Manchuria, occupied large and important parts of coastal China, and was eyeing other acquisitions, including France's rich colonies in southeast Asia. Italy had invaded Albania, had subjugated Ethiopia, and by September 1940 had driven into Egypt. After its occupation of France in the summer of 1940, Germany had laid plans to invade Britain through the southern and eastern English seacoasts.

Thus began the Battle of Britain, a desperate air war focused first on British ports, radar stations, and Royal Air Force fields, and, by the end of August, on London itself. The German bombers encountered spirited RAF fighter resistance and so, in early September, switched from day to night raids. Shortly thereafter, Hitler postponed his invasion plans, preferring to weaken the British through repeated bombings of London, the so-called London Blitz.

Pyle's first exposure to a war zone had been the heavily fortified eastern coast of England, to which he had flown from Lisbon in a sea plane. On the train to London, life had seemed normal enough, but then he had seen silver barrage balloons floating by the hundreds above an English city, followed by "a crater in a suburban street, then wrecked houses nearby, and a small factory burned. After that, for block after block, half the buildings we saw were wrecked."

Pyle had assumed the destruction would look different from that in newsreel pictures back home. But it didn't. "The only thing is that now it's real and you feel a revulsion and a small sinking knowledge of the awful power of a single bomb. You feel what it could do to you personally."

He arrived in London at night and found the streets dark and quiet, the windows and doors covered, cars and buses running without lights. The blacked-out city was "like something mysterious, darkly seen in a dream—shapes here, shadows there, tiny lights swimming toward you, dark bulks moving noiselessly away." A few nights later, the city was anything but dark. Fires set off by German bombs on the night of December 30 were the worst since the Great Fire of 1666.

A Dreadful Masterpiece

London, *December 30, 1940*—Someday when peace has returned to this odd world I want to come to London again and stand on a certain balcony on a moonlit night and look down upon the peaceful silver curve of the Thames with its dark bridges.

And standing there, I want to tell somebody who has never seen it how London looked on a certain night in the holiday season of the year 1940.

For on that night this old, old city—even though I must bite my tongue in shame for saying it—was the most beautiful sight I have ever seen.

It was a night when London was ringed and stabbed with fire.

*

They came just after dark, and somehow I could sense from the quick, bitter firing of the guns that there was to be no monkey business this night.

Shortly after the sirens wailed I could hear the Germans grinding overhead. In my room, with its black curtains drawn across the windows, you could feel the shake from the guns. You could hear the boom, crump, crump, crump, of heavy bombs at their work of tearing buildings apart. They were not too far away.

Half an hour after the firing started I gathered a couple of friends and went to a high, darkened balcony that gave us a view of one-third of the entire circle of London.

As we stepped out onto the balcony a vast inner excitement came over all of us—an excitement that had neither fear nor horror in it, because it was too full of awe.

You have all seen big fires, but I doubt if you have ever seen the whole horizon of a city lined with great fires—scores of them, perhaps hundreds.

The closest fires were near enough for us to hear the crackling flames and the yells of firemen. Little fires grew into big ones even as we watched. Big ones died down under the firemen's valor only to break out again later.

About every two minutes a new wave of planes would be over. The motors seemed to grind rather than roar, and to have an angry pulsation like a bee buzzing in blind fury.

The bombs did not make a constant overwhelming din as in those terrible days of last September. They were intermittent—sometimes a few seconds apart, sometimes a minute or more.

Their sound was sharp, when nearby, and soft and muffled, far away.

Into the dark, shadowed spaces below us, as we watched, whole batches of incendiary bombs fell. We saw two dozen go off in two seconds. They flashed terrifically, then quickly simmered down to pinpoints of dazzling white, burning ferociously.

These white pinpoints would go out one by one as the unseen heroes of the moment smothered them with sand. But also, as we watched, other pinpoints would burn on and pretty soon a yellow flame would leap up from the white center. They had done their work—another building was on fire.

The greatest of all the fires was directly in front of us. Flames seemed to whip hundreds of feet into the air. Pinkish-white smoke ballooned upward in a great cloud, and out of this cloud there gradually took shape—so faintly at first that we weren't sure we saw correctly—the gigantic dome and spires of St. Paul's Cathedral.

St. Paul's was surrounded by fire, but it came through. It stood there in its enormous proportions—growing slowly clearer and clearer, the way objects take shape at dawn. It was like a picture of some miraculous figure that appears before peace-hungry soldiers on a battlefield.

*

The streets below us were semi-illuminated from the glow.

Immediately above the fires the sky was red and angry, and overhead, making a ceiling in the vast heavens, there was a cloud of smoke all in pink. Up in that pink shrouding there were tiny, brilliant specks of flashing light—anti-aircraft shells bursting. After the flash you could hear the sound.

Up there, too, the barrage balloons were standing out as clearly as if it were daytime, but now they were pink instead of silver. And now and then through a hole in that pink shroud there twinkled incongruously a permanent, genuine star—the old-fashioned kind that has always been there.

Below us the Thames grew lighter, and all around below were the shadows—the dark shadows of buildings and bridges that formed the base of this dreadful masterpiece.

Later on I borrowed a tin hat and went out among the fires. That was exciting too, but the thing I shall always remember above all the other things in my life is the monstrous loveliness of that one single view of London on a holiday night—London stabbed with great fires, shaken by explosions, its dark regions along the Thames sparkling with the pinpoints of white-hot bombs, all of it roofed over with a ceiling of pink that held bursting shells, balloons, flares and the grind of vicious engines. And in yourself the excitement and anticipation and wonder in your soul that this could be happening at all.

These things all went together to make the most hateful, most beautiful single scene I have ever known.

Bombing Aftermath

LONDON, *December 31, 1940*—London learns a lesson from each new horror that the Germans bring over.

Through the school of experience it is gradually acquiring a superb efficiency at its new career of bomb-receiving.

It learned a keen lesson from Sunday night's fire-bombing. That lesson is that from now on the rooftops of London must be manned through every hour of darkness.

They say there are a million buildings in London. Of course there is not likely to be a watcher on every single little roof, but when Hitler sends his fire-sprayers again, I imagine there will be at least a quarter of a million pairs of hands and eyes waiting on the darkened rooftops to be ready to smother his fire bombs or direct the firemen to them.

The way it stands now any building in which more than thirty people are employed must have a spotter on its roof at night, and that is all. But there is apt to be a stricter compulsion soon, and in any event volunteer roof-spotting is just on the verge of becoming very fashionable.

*

Sunday night I watched incendiary bombs fall in dark places and saw great fires grow from them. Let me tell you how the thing works.

A fire bomb is about a foot long, and shaped like a miniature torpedo. It looks and feels like limestone. On the outside of it are four metal fins circled by a strip of metal on the top end. The bomb is made of a magnesium alloy, with a thermite core.

Each one weighs a little better than two pounds. One plane can scatter a thousand of them. Ten planes could easily start seven hundred fifty fires at once, over a large area.

Of course you don't see the bombs falling. They go off when they strike. If they hit the street they bounce crazily like a football, sputter violently for the first minute, throwing white fire about thirty feet, and then simmer down in an intense molten mass and burn about ten minutes more.

It is said they burn at a temperature of two thousand degrees. If one is left on a floor it will burn a hole and drop through. When they land in the open they are easily smothered with sand. Common ordinary citizens have smothered thousands of them.

Sunday night I saw one that fell within two feet of an emergency sandbox in the street. That was an easy one. But few of them land so conveniently.

That night I went to an office building that I visit frequently, and there two fire bombs had plunged through the roof and on down through three floors. One of them had gone through a heavy sheet of steel laid over an airshaft. It left an opening in that steel plate exactly the shape of the bomb, and as neat as though it had been cut in cardboard with a knife.

Now there was a lesson about roof spotters. The men on the roof of that building knew that those bombs had gone through, and they were quickly smothered. But there were hundreds of unwatched buildings in London that night into which fire bombs plunged unnoticed, and ten minutes later they were aflame.

That night as I wandered along Fleet Street I saw a five-story building suddenly leap into great flames. The firemen hadn't even known there was a fire in it.

*

At home, when a big fire starts, the police rope off the whole section, but it wasn't so in London Sunday night. What few pedestrians were there could go anywhere they liked, and they didn't have to feel their way that night, for there was no darkness.

Probably foolishly, I walked down a street that was afire on both sides, past walls that would soon be ready to fall. Hundreds of small motor pumps, carried in two-wheeled trailers behind cars, stood in the streets. The engines made such a whirr you couldn't have heard a plane overhead.

Firemen by the hundreds were working calmly, shouting orders to each other, smoking cigarets, and paying no attention to pedestrians.

I walked ten blocks. Every step had to be picked separately amidst an intertwined mass of fire hose.

Somehow I didn't have a feeling that this was war. I just felt as if I were seeing a terrific number of big "natural" fires. Even when I came upon two buildings that had been blown to dust by heavy bombs less than an hour before, there was still a feeling that it was all perfectly natural.

*

Although bombs are liable to fall anywhere, it happened that none came within six blocks of where we stood watching the early part of the fantastic show Sunday night. There were fires all around us, but we seemed to be in an island of immunity.

When we started out among the fires, the friends with whom I had been watching took another route and I did my fire wandering alone.

Oddly enough I was never afraid. As I remember it, my only concern was lest I get in the firemen's way.

When I returned to our oasis shortly before midnight, just as I stopped in the door the "raiders-passed" signal sounded. Up in my room I discovered that my feet were soaked and my coat drenched with spray from leaky hoses. And it will take a week to get the smoke out of my clothes.

When I turned out the light and pulled the blackout curtains from across the windows the room was bright from the glare of the fires, and it was hard to get to sleep. But I did sleep. And when I awakened around six o'clock in the morning the great light in the sky was gone. London again was almost as dark as it has been every night for a year and a half. Thus do the firemen of London work.

The coming of daylight is always a blessing. Things have a way of being overly grotesque at night. Today I can go out onto our balcony, where we stood watching London burn, and London will look just as it did the afternoon before the raiders came.

True, property was destroyed. Much property, valuable both materially and sentimentally. And lives were lost. But London is big and its lives are many. You feel a little abashed to realize the next morning that London as a whole is still here. The skyline looks just the same. The streets are jammed with humans.

Life is going on—where last night you felt that this must be the end of everything.

A City Beseiged

LONDON, *January 4, 1941*—This is indeed a city at war. A mere two-block walk will show you that.

I will try to describe all the little things that you would see on a short stroll. Just shut your eyes, try to transfer the details to your own city and see how odd it looks to you.

Every block is dotted with shelter signs. The official ones are black metal plates clamped to light posts, like street signs. They have a big white letter "S," and underneath in small letters the word "Shelter" and a white arrow pointing to the building in front of which the sign is affixed.

Each sign has a little V-shaped roof over it to keep the dim night-light from shining upward.

Every block has a dozen signs of white paper, pasted on building walls, saying, "Shelter Here During Business Hours" or "Shelter for Fifty Persons after 5 P.M."

A shelter is anything that protects you. It may be an underground restaurant, a store basement, a bank vault.

I know buildings in London that go six stories underground. When the banshee wails in London's West End you wouldn't have to run fifty yards in any direction to find a shelter.

Other signs, in yellow and black, say "To the Trenches." They point the way to shelters dug underneath small downtown parks such as Leicester Square. Every park and open space in London's West End has a newly built catacomb underneath.

Then there are surface shelters. You see these everywhere. They are simply long, windowless, flat-topped sheds, about eight feet high and ten feet wide, stretching for a block or more. They are built of a light-tan brick and divided into sections, each of which will hold about fifty persons.

Some of them are built right down the middle of wide streets. Others are on sidewalks, up against the buildings, leaving only a couple of feet of sidewalk room.

There are also signs with arrows pointing to first-aid posts and fire substations.

All over London, in little parks and areaways and alleys there are tanks of water for fire-fighting. Barrels and buckets of sand, for throwing on incendiary bombs, small pumps and auxiliary fire apparatus are scattered everywhere. Even in the halls of my holer.

*

A colossal amount of construction and repair work is going on all over London. Thirty-five thousand men are engaged in cleaning up the rubble of bombed buildings. Other scores of thousands work on the streets and under them on the maze of utility pipes and wires. Thousands more dig, build and hammer day and night, including Sundays, making more deep shelters, bricking up window openings, throwing up auxiliary walls.

Many a building has a brick wall standing in the middle of the sidewalk about three feet in front of its entrance, with a door in the middle. A few have built brick walls that entirely blanket their store fronts. And in some of London's most important buildings, which I cannot name, workmen today are bricking up every window opening, leaving only one little gunhole in the center, so that they become literally fortresses.

This is for the invasion, if it ever comes and if it gets this far.

Of course nobody dreams that it will get this far, but they are taking no chances. They are making ready to fight in every street, behind every wall, out of every window, if it must come to that.

*

Around some government buildings there are nasty-looking mazes of barbed wire. Some of the public statues are completely buried under mounds of sandbags, but most of them aren't.

Piles of sandbags buttress the foundations of thousands of stores. Many of these sandbag piles look ragged and ratty now, the bags have sprung leaks from long exposure to the weather and sand trickles out of them. Many of them, for that matter, have been stabbed by firefighters getting sand to put out incendiary bombs.

Army cars run about the streets. Huge, streamlined buses, camouflaged with a dull brown paint, come to town with soldiers on leave. You could hardly count the pedestrians in one block who are in uniform. At the cheaper restaurants the checkroom has more rifles than umbrellas.

Occasionally in some open space you see a flat sheet of brass-colored metal on top of a waist-high post. It looks something like a sundial. This is a gas detector. If gas ever comes, this metal will change color.

Great parks are all dug up with trenches and mounds of dirt to keep enemy planes from landing. St. James's Park has its honorable bomb craters, and its below-ground shelters, and even its barbed wire.

Occasionally you see a big gun on a rooftop.

All this panorama is in addition to the wreckage you see on every side.

Yes, London is a martial city. You can hardly conceive of Denver or Indianapolis looking like it. And yet people are so accustomed to it now that they hardly notice anything different.

Nobody, unless he is brand-new here, stops to look at bomb damage. Londoners seem barely aware of the barbed wire, the dugouts, the shelter signs. And I found that I too, after the first few days, could walk block after block without particularly noticing any of these things.

It is a new type of life, and that life has now become, through months of living with it, the normal life.

The Heroes Are All The People

LONDON, *January 10, 1941*—At home you all have read about London's amazing ability to take it, and about the almost annoying calm of Englishmen in the face of Hitler's bombs.

Well, I am not going to dwell on this, since it has been much written about already. But I just want to confirm that what you have read in this connection is all true. I got it the very minute I stepped off the plane from Lisbon, and I've been getting it ever since.

You get it in the attitudes of people, you get it in the casual way common folks talk, you get it just by looking around and seeing people going about their business.

The day before Christmas a hotel maid said, "I'll never forgive that old Hitler if he gives us a blitz on Christmas Day."

That's typical British conversation. The attitude of the people is not one of bravado. It is no self-injection of "Do or die for dear old Siwash."*

It isn't flag-waving, or our own sometimes silly brand of patriotism. In fact, I've never seen or heard the word patriotism since coming here.

No, it is none of these. It is simply a quaint old British idea that nobody is going to push them around with any lasting success.

There are millions of people in this world who fear that England may eventually lose this war. Such an ending is inconceivable to the British.

*

The whole spirit of this war is different from that of the World War.† Over here there doesn't seem to be the pumped-up, hysterical hatred that we had for Germany in the World War. I've heard Germans referred to as "the Boche" only once in London.

You don't hear atrocity stories told around here about the Germans. You don't hear people making outlandish remarks. You no longer hear yarns about Hitler being insane and a pervert. In fact, I've heard him referred to several times as a mighty smart man who has made very few mistakes. This isn't spoken sympathetically, or by pro-Nazis, but by common Englishmen willing to give the devil his due.

They say Hitler has made only one big mistake so far, and that was by starting the war in the first place.

*Siwash was a small provincial college in fiction by the American author George Fitch.
†World War I. Only later were the two wars distinguished by the appellations World War I and World War II.

*

And the spirit of bravery in the face of death is different in this war too. You all remember, or at least have read about, the eat-drink-and-be-merry-for-tomorrow-we-die-spirit of soldiers on leave in the World War. It was fatalistic, and dramatic, and what-the-hell. It was champagne and girls and on with the dance while there's still time.

That's not true in this war. There is night life in London, but not that daredevil kind of night life. People dance quietly. Late parties are rare. Drunkenness is not common. Soldiers on leave act much like civilians in peacetime. For in this war it isn't the soldiers who may die tomorrow—it's the people.

When the King goes out to inspect his heroes, they aren't long lines of straight-standing men in khaki with polished buttons. They are grimy firemen and wardens in blue overalls, so tired they can't even stand up straight for the King.

When just ordinary people at home may die tomorrow, heroics go out the window.

People aren't filled with a madly sweet compulsion to crowd a lifetime of fun into their few remaining hours. No, they are too busy, too poor, too tired, and too placidly determined to win by sticking it out.

It's a funny war. As someone remarked, the front-line trenches are four miles straight up above London, and the heroes are all the people.

*

It is true that all eyes in England look toward America.

My American accent alone is a key to unlock almost any door in London—except the doors of the extremely upper classes, of course.

And just as American public opinion about the war changes gradually,* so I believe the British feeling about the possibility of our entering the war is changing.

A few months ago, they say, all England was rabid for America to come in. But now many people are looking beyond the mere emotional effect of our entrance.

Many feel that if we came in, all our production would be kept

*President Franklin Roosevelt had created federal agencies to coordinate war production on Britain's behalf in September 1940. By November, he had proposed lend-lease, an aid program under which war matériel was to be provided to Britain and other anti-fascist nations with indefinite repayment terms. Public opinion was mixed. Individually and in groups, Americans had rallied to Britain's support by making bandages and donating blood and money to the Red Cross, but government assistance was another matter. Isolationists feared such a move would drag the country into a war. Interventionists, believing the nation should do its part to crush European fascism, favored helping Britain as a good first step.

at home and England would get less than she is getting now. About a third of the people I've discussed the matter with feel that way. But almost without exception they do feel that we should furnish cargo ships and convoy them with our warships.

*

Today every London conversation eventually switches around to, "He's up to something. What do you think it is?" Nine times out of ten, Hitler is referred to as "he" rather than by name. Even the newspapers do it sometimes.

Something is being cooked up—everybody is sure of that. Most people think he will attempt an invasion before spring. Many think he will unwind an aerial blitz over London this month that will make the September bombings seem tame.

Any night he may start it. Any night people expect it. And they are ready. They feel that Hitler has not got anything that they, ordinary people, can't take.

And after being here with them for a few weeks I somehow believe they are right.

January 13, 1941—. . . "Dispersal" is becoming more and more the theme of England in wartime—dispersal of troups, of factories, of children, of food. The bombings have brought that about.

Scatter every vital thing all over England in tiny units and small groups—that's the keynote.

Today only eighty thousand of London's one million children are left in the city. They are all over England.

They tell me that the soldiers, with some exceptions, eat and sleep in groups no larger than thirty. Army trucks are always parked a good fifty yards apart so a single bomb won't get more than one of them. Factories have branches everywhere. And as for food, it is stored in thousands of nooks and crannies all over Great Britain.

There are stocks of food in empty garages, in old meeting halls, in unused theaters, police stations, barns, cellars. No one-night blitz, no matter how terrific, is going to wipe out any notable portion of Britain's stored food.

And speaking of dispersal, the Ministry of Food keeps only a skeleton staff of two hundred fifty in London. The bulk of the ministry's staff of about twenty-five hundred are in the country.

England began working out a wartime food-control plan four years before the war started. It even had all the ration books printed and waiting months before the war.

The first rationing was not put in effect until four months after the war started—that is, last January. Bacon, butter and sugar were the first items dealt with. . . .

A Tube Shelter

LONDON, *January 29, 1941*— I got my very first view of an underground shelter crowd at the big Liverpool Street tube [subway] station. It was around eight o'clock on a raidless night. A policeman in the upper vestibule told us just to go down the escalator and take a look—as though it were a zoo. So we did.

Somehow I must have thought that there'd be nobody down there that night, or that if there were they'd be invisible or something, because I wasn't emotionally ready at all to see people lying around by the thousands on cold concrete.

In my first day in England I had seen terrible bomb damage. I had seen multitudinous preparations for war. I had talked with wounded soldiers. I had gone through London's great night of fire-bombing. I had listened for hours to the crack of guns and the crunch of bombs. And although I didn't especially know it at the time, none of these things went clear down deep inside and made me hurt.

It was not until I went down seventy feet into the bowels of the Liverpool Street tube and saw humanity sprawled there in childlike helplessness that my heart first jumped and my throat caught.

I know I must have stopped suddenly and drawn back.

I know I must have said to myself, "Oh my God!"

*

We hunted up the shelter marshal, and talked to him for a long time. He was immensely proud of his shelter, and I suppose he had a right to be, for they say it is paradise now compared to what it was in the beginning.

He told us to take a walk through the shelter and then meet him at the back entrance.

This is a new section of the tunnel, not yet used by trains. The tube is narrower than most of New York's subway excavations, and it is elliptical or egg-shaped. It is walled with steel casing.

We walked to the far end, about an eighth of a mile, through one tube, and then back in the parallel tube, which is just like the other.

On benches on each side, as though sitting and lying on a long streetcar seat, were the people, hundreds of them. And as we walked they stretched into thousands.

In addition, there was a row of sleeping forms on the wooden floor of the tube, stretched crosswise. Their bodies took up the whole space, so we had to watch closely when we put our feet down between the sleepers.

Many of these people were old—wretched and worn old people, people who had never known many of the good things of life and who were now winding up their days on this earth in desperate discomfort.

They were the bundled-up, patched-up people with lined faces that we have seen for years sitting dumbly in waiting lines at our own relief offices at home.

There were children too, some asleep and some playing. There were youngsters in groups, laughing and talking and even singing.

There were smart-alecks and there were quiet ones. There were hard-working people of middle age who had to rise at five and go to work.

Some people sat knitting or playing cards or talking. But mostly they just sat. And though it was only eight o'clock, many of the old people were already asleep.

It was the old people who seemed so tragic. Think of yourself at seventy or eighty, full of pain and of the dim memories of a lifetime that has probably all been bleak. And then think of yourself now, traveling at dusk every night to a subway station, wrapping your ragged overcoat about your old shoulders and sitting on a wooden bench with your back against a curved steel wall. Sitting there all night, in nodding and fitful sleep.

Think of that as your destiny—every night, every night from now on.

People looked up as we came along in our nice clothes and our obviously American hats. I had a terrible feeling of guilt as I walked through there—the same feeling that I have had when going through penitentiaries, staring at the prisoners. I felt ashamed to be there staring.

I couldn't look people in the face; consequently I didn't see very much of human visage that night, for I looked mostly at the floor. But I saw all I could bear. I saw enough.

*

Since that first night I have seen too much of it. I no longer feel that way about the shelterers in mass. Repetition makes the unusual become commonplace. Enough of anything dulls the emotions.

But I still think my first impression was a valid one. I still think it speaks the frightening poverty of character in this world more forcibly than do the bombs that cause it.

A bombed building looks like something you have seen before—

it looks as though a hurricane had struck. But the sight of thousands of poor, opportunityless people lying in weird positions against cold steel, with all their clothes on, hunched up in blankets, lights shining in their eyes, breathing fetid air—lying there far underground like rabbits, not fighting, not even mad, just helpless, scourged, weakly, waiting for the release of another dawn—that, I tell you, is life without redemption.

Pyle left London in early February to report on how the war was affecting people in the industrial cities, on the farms, and in the coal mines. He filed dispatches from York, Boroughbridge, Edinburgh, Glasgow, Birmingham, Coventry, Bristol, Shirehampton, and Dover.

Meanwhile, after much debate, Congress had approved President Roosevelt's lend-lease program. By this time, public opinion ran in favor of helping Britain, despite the risk of war with Germany, and Congress in late March 1941 voted to spend seven billion dollars in aid.

The United States was only nine months away from a formal declaration of war on the Axis powers when Pyle left Britain in the spring, but already the Battle of the Atlantic was underway, as American Navy ships escorted lend-lease shipments across the ocean, fighting with German submarines and warships. American lives and vessels were lost in this undeclared war. The Battle of Britain ended in June, when German planes were directed against Russia. In all, forty thousand civilians were killed in the bombings, and two hundred thousand injured.

NORTH AFRICA:

November 1942—June 1943

FROM *AN ERNIE PYLE ALBUM*

Much had happened in this war since Pyle's departure from England in the spring of 1941.

That summer, the Nazis had invaded the Balkans and then Russia. On December 7, 1941, the Japanese had attacked the American Navy at Pearl Harbor, thus drawing the United States into an alliance with twenty-five other nations, including Great Britain and the Soviet Union, against the Axis powers.

Pyle, meanwhile, had resumed his travel column, but the gravity of the war soon drew his attention, and in June 1942 he flew to Great Britain to report on the training of American troops.

Convinced of the need to relieve their Soviet ally by diverting Nazi attention, Prime Minister Winston Churchill and President Franklin Roosevelt had decided on an invasion of Axis-held North Africa. Operation Torch was the code name for what was to be a simultaneous three-pronged invasion of French Morocco and Algeria from two oceans, the Atlantic and the Mediterranean. It would be an ambitious undertaking, with troop convoys sailing from the United States and Great Britain, all under the command of General Dwight Eisenhower, then relatively unknown but soon to become supreme Allied commander in Europe.

The landings were made on the Atlantic coast of French Morocco and at Oran and Algiers in Algeria on November 8, 1942. The next day, the Germans occupied Tunisia, to the east of Algeria and just a short jump across the Mediterranean from Sicily. Dislodging them was to be a long, difficult process. But, as the Allies moved eastward (albeit slowly) through the winter mud, and as the British under General Bernard Montgomery pursued the German Afrika Korps westward through the Libyan desert after defeating it at El Alamein, the Germans and the Italians would be caught in a giant pincer movement—the largest of its kind ever and the beginning of the end for the Axis in North Africa.

Eisenhower had already moved his headquarters from Oran to Algiers when Pyle arrived in an eight-hundred-ship convoy bearing replacement troops for those killed and wounded in the initial landings. He had left London the day after the invasion began, "feeling self-conscious and ridiculous and old in Army uniform." Aboard ship (his was a British troop transport loaded with Americans), Pyle had closely observed the behavior of the officers and enlisted men, some of whom had no idea where they were headed.

The reaction of British waiters to American table habits had amused him, but he had been gratified when the stuffy British "finally broke down and entered into the spirit of the thing, and . . . eventually enjoyed the Wild West camaraderie as much as the Americans did." With this, Pyle had sounded one of his lasting and most comic themes—rambunctious Americans encountering traditional cultures, and forever being themselves.

As the convoy had passed through the Strait of Gibraltar, a radio message had reported that fifty German submarines were waiting for them. "The night by its very gentleness seemed in evil collusion with the plague that lay beneath the waters." The convoy was not attacked, however, and soon arrived at Oran, where "like twine from a hidden ball, the ships poured us out onto the docks in long brown lines. We lined up and marched away. . . . We marched at first gaily and finally with great weariness, but always with a feeling that at last we were beginning the final series of marches that would lead us home again—home, the one really profound goal that obsesses every one of the brown-clad Americans marching today on foreign shores."

Home—yearning for it, idealizing it, but too far removed from it to really fight in its name—this was to be another of Pyle's recurring themes. Unlike many of the soldiers, Pyle knew the war would last a long time. What he didn't know was that the exhilaration of life lived at the edge would soon give way to despair.

Killing Is All That Matters

WITH THE AMERICAN FORCES IN ALGIERS, *December 1, 1942*—From now onward, stretching for months and months into the future, life is completely changed for thousands of American boys on this side of the earth. For at last they are in there fighting.

The jump from camp life into front-line living is just as great as the original jump from civilian life into the Army. Only those who served in the last war can conceive of the makeshift, deadly urgent, always-moving-onward complexion of front-line existence. And existence is exactly the word: it is nothing more.

The last of the comforts are gone. From now on you sleep in bedrolls under little tents. You wash whenever and wherever you can. You carry your food on your back when you are fighting.

You dig ditches for protection from bullets and from the chill north wind off the Mediterranean. There are no more hot-water taps. There are no post exchanges where you can buy cigarets. There are no movies.

When you speak to a civilian you have to wrestle with a foreign language. You carry just enough clothing to cover you, and no more. You don't lug any knickknacks at all.

When our troops made their first landings in North Africa they went four days without even blankets, just catching a few hours' sleep on the ground.

Everybody either lost or chucked aside some of his equipment. Like most troops going into battle for the first time, they all carried too much at first. Gradually they shed it. The boys tossed out personal gear from their musette bags and filled them with ammunition. The countryside for twenty miles around Oran was strewn with overcoats, field jackets and mess kits as the soldiers moved on the city.

Arabs will be going around for a whole generation clad in odd pieces of American Army uniforms.

*

At the moment our troops are bivouacked for miles around each of three large centers of occupation—Casablanca, Oran and Algiers. They are consolidating, fitting in replacements, making repairs—spending a few days taking a deep breath before moving on to other theaters of action.

They are camped in every conceivable way. In the city of Oran some are billeted in office buildings, hotels and garages. Some are camping in parks and big vacant lots on the edge of town. Some are miles away, out in the country, living on treeless stretches of prairie. They are in tiny groups and in huge batches.

Some of the officers live in tents and sleep on the ground. Others have been lucky enough to commandeer a farmhouse or a barn, sometimes even a modern villa.

The tent camps look odd. The little low tents hold two men apiece and stretch as far as you can see.

There are Negro camps as well as white.

You see men washing mess kits and clothing in five-gallon gasoline cans, heated over an open fire made from sticks and pieces of packing cases. They strip naked and take sponge baths in the heat of the day. In the quick cold of night they cuddle up in their bedrolls.

You see Negroes playing baseball under the bright African sun during their spare hours of an afternoon.

*

The American soldier is quick in adapting himself to a new mode of living. Outfits which have been here only three days have dug vast networks of ditches three feet deep in the bare brown earth. They have rigged up a light here and there with a storage battery. They have gathered boards and made floors and sideboards for their tents to keep out the wind and sand. They have hung out their washing, and painted their names over the tent flaps. You even see a soldier sitting on his "front step" of an evening playing a violin.

They've been here only three days and they know they're unlikely to be here three days more, but they patch up some kind of home nevertheless.

Even in this short waiting period life is far from static. Motor convoys roar along the highways. Everything is on a basis of "not a minute to spare." There is a new spirit among the troops—a spirit of haste.

Planes pass constantly, eastbound. New detachments of troops wait for orders to move on. Old detachments tell you the stories of their first battle, and conjecture about the next one. People you've only recently met hand you slips of paper with their home addresses and say, "You know, in case something happens, would you mind writing . . ."

At last we are in it up to our necks, and everything is changed, even your outlook on life.

Swinging first and swinging to kill is all that matters now.

The town as a whole has been turned back to the French, but the Army keeps a hand raised and there will be no miscues.

December 8, 1942— . . . The Germans had stripped North Africa of everything. Foodstuffs went across the Mediterranean to France and on to Germany. The people here actually were in a pitiful condition. They were starving. The American occupation naturally stopped this flow to Germany. Our soldiers say that within a week they could see the effects. Food produced here in this fertile country now stays here. Further, our Army is donating huge food stocks to the city. The people are gradually starting to eat once more.

Americans, notoriously, are often foolishly generous. The troops in the first wave came ashore with only canned field rations carried on their backs, yet our soldiers gave much of this to the pitiful-looking Arab children. The result was that pretty soon the soldiers themselves hadn't much left to eat, so they lived for days on oranges.

In England, oranges are practically unknown, so here we've gorged ourselves on oranges. Some troops have eaten so many they got diarrhea and broke out in a rash. I buy tiny tangerines, very juicy, to carry around in my pockets. They cost a franc each, about one and a third cents. . . .

Scared Stiff

WITH THE AMERICAN FORCES IN ALGERIA, *December 9, 1942*—The hardest fighting in the whole original North African occupations seems to have been here in Oran. Many of my friends whom I knew in England went through it, and they have told me all about it. Without exception, they admit they were scared stiff.

Don't get the wrong idea from that. They kept going forward. But it was their first time under fire and, being human, they were frightened.

As one private said: "There was no constipation in our outfit those first few days."

I asked an officer how the men manifested fright. He said largely by just looking pitifully at each other and edging close together to have company in misery.

Now that the first phase is over, a new jubilance has come over the troops. There is a confidence and enthusiasm among them that didn't exist in England, even though morale was high there. They were impatient to get started and get it over, and now that they've started and feel sort of like veterans, they are eager to sweep on through.

That first night of landing, when they came ashore in big steel motorized invasion barges, many funny things happened. One famous officer intended to drive right ashore in a jeep, but they let the folding end of the barge down too soon and the jeep drove off into eight feet of water. Other barges rammed ashore so hard the men jumped off without even getting their feet wet.

It was moonlight, and the beach was deathly quiet. One small outfit I know didn't hear a shot till long after daylight the next morning, but the moonlight and shadows and surprising peacefulness gave them the creeps, and all night, as they worked their way inland over the hills, nobody spoke above a whisper.

Each outfit was provided with the password beforehand. In the shadows, soldiers couldn't tell who was who, and everyone was afraid of getting shot by his own men, so all night the hillsides around Oran hissed with the constantly whispered password directed at every approaching shadow. I wish I could tell you what the password was. You would think it very funny.

A friend of mine, Lt. Col. Ken Campbell, captured eight French soldiers with a pack of cigarets. It was all accidental. He stumbled onto an Arab sleeping on the beach who told him there were soldiers in the building up the hill. Campbell sneaked up, revolver in hand, and opened the door. The soldiers were all asleep. With quick decision, he stuck the gun back in its holster, then woke the soldiers. They were very startled and confused. Campbell speaks perfect French, so he passed around the cigarets, chatted with the soldiers, told them they were captured, and after a bit marched them away.

Pvt. Chuck Conick from Pittsburgh, telling me how the soldiers felt during that first advance, says everybody was scared but didn't talk about that in the rest periods between advances. He said they mainly wondered what the papers at home were saying about the battle. Time after time he heard the boys say: "If my folks could only see me now!"

Boys from New Mexico and Arizona were amazed at how much the country around here resembles their own desert Southwest. In the moonlight that first night the rolling treeless hills looked just like home country to them.

All through the advance the troops were followed in almost comic-opera fashion by hordes of Arab children, who would crowd around the guns until they were actually in the way. Soldiers tell me the Arabs were very calm and quiet and there was a fine dignity about even the most ragged. Our boys couldn't resist the sad and emaciated little faces of the children, and that was when they started giving their rations away.

It got hot in the daytime, so hot that the advancing soldiers kept stripping and abandoning their clothes until some were down to their undershirts, but at night it turned sharply chilly and they wished they hadn't.

French resistance seems to have run the scale all the way from eager cooperation clear up to bitter fighting to the death. In most sectors the French seemed to fire only when fired on. It has been established now that many French troops had only three bullets for their rifles, but in other places 75-mm guns did devastating work.

Our oldsters say they didn't mind machine-gun and rifle fire so much, but it was the awful noise and uncanny accuracy of the 75's that made their hearts stand still.

The boys who went through it have memories forever. Many say that most of all they remember little things of beauty like the hills shadowed in moonlight and the eerie peacefulness of the beach when they landed.

December 15, 1942—. . . We are now in the first month of [the North African] winter season. From now till late March there are few mosquitoes, and there isn't much danger of malaria. The hospitals rcport only an occasional case. On the average the nights are quite chilly. It starts getting cold as soon as the sun gets low, around four o'clock. By dark it is usually cold enough for an overcoat. You sleep under all the blankets you can get. In the morning the sun isn't well up until after eight. Usually the sky is a clear blue before noon. It seems to be a larger sky than ours back home. Maybe that's because we are out where we can see more sky than ordinarily. Some days high white clouds cover the sky. Some days go by entirely cloudless, and then the sun is quite warm and it is really like a day in late June at home. . . .

December 24, 1942—Oran, as a city, is not a bad place at all. But most of the Americans here would trade the whole layout for the worst town in the United States, and throw in a hundred dollars to boot.

That's the way Americans are, including me. Most of us had never heard of Oran till the war started. Yet it is bigger than El Paso. It has palm-lined streets, broad sidewalks, outdoor cafés, a beautiful harbor, restaurants with soft-colored lighting, and apartments with elevators.

On the other hand it has Arabs dressed in ragged sheets, garbage in the gutters, dogs that are shockingly gaunt, and more horse carts than autos.

Most of the Americans talk about how dirty Oran is. Which just goes to show they haven't been around. Oran is cleaner than some of the poorer Latin cities in our own hemisphere. And at this season it doesn't even smell very bad.

World travelers had told me that Oran had an Oriental atmosphere, but I can't sense it. It seems much more like a Latin city than an Oriental one.

You could compare it in many ways with El Paso if you discounted the harbor. The climate is roughly the same. Both cities are in semi-arid country. Both are dusty in the spring and very hot in summer. Both are surrounded by fertile, irrigated land that produces fruit and vegetables and grain. And if you just substitute Mexicans for Arabs, the proportion to whites is about the same.

The population of Oran is actually mostly French, Spanish and Jewish. The Arabs are a minority. They run all the way from hideous beggars up to solemn men in long white robes and bright turbans, sitting in the most expensive cafés and sipping tall drinks. But you see many more Europeans than Arabs. . . .

December 31, 1942—. . . The Arabs are strange people. I don't pretend to know anything about them yet. They are poor, and they look as tight-lipped and unfriendly as the Indians in some of the Latin countries, yet they're friendly and happy when you get close to them. As you drive through the country, Arab farmers by hundreds wave at you along the road, and small children invariably shout their few American words—"goodbye," or "okay"—as you pass, and either salute like soldiers or give the "V" sign with their fingers.

In half a day's driving here I get more "V" signs than I saw the whole time I was in England.

I still haven't got the religion question straight. Some Arab women wear white sheets and hoods that cover the face, except for one eye sticking out. The soldiers call them "One-Eyed Flossies." But they are in the minority. Most of the women show their faces.

As far as I can figure out, the ones who cover their faces are the severely religious, just as at home only a few of the Jewish people are what they call orthodox. The rest are good people, but they don't observe the ancient customs and restrictions.

Just at sunset yesterday we passed a team and a wagon carrying a whole Arab family. The man was down on his knees and elbows at the edge of the pavement, facing east toward Mecca, but the women and children were sitting in the wagon just as usual.

One of our party wisecracked, "I guess he's making a deal for the whole family."

That was the only Arab I've seen praying. . . .

Operation Torch was an Anglo-American undertaking that assumed a decidedly American face, a public-relations move to minimize resistance from the Axis-aligned French Vichyites, who intensely disliked the British. The following two columns on the American policy of leniency toward the Vichyites were widely quoted in the stateside press, much to the chagrin of American officials, who were faced with a difficult situation. How the pieces passed the censors was the question of the hour.

Snakes in Our Midst

ORAN, ALGERIA, *January 4, 1943*—Men who bring our convoys from America, some of whom have just recently arrived, tell me the people at home don't have a correct impression of things over here.

Merchant Marine officers who have been here a couple of days are astonished by the difference between what they thought the situation was and what it actually is. They say people at home think the North African campaign is a walkaway and will be over quickly; that our losses have been practically nil; that the French here love us to death; and that all German influence has been cleaned out.

If you think that, it is because we newspapermen here have failed at getting the finer points over to you.

Because this campaign at first was as much diplomatic as military, the powers that be didn't permit our itchy typewriter fingers to delve into things internationally, which were ticklish enough without that. I believe misconceptions at home must have grown out of some missing part of the picture.

It would be very bad for another wave of extreme optimism to sweep over the United States. So maybe I can explain a little bit about why things over here, though all right for the long run, are not all strawberries and cream right now.

In Tunisia, for instance, we seem to be stalemated for the moment. The reasons are two. Our Army is a green army, and most of our Tunisian troops are in actual battle for the first time against seasoned troops and commanders. It will take us months of fighting to gain the experience our enemies start with.

In the second place, nobody knew exactly how much resistance the French would put up here, so we had to be set for full resistance. That meant, when the French capitulated in three days, we had to move eastward at once, or leave the Germans unhampered to build a big force in Tunisia.

So we moved several hundred miles and, with the British, began fighting. But we simply didn't have enough stuff on hand to knock the Germans out instantly. Nobody is to blame for this. I think our Army is doing wonderfully—both in fighting with what we have and in getting more here—but we are fighting an army as tough in spirit as ours, vastly more experienced, and more easily supplied.

So you must expect to wait awhile before Tunisia is cleared and Rommel jumps into the sea.

*

Our losses in men so far are not appalling, by any means, but we are losing men. The other day an American ship brought the first newspaper from home I had seen since the occupation, and it said only twelve men were lost in taking Oran.

The losses, in fact, were not great, but they were a good many twelves times twelve.

Most of our convalescent wounded have been sent to England. Some newly arrived Americans feel that, if more of the wounded were sent home, it would put new grim vigor into the American people. We aren't the sort of people from whom wounded men have to be concealed.

*

The biggest puzzle to us who are on the scene is our policy of dealing with Axis agents and sympathizers in North Africa. We have taken into custody only the most out-and-out Axis agents, such as the German armistice missions and a few others. That done, we have turned the authority of arrest back to the French.

The procedure is that we investigate, and they arrest. As it winds up, we investigate period.

Our policy is still appeasement. It stems from what might be called the national hodgepodge of French emotions. Frenchmen today think and feel in lots of different directions. We moved softly at first, in order to capture as many French hearts as French square miles. Now that phase is over. We are here in full swing. We occupy countries and pretend not to. We are tender in order to avoid offending our friends, the French, in line with the policy of interfering as little as possible with French municipal life.

We have left in office most of the small-fry officials put there by the Germans before we came. We are permitting fascist societies to continue to exist. Actual sniping has been stopped, but there is still sabotage.

The loyal French see this and wonder what manner of people we are. They are used to force, and expect us to use it against the common enemy, which includes the French Nazis. Our enemies see it, laugh, and call us soft.

Both sides are puzzled by a country at war which still lets enemies run loose to work against it.

*

There are an astonishing number of Axis sympathizers among the French in North Africa. Not a majority, of course, but more than you would imagine. This in itself is a great puzzle to me. I can't fathom the thought processes of a Frenchman who prefers German victory and perpetual domination rather than a temporary occupation resulting in eventual French freedom.

But there are such people, and they are hindering us, and we over here think you folks at home should know three things:

That the going will be tough and probably long before we have cleaned up Africa and are ready to move to bigger fronts. That the

French are fundamentally behind us, but that a strange, illogical stratum is against us. And that our fundamental policy still is one of soft-gloving snakes in our midst.

A Mixed-Up Situation

WITH THE AMERICAN FORCES IN ALGERIA, *January 5, 1943*—I have been delving further into this strange business of Axis sympathies among the people of French North Africa. It is very involved.

The population is all mixed up—Arabs, Jews, Spanish and French. And there doesn't seem to be much national loyalty. It looks as if the people, being without any deep love of the country, favor whichever side appears most likely to feather their nest.

Outside the big cities, Algeria hasn't fared badly under the Germans. The cities were actually starving, because the Germans bought produce direct from the farms, and the cities didn't get it.

America has already contributed shiploads of food to the Algerian people, but for some reason little of it has showed up in the public markets. City housewives find the stalls bare as usual, and mutter about "les Américains."

The Germans paid high prices to the farmers for their crops, and paid in French money. They didn't levy the terrific indemnities here that they did in France. Hence the farm population actually prospered, and had almost nothing to kick about.

Now this year Algeria has the biggest orange crop since the war started. In distant sections oranges are actually rotting on the trees for lack of transportation. The farmers blame the Americans for this, and I suppose with some justice. True, we have already arranged to ship vast cargoes of oranges to England in returning convoys, but we can't spare enough transportation to get the whole crop to the docks.

As far as I can see, the only way to get the Arab, French and Spanish farmers on our side would be to buy the whole orange crop, even at the high prices the Germans paid.

*

When the Germans took control they demobilized the French North African army. That suited the people fine. They didn't want to fight anyway. But now the army is being mobilized again, and people are saying:

"Under the Germans we didn't have to fight. Under the Americans our leaders make us go into the Army again."

They are passive about it, but many of them are not happy.

There was a deep fascist tinge among some of the officers of the regular army. I've tried to find out the reason. And as far as I can learn, it was mostly a seeking for an ordered world to live in.

The people and the army alike were disillusioned and shattered by the foul mess into which Paris had fallen—the mess that resulted in catastrophe to France. They were, and are, bitter against the politicians and the general slovenliness in high places. They want no more of it.

They want things to run smoothly. They want security—and they visualize it as guaranteed by the methodical rule of the Axis.

*

The German propaganda here has been expert. The people have been convinced that Germany will win. Lacking any great nationalistic feeling, the people jump onto whatever seems to be the leading bandwagon, and they think it's Germany.

Propaganda also has made them think America is very weak. Literally, they believe we don't have enough steel to run our factories nor enough oil for our motors.

German propaganda has drilled into them the glories of the New Order. These people believe that life for them under German control would be milk and honey, perpetual security and prosperity. They really believe it.

*

Also, our troops have made a poor impression, in contrast to the few Germans they've seen. We admittedly are not rigid-minded people. Our Army doesn't have the strict and snappy discipline of the Germans. Our boys sing in the streets, unbutton their shirt collars, laugh and shout, and forget to salute. A lot of Algerians misinterpret this as inefficiency. They think such a carefree army can't possibly whip the grim Germans. Most of the minor peoples of the world expect discipline. They admire strict rulers because to them strictness is synonymous with strength. They can't conceive of the fact that our strength lies in our freedom.

Out of it all I gather a new respect for Americans, sloppy though we may be. They may call us Uncle Shylock, but I know of no other country on earth that actually is less grabby. In all my traveling both before and during the war I have been revolted by the nasty, shriveled greediness of soul that inhabits so much of the world. The more I see of the Americans and the British, the more I like us. And although Germany is our bitter enemy, at least the Germans have the character to be wholly loyal to their own country.

Once more I want to say that this stratum about which I am

writing is not a majority of the people of North Africa. Much of the population is just as fervent for Allied victory as we are. But there is this Axis tinge, and I wanted to try to explain why it existed. Personally, I don't feel that it can do us any grave harm.

January 8, 1943—. . . They say here that a soldier's three first needs are: (1) good mail service, (2) movies, radios and phonographs, and (3) cigarets and candy.

Cigarets are being issued free now, six packs a week. But the other items are very short in Africa.

Every radio in Oran has been bought up by the Army. Music stores are cleaned out. All the camps want more musical instruments. There is even advertising in the newspapers for second-hand ones.

Many camps have rigged up their own forms of entertainment. Some already have bands, and have given big dances. Dancing has been banned here during more than two years of German rule.

Boxing is popular in the camps, and tournaments are being arranged. Boxing gloves are one thing that did show up here in sizable amounts.

But it is simple athletic games in which lots of men can participate that the Special Services Branch is concentrating on in lieu of better things. Three such games—kick baseball, speedball, and touch football—have been inaugurated. In addition, I've seen lots of handball and even badminton being played at the more remote camps. . . .

Doctors in Battle

WITH THE AMERICAN FORCES IN ALGERIA, *January 12, 1943*—Back in England last summer I spent some time with the Army's Medical Corps, intending to write about our preparations for tending wounded soldiers.

But I never wrote the columns. The sight of surgeons being taught to operate at the front, of huge warehouses filled to the roofs with bandages, of scores of hospitals built for men then healthy who would soon be cripples—it was shocking and too morbid, and I couldn't write about it.

But now all that preparation is being put to use. Our doctors and nurses and medical aides have had their first battle experience. The hospitals are going full blast. And it doesn't seem morbid in actuality, as it did in contemplation.

In the Oran area, where our heaviest casualties occurred, the wounded are in five big hospitals. Three are French hospitals taken over by the Army. One is an abandoned French barracks turned into a hospital. And one is a huge tent hospital out in an oats field. It is the most amazing thing I have seen, and I'll write about it later.

*

So far the doctors can be, and are, proud of their work. The nurses have already covered themselves with glory. The wounded have only praise for those who pulled them through.

Our only deaths in the original occupation were those killed outright and those so badly wounded nothing could have saved them. In other words, we lost almost nobody from infection, or from medical shortcomings in the hurly-burly of battle.

You've already read of the miracles wrought by sulfanilamide in the first battles of Africa. Doctors and men both still talk about it constantly, almost with awe. Doctors knew it was practically a miracle drug, but they hadn't realized quite how miraculous.

Every soldier was issued a sulfanilamide packet before he left England, some even before they left America. It consisted of twelve tablets for swallowing, and a small sack of the same stuff in powdered form for sprinkling on wounds.

The soldiers used it as instructed, and the result was an almost complete lack of infection. Hundreds are alive today who would have been dead without it. Men lay out for twenty-four hours and more before they could be taken in, and the sulfanilamide saved them.

It's amusing to hear the soldiers talk about it. Sulfanilamide is a pretty big word for many of them. They call it everything from *snuffalide* to *sulphermillanoid.*

There's one interesting sidelight about it—some of the wounded soldiers didn't have any sulfanilamide left, because they had surreptitiously taken it all to cure venereal diseases. They say you can knock a venereal case in four or five days with it, and thus don't have to report in sick.

One doctor told me that most American wounds were in the legs, while most of the French wounds were in the head. The explanation seems to be that we were advancing and thus out in the open, while the French were behind barracks with just their heads showing.

Both sides treated the wounded of the other side all during the battle. Our soldiers are full of gratitude for the way they were treated in the French hospitals. They say the French nurses would even steal cigarets for them.

The mixup of French emotions that showed itself during the fighting was fantastic. One French motor launch went about Oran Harbor firing with a machine gun at wounded Americans, while other Frenchmen in rowboats were facing the bullets trying to rescue them.

I know of one landing party sent ashore with the special mission of capturing four merchant ships. They took them all without firing a shot. The captain of one ship greeted the party with "What was the matter? We expected you last night!" and the skipper of another met the party at the gangway with a bottle of gin.

There was much fraternization. In one town where fighting was heavy, the bodies of five men were found in a burned truck. Three were Americans and two were French.

Morphine was a great life-saver. Pure shock is the cause of many deaths; but if morphine can be given to deaden the pain, shock cases often pull through. Many officers carried morphine and gave injections right on the field. My friend Lt. Col. Louis Plain of the Marine Corps, who had never given an injection in his life, gave six on the beach at Arzew.

Many of our wounded men already have returned to duty. Those permanently disabled will be sent home as soon as they are able. Those still recovering are anxious to return to their outfits. I've inquired especially among the wounded soldiers about this, and it's a fact that they are busting to get back into the fray again. Morale was never higher.

Pyle moved inland to a desert airfield, nicknamed the Garden of Allah, at Biskra in Algeria. The attack described here was the first of a long series he would endure in his two-and-a-half years of war reporting.

Under Fire

A FORWARD AIRDROME IN FRENCH NORTH AFRICA, *January 19, 1943*—While bad weather stymies the ground fighting in Tunisia, the air war on both sides has been daily increasing in intensity until it has reached a really violent tempo.

Not a day passes without heavy bombing of Axis ports, vicious strafing of cities and airdromes, losses on both sides, and constant watchful patrolling.

Here at one of our airdromes, all of us can assure you that being bombed is no fun. Yet these tired, hard-worked Americans jokingly decided to send a telegram to Allied headquarters asking them to arrange for the Jerries to stop there each evening and pick up our mail.

I am living at this airdrome for a while. It can't be named, although the Germans obviously know where it is since they call on us frequently. Furthermore, they announced quite a while ago by radio that they would destroy the place within three days.

I hadn't been here three hours till the Germans came. They arrived just at dusk. And they came arrogantly, flying low. Some of them must have regretted their audacity, for they never got home. The fireworks that met them were beautiful from the ground, but must have been hideous up where they were.

They dropped bombs on several parts of the field, but their aim was marred at the last minute. There were no direct hits on anything. Not a man was scratched, though the stories of near misses multiplied into the hundreds by the next day.

One soldier who had found a bottle of wine was lying in a pup tent drinking. He never got up during the raid—just lay there cussing at the Germans.

"You can't touch me, you blankety-blanks! Go to hell, you so-and-so's!"

When the raid was over he was untouched, but the tent a foot above him was riddled with shrapnel.

Another soldier made a practice of keeping a canteen hanging just above his head. That night when he went to take a drink the canteen was empty. Investigation revealed a shrapnel hole, through which the water had run out.

Another soldier had the front sight of his rifle shot off by a German machine-gun bullet.

Some of the soldiers were actually picking tiny bits of shrapnel our of their coats all the next day. Yet, as I said, not a drop of American blood was shed.

*

When this airdrome was first set up the soldiers dug slit trenches just deep enough to lie down in during a raid, but after each new bombing the trenches get deeper.

Everybody makes fun of himself—but keeps on digging. Today some of these trenches are more than eight feet deep. I'll bet there has been more wholehearted digging here in two weeks than the WPA* did in two years.

*Works Progress Administration. A New Deal program created by President Roosevelt during the Depression to employ out-of-work Americans.

The officers don't have to hound their men. They dig with a will of their own, and with a vengeance. Nowhere on the field—and it is a huge one—do you have to run more than fifty yards to drop into a trench.

If we stay here long enough we'll probably have to install elevators to get to the bottom of the trenches. Many of them are getting so deep the boys have dug steps at each end.

After supper you see officers as well as men out digging. Each little group has its own trench design. Some are just square holes. Some form an L. Some are regulation zigzag. Some of the bigger ones make a Chinese puzzle.

Some of the trenches have been covered with boards and mounds of dirt like regular bomb shelters.

The ground here is dry, and the trenches don't fill up with water as they do in the coastal and mountain camps. The earth is as hard as concrete. You have to use an ax as well as a pick and shovel.

*

You'd love our air-raid alarm system. It consists of a dinner bell hanging from a date palm tree outside headquarters, When the radio watchers give the order the dinner bell is rung. Then the warning is carried to the far ends of the vast airdrome by sentries shooting revolvers and rifles into the air. At night it sounds like a small battle. When the alarm goes the soldiers get excited, and mad too. When the Germans come over, the anti-aircraft guns throw up a fantastic Fourth of July torrent of red tracer bullets. But to the soldiers on the ground that isn't enough, so they let loose with everything from Colt .45's up to Tommy guns.

If the Germans don't kill us we'll probably shoot ourselves.

January 20, 1943—This airdrome is away from the dark and rainy coastal belt of the Mediterranean.

The only way I can picture it for you is to suggest that you try to visualize some flat endless space in the desert of our own Southwest, with purple mountains in the distance and sand everywhere. Put an oasis of date palms down upon it, so big it would take an hour to walk from one end to the other.

Here the sun shines down warmly out of an incredibly blue sky. At night there are stars by the million, but a dry and piercing chill comes down with the darkness.

Here is Africa as we have pictured it back home. The green fields and European-type cities of the coast have been left behind. Here the villages are sun-caked adobe. Arabs in their rags dominate the population.

It is a long way between villages. Now and then you see a camel on the road. The wind blows some days, suffocating you with flying sand. It is hard on men and engines both. Little rippled drifts of yellow sand form around shrubs in the desert, and our soldiers wear tinted dust goggles.

It does rain here, but very seldom. Soldiers who have lived knee-deep in the perpetual winter mud of the coastal belt call this the best place in Africa to be.

*

We are not far from the enemy, as the crow flies. All day our air patrols cover the desert for hundreds of miles, keeping track of enemy movements in our direction. Even camel trains are on patrol, under the French army. All troops are constantly in readiness for a descent by enemy parachutists.

Infantry and anti-tank units arrive and bivouac around the countryside for our protection. Truck trains come across the mountains bringing new loads of gasoline and bombs. American cargo planes, flying in formation with fighter escort, arrive daily with airplane parts and other urgent supplies—and sometimes with mail. . . .

January 21, 1943—. . . There is never a moment during daylight when there are not planes in the air. The first patrols take off before dawn and the last ones land after dark. All day there is a ceaseless coming and going. New bunches of replacement planes arrive and depart in workhorse manner. Casuals drop in just a few days out of America, England or India. Actually the air above seems much like Bolling Field at Washington.

It is hard to believe the whole thing was set up with one purpose only—destruction and death. It is just as hard to believe that destruction and death can likewise come to us out of the same blue sky. But as one officer said:

"We've got to realize it, for believe me, everything is for keeps now."

January 27, 1943—The American soldier is a born housewife, I've become convinced. I'll bet there's not another army in the world that fixes itself a "home away from home" as quickly as ours does.

I've seen the little home touches created by our soldiers in their barns and castles and barracks and tents all over America, Ireland,

England and Africa. But nowhere has this sort of thing been given such a play as here at this desert airdrome.

The reason is twofold: first the climate here is so dry you can fix up something with a fair certainty that it won't be washed away in the morning. Second, because of the constant danger of a German bashing, the boys have dug into the ground to make their homes, and the things they can do with a cave are endless, as every farm boy knows.

The basic shelter here is a pup tent, but the soldiers have dug holes and set their tents over these. And the accessories inside provide one of the greatest shows on earth. Wandering among them is better than going to a state fair. The variations are endless. . . .

Pyle began to clarify for himself and his readers the moral adjustments forced upon young men at war. His invocation of teamwork in the third paragraph was a perfect expression of the democratic ethic that would saturate his war reportage.

Schoolboys Turned Killers

A FORWARD AIRDROME IN FRENCH NORTH AFRICA, *February 9, 1943*—It is hard for a layman to understand the fine points of aerial combat as practiced at the moment in North Africa. It is hard even for the pilots themselves to keep up, for there are changes in tactics from week to week.

We will have some new idea and surprise Germans with it. Then they'll come across with a surprise maneuver, and we will have to change everything to counteract it.

But basically, at the moment, you can say that everything depends on teamwork. The lone dashing hero in this war is certain to be a dead hero within a week. Sticking with the team and playing it all together is the only guarantee of safety for everybody.

Our fighters go in groups with the bombers, ranging the sky above them, flying back and forth, watching for anything that may appear. But if they see some Germans in the distance nobody goes after them. That would be playing into the Germans' hands. So they stick to their formation above the bombers, making an umbrella.

The German has two choices—to dive down through them, or to wait until somebody is hit by flak and has to drop back. Then they are on him in a flash.

When that happens the fighters attack, but still in formation.

Keeping that formation always and forever tight is what the flight leaders constantly drill into the boys' heads. It is a great temptation to dash out and take a shot at some fellow, but by now they've seen too many cases of the tragedy of such action.

The result is that this war doesn't have many individual air heroes. A team may be a composite hero, but not an individual.

One group leader told me: "If everything went according to schedule we'd never shoot down a German plane. We'd cover our bombers and keep ourselves covered and everybody would come home safe."

*

The fighter pilots seem a little different from the bomber men. Usually they are younger. Many of them were still in school when they joined up. Ordinarily they might be inclined to be more harum-scarum, but their work is so deadly, and the sobering dark cloud of personal tragedy is over them so constantly, that it seems to have humbled them. In fact I think it makes them nicer people than if they were cocky.

They have to get up early. Often I've gone to the room of my special friends at nine-thirty in the evening and found them all asleep.

They fly so frequently they can't do much drinking. One night recently when one of the most popular fighter pilots was killed right on the home field, in an accident, some of them assuaged their grief with gin.

"Somehow you feel it more when it happens right here than when a fellow just doesn't come back," they said.

When they first came over here, you'd frequently hear pilots say they didn't hate the Germans, but you don't hear that anymore. They have lost too many friends, too many roommates.

*

Now it is killing that animates them.

The highest spirits I've seen in that room were displayed one evening after they came back from a strafing mission. That's what they like to do best, but they get little of it. It's a great holiday from escorting bombers, which they hate to do. Going out free-lancing to shoot up whatever they see, and going in enough force to be pretty sure they'll be superior to the enemy—that's Utopia.

That's what they had done that day. And they really had a field day. They ran onto a German truck convoy and blew it to pieces. They laughed and got excited as they told about it. The trucks were all full of men, and "they flew out like firecrackers." Motorcyclists got hit and dived forty feet before they stopped skidding.

Two Messerschmitt 109's made the mistake of coming after our planes. They never had a chance. After firing a couple of wild bursts they went down smoking, and one of them seemed to blow up.

The boys were full of laughter when they told about it as they sat there on their cots in the dimly lighted room. I couldn't help having a funny feeling about them. They were all so young, so genuine, so enthusiastic. And they were so casual about everything —not casual in a hard, knowing way, but they talked about their flights and killing and being killed exactly as they would discuss girls or their school lessons.

Maybe they won't talk at all when they finally get home. If they don't it will be because they know this is a world apart and nobody else could ever understand.

Fighter Pilot

A FORWARD AIRDROME IN FRENCH NORTH AFRICA, *February 10, 1943*— Lt. Jack Ilfrey is the leading American ace in North Africa at the moment. However, that's not my reason for writing about him.

In the first place, the theory over here is not to become an individual fighter and shoot down a lot of planes, so being an ace doesn't mean so much. In the second place, somebody else might be ahead of Ilfrey by this evening, with fate pulling the strings the way she does.

So I'm writing about him largely because he is a fine person and more or less typical of all boys who fly our deadly fighters.

Jack Ilfrey is from Houston. His father is cashier of the First National Bank.

Jack is only twenty-two. He has two younger sisters. He went to Texas A & M for two years, and then to the University of Houston, working at the same time for the Hughes Tool Company. He will soon have been in the Army two years.

It is hard to conceive of his ever having killed anybody. For he looks even younger than his twenty-two years. His face is good-humored. His darkish hair is childishly uncontrollable and pops up into a little curlicue at the front of his head. He talks fast, but his voice is soft and he has a very slight hesitation in his speech that somehow seems to make him a gentle and harmless person.

There is not the least trace of the smart aleck or wise guy about him. He is wholly thoughtful and sincere. Yet he mows 'em down.

*

Here in Africa Ilfrey has been through the mill. He got two Focke-Wulf 190's one day, two Messerschmitt 109's another day. His fifth victory was over a twin-motored Messerschmitt 110, which carries three men. And he has another kill that has not yet been confirmed.

He hasn't had all smooth sailing by any means. In fact he's very lucky to be here at all. He got caught in a trap one day and came home with two hundred sixty-eight bullet holes in his plane. His armor plate stopped at least a dozen that would have killed him.

Jack's closest shave, however, wasn't from being shot at. It happened one day when he saw a German fighter duck into a cloud. Jack figured the German would emerge at the far end of the cloud, so he scooted along below to where he thought the German would pop out, and pop out he did—right smack into him, almost.

They both kicked rudder violently, and they missed practically by inches. Neither man fired a shot, they were so busy getting out of each other's way. Jack says he was weak for an hour afterward.

*

There is nothing "heroic" about Lt. Ilfrey. He isn't afraid to run when that is the only thing to do.

He was telling about getting caught all alone one day at a low altitude. Two Germans got on his tail.

"I just had two chances," he says. "Either stay and fight, and almost surely get shot down, or pour on everything I had and try to get away. I ran a chance of burning up my engines and having to land in enemy territory, but I got away. Luckily the engines stood up."

Ilfrey, like all the others here, has little in the way of entertainment and personal pleasure. I walked into his room late one afternoon, after he had come back from a mission, and found him sitting there at a table, all alone, killing flies with a folded newspaper.

And yet they say being an ace is romantic.

Pyle left the airmen at the Garden of Allah and joined the infantry of General Fredenhall's II Corps in Tunisia. The infantryman's life so impressed Pyle that he undertook to explain to stateside readers in great detail just how rough front-line existence was.

Night Convoy

AT THE FRONT IN TUNISIA, *February 16, 1943*—A big military convoy moving at night across the mountains and deserts of Tunisia is something that nobody who has been in one can ever forget.

Recently I have been living with a front-line outfit. Late one afternoon it received sudden orders to move that night, bag and baggage. It had to pull out of its battle positions, time the departures of its various units to fit into the flow of traffic at the first control point on the highway, and then drive all night and go into action on another front.

All the big convoys in the war area move at night. German planes would spot a daytime convoy and play havoc with it.

It is extremely difficult and dangerous, this moving at night in total blackness over strange and rough roads. But it has to be done.

Our convoy was an immense one. There were hundreds of vehicles and thousands of men. It took seven–and–a–half hours to pass one point.

The convoy started moving at five-thirty in the evening, just before dusk. The last vehicle didn't clear till one o'clock the next morning.

*

I rode in a jeep with Capt. Pat Riddleberger of Woodstock, Virginia, and Pvt. John Coughlin of Manchester, New Hampshire. Ahead of us was a small covered truck which belonged to Riddleberger's tank-destroyer section. We were a little two-vehicle convoy within ourselves.

We were to fall in near the tail end, so we had half the night to kill before starting. We stood around the truck, parked in a barnlot, for an hour or two, just talking in the dark. Then we went into the kitchen of the farmhouse which had been used as a command post and which was empty now.

There was an electric light, and we built a fire in the kitchen fireplace out of boxes. But the chimney wouldn't draw, and we almost choked from the smoke.

Some officers had left a stack of copies of the *New York Times* for October and November lying on the floor, so we read those for an hour or so. We looked at the book sections and the movie ads. None of us had ever heard of the new books or the current movies. It made us feel keenly how long we had been away and how cut off we were from home.

"They could make money just showing all the movies over again for a year after we get back," one of the boys said.

We finished the papers and there were still three hours to kill, so we got blankets out of the truck and lay down on the concrete floor. We were sleeping soundly when Capt. Riddleberger awakened us at one A.M. and said we were off.

The moon was just coming out. The sky was crystal-clear, and the night bitter cold. The jeep's top was down.

We all put on all the clothes we had. In addition to my usual polar-bear wardrobe, which includes heavy underwear and two sweaters, I wore that night a pair of coveralls, a heavy combat suit that a tank man lent me, a pair of overshoes, two caps—one on top of the other—and over them a pair of goggles. And all three of us in the jeep wrapped up in blankets.

In spite of all that, we almost froze before the night was over.

*

We moved out of the barnlot, and a half a mile away we swung onto the main road, at the direction of motorcyclists who stood there guiding the traffic.

Gradually our eyes grew accustomed to the half-darkness, and it wasn't hard to follow the road. We had orders to drive in very close formation, so we kept within fifty feet of each other.

*

After a few miles we had to cross over a mountain range. There were steep grades and switchback turns, and some of the trucks had to back and fill to make the sharper turns.

There was considerable delay on the mountain. French trucks and buses would pass and tie up traffic, swinging in and out. And right in the center of these tortuous mountains we met a huge American hospital unit, in dozens of trucks, moving up to the front. They were on the outside of the road, and at times their wheels seemed about to slide off into the chasm.

We had long waits while traffic jams ahead were cleared. We would shut off our motors and the night would be deathly silent except for a subdued undertone of grinding motors far ahead. At times we could hear great trucks groaning in low gear on steep grades far below, or the angry clanking of tanks as they took sharp turns behind us.

Finally the road straightened out on a high plateau. There we met a big contingent of French troops moving silently toward the front we had just vacated. The marching soldiers seemed like dark ghosts in the night. Hundreds of horses were carrying their artillery, ammunition and supplies.

I couldn't help feeling the immensity of the catastrophe that has put men all over the world, millions of us, to moving in machinelike precision throughout long foreign nights—men who should be comfortably asleep in their own warm beds at home.

War makes strange giant creatures out of us little routine men who inhabit the earth.

Life At The Front

THE TUNISIAN FRONT, *February 19, 1943*—It must be hard for you folks at home to conceive how our troops right at the front actually live. In fact it is hard to describe it to you even when I'm among them, living in somewhat the same way they are.

You can scarcely credit the fact that human beings—the same people you've known all your life—could adjust themselves so acceptingly to a type of living that is only slightly above the caveman stage.

*

Some of our troops came directly to the Tunisian front after the original occupation of North and West Africa, and have been here ever since. They have not slept in a bed for months. They've lived through this vicious winter sleeping outdoors on the ground. They haven't been paid in three months. They have been on British rations most of the time, and British rations, though good, get mighty tiresome.

They never take off their clothes at night, except their shoes. They don't get a bath oftener than once a month. One small detachment acquired lice and had to be fumigated, but all the rest have escaped so far. They move so frequently they don't attempt to put in many home touches, as the men do at the more permanent camps toward the rear. Very few of the front-line troops have ever had any leave. They never go to town for an evening's fun. They work all the time.

Nobody keeps track of the days or weeks. I'll wager that ninety percent of our front-line troops never know when Sunday comes.

Furthermore, the old traditional differences between day and night have almost ceased to exist. Nighttime no longer necessarily means rest, nor daytime work. Often it's just reversed. The bulk of our convoying of supplies and shifting of troops is done at night. The soldiers are accustomed to traveling all night, sometimes three or four nights in a row. Irregularity of sleep becomes normal. One soldier told me he once went three days and nights without sleep.

You see men sleeping anywhere, anytime. The other day I saw a soldier asleep in blankets under an olive tree at two in the afternoon. A few feet away a full colonel was sleeping soundly on the ground. In battle you just go until you drop.

It isn't always possible to get enough food up to the fighting soldiers. I have just been with one artillery outfit in the mountains whose members were getting only one cold meal a day.

Nurses tell me that when the more seriously wounded reach the hospital they are often so exhausted they fall asleep without drugs, despite their pain.

*

The war coarsens most people. You live rough and talk rough, and if you didn't toughen up inside you simply wouldn't be able to take it. An officer friend of mine, Lt. Lennie Bessman of Milwaukee, was telling me two incidents of a recent battle that touched him deeply.

One evening he and another officer came up to a tiny farmhouse, which was apparently empty. To be on the safe side he called out "Who's there?" before going in. The answer came back: "Capt. Blank, and who the hell wants to know?"

They went in and found the captain, his clothes covered with blood, heating a can of rations over a gasoline flame. They asked if they could stay all night with him. He said he didn't give a damn. They started to throw their blankets down, and the captain said: "Look out for that man over there."

There was a dead soldier lying in a corner.

The captain was cooking his supper and preparing to stay all night alone in that same room. The flood and fury of death about him that day had left him utterly indifferent both to the companionship of the living and the presence of the dead.

The other incident was just the opposite. Another captain happened to be standing beside Bessman. It was just at dusk and they were on the desert. The night chill was coming down. The captain looked to the far horizon and said, sort of to himself: "You fight all day here in the desert and what's the end of it all? Night just closes down over you and chokes you."

A little later Bessman got out a partly filled bottle of gin he had with him and asked this same sensitive captain if he'd like a drink. The captain didn't even reach out his hand. He simply answered: "Have you got enough for my men too?"

He wouldn't take a drink himself unless the enlisted men under him could have some.

All officers are not like that, but the battlefield does produce a brotherhood. The common bond of death draws humans toward each other over the artificial barrier of rank.

The Velvet Is Gone

THE TUNISIAN FRONT, *February 20, 1943*—After a few weeks of front-line living your whole perspective on the niceties and necessities of life changes.

You used to be sore when you couldn't get a taxi. Now you've struck gold when you find a spot where you can lie down out of the wind.

Even my own perspective has changed, and as a correspondent I've had only the barest taste of the rough life. For a lifetime I have bathed with becoming regularity, and I thought the world would come to an end unless I changed my socks every day. Now I have just had my first bath in a month, and I go two weeks at a time without even taking off my socks. Oddly enough, it doesn't seem to make much difference.

*

The other day I had to laugh at myself over a little emotion I experienced. We had arrived one evening at a new front-line headquarters. It was centered on a Tunisian farmhouse, as practically all command posts are.

Soldiers and officers alike were sleeping just anywhere they could —in trucks, under trees, in the barn and chicken houses. It was cold and damp, as usual.

Nobody tells a correspondent where to sleep or what to do when he is gypsying around the front. He shifts for himself. So I nosed around and found a place to sleep. It was under a big French grain wagon sitting in the barnlot.

Some soldiers had found several strips of corrugated tin roofing and set them around three sides of the wagon, making walls. The wagon bed formed a roof overhead. They had brought straw from a nearby stack and put it on the ground under the wagon. There we threw our bedding rolls.

It was the coziest place I'd slept in for a week. It had two magnificent features—the ground was dry, and the wind was cut off.

I was so pleased at finding such a wonderful place that I could feel my general spirits go up like an elevator.

When the detachment got orders to move the next day, I felt a genuine regret at leaving this little haven. And to think, after all, it was only some pitiful straw on the hard ground under a wagon.

*

As we were going to bed that night, Hal Boyle of the Associated Press, who was sleeping next to me, said:

"I believe that in wartime your physical discomfort becomes a more dominant thing in your life than the danger you're in."

I believe that's true. The danger comes in spurts. The discomfort is perpetual. You're always cold and almost always dirty. Outside of food and cigarets you have absolutely none of the little things that made life normal back home. You don't have chairs, lights, floors, or tables. You don't have any place to set anything, or any store to buy things from. There are no newspapers, milk, beds, sheets, radiators, beer, ice cream, or hot water. You just sort of exist, either standing up working or lying down asleep. There is no pleasant in-between. The velvet is all gone from living.

*

It doesn't get much below freezing here in central Tunisia, but you must believe me when I say we all suffer agonies from the cold. Any soldier will back me up.

The days are sunshiny, and often really warm, but the nights are almost inhuman. Everybody wears heavy underwear and all the sweaters he can find, plus overcoat and gloves and knitted cap. And still he's cold. We have snow on the mountains here.

The soldiers somehow resent the fact that so many of you folks at home think just because we're in Africa that we're passing out with the heat. Any number of soldiers have showed me letters from their families full of sympathy because of the heat prostrations they must be suffering.

Soldiers ask me for heaven's sake to get over to the folks at home that Africa in winter is frigid. I'll tell you, in one little incident, just how cold it is, and also how little money means compared to bodily necessities.

When not traveling around the fronts I'm living in a small igloo tent among fir trees at a certain forward camp. There I hole up for days at a time to write these columns. The tent is fine except that there's no heat in it and no way to get any heat.

So the other day, along the road, I ran into a soldier in a half-track who had a kerosene stove—the old-fashioned kind they used to heat the school with, you know. I offered him fifty dollars for it—back home it would be worth about three dollars.

He didn't hesitate a second. He just said, "No sir," and that was the end of that.

It would have been just the same if I'd offered him five hundred dollars. He couldn't use the money, and without the stove he'd be miserable.

Now do you see how things are different over here with us?

February 22, 1943—. . . Soldiers cook their own meals when on the move. They make a fire in one of two ways, each involving the use of gasoline. For a short fire they dig a hole about the size of your hand, pour gasoline in the hole, sprinkle sand over the gasoline, and then throw in a match. The sand keeps the gas from burning too quickly. On a small fire like that they can heat a canteen or a cup of coffee.

For a bigger fire, first they fill a small can with gasoline and bury it even with the surface of the ground. They pile rocks around to set their cooking utensils on, and then toss a match at the gas.

I've never yet seen a real skillet, pan or stewpot over here. The soldiers make their own utensils out of those famous five-gallon gasoline tins. I don't believe there's anything in the world that can't be made out of a five-gallon gasoline tin.

The soldiers have learned not to be lax about keeping their mess kits clean, for they know from bitter experience that a dirty mess kit is the quickest way to violent nausea through poisoning.

To wash their mess kits they scour them with sand and then polish them with toilet paper. The best dishrag I've ever found is toilet paper. . . .

February 23, 1943—. . . You become eminently practical in wartime. A chaplain who recently went through the pockets of ten Americans killed in battle said the dominant thing he found was toilet paper. Careless soldiers who were caught without such preparedness have to use twenty-franc notes.

Everything is so scarce you always take anything that's offered you whether you need it or not. I've taken a proffered cigaret while already smoking one. I've drunk wine, which I detest, just because somebody was sharing his bottle. I no longer have any shame about accepting candy, cigarets, clothing, or anything else anybody offers.

We have all been living for months on the policy which the famous Col. Edson Raff put in these words:

"I never refuse anything."

If somebody offered me a bottle of castor oil I'd accept it and hide it away.

Soldiers at the front are good about sharing whatever they have. The average soldier, when he has a windfall and gets a package of candy or cigarets from home, doles out to his friends. It's sort of share and share alike, for times are tough. . . .

On February 14, 1943, German tanks under the command of Field Marshal Erwin Rommel lunged at Allied positions in western Tunisia, pushing the green Americans some fifty miles back through Kasserine Pass. For many American troops, Kasserine Pass was their first taste of battle—and defeat. Pyle was set to take a breather from the front, but he stayed on to cover the retreat. About twenty-three hundred American GIs surrendered to the advancing Germans. The Allies eventually recovered the lost territory.

A Humiliating Predicament

AT THE TUNISIAN FRONT, *February 23, 1943*—You folks at home must be disappointed at what happened to our American troops in Tunisia. So are we over here.

Our predicament is damned humiliating, as Gen. Joe Stilwell said about our getting kicked out of Burma a year ago. We've lost a great deal of equipment, many American lives, and valuable time and territory—to say nothing of face. Yet no one over here has the slightest doubt that the Germans will be thrown out of Tunisia. It is simply in the cards.

It is even possible that our defeat may not even delay Rommel's exodus, for actually our troops formed only a small part of the total Allied forces in Tunisia. Estimates among men at the front run anywhere from two to six months for finishing the Tunisian campaign.

One thing you folks at home must realize is that this Tunisian business is mainly a British show. Our part in it is small. Consequently our defeat is not as disastrous to the whole picture as it would have been had we had been bearing the major portion of the task.

We Americans did the North African landings and got all the credit, although the British did help us. The British are doing the Tunisia job and will get the credit, though we are giving them a hand. That's the way it has been planned all the time. That's the way it will be carried out.

When the time comes the British 1st Army will squeeze on the north, the British 8th Army will squeeze on the south, and we will hold in the middle. And it will really be the British who will run Rommel out of Tunisia.

The fundamental cause of our trouble over here lies in two things: we had too little to work with, as usual, and we underestimated Rommel's strength and especially his audacity.

Both military men and correspondents knew we were too thinly spread in our sector to hold if the Germans were really to launch a big-scale attack. Where everybody was wrong was in believing they didn't have the stuff to do it with.

Correspondents are not now permitted to write anything critical concerning the Tunisian situation, or to tell what we think was wrong. The powers that be feel that this would be bad for "home morale." So you just have to trust that our forces are learning to do better next time.

Personally, I feel that some such setback as this—tragic though it is for many Americans, for whom it is now too late—is not entirely a bad thing for us. It is all right to have a good opinion of yourself, but we Americans are so smug with our cockiness. We somehow feel that just because we're Americans we can whip our weight in wildcats. And we have got it into our heads that production alone will win the war.

There are two things we must learn, and we may be learning them right now—we must spread ourselves thicker on the front lines and we must streamline our commands for quick and positive action in emergencies.

*

As for our soldiers themselves, you need feel no shame nor concern about their ability. I have seen them in battle and afterwards and there is nothing wrong with the common American soldier. His fighting spirit is good. His morale is okay. The deeper he gets into a fight the more of a fighting man he becomes.

I've seen crews that have had two tanks shot out from under them but whose only thought was to get a third tank and "have another crack at them blankety-blanks."

It is true that they are not such seasoned battle veterans as the British and Germans. But they had had some battle experience before this last encounter, and I don't believe their so-called greenness was the cause of our defeat. One good man simply can't whip two good men. That's about the only way I know to put it. Everywhere on every front we simply have got to have more stuff before we start going forward instead of backward.

I happened to be in on the Battle of Sbeïtla, where we fought the German breakthrough for four days before withdrawing. In the next few days I shall try to describe to you what it was like.

THE TUNISIAN FRONT, *February 24, 1943*—On the morning the big German push started against the American troops in Tunisia, our forward command post in that area was hidden in a patch of cactus about a mile from the town of Sidi-Bou-Zid.*

It had been there more than a week, and I had visited there myself only three days previously. I had spent a lot of time with our forward troops in the hills, and I knew most of the officers.

A command post is really the headquarters of a unit. In this case a brigadier general was in command. His staff included intelligence and planning officers, unit commanders, a medical detachment, kitchens and various odds and ends.

A command post of this size has several score vehicles and two or three hundred men. Its work is all done in trucks, half-tracks or tents. It is always prepared to move, when at the front. And it does move every few days, so the enemy won't spot it.

This special command post was about ten miles back from the nearest known enemy position. Our artillery and infantry and some tanks were between it and the enemy.

*

I am describing all this because I will use the men of this command post as characters in our story as I try to picture the tragedy of that first day's surprise push.

That Sunday morning hordes of German tanks and troops came swarming out from behind the mountains around Faïd Pass. We didn't know so many tanks were back there, and didn't know so many Germans were either, for our patrols had been bringing in mostly Italian prisoners from their raids.

The attack was so sudden nobody could believe it was in full force. Our forward troops were overrun before they knew what was happening. The command post itself didn't start moving back till after lunch. By then it was too late—or almost too late.

Command cars, half-tracks and jeeps started west across the fields of semi-cultivated desert, for by then the good road to the north was already cut off. The column had moved about eight miles when German tanks came charging in upon the helpless vehicles from both sides.

A headquarters command post is not heavily armed. It has little to fight back with. All that these men and cars could do was duck and dodge and run like hell. There was no such thing as a fighting line. Everything was mixed up over an area of ten miles or more.

It was a complete melee. Every jeep was on its own. The accompanying tanks fought till knocked out, and their crews then

*In north-central Tunisia, about ten miles behind what had been the Allies' lines.

got out and moved along on foot. One tank commander whose whole crew escaped after the tank caught fire said that at least the Germans didn't machine-gun them when they jumped from the burning tank.

Practically every vehicle reported gasoline trouble that afternoon. Apparently there was water in the gas, yet nobody feels that it was sabotage. They say there had been similar trouble before, but never so bad.

*

A friend of mine, Maj. Ronald Elkins of College Station, Texas, had his half-track hit three times by German shells. They were standing still, cleaning a carburetor filter, when the third shell hit. It set them afire. Some of the crew eventually got back safely, but others are still missing. Maj. Elkins said they could have got clear back with the car "if the damned engine had only kept running."

The Germans just overran our troops that afternoon. They used tanks, artillery, infantry, and planes divebombing our troops continuously. Our artillery was run over in the first rush. We were swamped, scattered, consumed, by the German surprise.

Twilight found our men and machines straggling over an area extending some ten miles back of Sidi-Bou-Zid. Darkness saved those who were saved.

During the night the command post assembled what was left of itself in another cactus patch about fifteen miles behind its first position. Throughout the night, and for days afterward, tired men came straggling in from the desert afoot.

That night the Germans withdrew from the area they'd taken, and next morning we sent trucks back to bury the dead and tow out what damaged vehicles they could. But by next afternoon the battle was on again.

THE TUNISIAN FRONT, *February 26, 1943*—On the morning of the Germans' surprise breakthrough out of Faïd Pass, I was up in the Ousseltia Valley with another contingent of our troops.

Word came to us about noon that the Germans were advancing upon Sbeïtla from Faïd. So I packed into my jeep and started alone on the familiar eighty-five-mile drive south to Sbeïtla. It was a bright day and everything seemed peaceful. I expected to see German planes as I neared Sbeïtla, but there were none, and I drove into my cactus-patch destination about an hour before sundown.

I hadn't been there fifteen minutes when the dive bombers came, but that's another story, which will come later.

I checked in at the intelligence tent to see what was going on, and found that things were dying down with the coming of dusk. So I pitched my tent and went to bed right after supper. Next morning I got up before daylight and caught a ride, just after sunrise, with two officers going up to the new position of our forward command post. We drove very slowly, and all kept a keen eye on the sky. I didn't have a gun, as correspondents are not supposed to carry arms. Occasionally we stopped the jeep and got far off the road behind some cactus hedges, but the German dive bombers were interested only in our troop concentrations far ahead.

Finally we spotted a small cactus patch about half a mile off the road. We figured this was the new home of the forward command post, and it was. They had straggled in during the night and were still straggling in.

*

The cactus patch covered about two acres. In it were hidden half a dozen half-tracks, a couple of jeeps, three light tanks and a couple of motorcycles—all that was left of the impressive array of the traveling headquarters that had fled Sidi-Bou-Zid eighteen hours before.

The commanding general had already gone forward again, in a tank, to participate in the day's coming battle. The remainder of the command post were just sitting around on the ground. Half of their comrades were missing. There was nothing left for them to work with, nothing to do.

When I came into this cactus patch the officers whom I knew, and had left only four days before, jumped up and shook hands as though we hadn't seen each other in years. Enlisted men did the same thing.

I thought this was odd, at first, but now I know how they felt. They had been away—far along on the road that doesn't come back—and now that they were still miraculously alive it was like returning from a voyage of many years, and naturally you shake hands.

During the next few hours there in the cactus patch I listened to dozens of personal escape stories. Every time I would get within earshot of another officer or enlisted man he'd begin telling what had happened to him the day before.

*

Talk about having to pull stories out of people—you couldn't keep these guys from talking. There was something pathetic and terribly touching about it. Not one of them had ever thought he'd see this dawn, and now that he had seen it his emotions had to pour out. And since I was the only newcomer to show up since their escape, I made a perfect sounding board.

The minute a man would start talking he'd begin drawing lines on the ground with his shoe or a stick, to show the roads and how he came. I'll bet I had that battleground scratched in the sand for me fifty times during the forenoon. It got so I could hardly keep from laughing at the consistency of their patterns.

That morning should have been by all rights a newspaperman's dream. There were fantastic stories of escape, intimate recountings of fear and elation. Any one of them would have made a first-page feature story in any newspaper. Yet I was defeated by the flood of experiences. I listened until the stories finally became merged, overlapping and paralleling and contradicting until the whole adventure became a composite, and today it is in my mind as in theirs a sort of generalized blur.

The sun came out warmly as though to soothe their jagged feelings, and one by one the men in the cactus patch stretched on the ground and fell wearily asleep at midday. And I, satiated with the adventures of the day before, lay down and slept too, waiting for the day's new battle to begin.

February 28, 1943—The withdrawal of our American forces from the vast Sbeïtla Valley, back through Kasserine Pass, was a majestic thing in a way. It started before dawn one morning, and continued without a break for twenty-four hours.

It had no earmarks of a retreat whatever, it was carried out so calmly and methodically. It differed in no way, except size, from the normal daily convoys of troops and supplies. . . .

. . . First, before daylight, came the kitchen trucks and engineers to prepare things ahead. Then came rolling guns, and some infantry to set up protection along the roads. Then the great vast bulk of long supply trains, field hospitals, command posts, ammunition wagons, infantry, artillery, and finally—when night came again—the tanks started and moved on until the next dawn. The whole thing was completely motorized. Nobody was walking.

It was hard to realize, when you were a part of it, that this was a retreat—that American forces in large numbers were retreating in foreign battle one of the few times in our history.

We couldn't help feel a slight sense of humiliation. Yet, while it was happening, that humiliation was somewhat overcome by our pride in the orderliness of the accomplishment. . . .

Sidi-Bou-Zid lay in the path of the Germans as they stormed through Faïd Pass and into Allied territory. The surprised Americans and their tanks were no match for Field Marshal Erwin Rommel's new Tiger tanks.

Tank Battle at Sidi-Bou-Zid

THE TUNISIAN FRONT, *March 1, 1943*—This and the next few columns will be an attempt to describe what a tank battle looks like.

Words will be poor instruments for it. Neither can isolated camera shots tell you the story. Probably only Hollywood with its machinery of many dimensions is capable of transferring to your senses a clear impression of a tank battle.

The fight in question was the American counterattack on the second day of the battle at Sidi-Bou-Zid which eventually resulted in our withdrawal.

It was the biggest tank battle fought so far in this part of the world. On that morning I had a talk with the commanding general some ten miles behind the front lines before starting for the battle scene.

He took me into his tent and showed me just what the battle plan was for the day. He picked out a point close to the expected battle area and said that would be a good place for me to watch from.

The only danger, he said, would be one of being encircled and cut off if the battle should go against us.

"But it won't," he said, "for we are going to kick hell out of them today and we've got the stuff to do it with."

Unfortunately, we didn't kick hell out of them. In fact, the boot was on the other foot.

I spent the forenoon in the newly picked, badly shattered forward command post. All morning I tried to get on up where the tanks were but there was no transportation left around the post and their communications were cut off at noontime.

We sat on the ground and ate some British crackers with jam and drank some hot tea. The day was bright and mellow. Shortly after lunch a young lieutenant dug up a spare jeep and said he'd take me on up to the front.

We drove a couple of miles east along a highway to a crossroads which was the very heart center of our troops' bivouacs. German airmen had been after this crossroads all morning. They had hit it again just a few minutes before we got there. In the road was a large crater and a few yards away a tank was off to one side, burning.

The roads at that point were high and we could see a long way.

In every direction was a huge semi-irrigated desert valley. It looked very much like the valley at Phoenix, Arizona—no trees but patches of wild growth, shoulder-high cactus of the prickly-pear variety. In other parts of the valley were spotted cultivated fields and the tiny square stucco houses of Arab farmers. The whole vast scene was treeless, with slightly rolling big mountains in the distance.

As far as you could see out across the rolling desert, in all four sections of the "pie" formed by the intersecting roads, was American equipment—tanks, half-tracks, artillery, infantry—hundreds, yes, thousands of vehicles extending miles and miles and everything standing still. We were in time; the battle had not yet started.

We put our jeep in super low gear and drove out across the sands among the tanks. Ten miles or so east and southeast were the Germans but there was no activity anywhere, no smoke on the horizon, no planes in the sky.

It all had the appearance of an after-lunch siesta but no one was asleep.

As we drove past tank after tank we found each one's crew at its post inside—the driver at his control, the commander standing with head sticking out of the open turret door, standing there silent and motionless, just looking ahead like the Indian on the calendars.

We stopped and inquired of several what they were doing. They said they didn't know what the plan was—they were merely ready in place and waiting for orders. Somehow it seemed like the cars lined up at Indianapolis just before the race starts—their weeks of training over, everything mechanically perfect, just a few quiet minutes of immobility before the great struggle for which they had waited so long.

Suddenly out of this siesta-like doze the order came. We didn't hear it for it came to the tanks over their radios but we knew it quickly for all over the desert tanks began roaring and pouring out blue smoke from the cylinders. Then they started off, kicking up dust and clanking in that peculiar "tank sound" we have all come to know so well.

They poured around us, charging forward. They weren't close together—probably a couple of hundred yards apart. There weren't lines or any specific formation. They were just everywhere. They covered the desert to the right and left, ahead and behind as far as we could see, trailing their eager dust tails behind. It was almost as though some official starter had fired his blank pistol. The battle was on.

THE TUNISIAN FRONT, *March 2, 1943*—We were in the midst of the forward-rushing tanks, but didn't know what the score was. So I pulled the jeep to the side, gradually easing out.

We decided to get to a high spot and take a look at what was happening, before we got caught. So we bounced over gullies and ditches, up the side of a rocky hill.

There—in a hidden gully—we found the commanding colonel, standing beside a radio half-track. We stood close enough to the radio to hear the voice of the battalion commander, who was leading the tank attack. At the same time, through binoculars, we watched the fantastic surge of caterpillar metal move forward amidst its own dust.

Far across the desert, in front of us, lay the town of Sidi-Bou-Zid. Through the glasses we could see it only as a great oasis whose green trees stood out against the bare brown of the desert. On beyond were high hills, where some of our troops were still trapped after the surprise attack of the day before.

Behind our tanks, leading the attack, other armored vehicles puffed blue smoke. New formations began to move forward swiftly. The artillery went first, followed by armored infantry in half-tracks and even in jeeps. Now the entire desert was surging in one gigantic movement.

Over the radio came the voice of the battalion commander:

"We're in the edge of Sidi-Bou-Zid, and have struck no opposition yet." So our tanks were across the vast plain, which the Germans had abandoned during the night—after the chaos of the previous day.

This peaceful report from our tank charge brought no comment from anyone around the command truck. Faces were grave: it wasn't right—this business of no opposition at all; there must be a trick in it somewhere . . .

Suddenly, brown geysers of earth and smoke began to spout. We watched through our glasses. Then, from far off, came the sound of explosions.

Again the voice from the radio:

"We're getting shelled, but can't make out where it's coming from." Then a long silence, while the geysers continued to burst . . .

"I'm not sure, but I think it's artillery along the road north of town . . . Now there is some from the south."

We looked, and could see through our glasses the enemy advancing. They were far away, perhaps ten miles—narrow little streaks of dust, like plumes, speeding down the low sloping plain from the mountain base toward the oasis of Sidi-Bou-Zid.

We could not see the German tanks, only dust plumes extending and pushing forward.

Just then I realized that although we were standing on the very hill the general had picked out for me on his map that morning, it was not good enough. I said to the young lieutenant: "Let's get on up there." He replied: "I'm ready."

So we got into the jeep, and went leaping and bounding up toward what was—but we didn't know it then—the most ghastly armored melee that has occurred so far in Tunisia.

THE TUNISIAN FRONT, *March 3, 1943*—It was odd, the way we went up into the thick of the battle in our jeep. We didn't attach ourselves to anybody. We didn't ask anybody if we could go. We just started the motor and went.

Vehicles ahead of us had worn a sort of track across the desert and through irrigated fields. We followed them awhile, keeping our place in the forward-moving procession. We were just a jeep with two brown-clad figures in it, indistinguishable from anyone else.

The line was moving cautiously. Every now and then the procession would stop. A few times we stopped too. We shut off our motor to listen for planes. But, finally, we tired of the slow progress. We dashed out across the sand and the Arabs' plowed fields, skirting cactus fences and small farmyards.

As we did this, a sensation of anxiety—which had not touched me before—came over me. It was fear of mines in the freshly dug earth; the touch of the wheel—we could so easily be blown into little bits. I spoke of this to the lieutenant, but he said he didn't think they had had time to plant mines.

I thought to myself: "Hell, it doesn't take all night to plant a mine." We did not—it is obvious to report—hit any mines.

*

The battlefield was an incongruous thing. Always there is some ridiculous impingement of normalcy on a field of battle.

Here on this day were the Arabs. They were herding their camels, just as usual. Some of them continued to plow their fields. Children walked along, driving their little sack-laden burros, as tanks and guns clanked past them. The sky was filled with planes and smoke bursts from screaming shells.

As we smashed along over a field of new grain, which pushed its small shoots just a few inches above earth, the asinine thought popped into my head: "I wonder if the Army got permission to use this land before starting the attack."

Both sides had crossed and recrossed these farms in the past twenty-four hours. The fields were riddled by deep ruts and by the wide spooky tracks of the almost-mythical Mark VI tanks.

Evidence of the previous day's battle was still strewn across the desert. We passed charred half-tracks. We stopped to look into a burned-out tank, named *Temes,* from which a lieutenant-colonel friend of mine and his crew had demolished four German tanks before being put out of commission themselves.

We passed a trailer still full of American ammunition, which had been abandoned. The young lieutenant wanted to hook our own jeep to it as a tow when we returned, but I talked him out of it. I feared the Germans had booby-trapped it during the night.

We moved on closer to the actual tank battle ahead, but never went right into it—for in a jeep that would have been a fantastic form of suicide. We stopped, I should judge, about a mile behind the foremost tanks.

Behind us the desert was still alive with men and machines moving up. Later we learned that some German tanks had maneuvered in behind us, and were shooting up our half-tracks and jeeps. But, fortunately, we didn't know all this at the time.

Light American tanks came up from the rear and stopped near us. They were to be held there in reserve, in case they had to be called into the game in this league which was much too heavy and hot for them. Their crews jumped out the moment they stopped, and began digging foxholes against the inevitable arrival of the dive bombers.

Soon the dive bombers came. They set fires behind us. American and German tanks were burning ahead of us.

Our planes came over, too, strafing and bombing the enemy.

One of our half-tracks, full of ammunition, was livid red, with flames leaping and swaying. Every few seconds one of its shells would go off, and the projectile would tear into the sky with a weird whanging sort of noise.

Field artillery had stopped just on our right. They began shelling the German artillery beyond our tanks. It didn't take long for the Germans to answer.

The scream of an approaching shell is an appalling thing. We could hear them coming. (You sort of duck inside yourself, without actually ducking at all.)

Then we could see the dust kick up a couple of hundred yards away. The shells hit the ground and ricocheted like armor-piercing shells, which do not explode but skip along the ground until they finally lose momentum or hit something.

*

War has its own peculiar sounds. They are not really very much different from sounds in the world of peace. But they clothe themselves in an unforgettable fierceness, just because born in danger and death.

The clank of a starting tank, the scream of a shell through the air, the ever-rising whine of fiendishness as a bomber dives—these sounds have their counterparts in normal life, and you would be hard put to distinguish them in a blindfold test. But, once heard in war, they remain with you forever.

Their nervous memories come back to you in a thousand ways —in the grind of a truck starting in low gear, in high wind around the eaves, in somebody merely whistling a tune. Even the sound of a shoe, dropped to the floor in a hotel room above you, becomes indistinguishable from the faint boom of a big gun far away. A mere rustling curtain can paralyze a man with memories.

March 10, 1943— . . . Is war dramatic, or isn't it? Certainly there are great tragedies, unbelievable heroics, even a constant undertone of comedy. It is the job of us writers to transfer all that drama back to you folks at home. Most of the other correspondents have the ability to do it. But when I sit down to write, here is what I see instead:

Men at the front suffering and wishing they were somewhere else, men in routine jobs just behind the lines bellyaching because they can't get to the front, all of them desperately hungry for somebody to talk to besides themselves, no women to be heroes in front of, damn little wine to drink, precious little song, cold and fairly dirty, just toiling from day to day in a world full of insecurity, discomfort, homesickness and a dulled sense of danger. . . .

Pyle accompanied a salvage crew into the Sahara to retrieve parts from American bombers that had crashed near German lines.

Digging and Grousing

ON THE NORTH AFRICAN DESERT, *March 23, 1943*—When our Sahara salvage expedition finally found the wrecked airplanes far out on the endless desert, the mechanics went to work taking off usable parts, and four others of us appointed ourselves the official ditchdiggers of the day.

We were all afraid of being strafed if the Germans came over and saw men working around the planes, and we wanted a nice ditch handy for diving into. The way to have a nice ditch is to dig one. We wasted no time.

Would that all slit trenches could be dug in soil like that. The sand was soft and moist; just the kind children like to play in. The four of us dug a winding ditch forty feet long and three feet deep in about an hour and a half.

*

The day got hot, and we took off our shirts. One sweating soldier said: "Five years ago you couldn't a got me to dig a ditch for five dollars an hour. Now look at me.

"You can't stop me digging ditches. I don't even want pay for it; I just dig for love. And I sure do hope this digging today is all wasted effort; I never wanted to do useless work so bad in my life.

"Any time I get fifty feet from my home ditch you'll find me digging a new ditch, and brother I ain't joking. I love to dig ditches."

Digging out here in the soft desert sand was paradise compared with the claylike digging back at our base. The ditch went forward like a prairie fire. We measured it with our eyes to see if it would hold everybody.

"Throw up some more right here," one of the boys said, indicating a low spot in the bank on either side. "Do you think we've got it deep enough?"

"It don't have to be so deep," another one said. "A bullet won't go through more than three inches of sand. Sand is the best thing there is for stopping bullets."

A growth of sagebrush hung over the ditch on one side. "Let's leave it right there," one of the boys said. "It's good for the imagination. Makes you think you're covered up even when you ain't."

That's the new outlook, the new type of conversation, among thousands of American boys today. It's hard for you to realize, but there are certain moments when a plain old ditch can be dearer to you than any possession on earth. For all bombs, no matter where they may land eventually, do all their falling right straight at your head. Only those of you who know about that can ever know all about ditches.

*

While we were digging, one of the boys brought up for the thousandth time the question of that letter in *Time* magazine. What letter, you ask? Why, it's a letter you probably don't remember, but it has become famous around these parts.

It was in the November 23 [1942] issue, which eventually found its way over here. Somebody read it, spoke to a few friends, and pretty soon thousands of men were commenting on this letter in terms which the fire department won't permit me to set to paper.

To get to the point, it was written by a soldier, and it said: "The greatest Christmas present that can be given to us this year is not smoking jackets, ties, pipes or games. If people will only take the money and buy war bonds . . . they will be helping themselves and helping us to be home next Christmas. Being home next Christmas is something which would be appreciated by all of us boys in service!"

The letter was all right with the soldiers over here until they got down to the address of the writer and discovered he was still in camp in the States. For a soldier back home to open his trap about anything concerning the war is like waving a red flag at the troops over here. They say they can do whatever talking is necessary.

"Them poor dogfaces back home," said one of the ditch-diggers with fine soldier sarcasm, "they've really got it rugged. Nothing to eat but them old greasy pork chops and them three-inch steaks all the time. I wouldn't be surprised if they don't have to eat eggs several times a week."

"And they're so lonely," said another. "No entertainment except to rassle them old dames around the dance floor. The USO closes at ten o'clock and the nightclubs at three. It's mighty tough on them. No wonder they want to get home."

"And they probably don't get no sleep," said another, "sleeping on them old cots with springs and everything, and scalding themselves in hot baths all the time."

"And nothing to drink but that nasty old ten-cent beer and that awful Canadian Club whiskey," chimed in another philosopher with a shovel.

"And when they put a nickel in the box nothing comes out but Glenn Miller and Artie Shaw and such trash as that. My heart just bleeds for them poor guys."

"And did you see where he was?" asked another. "At the Albuquerque Air Base. And he wants to be home by next Christmas. Hell, if I could just see the Albuquerque Air Base again I'd think I was in heaven."

That's the way it goes. The boys feel a soldier isn't qualified to comment unless he's on the wrong side of the ocean. They're gay and full of their own wit when they get started that way, but just the same they mean it. It's a new form of the age-old soldier pastime of grousing. It helps take your mind off things.

Pyle took a vacation in late February and early March, during which he toured the Belgian Congo. When he returned, Montgomery's British 8th Army had chased the Afrika Korps well into Tunisia, and the Allies were taking German and Italian prisoners. Pyle, like most Americans, was curious about the Germans. What were they like, these members of a supposedly superior race who had ruthlessly subjugated so many? The following was the first of a series of reports Pyle filed on Germans captured in the Tunisian campaign.

Prisoners

IN TUNISIA, *April 19, 1943*—The men who interrogate captured prisoners have interesting jobs. In addition to being linguists, they have to be good psychologists to wheedle information out of reluctant German soldiers.

They never have any trouble getting the Italians to talk, but unfortunately the Italians don't know anything. According to interrogators they are a pretty sorry lot. Some of them didn't even know they were fighting against Americans till they got captured.

One batch I know of thought we would execute them, and were pathetically happy when they discovered they would live. The first thing they usually ask is to be allowed to write their families that they're all right, and of course permission is granted.

Most of them keep diaries. All of them, Italians and Germans alike, seem to have plenty of money in their pockets. The Italians all carry Catholic medals and crosses, and are grateful on learning they can keep these. Nearly everybody has a picture of a wife or sweetheart or children, and these too they are allowed to keep.

A few of the captured Germans and Italians up north had on thin clothing, and no underwear at all. But most of them are warmly dressed and well equipped. The first thing our soldiers take away from a German is his mess kit. It is superior in quality and design to ours; is made of steel, easy to keep clean, more compact, and even has a can opener with it.

The Italians have a shovel that is quite a gadget. It is small, sort of like a fireplace coal shovel. The shovel part is swiveled onto the handle, so that you can turn it down, lock it, and the shovel then becomes a pick.

*

Italian enlisted men wear as lapel insignia a tin star, exactly like the stars an American general wears. I know at least two generals now wearing these Italian stars on their shoulders. And I heard of a private who pinned one on his cap unthinkingly, and went around for an hour wondering why everybody in the Army was suddenly saluting him.

The Italians are almost unanimously happy to be captured, but you never can tell what a German's attitude will be. Some are friendly and glad to be out of it. Others are arrogant. They tell of one wounded German who came to in the operating room of one of our hospitals, and instantly came off the table swinging with both fists. Nurses say the wounded Germans usually are sullen and autocratic.

There is one conscripted German regiment made up of people rejected earlier in the war—men with one eye or one finger missing, older people, men from occupied countries. But mostly the Germans and Italians both are in excellent physical condition.

The Germans get paid every ten days, and nearly half their money is automatically sent home. They are usually short on cigarets. Often you'll see Americans going past a batch of newly captured prisoners and stopping to give them cigarets.

Stories differ as to how the Axis treats our prisoners. Some of those who have escaped say the Italians are worse than the Germans. I know Americans who say they'll commit suicide before they'll be captured again. I guess it depends on the individual who gets his hands on you.

The End is Near

NORTHERN TUNISIA, *April 21, 1943*—Now we have left central Tunisia behind us. We are in the north now, Americans as well as British, and the end of the long Tunisian trail is in sight. Surely the kill cannot now be long delayed.

Except in the air, the American troops are playing a rather minor part in this final act. In the air we are all-out, and great formations of American planes are overhead constantly. But on the ground it is the British 8th and 1st Armies who are giving Rommel the main squeeze.

The troops have been so distributed for this last phase that the Americans and the French are holding only a small slice of the quarter circle that is penning the Germans into the Tunis corner. True, we will do some hard fighting, but the bulk of the knockout blow on the ground will be British.

You at home will be wrong if you try to make anything sinister out of that, for it's the way it should be, as I tried to tell you once before.

The British have more troops, and more experienced troops, in Tunisia than we have. We had sort of divided the load earlier, but with the arrival of the 8th Army the affair has become predominantly British.

Since Montgomery has chased Rommel all the way from Egypt in one of the great military achievements of history, it is only right that the British should have the kill.

*

The 8th Army is a magnificent organization. We correspondents have been thrilled by its perfection. So have our troops. It must surely be one of the outstanding armies of all time. We trailed it several days up the Tunisian coast, and we came to look upon it almost with awe.

Its organization for continuous movement is so perfect that it seems more like a big business firm than a destructive army. The men of the 8th are brown-skinned and white-eyebrowed from the desert sun. Most of them are in shorts, and they are a healthy-looking lot. Their spirit is like a tonic. The spirit of our own troops is good, but these boys from the burning sands are throbbing with the vitality of conquerors.

They are friendly, cocky, and confident. They've been three years in the desert, and now they wear the expression of victory on their faces. We envy them, and are proud of them.

*

This north country is entirely different from the semi-desert where we Americans spent the winter. Up here the land is fertile and everything is violently green.

Northern Tunisia is all hills and valleys. There are no trees at all, but now in spring the earth is solidly covered with deep green—pastures and freshly growing fields of grain. Small wild flowers spatter the countryside.

I have never seen lovelier or more gentle country. It gives you a sense of peacefulness. It seems to speak its richness to you. It is a full, ripe country, and here in the springtime living seems sweet and worthwhile.

There are winding gravel roads everywhere, and many roads of fine macadam. Villages are perched on the hillsides, and some of them look like picture postcards. This is all so different from the Tunisia we've known that all of us, driving up suddenly one sunny afternoon into this clean cool greenness, felt like holding out our arms and saying: "This is the country we love."

Yet this peaceful green is gradually turning red with blood. The roads are packed with brown-painted convoys, and the trailers sprout long rifle barrels. The incredibly blue sky with its big white clouds is streaked with war planes in great throbbing formations. And soon the whole northeastern corner of Tunisia will roar and rage with a violence utterly out of character with a landscape so rich in nature's kindness.

The only thing we can say in behalf of ourselves is that the human race even in the process of defiling beauty still has the capacity to appreciate it.

Many American soldiers underwent their blooding at Kasserine Pass and in the two months since had become hardened, crafty fighters.

"Brave Men, Brave Men!"

NORTHERN TUNISIA, *April 22, 1943*—I was away from the front lines for a while this spring, living with other troops, and considerable fighting took place while I was gone. When I got ready to return to my old friends at the front I wondered if I would sense any change in them.

I did, and definitely.

The most vivid change is the casual and workshop manner in which they now talk about killing. They have made the psychological transition from the normal belief that taking human life is sinful, over to a new professional outlook where killing is a craft. To them now there is nothing morally wrong about killing. In fact it is an admirable thing.

I think I am so impressed by this new attitude because it hasn't been necessary for me to make this change along with them. As a noncombatant, my own life is in danger only by occasional chance or circumstance. Consequently I need not think of killing in personal terms, and killing to me is still murder.

Even after a winter of living with wholesale death and vile destruction, it is only spasmodically that I seem capable of realizing how real and how awful this war is. My emotions seem dead and crusty when presented with the tangibles of war. I find I can look on rows of fresh graves without a lump in my throat. Somehow I can look on mutilated bodies without flinching or feeling deeply.

It is only when I sit alone away from it all, or lie at night in my bedroll recreating with closed eyes what I have seen, thinking and thinking and thinking, that at last the enormity of all these newly dead strikes like a living nightmare. And there are times when I feel that I can't stand it and will have to leave.

*

But to the fighting soldier that phase of the war is behind. It was left behind after his first battle. His blood is up. He is fighting for his life, and killing now for him is as much a profession as writing is for me.

He wants to kill individually or in vast numbers. He wants to see the Germans overrun, mangled, butchered in the Tunisian trap. He speaks excitedly of seeing great heaps of dead, of our bombers sinking whole shiploads of fleeing men, of Germans by the thousands dying miserably in a final Tunisian holocaust of his own creation.

In this one respect the front-line soldier differs from all the rest of us. All the rest of us—you and me and even the thousands of soldiers behind the lines in Africa—we want terribly yet only academically for the war to get over. The front-line soldier wants it to be got over by the physical process of his destroying enough Germans to end it. He is truly at war. The rest of us, no matter how hard we work, are not.

*

Say what you will, nothing can make a complete soldier except battle experience.

In the semifinals of this campaign—the cleaning out of central Tunisia—we had large units in battle for the first time. Frankly, they didn't all excel. Their own commanders admit it, and admirably they don't try to alibi. The British had to help us out a few times, but neither American nor British commanders are worried about that, for there was no lack of bravery. There was only lack of experience. They all know we will do better next time.

The 1st Infantry Division is an example of what our American units can be after they have gone through the mill of experience. Those boys did themselves proud in the semifinals. Everybody speaks about it. Our casualties included few taken prisoners. All the other casualties were wounded or died fighting.

"They never gave an inch," a general says. "They died right in their foxholes."

I heard of a high British officer who went over this battlefield just after the action was over. American boys were still lying dead in their foxholes, their rifles still grasped in firing position in their dead hands. And the veteran English soldier remarked time and again, in a sort of hushed eulogy spoken only to himself:

"Brave men. Brave men."*

Pyle thought human behavior generally aberrant, but he took solace in the regenerative powers of nature. By the time this column saw print stateside, the final attack on Axis troops was well under way.

War Leaves Few Traces

NORTHERN TUNISIA, *April 23, 1943*—Thousands are the soldiers who want someday to bring their wives and children back to Tunisia, in times of peace, and take them over the battlefields we have come to know so well. But except for the cities they will not find much to remind them of the ferocity that existed here.

I have recently traveled over the Tunisian battle area—both the part we knew so intimately because it was on our side and the part we didn't know at all because the Germans lived there at the time.

You don't see the desolated countryside we remember from pictures of France in the last war. That is because the fighting has been mobile, because neither side used permanent huge guns, and because the country is mostly treeless and empty. But there are some marks left, and I'll try to give you examples in this and tomorrow's column.

*

East of El-Guettar down a broad valley through which runs a nice macadam road, you see dark objects sitting far off on the plain. These are burned-out tanks of both sides.

A certain two sit close together like twins, about a mile off the road. The immense caterpillar track is off one of them and lies trailed out behind for fifty feet. The insides are a shambles. Seared and jumbled personal and mechanical debris is scattered around outside. Our soldiers have already retrieved everything worthwhile from the German debris, but you can still find big wrenches, oil-soaked gloves, and twisted shell cases.

And in the shade of one tank, not five feet from the great metal skeleton, is the fresh grave of a German tanker, marked by a rough wooden cross without a name.

There are many of these tanks scattered miles apart through the valley.

*Pyle used this quotation as the title of his third collection of war columns.

On the hillsides you can still see white splotches—powder marks from our exploding artillery shells. Gnarled lengths of Signal Corps telephone wire, too mauled to retrieve, string for yards along the roadsides.

There are frequent filled-in holes in the macadam where artillery dive bombers took their toll. Now and then a little graveyard with wooden crosses stands lonesomely at the roadside. Some of the telephone poles have been chopped down. There are clumps of empty ammunition boxes.

But for all these things you must look closely. There was once a holocaust here but it left only a slight permanent mark. It is sort of hard to disfigure acres of marigolds and billions of blades of fresh desert grass.

*

Sidi-Bou-Zid is the little white village I saw destroyed by shellfire back in February. It was weeks later before I could get close enough to see the details, for the village remained German territory for some time.

This was one of the little towns I knew so well, and now it is pitiful to look at. The village almost doesn't exist anymore. Its dozens of low stone adobe buildings, stuccoed a snowy white, are nothing now but rock piles. This village has died. The reason for the destruction of Sidi-Bou-Zid was that German and American tank columns, advancing toward each other, met there. Artillery from both sides poured its long-distance fury into the town for hours. There will have to be a new Sidi-Bou-Zid.

Faïd Pass is the last pass in the Grand Dorsal before the drive eastward onto the long flat plain that leads to the Mediterranean at Sfax. For months we looked with longing eyes at Faïd. A number of times we tried to take it and failed. But when the Germans' big retreat came they left Faïd Pass voluntarily. And they left it so thoroughly and maliciously mined that even today you don't dare drive off onto the shoulder of the road, or you may get blown to kingdom come.

Our engineers go through these mine fields with electrical instruments, locate the mines, and surround them with warning notices until they can later be dug up or exploded. These notices are of two types—either a white ribbon strung around the mine area on knee-high sticks, or else stakes with oppositely pointing arrows on top. The white arrow pointing to the left meaning that side is safe, the red arrow pointing to the right meaning that side is mined.

And believe me, after seeing a few mine-wrecked trucks and jeeps, you fear mines so dreadfully that you find yourself actually leaning away from the side of the road where the signs are, as you drive past.

Little Boys Lost in the Dark

NORTHERN TUNISIA, *April 27, 1943*—We moved one afternoon to a new position just a few miles behind the invisible line of armor that separates us from the Germans in northern Tunisia. Nothing happened that first night that was spectacular, yet somehow the whole night became obsessed with a spookiness that leaves it standing like a landmark in my memory.

We had been at the new camp about an hour and were still setting up our tents when German planes appeared overhead. We stopped work to watch them. It was the usual display of darting planes, with the conglomerate sounds of ack-ack on the ground and in the sky.

Suddenly we realized that one plane was diving straight at us, and we made a mad scramble for foxholes. Two officer friends of mine had dug a three-foot hole and set their tent over it. So they made for their tent, and I was tramping on their heels. The tent flap wouldn't come open, and we wound up in a silly heap. Finally it did open, and we all dived through the narrow opening at once.

We lay there in the hole, face down, as the plane came smack overhead with a terrible roar. We were all drawn up inside, waiting for the blow. Explosions around us were shatteringly loud, and yet when it was all over we couldn't find any bomb holes or anybody hurt.

But you could find a lot of nervous people.

*

Dusk came on, and with dusk began the steady boom of big guns in the mountains ahead of us. They weren't near enough for the sound to be crashing. Rather it was like the lonely roll of an approaching thunderstorm—a sound which since childhood has always made me sad with a kind of portent of inevitable doom.

We went to bed in our tents. A nearby farmyard was full of dogs and they began a howling that lasted all night. The roll of artillery was constant. It never stopped once in twenty-four hours. Once in a while there were nearer shots which might have been German patrols or might not.

We lay uneasily in our cots. Sleep wouldn't come. We turned and turned. I snapped on a flashlight.

"What time is it?" asked Chris Cunningham from the next cot.

"Quarter to one," I answered. "Haven't you been asleep?"

He hadn't.

A plane droned faintly in the distance and came nearer and nearer until it was overhead.

"Is that a Jerry or a Beaufighter?*" Chris asked out of the darkness.

"It hasn't got that throb-throb to it," I said, "so it must be a Beaufighter. But hell, I never can tell really. Don't know what it is."

The plane passed on, out of hearing. The artillery rolled and rolled. A nearer shot went off uncannily somewhere in the darkness. Some guinea hens set up a terrific cackling.

I remembered that just before dusk a soldier had shot at a snake in our new camp, and they thought it was a cobra. We'd just heard our first stories of scorpions, too. I began to feel creepy and wondered if our tent flaps were tight.

Another plane throbbed in the sky, and we lay listening with an awful anticipation. One of the dogs suddenly broke into a frenzied barking and went tearing through our little camp as though chasing a demon.

My mind seemed to lose all sense of proportion, and I was jumpy and mad at myself.

Concussion ghosts, traveling in waves, touched our tent walls and made them quiver. Ghosts were shaking the ground ever so lightly. Ghosts were stirring the dogs to hysteria. Ghosts were wandering in the sky peering for us in our cringing hideout. Ghosts were everywhere, and their hordes were multiplying as every hour added its production of new battlefield dead.

You lie and think of the graveyards and the dirty men and the shocking blast of the big guns, and you can't sleep.

"What time is it?" comes out of darkness from the next cot. I snap on the flashlight.

"Half past four, and for God's sake go to sleep!"

Finally just before dawn you do sleep, in spite of everything.

*

Next morning we spoke around among ourselves and found one by one that all of us had tossed away all night. It was an unexplainable thing. For all of us had been through dangers greater than this. On another night the roll of the guns would have lulled us to sleep.

It's just that on some nights the air becomes sick and there is an

*A British fighter-bomber.

unspoken contagion of spiritual dread, and you are little boys again, lost in the dark.

April 28, 1943— . . . I have stopped now and then to see some of the battle graveyards. The Germans bury their dead in small cemeteries along the roadsides, but we concentrate in fewer and bigger graveyards, usually on the edge of some town. Arabs are hired to dig the graves.

At Gafsa there is an American cemetery with more than six hundred graves. It is in desertlike country, and the graves are aligned in precise rows in the naked gray earth. Each is marked with a waist-high wooden cross.

In a nearby tent is a great pile of ready-made crosses, and a stack of newly carpentered wood markers in the form of the Star of David, for the Jewish dead.

As all the American dead in the Gafsa area have been located and reburied in the permanent graveyard, this cemetery section will move on to other fronts.

The little German cemeteries are always bordered with rows of white rocks, and in some there will be a phrase neatly spelled out in white rocks with a border around it. One that I remember said, in rough translation:

"These dead gave their spirits for the glory of Greater Germany."

In one German cemetery of about a hundred graves we found eleven Americans. They lay among the Germans, not segregated in any way. Their graves are identical with those of the Germans except that beneath the names on the wooden crosses is printed "Amerikaner," and below that the Army serial number. We presume their dog tags were buried with them.

On one of the graves, beneath the soldier's serial number, is also printed: "T-40." The Germans apparently thought that was part of his number. Actually it only showed that the man had had his first anti-tetanus shot in 1940.

My friend Sgt. Pat Donadeo of Pittsburgh was with me when we looked at this graveyard, and as we left he said:

"They respect our dead the same as we do theirs. It's comforting to know that." . . .

The Germans leave very clean country behind them. Their salvage organization must be one of the best in the world—probably because of desperate necessity. We've gone all over the Tunisian country from which they have fled, and evidences that they have been there are slight. You see burned-out tanks in the fields, and some wrecked scout cars and Italian trucks lying in roadside ditches, and that is about all. Nothing is left behind that is repairable. Wrecked cars are stripped of their tires, instruments and lights. They leave no tin cans, boxes or other junk as we do. . . .

An Inconceivable Life

AT THE FRONT LINES IN TUNISIA, *May 1, 1943*—When our infantry goes into a big push in northern Tunisia each man is issued three bars of D-ration chocolate, enough to last one day. He takes no other food.

He carries two canteens of water instead of the usual one. He carries no blankets. He leaves behind all extra clothes except his raincoat. In his pockets he may have a few toilet articles. Some men carry their money. Others give it to friends to keep.

In the days that follow they live in a way that is inconceivable to us at home. They walk and fight all night without sleep. Next day they lie flat in foxholes, or hide in fields of freshly green, knee-high wheat.

If they're in the fields they dare not even move enough to dig foxholes, for that would bring the German artillery. They can't rise even for nature's calls. The German feels for them continually with his artillery.

*

The slow drag of these motionless daylight hours is nearly unendurable. Lt. Mickey Miller of Morgantown, Indiana, says this lifeless waiting in a wheatfield is almost the worst part of the whole battle.

The second evening after the attack begins, C-rations and five-gallon cans of water are brought up across country in jeeps, after dark. You eat in the dark, and you can't see the can you are eating from. You just eat by feel. You make cold coffee from cold water.

One night a German shell landed close and fragments punctured fifteen cans of water.

Each night enough canned rations for three meals are brought up, but when the men move on after supper most of them either lose or leave behind the next day's rations, because they're too heavy to carry. But, as they say, when you're in battle and excited you sort of go on your nerve. You don't think much about being hungry.

The men fight at night and lie low by day, when the artillery takes over its blasting job. Weariness gradually creeps over them. What sleeping they do is in daytime. But, as they say, at night it's too cold and in daytime it's too hot. Also the fury of the artillery makes daytime sleeping next to impossible. So does the heat of the sun. Some men have passed out from heat prostration. Many of them get upset stomachs from the heat.

But as the third and fourth days roll on weariness overcomes all obstacles to sleep. Men who sit down for a moment's rest fall asleep in the grass. There are even men who say they can march while asleep.

Lt. Col. Charlie Stone of New Brunswick, New Jersey, actually went to sleep while standing up talking on a field telephone—not while listening, but in the middle of a spoken sentence.

When sometimes they do lie down at night the men have only their raincoats to lie on. It is cold, and the dew makes the grass as wet as rain. They don't dare start a fire to heat their food, even in daytime, for the smoke would attract enemy fire. At night they can't even light cigarets in the open, so after digging their foxholes they get down and make hoods over their heads with their raincoats, and light up under the coats.

They have plenty of cigarets. Those who run out during battle are supplied by others. Every night new supplies of water and C-rations are brought up in jeeps.

*

You can't conceive how hard it is to move and fight at night. The country is rugged, the ground rough. Everything is new and strange. The nights are pitch black. You grope with your feet. You step into holes, and fall sprawling in little gullies and creeks. You trudge over plowed ground and push through waist-high shrubs. You go as a man blindfolded, feeling unsure and off balance, but you keep on going.

Through it all there is the fear of mines. The Germans have mined the country behind them beyond anything ever known before. We simply can't take time to go over each inch of ground with mine detectors, so we have to discover the mine fields by stumbling into them or driving over them. Naturally there are casualties, but they are smaller than you might think—just a few men each day.

The greatest damage is psychological—the intense watchfulness our troops must maintain.

The Germans have been utterly profligate with their mines. We dug out four hundred from one field. We've found so many fields and so many isolated mines that we have run out of white tape to mark them with. But still we go on.

The last two sections of the following column are Pyle's most eloquent celebration of the infantry. They have been widely reprinted.

The God-Damned Infantry

IN THE FRONT LINES BEFORE MATEUR, NORTHERN TUNISIA, *May 2, 1943*—We're now with an infantry outfit that has battled ceaselessly for four days and nights.

This northern warfare has been in the mountains. You don't ride much anymore. It is walking and climbing and crawling country. The mountains aren't big, but they are constant. They are largely treeless. They are easy to defend and bitter to take. But we are taking them.

The Germans lie on the back slope of every ridge, deeply dug into foxholes. In front of them the fields and pastures are hideous with thousands of hidden mines. The forward slopes are left open, untenanted, and if the Americans tried to scale these slopes they would be murdered wholesale in an inferno of machine-gun crossfire plus mortars and grenades.

Consequently we don't do it that way. We have fallen back to the old warfare of first pulverizing the enemy with artillery, then sweeping around the ends of the hill with infantry and taking them from the sides and behind.

*

I've written before how the big guns crack and roar almost constantly throughout the day and night. They lay a screen ahead of our troops. By magnificent shooting they drop shells on the back slopes. By means of shells timed to burst in the air a few feet from the ground, they get the Germans even in their foxholes. Our troops have found that the Germans dig foxholes down and then under, trying to get cover from the shell bursts that shower death from above.

Our artillery has really been sensational. For once we have enough of something and at the right time. Officers tell me they actually have more guns than they know what to do with.

All the guns in any one sector can be centered to shoot at one spot. And when we lay the whole business on a German hill the whole slope seems to erupt. It becomes an unbelievable cauldron of fire and smoke and dirt. Veteran German soldiers say they have never been through anything like it.

*

Now to the infantry—the God-damned infantry, as they like to call themselves.

I love the infantry because they are the underdogs. They are the mud-rain-frost-and-wind boys. They have no comforts, and they even learn to live without the necessities. And in the end they are the guys that wars can't be won without.

I wish you could see just one of the ineradicable pictures I have in my mind today. In this particular picture I am sitting among clumps of sword-grass on a steep and rocky hillside that we have just taken. We are looking out over a vast rolling country to the rear.

A narrow path comes like a ribbon over a hill miles away, down a long slope, across a creek, up a slope and over another hill.

All along the length of this ribbon there is now a thin line of men. For four days and nights they have fought hard, eaten little, washed none, and slept hardly at all. Their nights have been violent with attack, fright, butchery, and their days sleepless and miserable with the crash of artillery.

The men are walking. They are fifty feet apart, for dispersal. Their walk is slow, for they are dead weary, as you can tell even when looking at them from behind. Every line and sag of their bodies speaks their inhuman exhaustion.

On their shoulders and backs they carry heavy steel tripods, machine-gun barrels, leaden boxes of ammunition. Their feet seem to sink into the ground from the overload they are bearing.

They don't slouch. It is the terrible deliberation of each step that spells out their appalling tiredness. Their faces are black and unshaven. They are young men, but the grime and whiskers and exhaustion make them look middle-aged.

In their eyes as they pass is not hatred, not excitement, not despair, not the tonic of their victory—there is just the simple expression of being here as though they had been here doing this forever, and nothing else.

The line moves on, but it never ends. All afternoon men keep coming round the hill and vanishing eventually over the horizon. It is one long tired line of antlike men.

*

There is an agony in your heart and you almost feel ashamed to look at them. They are just guys from Broadway and Main Street, but you wouldn't remember them. They are too far away now. They are too tired. Their world can never be known to you, but if you could see them just once, just for an instant, you would know that no matter how hard people work back home they are not keeping pace with these infantrymen in Tunisia.

INTERMISSION

IN THE FRONT LINES BEFORE MATEUR, *May 3, 1943*—After four days in battle the famous infantry outfit that I'm with sat on its newly won hill and took two days' rest while companion units on each side of it leap-frogged ahead.

The men dig in on the back slope of the hill before any rest begins. Everybody digs in. This is an inviolate rule of the commanding officers and nobody wants to disobey it. Every time you pause, even if you think you're dying of weariness, you dig yourself a hole before you sit down.

The startling thing to me about these rest periods is how quickly the human body can recuperate from critical exhaustion, how rapidly the human mind snaps back to the normal state of laughing, grousing, yarn-spinning, and yearning for home.

*

Here is what happens when a unit stops to rest.

My unit stops just after daybreak on Hill 394. Foxholes are dug, outposts placed, phone wires strung on the ground. Some patrol work goes on as usual. Then the men lie down and sleep till the blistering heat of the sun wakes them up.

After that you sit around in bunches recounting things. You don't do much of anything. The day just easily kills itself.

That first evening is when life begins to seem like Christmas Eve. The mail comes up in jeeps just before dark. Then comes the men's blanket rolls. At dark, hot food arrives—the first hot food in four days.

This food is cooked in rolling kitchens several miles back and brought up by jeep, in big thermos containers, to the foot of the hill. Men carry the containers, slung on poles over their shoulders, up goat paths in the darkness to all parts of the mountain.

Hot food and hot coffee put life in a man, and then in a pathetic kind of contentment, you lie down and you sleep. The all-night crash of the artillery behind you is completely unheard through your weariness.

There are no mosquitoes so far in the mountains, and very few fleas, but there are lots of ants.

Hot food arrives again in the morning, before daylight. You eat breakfast at four A.M. Then begins a day of reassembling yourself.

Word is passed that mail will be collected that evening, so the boys sit on the ground and write letters. But writing is hard, for they can't tell in their letters what they've just been through.

The men put water in their steel helmets and wash and shave for the first time in days. A few men at a time are sent to the creek in the valley to take baths. The remainder sit in groups on the ground talking, or individually in foxholes cleaning their guns, reading, or just relaxing.

A two-months-old batch of copies of the magazine *Yank** arrives, and a two-weeks-old bunch of the *Stars and Stripes*. Others read detective magazines and comic books that have come up with their bedrolls.

At noon everybody opens cans of cold C-ration. Cold coffee in five-gallon water cans is put in the sun to warm.

Soldiers cut each other's hair. It doesn't matter how it looks, for they aren't going anywhere fancy, anyhow. Some of them strip nearly naked and lie on their blankets for a sunbath. By now their bodies are tanned as though they had been wintering at Miami Beach. They wear the inner part of their helmets, for the noonday sun is dangerous.

Their knees are skinned from crawling over rocks. They find little unimportant injuries that they didn't know they had. Some take off their shoes and socks and look over their feet, which are violently purple with athlete's-foot ointment.

*

I sit around with them, and they get to telling stories, both funny and serious, about their battle. They are all disappointed when they learn I am not permitted to name the outfit they're in, for they are all proud of it and would like the folks at home to know what they've done.

"We always get it the toughest," they say. "This is our third big battle now since coming to Africa. The Jerry is really afraid of us now. He knows what outfit we are, and he doesn't like us."

Thus they talk and boast and laugh and speak of fear. Evening draws down and the chill sets in once more. Hot chow arrives just after dusk.

And then the word is passed around. Orders have come by telephone.

There is no excitement, no grouching, no eagerness either. They had expected it.

Quietly they roll their packs, strap them on, lift their rifles and fall into line.

There is not a sound as they move like wraiths in single file down

Yank was a weekly military magazine; *Stars and Stripes* was the daily newspaper for all service personnel.

tortuous goat paths, walking slowly, feeling the ground with their toes, stumbling and hushfully cussing. They will walk all night and attack before dawn.

They move like ghosts. You don't hear or see them three feet away. Now and then a light flashes lividly from a blast by our big guns, and then for just an instant you see a long slow line of dark-helmeted forms silhouetted in the flash.

Then darkness and silence consume them again, and somehow you are terribly moved.

Night March

IN THE FRONT LINES BEFORE MATEUR, *May 4, 1943*—Rest periods for our front-line troops in Tunisia are few and far between. And when they do come they are only for a day or two, and subject to being ended at any moment.

The infantry battalion that I've attached myself to had its rest cut short just after dark on the second evening. Word came to move again into the lines, which were only a mile and a half away.

We had been dug in on a high, rocky ridge. German shells pounded continuously on the back side of the ridge, just a hundred yards off. The whole solid mountain seemed to tremble with each blast, but of course it didn't actually. And we were perfectly safe.

Our view there was beautiful and majestic. Yet I personally was not reluctant to leave. For we had discovered that our ridge was inhabited by a frightening menagerie of snakes, two-legged lizards, scorpions, centipedes, overgrown chiggers and man-eating ants.

Our battalion marched in two sections. The first left early, with orders to attack a certain forward hill at three A.M. The other half was to start after midnight, reach a certain protected wadi [ravine] before dawn, dig itself in and stand by for use whenever needed. I went with the second batch.

The men weren't upset about going into the line again so soon. They just accepted it. They feel they have already done more than their share of this war's fighting, but there is in their manner a touchingly simple compliance with whatever is asked of them.

At one A.M. we were ready to go. Blanket rolls and personal gear were left behind. I carried only my mackinaw and small hand shovel.

In columns of twos we plowed down a half-mile slope waist-high in wild grass. The slope was full of big bomb craters. We had to feel for them with our feet and walk around them. There were big rocks hidden in the grass, and soldiers would stumble and fall down awkwardly in their heavy gear, and get up cussing.

Finally we hit a sort of path and fell into a single line of march. It was very slow at first, for we were crowding the last stragglers of the first section. For long periods we would stop for some unexplained reason and just sit on the ground.

The man ahead of me, Pvt. Lee Hawkins of Everett, Pennsylvania, had a fifty-pound radio strapped onto his back, plus two boxes of ammunition. How he kept on his feet in that rough sightless march I don't know.

After a couple of hours the route ahead seemed to clear up. We walked briskly in single file. You had to keep your eyes on the ground and watch every step.

The moon came up, but it was behind a great black cloud and gave only a little light. We talked some, but not much.

We made a couple of brief unexplained stops, and then suddenly word came down the column:

"No more talking. Pass it back."

From then on we marched in silence except for the splitting crash of German artillery ahead and of ours behind. The artillery of both sides was firing almost continuously. There would be the heavy blast of the guns, then an eerie rustle from each shell as it sped unseen across the sky far above our heads. It gave the night a strange sense of greatness.

As a first-timer I couldn't help but feel a sort of exaltation from this tense, stumbling march through foreign darkness up into the unknown.

*

It did have its lighter touch, if you were inclined to hunt for a laugh. One soldier with a portable radio had been trying since early evening to get contact with our leading column. He was having static trouble, and kept walking around trying various locations all night long. Wherever you turned, wherever you stopped, you could always hear this same voice, gradually growing pitiful in its vain quest, calling softly:

"Lippman to Howell. Come in, Howell."

As the night wore on and this voice kept up its persistent wandering and fruitless calling for its mate it got to be like a scene out of a Saroyan play, and I had a private giggle over it.

*

Shells from both sides kept going far over our heads. They were landing miles away. Then all of a sudden they weren't. With the quickness of an auto accident a German shell screamed toward us.

Instinct tells you, from the timbre of the tone, how near a shell is coming to you. Our whole column fell flat automatically and in unison.

The shell landed with a frightening blast two hundred yards to our right. We got up and started, and it happened again, this time to our left.

I felt weak all over, and all the others had the creeps too.

Then off to the left we heard German machine-gun fire. You can always tell it from American machine-gun fire because it is so much faster. Word was passed down the line for us to squat down. We sat silently on our haunches for a minute, and then on another order we all crept over into some grass and lay hidden there for about five minutes. Then we started on.

We got to where we were gong half an hour before dawn. It was an outcropping of big white rocks, covering several acres, just back of the rise where the earlier half of our unit was already fighting.

The commanding officer told us to find good places among the rocks, get well scattered, and dig in immediately. He didn't have to do any urging. Machine guns were crashing a few hundred yards off. Now and then a bullet would ricochet down among us.

The order went around to dig only with shovels, for the sound of picks hitting rocks might give us away to the Germans. We talked only in low voices. The white rocks were like ghosts and gave an illusion of moving when you looked at them.

I picked out an L-shaped niche formed by two knee-high rocks, and began shoveling out a hole in front of them. At dawn we were all dug in, and the artillery had increased to a frenzy that seemed to consume the sky.

We had now been without sleep for twenty-four hours, and we lay in our holes and slept wearily, oblivious of the bedlam around us and the heat of the bright early sun.

Just as I fell off to sleep I heard a low voice just behind my rock, pleading, it seemed to me now, a little hoarsely, but still determinedly:

"Come in, Howell. Come in, Howell."

A Day of Ceaseless Shelling

IN THE FRONT LINES NEAR MATEUR, *May 5, 1943*—The day I'm writing about in this column is one of those days when you sit down on a rock about once an hour, put your chin in your hand, and think to yourself:

"What the hell am I doing here, anyway?"

On this unforgettable Tunisian day between three and four thousand shells have passed over our heads. True, most of them were in transit, en route to somewhere else, but enough of them were intended for us to make a fellow very somber before the day was over. And just as a sideline, a battle was going on a couple of hundred yards to one side, mines were blowing up jeeps on the other side, and German machine-gun bullets were zinging past with annoying persistency.

My outfit was in what was laughingly called "reserve" for the day. But when you hear soldiers who have been through four big battles say with dead seriousness, "Brother, this is getting rugged!" you feel that you would rather be in complete retirement than in reserve.

*

All day we were a sort of crossroads for shells and bullets. All day guns roared in a complete circle around us. About three-eighths of this circle was German, and five-eighths of it American. Our guns were blasting the Hun's hill positions ahead of us, and the Germans were blasting our gun positions behind us. Shells roared over us from every point of the compass. I can't believe there was a whole minute in fourteen hours of daylight when the air above us was silent.

The guns themselves were close enough to be brutal in their noise, and between shots the air above us was filled with the intermixed rustle and whine of traveling shells.

You can't see a shell, unless you're standing near the gun when it is fired, but its rush through the air makes such a loud sound that it seems impossible you can't see them. Some shells whine loudly throughout their flight. Others make only a toneless rustle. It's an indescribable sound. The nearest I can come to it is the sound of jerking a stick through water.

Some apparently defective shells get out of shape and make queer noises. I remember one that sounded like a locomotive puffing hard at about forty miles an hour. Another one made a rhythmic knocking sound as though turning end over end. We all had to laugh when it went over.

They say you never hear the shell that hits you. Fortunately I don't know about that, but I do know that the closer they hit the less time you hear them. Those landing within a hundred yards you hear only about a second before they hit. The sound produces a special kind of horror inside you that is something more than mere fright. It is a confused form of acute desperation.

Each time, you are sure this is the one. You can't help but duck.

Whether you shut your eyes or not I don't know, but I do know you become instantly so weak that your joints feel all gone. It takes about ten minutes to get back to normal.

Shells that come too close make veterans jump just the same as neophytes. Once we heard three shells in the air at the same time, all headed for us. It wasn't possible for me to get three times as weak as usual, but after they had all crashed safely a hundred yards away I know I would have had to grunt and strain mightily to lift a soda cracker.

*

Sometimes this enemy fire quiets down and you think the Germans are pulling back, until suddenly you are rudely awakened by a heinous bedlam of screaming shells, mortar bursts, and even machine-gun bullets.

Here is an example of these sudden changes. As things had died down late one afternoon, and the enemy was said to be several hills back, I was wandering around among some soldiers who were sitting and standing outside their foxholes during the lull. Somebody told me about a new man who had had a miraculous escape, so I walked around till I found him.

He was Pvt. Malcolm Harblin of Peru, New York, a twenty-four-year-old farmer who has been in the Army only since June. Harblin is a small, pale fellow, quiet as a mouse. He wears silver-rimmed glasses. His steel helmet is too big for him.

He looks incongruous on a battlefield, But he was all right in his very first battle, back at El Guettar—an 88-mm shell hit right beside him, and a big fragment went between his left arm and his chest, tearing his jacket, shirt, and undershirt all to pieces. But he wasn't scratched.

He still wears that ragged uniform, for it's all he has. He was showing me the holes, and we were talking along nice and peaceful-like, when all of a sudden here came that noise, and boy this one had all the tags on it.

Harblin dived into his foxhole and I was right on top of him. But sometimes you don't hear them soon enough. And in this case we would have been too late, except that the shell was a dud.

It hit the ground about thirty feet ahead of us, bounced past us so close we could almost have grabbed it, and finally wound up less than a hundred yards back of us.

Harblin looked at me, and I looked at Harblin. And I just had strength enough to whisper bitterly at him:

"You and your narrow escapes!"

May 6, 1943— . . . Two German prisoners came down the hill, with a doughboy [infantryman] behind them making dangerous motions at their behinds with his bayonet.

The captor was a straight American of the drawling hillbilly type, who talked through his nose. I'm sorry I didn't get his name. When he walked the Germans back to his sergeant he said, in his tobacco-patch twang:

"Hey Sarge, here's two uv Hitler's supermen fer yuh."

The two prisoners were young and looked very well fed. Their uniforms were loose-fitting khaki, sort of like men's beach suits at home. With their guns and all their other soldier gear taken away, they had the appearance of being half-dressed. The expression on their faces was one of wondering what came next.

They were turned over to another soldier, who marched them across the fields to the rear. I couldn't help grinning as I watched, for the new guardian stayed well behind them and walked as though he were treading on ice. . . .

*

We've heard stories about the Germans shooting up ambulances and bombing hospitals, and I personally know of instances where those stories are true. But there are also stories of just the opposite nature. Many of our officers tell me the Germans have fought a pretty clean war in Tunisia. They do have scores of crafty, brutal little tricks that we don't have, but as for their observance of the broader ethics of war, our side has no complaint.

One battalion surgeon told me of running his ambulance out onto a battlefield under heavy artillery fire—whereupon the Germans stopped shelling and stayed stopped while he evacuated the dead and wounded for eight hours.

I've heard other stories where our ambulances got past German machine-gun nests without knowing it until the Germans came out and stopped them and, seeing they had wounded, waved them on. And so far as our doctors know, the German doctors give our captured wounded good medical care—as we do theirs also, of course. . . .

The End in Tunisia

TUNISIAN FRONT, *May 7, 1943*—The thing that Americans in Africa had fought and worked six months to get came today. When it did come, it was an avalanche almost impossible to describe. The flood of prisoners choked the roads.* There were acres of captured materials.

I'll try to tell you what the spirit of the day was like.

It was a holiday, though everybody kept on working. Everybody felt suddenly free inside, as though personal worry had been lifted. It was like the way we used to feel as children on the farm, when parents surprised us by saying work was finished and we were going to the state fair for a day. And when you have looked, goggle-eyed, all day, at more Germans than you ever expected to see in your life, you really feel as if you have been to a fair.

Today you saw Germans walking alone along highways. You saw them riding, stacked up in our jeeps, with one lone American driver. You saw them by hundreds, crammed as in a subway in their own trucks, with their own drivers. And in the forward areas our fairgrounds of mile after mile contained more Germans than Americans. Germans were everywhere.

It made you a little lightheaded to stand in the center of a crowd, the only American among scores of German soldiers, and not have to feel afraid of them. Their 88's stood abandoned. In the fields dead Germans still lay on the grass. By the roadside scores of tanks and trucks still burned. Dumps flamed, and German command posts lay littered where they had tried to wreck as much as possible before surrendering.

But all those were sideshows—the big show was the mass of men in strange uniforms, lining roads, swamping farmyards, blackening fields, waiting for us to tell them where to go.

High German officers were obviously down in the mouth over the tragic end of their campaign. We saw some tears. Officers wept over the ghastly death toll taken of their men during the last few days. Officers were meticulously correct in their military behavior, but otherwise standoffish and silent.

Not so the common soldiers. I mingled with them all day and sensed no sadness among them. Theirs was not the delight of the Italians, but rather an acceptance of defeat in a war well-fought—why be surly about it?

They were friendly, very friendly. Being prisoners, it obviously paid them to be friendly; yet their friendliness seemed genuine. Just as when the French and Americans first met, the Germans started

*Between May 7, when Tunis and Bizerte fell, and May 13, when the last prisoner gave up, two hundred seventy-five thousand Germans had surrendered to Allied Forces. General Rommel and several hundred other Germans escaped, however.

learning English words and teaching us German words.

But circumstances didn't permit much communion between them and our troops. Those Americans who came in direct contact with them gave necessary orders and herded them into trucks. All other Americans just stared curiously as they passed. I saw very little fraternizing with prisoners.

I saw no acts of belligerence and heard neither boos nor cheers. But I did hear a hundred times: "This is the way it should be. Now we can go on from here."

German boys were as curious about us as we were about them. Every time I stopped, a crowd would form quickly. In almost every group was one who spoke English. In all honesty I can't say their bearing or personality was a bit different from that of a similar bunch of American prisoners. They gave us their cigarets and accepted ours. They examined the jeep, and asked questions about our uniforms. If you passed one walking alone, usually he would smile and speak.

One high American officer told me he found himself feeling sorry for them—until he remembered how they had killed so many of his men with their sneaking mines, how they had him pinned down a few days ago with bullets flying; then he hated them.

I am always a sucker for the guy who loses, but somehow it never occurred to me today to feel sorry for those prisoners. They didn't give you a feeling they needed any sorrowing over. They were loyal to their country and sorry they lost but, now that it was over for them, they personally seemed glad to be out of it.

Tonight they still lounge by thousands in fields along the roads. Our trucks, and theirs too, are not sufficient to haul them away. They will just have to wait their turn to be taken off to prison camps. No guards are necessary to keep them from running off into the darkness tonight. They have already done their running and now they await our pleasure, rather humbly and with a curious eagerness to see what comes next for them.

German Supermen Up Close

NORTHERN TUNISIA, *May 8, 1943*—Before the first day of the great surrender on the Bizerte–Tunis front was over, I believe half the Americans in the area had German souvenirs of some sort.

There was very little of what one would call looting of German supply dumps. The Germans gave away helmets, goggles and map cases, which they will not be needing anymore. The spoils of war which the average doughboy has on him are legitimate, and little enough recompense for his fighting.

Practically every American truck has a German or Italian helmet fastened to its radiator. Our motorcycles are decorated like a carnival, with French flags and the colorful little black-and-yellow death's-head pennants the Germans use for marking their own mine fields.

Many soldiers have new Lugers in their holsters. Lots of our men clowningly wear German field caps. German goggles are frequently seen on American heads. I got in on the souvenirs, too. I got one memento that is a little gem. It's an automobile—yep, a real automobile that runs.

I drove back to camp that first evening in my German "Volkswagen," the bantam car the Nazis use as we use our jeep. It is a topless two-seater with a rear motor, camouflaged a dirty brown.

Mine was given me by our 1st Armored Division for—as they said —"sweating it out with us at Faïd Pass all winter." As I drove back from the lines, Americans in the rear would stare, startled-like and belligerent; then, seeing an American at the wheel they would laugh and wave. I have owned half a dozen autos in my life, but I've never been so proud of one as of my clattering little Volkswagen.

*

On that first day of surrender the Germans sat in groups of hundreds in the fields, just waiting. They lay on their overcoats, resting. They took off their shirts to sun themselves. They took off their shoes to rest their feet.

They were a tired army but not a nondescript one. All were extremely well equipped. Their uniforms were good. They had plenty in the way of little personal things, money, cigarets, and food. Their equipment was of the best materials.

One English-appearing soldier had a Gem nail-clipper. He said he paid twenty-five cents for it in New York in 1939.

Some were cleanly shaven, some had three- or four-day beards, just like our soldiers. Lots of them had red-rimmed eyes from lack of sleep.

As a whole, they seemed younger than our men, and I was surprised that on the average they didn't seem as big. But they did appear well fed and in excellent health.

They think Americans are fine fighters. They express only good-natured contempt for their allies, the Italians. As one of them said:

"It isn't just that Italians don't fight well. It's simply that Germans don't like Italians very much in the first place."

Wherever any American correspondents stopped, prisoners immediately gathered around. They all seemed in good spirits. Even those who couldn't speak a word of English would try hard to tell you something.

*

The main impression I got, seeing German prisoners, was that they were human like anybody else, fundamentally friendly, a little vain. Certainly they are not supermen. Whenever a group of them would form, some American soldier would pop up with a camera to get a souvenir picture. And every time, all the prisoners in the vicinity would crowd into the picture like kids.

One German boy had found a broken armchair leaning against a barn, and was sitting in it. When I passed he grinned, pointed to his feet and then to the chair arms, and put back his head in the international sign language for "Boy, does this chair feel good!"

This colossal German surrender has done more for American morale here than anything that could possibly have happened. Winning in battle is like winning at poker or catching lots of fish—it's damned pleasant and it sets a man up. As a result, the hundreds of thousands of Americans in North Africa now are happy men, laughing and working with new spirits that bubble.

May 17, 1943— . . . The Germans didn't quite hew to the ethical line in one thing—they continued trying to destroy their own stuff after the surrender. Vehicles were set afire, and soldiers broke their rifles over bridge abutments as they walked along. Sometimes their destructive frenzy was almost laughable. I saw one bivouac where they had left all their big guns, their ten-wheelers, all their heavy gear intact, yet they had smashed such things as personal radios, toilet kits, chairs, and even an accordion.

However, what they put out of action was trivial. The collapse was so huge that most of their stuff was taken intact. Today you see long convoys of German trucks on the Tunisian highways, but they have American drivers, and the yellow star of the U.S. Army is painted on their sides. Our Military Police acted quickly to throw guards around all captured supply dumps and preserve them until the Army can collect, sort, and put to use all the captured material.

*

A little scene on the day of the surrender sticks in my mind. Hundreds of Germans were standing and sitting around a Tunisian farmyard. There was a sprinkling of Italian prisoners too, and a scattering of American, British and French soldiers on various errands. It was indeed an international assembly.

In this far foreign farmyard there was a windmill. The printing on the windmill's big fan seemed so incongruous that I had to jot it down, for it said "Flint & Walling Manufacturing Co., Kendallville, Indiana." You just can't get foreign enough to lose us Hoosiers.

One of the English-speaking German soldiers asked me why I was copying that down, and when I told him it was because the windmill came from my home state he smiled and said oh yes, he'd been in Indiana several times himself! . . .

May 18, 1943— . . . Although they are usually friendly and pleasant, you seldom find a prisoner who has any doubt that Germany will win the war. They say they lost here because we finally got more stuff into Tunisia than they had. But they laugh at the idea of our invading the Continent. On the whole they can't understand why America is in the war at all, figuring it is not our business.

Whether from deliberate Nazi propaganda or mere natural rumor I don't know, but the prisoners have a lot of false news in their heads. For instance, some of them had heard that Japan had been at war with Russia for six months and had practically cleaned the Russians out of Siberia. One of them heard that the Luftwaffe had bombed New York. When told that this was ridiculous, he said he didn't see himself how it could be possible.

*

Pvt. Bill Connell of Brooklyn had a funny experience. He was talking with an English-speaking prisoner, and the conversation finally unearthed the information that, as Pvt. Connell says, "We know different people together"—meaning, I'm sure, that they had once actually lived in adjoining houses in Brooklyn. But that coincidence didn't cause any old-palship to spring up between them, for the prisoner was one of those bullheaded Nazis and Connell got so disgusted he didn't even ask his name.

The prisoner was very sarcastic, and said to Connell:

"You Americans are saps. You're still in the war, and I'm out of it."

I thought Connell's answer was pretty good. He replied:

"You're such a hot Nazi, but it's lots of good you're going to do your country from now on." . . .

*

Captured supplies show that the Germans use excellent materials in all their stuff. However, it seems to us that there is some room for improvement in their vaunted efficiency. They have more of a hodgepodge and more overlapping designs than we do. They have big ten-wheeler troop carriers with seats running crosswise, but it is far too much vehicle for the service it performs. It can't possibly be used for any other work than troop-carrying, and even for that it is an easy target, with men sitting up there in the open. And it is slow.

They also have a gadget that resembles a motorcycle except that the back end runs on two small caterpillar tracks [treads] instead of wheels. It's a novel idea, but as somebody says, it can carry only three men and there's enough material wasted to make a young tank. . . .

The campaign was over, but Pyle still had to provide his newspapers copy. He settled in at a press camp near Algiers and wrote out his gathered material.

TUNISIAN AFTERMATH

IN TUNISIA, *May 19, 1943*—A few weeks ago I wrote a column describing the winter's battleground in Tunisia, in which I said there wasn't much evidence over the countryside of the fighting that had gone on. That was the central Tunisian battlefield—the one we fought over all winter.

But now we have a new battlefield to look over, the northern one, and it looks vastly more warlike than the southern one. There are two reasons for this—the fighting was more concentrated and on a much greater scale, and the Germans collapsed so quickly they had no time to retrieve vehicles and clean up the battlefields as they did in the South.

Today there are roads in northern Tunisia that are littered for miles at a stretch with wrecked and burned-out vehicles. Sometimes a skeleton of a tank or a big truck sits right in the middle of a road and you have to drive around it. In spots you can see two or three dozen wrecked tanks scattered across a mile-wide valley. In many places the roads are rough from filled-in shell holes.

*

In the first day or two after the finish you would still see an occasional blanket-covered body lying at the roadside. Frequently you see one or two German graves, where victims of vehicle strafing are buried. And as you drive along, your nose tells you now and then of one that the burial parties missed.

I am constantly amazed and touched at the number of dogs and mules killed on the highways by artillery and strafing planes.

Practically all the bridges in northern Tunisia have been blown up. You detour around the smaller ones. Over the larger streams American and British engineers have thrown up sudden and magnificent steel bridges, or laid pontoon bridges.

Only a few of the towns in central Tunisia were really wrecked by shellfire, but in northern Tunisia all the towns along the line of battle have been truly destroyed. Bizerte is the most completely wrecked place I have ever seen. It was a large city, and a beautiful one. It is impossible to picture in words what it looks like now.

If you remember World War I pictures of such places as Verdun, that is the way it is. Nothing could possibly have lived through the months-long bombing that Bizerte took. Those who say a city can't be destroyed by bombing should come and see Bizerte.

*

As soon as the Tunisian war was over the Arabs began flocking back to their homes. They had been cleaned out of the battle area by both sides, for two reasons—to keep them from getting hurt, and because neither side trusted them.

Most of them were simply evacuated to safe hills in the rear, but those under suspicion were arrested and put in outdoor prison camps while the fighting was going on.

They come back across country now in long caravans. Scores of Arabs are in each group, with their sheep and their cattle, their burros and their kids. They are a dirty and disheartening lot.

Their junklike belongings are piled high on two-wheeled carts. I saw one car with fourteen oxen hitched to it.

The women usually have large bundles on their backs. Now and then one Arab will give you the Victory sign and say "*Bon jour,*" but most of them pass in silence. For the Tunisian Arab was well sold by German propaganda.

*

Ferryville* and Tunis are the two places where fantastic demonstrations were put on as the Americans and British entered and released the cities from their captivity. The wild Ferryville demonstration has already been written about, but I am mentioning it again in order to tell a little story.

Chris Cunningham of the United Press and I shared a tent and traveled together quite a bit in this northern campaign. Chris is a

*Now Menzel-Bourguiba.

stocky fellow, with black whiskers. He looks pretty tough, although he is actually rather bashful.

When he drove in to Ferryville in his jeep he was immediately surrounded and overpowered by jubilant men, women and children, throwing flowers and shouting, "*Vive la France!*" and "*Vive l'Amérique!*"

In the midst of this hubbub a pompous-looking gentleman, a gruffly dignified Frenchman of the old school, arrived on the scene. He stood for a moment at the curb, surveying the outburst with what appeared to be disapproval. Then he took a deep breath, brushed the common herd aside with both hands as though he were swimming, reached over into the jeep and kissed Chris first on one cheek and then on the other. That accomplished, he turned and strode pompously away.

Chris hasn't heard the last of it yet.

An Intense Weariness

IN TUNISIA, *May 21, 1943*—While with the infantry in the north Tunisian campaign I had to live just as they did. Our home was on the ground. We sat, ate and slept on the ground.

We were in a different place almost every night, for we were constantly moving forward from hill to hill. Establishing a new bivouac consisted of nothing more than digging new foxholes. We never took off our clothes, not even our shoes. Nobody had more than one blanket, and many had none at all.

For three nights I slept on the ground with nothing under or over me. Finally I got one blanket and my shelter halves sent up.

We had no warm food for days. Each man kept his own rations and ate whenever he pleased. Oddly enough I was never conscious of the lack of warm food. Water was brought to us in cans, but very little washing was done.

*

Sometimes we were up all night on the march and then would sleep in the daytime till the hot sun made sleep impossible. Some of the men slept right in their foxholes, others on the ground alongside. Since rocks were so abundant, most of us buttressed our foxholes with little rock walls around them.

During that week we were shot at by 88's, 47's, machine guns and tanks. Despite our own air superiority we were dive-bombed numerous times, but they were always in such a hurry to get it over and get home that usually their aim was bad and the bombs fell harmlessly in open spaces. You could always count on being awakened at dawn by a dive-bombing.

Having now been both shelled and bombed, I believe an artillery barrage is the worst of the two. A prolonged artillery barrage comes very close to being unbearable, and we saw many pitiful cases of "anxiety neurosis."

The nights were sometimes fantastic. The skies would flash all night from the muzzle blasts of big guns. Flares shot from the ground and dropped from planes would hang in the sky. Armored vehicles would rumble across country all night. German planes would thrum through the skies seeking some flash of light on the ground.

At dusk groups of litter-bearers would set out to carry the wounded from forward companies. Just after dawn each morning the stretchers and the walking wounded would come slowly downhill from the night's fighting. Ammunition carriers in long lines toiled up to us, carrying those triple clusters of heavy mortar shells on their shoulders.

A couple of miles behind us the engineers worked day and night without cease, digging and blasting and bulldozing passes through the hills so our wheeled vehicles could follow the advance.

Sometimes we didn't sleep at all for thirty hours or more. At first the activity and excitement and everything kept me awake. I didn't want to go to sleep for fear of missing something. Also, at first the terrific noise of the artillery kept us awake. But on my last two nights in the lines I slept eight hours solid and never heard a thing.

*

During all the time we were under fire I felt fine. The catch-as-catch-can sleep didn't seem to bother me. I never felt physically tired even after the marches. The days were so diverse and so unregimented that a week sped by before I knew it. I never felt that I was excited or tense except during certain fast-moving periods of shelling or bombing, and these were quickly over. When I finally left the line just after daylight one morning I never felt better in my life.

And yet, once I was safely back in camp an intense weariness came over me. I slept almost every minute of two days and nights. I just didn't have the will to get up, except to eat. My mind was as blank as my body was lifeless. I felt as though every cell in my makeup had been consumed. It was utter exhaustion such as I had never known before. Apparently it was the let down from a week of being uncommonly tense without realizing I was tense. It was not until the fourth day that I began to feel really normal again, and even now I'm afraid I think too much about the wounded men.

They Fought Like Veterans

IN TUNISIA, *May 22, 1943*—The major portion of my time during the Tunisian campaign was spent with the 1st Infantry Division and the 1st Armored Division. That was because they were the earliest ones on the scene and I was best acquainted with them.

But there were other divisions in Tunisia too, and in the final phase all contributed their part to the cracking of the Hun. If the war had lasted longer I would have swung over and written about these other units too, but since that chance didn't come, those of you at home who have men in these divisions may know that what I've written about one is largely representative of all.

The 1st Armored Division was the one that made the kill and got the mass of prisoners. Yet their fighting was no better and no greater than that of the 1st Infantry Division, which lost so heavily cleaning out the mountains, or of the 34th Division, which took the key Hill 609 and made the victory possible, or of the 9th Division, which swept the Heinies out of the rough coastal country in the north, or of the artillery that softened up the enemy, or of the fighting engineers who kept streams bridged and highways passable. Or of any other of the countless units that contributed to the whole, and without a single one of which all the others would have been lost.

*

In this final phase of the Tunisian campaign we have yet to hear a word of criticism of our men. They fought like veterans. They were well handled. We had enough of what we needed. Everything meshed perfectly, and the end was inevitable. So you at home need never be ashamed of our American fighers. Even though they didn't do too well in the beginning, there was never at any time any question about the Americans' bravery.

It is a matter of being hardened and practiced by going through the flames. Tunisia has been a good warm-up field for our armies. We will take an increasingly big part in the battles ahead.

The greatest disservice you folks at home can do our men over here is to believe we are at last over the hump. For actually—and over here we all know it—the worst is yet to come.

*

Our front-line troops by now are getting pretty well saturated with little personal things they got from the Germans. Nearly everybody has a souvenir of some kind, running all the way from machine guns to writing paper.

A good many soldiers have made new pistol grips for themselves out of the windshields of shot-down German planes. The main advantage of this switch from the regulation handle is that the composition is transparent; you can put your girl's picture under the grip and it will show through.

Sgt. Gibson Fryer of Troy, Alabama, has a picture of his wife on each side of the handle of his .45. Sgt. Fryer has noticed that the Germans are very neat in ways. They have little toilet kits in their pockets. Among his souvenirs is a pair of manicure scissors he got from a prisoner long before the big surrender came.

Sgt. Fryer had an experience on one of the last few days of the campaign that will be worth telling his grandchildren about. He was in a foxhole on a steep hillside. An 88-mm shell landed three feet away and blew him out of his hole. He rolled, out of control, fifty yards down the rocky hillside. He didn't seem to be wounded, but all his breath was gone. He couldn't move. He couldn't make a sound. His chest hurt. His legs wouldn't work.

A medic came past and poked him. Sgt. Fryer couldn't say anything, so the medic went on. Pretty soon two of Fryer's best friends walked past and he heard one of them say, "There's Sgt. Fryer. I guess he's dead." And they went right on, too.

It was more than an hour before Fryer could move, but within a few hours he was perfectly normal again. He laughs and says that if his wife sees this in print she'll think for sure he's a hero.

With the defeat of the Axis in North Africa, it was apparent the fall of 1942 had been the turning point of the war. Not only had the Allies begun to act in concert to defeat an aggressive enemy, but the Axis powers had also begun to pay the price for overextending themselves.

Germany's misadventure in Russia had reached a climax in January, when its 6th Army—depleted, starved, and frozen—had surrendered at Stalingrad. Japan, too, had sustained a major defeat that month—a total loss in the Guadalcanal campaigns, which ended with the Allies on the offensive. By late spring 1943, Italy had lost its African colonies and Mussolini his dream of a new Roman empire; Germany had lost its crack Afrika Korps. Both nations had suffered heavy casualties and had many troops taken prisoner.

Most important, these defeats had destroyed the myth of fascist invincibility and shaken the confidence of the Axis, at best a loose confederation and soon to be even more disjointed.

It was different with the Allies. The war in North Africa had welded them into an efficient multinational fighting force under a single command, a development that would bode well in the months of bitter fighting to come. The Axis powers knew they faced a formidable enemy, and just as they had been nothing short of strident in their conquests, the Allies, emboldened by the success of the North African landings, had taken on a strident stripe of their own: unconditional surrender was the price they sought to extract from their enemies.

Pyle spent the early part of summer 1943 at a press camp on the shore of the Mediterranean near Algiers, where he prepared some concluding remarks on the North Africa campaign for his soon-to-be-published book, Here Is Your War: The Story of G.I. Joe. *"It may be that the war has changed me, along with the rest [of the men]," Pyle wrote. "It is hard for anyone to analyze himself. I know that I find more and more that I wish to be alone, and yet contradictorily I believe I have a new patience with humanity that I've never had before. When you've lived with the unnatural mass cruelty that mankind is capable of inflicting upon itself, you find yourself dispossessed of the faculty for blaming one poor man for the triviality of his faults. I don't see how any survivor of war can ever be cruel to anything, ever again."*

Pyle explained that his perspective on the war was a "worm's-eye view" composed of "tired and dirty soldiers who are alive and don't want to die; of long darkened convoys in the middle of the night; of shocked silent men wandering back down the hill from battle; of chow lines and Atabrine tablets and foxholes and burning tanks and Arabs holding up eggs and the rustle of high-flown shells; of jeeps and petrol dumps and smelly bedding rolls and C-rations and cactus patches and blown bridges and dead mules and hospital tents and shirt collars greasy-black from months of wearing; and of laughter too, and anger and wine and lovely flowers and constant cussing. All these it is composed of; and of graves and graves and graves."

He had resigned himself to more of the same. "It has to be that way, and wishing doesn't change it." Still, he thought about the dead, "those whose final awareness was a bedlam of fire and noise and uproar." "They died and others lived and nobody knows why it is so. They died and thereby the rest of us can go on and on. When we leave here for the next shore, there is nothing we can do for the ones beneath the wooden crosses, except perhaps to pause and murmur, 'Thanks, pal.' "

The next shore was Sicily.

SICILY:

July 1943—September 1943

UPI

At the Casablanca conference in Morocco in January 1943, Churchill and Roosevelt decided on the invasion of Sicily as a prelude to the invasion of mainland Italy—the "soft underbelly" of Europe, as Churchill called it.

The mission in Sicily—Operation Husky—would further divert German attention from Russia and pressure the Italians to desert Germany. With Italy out of the war, the Allies reasoned, German acquiescence would be easier to get.

It was also at Casablanca that the phrase "unconditional surrender" was first uttered publicly—by Roosevelt, who later admitted the words came to him as he spoke to the press. This prompted a flurry of eloquent but ineffectual qualifying statements from Churchill and from Roosevelt as well, who feared his hasty choice of words would make the Axis even more intransigent.

At Casablanca, too, the Allies began to plan for the invasion of Hitler's Fortress Europe from the west, by crossing the English Channel from Britain and landing in France.

During early summer of 1943, the Allies began bombing Axis defenses in Sicily, Sardinia, and southern Italy, while brilliant counterintelligence measures obscured Allied invasion intentions. Singly and in small groups, correspondents were called from their press camp near Algiers and assigned to their positions among the invasion fleet. Pyle was "somewhat surreptitiously whisked away by air about ten days ahead of time," unable to cable news of his whereabouts to Scripps-Howard.

At Bizerte Harbor, Pyle boarded a headquarters ship, the USS Biscayne, *and sunk "into the blessedness of a world that is orderly and civilized compared with the animal-like existence of living in the field." He agreed to edit the ship's mimeographed newspaper and rose daily at three* A.M. *to begin the task. Though Bizerte and its harbor were in Allied hands, German planes routinely bombed both, aided by the harbor lights that enabled crews to load invasion matériel through the night.*

This Time It Was Real

ABOARD A U.S. NAVY SHIP ON THE INVASION FLEET, *July 13, 1943*—Before sailing on the invasion, our ship had been lying far out in the harbor tied to a buoy for several days. Several times a day "General Quarters" would sound and the crew would dash to their battle stations but always it was a photo plane or perhaps one of our own.

Then we moved into a pier. That very night the raiders came and our ship got its baptism of fire—she lost her virginity, as the sailors put it. I had got out of bed at three A.M. as usual to stumble sleepily up to the radio shack to go over the news reports which the wireless had picked up. There were several radio operators on watch and we were sitting around drinking coffee while we worked. Then around four A.M. all of a sudden "General Quarters" sounded. It was still pitch dark. The whole ship came to life with a scurry and rattling, sailors dashing to stations before you'd have thought they could get their shoes on.

Shooting had already started around the harbor so we knew this time it was real. I kept on working and the radio operators did too, or rather tried to work. So many people were going in and out of the radio shack that we were in darkness half the time since the lights automatically go off when the door opens.

Then the biggest guns of our ship let loose. They made such a horrifying noise we thought we'd been hit by a bomb every time they went off. Dust and debris came drifting down from the ceiling to smear up everything. Nearby bombs shook us up, too.

One by one the electric light bulbs were shattered from the blasts. The thick steel walls of the cabin shook and rattled as though they were tin. The entire vessel shivered under each blast. The harbor was lousy with ships and they were all shooting. The raiders were dropping flares all over the sky and the searchlights on the warships were fanning the heavens.

Shrapnel rained down on the decks, making a terrific clatter. All this went on for an hour and a half. When it was over and everything was added up we found four planes had been shot down. Our casualties were negligible and no damage was done the ship except little holes from near-misses. Three men on our ship had been wounded.

Best of all, we were credited with shooting down one of the planes!

*

Now this raid, of course, was only one of scores of thousands that have been conducted in this war. Standing alone it wouldn't even be worth mentioning. I'm mentioning it to show you what a little taste of the genuine thing can do for a bunch of young Americans.

As I wrote the other day, our kids on this ship had never been in action. The majority of them were strictly wartime sailors, still half-civilian in character. They'd never been shot at, never shot one of their own guns except in practice, and because of this they had been very sober, a little unsure and more than a little worried about the invasion ordeal that lay so near ahead of them. And then, all within an hour and a half, they became veterans. Their zeal went up like one of those shooting graph lines in the movies when business is good. Boys who had been all butterfingers were loading shells like machinery after fifteen minutes when it became real. Boys who previously had gone through their routine lifelessly were now yelling with bitter seriousness, "Dammit, can't you pass them shells faster."

The gunnery officer, making his official report to the Captain, did it in these gleefully robust words: "Sir, we got the son of a bitch."

One of my friends aboard ship is Norman Somberg, aerographer, third class, of Miami. We had been talking the day before and he told me how he had gone two years to the University of Georgia studying journalism and wanted to get in it after the war. I noticed he always added: "If I live through it."

Just at dawn, as the raid ended, he came running up to me full of steam and yelled, "Did you see that plane go down smoking! Boy, if I would get off the train at Miami right now with the folks and my girl there to meet me, I couldn't be any happier than I was when I saw we'd got that guy."

It was worth a day's pay to be on this ship the day after the raid. All day long the sailors went gabble, gabble, gabble, each telling the other how they did it, what they saw, what they thought. After that raid a great part of their reluctance to start for the unknown vanished, their guns had become their pals, the enemy became real and the war came alive for them and they didn't fear it so much anymore. This crew of sailors had just gone through what hundreds of thousands of other soldiers and sailors had already experienced—the conversion from peaceful people into fighters. There's nothing especially remarkable about it but it is moving to be on hand and see it happen.

July 12, 1943— . . . The night before we sailed I sat in the darkness of the forward deck helping half a dozen sailors eat a can of stolen pineapple. Some of the men of our little group were hardened and mature. Others were almost children. They all talked seriously and their gravity was touching. The older ones tried to rationalize how the law of averages made it unlikely our ship out of all the hundreds in action would be hit. They spoke of the inferiority of the Italian fleet and argued pro and con over whether Germany has some hidden Luftwaffe up her sleeve she might whisk out to destroy us. Younger ones spoke but little. They talked to me of their plans and hopes for going to college or getting married after the war, always epilogued by the phrase: "If I get through this fracas alive." . . .

*

As we sat there on the hard deck, squatting in a circle around our pineapple can like Indians, we all seemed terribly pathetic to me. Even the dizziest of us knew that within less than forty-eight hours many of us stood an excellent chance of being in this world no more. I don't believe one of us was afraid of the physical part of dying. That isn't the way it is. Your emotion is rather one of almost desperate reluctance to give up your future. I suppose that seems like splitting hairs and that it really all comes under the heading of fear, yet somehow to us there is a difference.

These gravely yearned-for futures of men going into battle include so many things—things such as seeing "the old lady" again, of going to college, of staying in the Navy for a career, of holding on your knee just once your own kid whom you've never seen, of becoming again champion salesman of your territory, of driving a coal truck around the streets of Kansas City once more and, yes, even of just sitting in the sun once more on the south side of a house in New Mexico. . . .

. . . I never heard anybody say anything patriotic like the storybooks have people saying. There was philosophizing but it was simple and undramatic. I'm sure no man would have stayed ashore if given the chance. There was something bigger than the awful dread that would have kept them there. With me it probably was an irresistible egotism in seeing myself part of the historic naval movement. With others it was, I think, just the application of plain, ordinary, unspoken, even unrecognized, patriotism.

July 16, 1943— . . . I got to know a great many of the sailors personally and almost all of them by nodding acquaintance. I found them to be just people and nice people like the soldiers. They are fundamentally friendly. They all want to get home. They are willing to do everything they can to win the war. They all would kind of like to have their names in the paper and deep down they're all a little afraid.

There is one rather subtle difference between sailors and soldiers I did sense (although many of the sailors will probably resent it) and that is—the sailors aren't hardened and roughened as much as the soldiers. It's understandable.

The front-line soldier has lived like an animal for months and is a veteran of the cruel fierce world of death. Everything has been abnormal and unstable in his life for months. He has been filthy dirty, has eaten if and when, has slept on the hard ground without cover. His clothes have been greasy, he has lived in a constant haze of dust, pestered by flies and the heat, moving constantly, deprived of all the things that once meant stability. Things such as walls, chairs, floors, windows, faucets, shelves, Coca-Colas and the greatly important little matter of knowing that you'll go to bed tonight in the same place you got up in this morning.

The front-line soldier has had to harden his inside as well as his outside or he would crack under the strain. Sailors aren't sissies—neither by tradition nor currently—but they aren't as rough and tough as the Tunisian soldiers, at least the gang I was with.

A ship is a home, and the security of home has kept them more as they were. They don't cuss as much nor as foully as soldiers. They don't bust loose as riotously when they hit town. They aren't as all-around hard in outlook. They've not drifted as far from normal life as soldiers—for they have world news every morning in mimeographed sheets, have radios, movies nearly every night, ice cream. Their clothes, their beds are clean. They walk through the same doors, up the same steps every day for months. . . .

Of course, when they die, death for them is just as horrible—and sometimes they die in greater masses than soldiers. But until the enemy comes over the horizon a sailor doesn't have to fight. A front-line soldier has to fight everything all the time. It makes a difference in a man's character. . . .

Sailing out of the harbor and into the Mediterranean, the Biscayne *moved toward the assembled invasion fleet, which on the horizon "resembled a distant city. It covered half the skyline, and the full-colored camouflaged ships stood indistinctly against the curve of the dark waters as a solid formation of uncountable structures blending together. Even to be a part of it was frightening."*

The officers who staffed the invasion ships were "youngsters of scant experience," and the voice of one, the commander of a subchaser, conveyed across the water by megaphone at dusk, prompted Pyle to reflect that the skipper was likely a "young man who had so recently been so normally unaware of any sea at all—the bookkeeper in your bank, perhaps, and now here he was a strange new man in command of a ship, suddenly transformed into a person with awful responsibilities carrying out with great intentness his special small part of the enormous aggregate that is our war on all the lands and seas of the globe."

The war had changed everything, Pyle wrote, and now, cruising toward an uncertain fate were hundreds of ships, "carrying across this ageless and indifferent sea tens of thousands of young men of new professions, fighting for . . . for . . . well, at least for each other."

Just as the Biscayne *was set to anchor three-and-a-half miles off the southern coast of Sicily, the crew underwent a terrifying experience. The beams of five high-powered searchlights on the Sicilian shore came to rest on the ship. The lights "pinioned us in their white shafts as we sat there as naked as babies and just as scared. . . . We were stuck on the end of five merciless poles of light. We were utterly helpless." The crew held its fire, and, inexplicably, the searchlights were switched off, leaving the ship "alone in the blessed darkness."*

A few minutes later, assault boats landed on the beach.

An Easy Landing

SOUTHERN SICILY, *July 17, 1943*—At the end of the first of our invasion of Sicily we Americans looked about us with awe and unbelief and not a little alarm.

It had all been so easy it gave you a jumpy, insecure feeling of something dreadfully wrong somewhere. We had expected a terrific slaughter on the beaches and there was none. Instead of thousands of casualties along the fourteen-mile front of our special sector we added up a total that was astonishingly small.

By sunset of the first day the Army had taken everything we had hoped to get during the first five days. Even by midafternoon the country for miles inland was so saturated with American troops and vehicles it looked like Tunisia after months of our habitation instead of a hostile land just attacked that morning. And the Navy, which had the job of bringing the vast invading force to Sicily, was three days ahead of its schedule of unloading ships.

Convoys had started back to Africa for new loads before the first day was over. The invading fleet had escaped without losses other than normal, mechanical breakdowns. Reports from the other two sectors of the American assault front indicated they had much the same surprising welcome we got.

It was wonderful and yet it all was so illogical. Even if the Italians did want to quit, why did the Germans let them? What had happened? What did the enemy have up its sleeve?

As this is written on the morning of the second day, we don't yet know. Nobody is under any illusion that the battle of Sicily is over. Strong counterattacks are inevitable. Already German dive-bombings are coming at the scale of two per hour but whatever happens we've got a head start that is all in our favor.

For this invasion I was accredited to the Navy. I intended writing mainly about the seaborne aspect of the invasion and had not intended to go ashore at all for several days, but the way things went I couldn't resist the chance to see what it was like over there on land, so I hopped an assault barge and spent all the first day ashore.

*

When we got our first look at Sicily we were all disappointed. I for one had always romanticized it in my mind as a lush green, picturesque island. I guess I must have been thinking of the Isle of Capri. The south coast of Sicily is a drab, light-brown country. There aren't many trees. The fields of grain had been harvested and they were dry and naked and dusty. The villages are pale gray and indistinguishable at a distance from the rest of the country. Water is extremely scarce. Good-sized hills rise a half mile or so back of the beach and on the hillsides grass fires started by the shells of our gunboats burn smokily by day and flamingly by night.

It is cooler than North Africa; in fact it would be delightful were it not for the violent wind that rises in the afternoon and blows so fiercely you can hardly talk in the open. This wind, whipping our barges about in the shallow water, delayed us more than the Italian soldiers did.

*

The people of Sicily on that first day seemed relieved and friendly. They seemed like people who had just been liberated rather than conquered. Prisoners came in grinning, calling greetings to their captors. Civilians on the roads and in the towns smiled and waved. Kids saluted. Many gave their version of the V sign by holding up both arms. The people told us they didn't want to fight.

Our soldiers weren't very responsive to the Sicilians' greetings. They were too busy getting all possible equipment ashore, rounding up the real enemies and establishing a foothold, to indulge in the hand-waving monkey business. After all, we are still at war and these people, though absurd and pathetic, are enemies and caused us misery coming all this way to whip them.

On the whole the people were a pretty third-rate-looking lot. They were poorly dressed and looked like they always had been. Most of them hadn't much expression at all and they kept getting in the way of traffic just like the Arabs. Most of our invading soldiers, at the end of the first day in Sicily, summed up their impressions of their newly acquired soil and its inhabitants by saying:

"Hell, this is just as bad as Africa."

August 6, 1943— . . . Sicily is really a beautiful country. Up here in the north it is all mountainous, and all but the most rugged of the mountains are covered with fields or orchards. Right now everything is dry and burned up, as we so often see our own Midwest in dry summers. They say this is the driest summer in years.

Our ceaseless convoys chew up the gravel roads, and the dust becomes suffocating, but in springtime Sicily must look like the Garden of Eden. The land is wonderfully fertile. Sicilians would not have to be poor and starving if they were capable of organizing and using their land to its fullest.

*

Driving over Sicily you have a feeling of far greater antiquity than you get even from looking at the Roman ruins in North Africa. Towns sit right smack on the top of needle-point mountain peaks. They were built that way in the old days for protection. Today a motor car can't even get up to many of them.

The houses are of a cement-colored stone, and they so blend into the mountains that often you can't see a city at all from a few miles away.

In these mountain towns the streets are too narrow for vehicles, the passageways are dirty, and the goat and burro are common.

In the remotest and most ancient town you'll find that half the people have relatives in America, and there is always somebody popping up from behind every bush or around every corner who lived for twelve years in Buffalo or thirty years in Chicago.

Farming is still done in Biblical style. The grain-threshing season is now on, and how do you suppose they do it? Simply by tying three mules together and running them around in a small circle all day long while another fellow keeps throwing grain under their hoofs with a wooden pitchfork. . . .

Five days after he went ashore, Pyle came down with a case of "battlefield fever" and spent several days in a hospital tent. The symptoms: "You ache all over and have a very high temperature. The doctors say it is caused by a combination of too much dust, bad eating, not enough sleep, exhaustion, and the unconscious nerve tension that comes to everybody in a front-line area. You don't die of battlefield fever, but you think you're going to."

August 9, 1943— . . . When I took sick I was with the 45th Division, made up largely of men from Oklahoma and west Texas. You don't realize how different certain parts of our country are from others until you see their men set off in a frame, as it were, in some strange faraway place like this.

The men of Oklahoma are drawling and soft-spoken. They are not smart-alecks. Something of the purity of the soil seems to be in them. Even their cussing is simpler and more profound than the torrential obscenities of Eastern city men. An Oklahoman of the plains is straight and direct. He is slow to criticize and hard to anger, but once he is convinced of the wrong of something, brother, watch out.

These wounded men of Oklahoma have gotten madder about the war than anybody I have seen on this side of the ocean. They weren't so mad before they got into action, but now to them the Germans across the hill are all "sonsabitches."

And these quiet men of the 45th, the newest division over here, have already fought so well they have drawn the high praise of the commanding general of the corps of which the division is a part. . . .

*

Dying men were brought into our tent, men whose death rattle silenced the conversation and made all the rest of us grave.

When a man was almost gone the surgeons would put a piece of gauze over his face. He could breathe through it but we couldn't see his face well.

Twice within five minutes chaplains came running. One of these occasions haunted me for hours.

The man was still semi-conscious. The chaplain knelt down beside him, and two ward boys squatted alongside. The chaplain said:

"John, I'm going to say a prayer for you."

Somehow this stark announcement hit me like a hammer. He didn't say, "I'm going to pray for you to get well," he just said he was going to say a prayer, and it was obvious he meant the final prayer. It was as though he had said, "Brother, you may not know it, but your goose is cooked."

He said a short prayer, and the weak, gasping man tried in vain to repeat the words after him. When he had finished, the chaplain said, "John, you're doing fine, you're doing fine." Then he rose and dashed off on other business, and the ward boys went about their duties.

The dying man was left utterly alone, just lying there on his litter on the ground, lying in an aisle, because the tent was full. Of course it couldn't be otherwise, but the awful aloneness of that man as he went through the last few minutes of his life was what tormented me. I felt like going over and at least holding his hand while he died, but it would have been out of order and I didn't do it. I wish now I had.

As Proficient As a Circus

SOMEWHERE IN SICILY, *August 11, 1943*—Probably it isn't clear to you just how the Army's setup for the care of the sick and wounded works on a battlefront. So I'll try to picture it for you.

Let's take the medical structure for a whole division, such as the 45th, which I have been with recently. A division runs roughly fifteen thousand men. And almost a thousand of that number are medical men.

To begin right at the front, three enlisted medical-aid men go along with every company. They give what first aid they can on the battlefield. Then litter-bearers carry the wounded back to a battalion aid station.

Sometimes a wounded man is taken back right away. Other times he may be pinned down by fire so that the aid men can't get to him, and he will have to lie out there for hours before help comes. Right there in the beginning is the biggest obstacle, and the weakest feature of the army's medical setup.

Once a soldier is removed from the battlefield his treatment is superb. The battalion aid station is his first of many stops as he is worked to the rear and finally to a hospital. An aid station is merely where the battalion surgeon and his assistant happen to be. It isn't a tent or anything like that—it's just the surgeon's medical chest and a few stretchers under a tree. Each station is staffed by two doctors and thirty-six enlisted men. They are very frequently under fire.

At an aid station a wounded man gets what is immediately necessary, depending on the severity of his wounds. The idea all along is to do as little actual surgical work as possible, but at each stop merely to keep a man in good enough condition to stand the trip on back to the hospital, where they have full facilities for any kind of work. Hence if a soldier's stomach is ripped open they do an emergency operation right at the front but leave further operating to be done at a hospital. If his leg is shattered by shrapnel they bind it up in a metal rack, but the operating and setting isn't done till he gets back to the hospital. They use morphine and blood plasma copiously at the forward stations to keep sinking men going.

*

From the battalion aid station the wounded are taken by ambulance, jeep, truck or any other means back to a collecting station. This is a few tents run by five doctors and a hundred enlisted men, anywhere from a quarter of a mile to several miles behind the lines. There is one collecting station for each regiment, making three to a division.

Here they have facilities for doing things the aid station can't do. If the need is urgent they redress the wounds and give the men more morphine, and they perform quite a lot of operations. Then the men are sent by ambulance on back to a clearing station.

The 45th Division has two clearing stations. Only one works at a time. While one works, the other takes a few hours' rest, then leapfrogs ahead of the other one, sets up its tents and begins taking the patients. In emergencies both clearing stations work at once, temporarily abandoning their rest-and-leapfrog routine.

All these various crews—the company aid men, the battalion aid station, the collecting station and the clearing station—are all part of the division. They move with it, fight when it does, and rest when it does.

*

Then back of the clearing stations the hospitals begin. The first hospitals are usually forty miles or more back of the fighting. The hospitals are separate things. They belong to no division, but take patients from everywhere.

They get bigger as you go back, and in the case of Sicily patients are evacuated from the hospitals right onto hospital ships and taken back to still bigger hospitals in Africa.

The main underlying motive of all front-line stations is to get patients evacuated quickly and keep the decks clear so they will always have room for any sudden catastrophic run of battle casualties.

A clearing station such as the one I was in is really a small hospital. It consists of five doctors, one dentist, one chaplain, and sixty enlisted men. It is contained in six big tents and a few little ones for the fluroscope room, the office, and so forth. Everybody sleeps outdoors on the ground, including the commanding officer. The mess is outdoors under a tree.

The station can knock down, move, and set up again in an incredibly short time. They are as proficient as a circus. Once, during a rapid advance, my station moved three times in one day.

Operating in the Rough

SOMEWHERE IN SICILY, *August 12, 1943*—Army ambulances carry four stretchers each, or nine sitting wounded. When they reach a clearing station they back up to the surgical tent and unload.

The men lie there on their stretchers on the floor of the tent while the aid men look at their tags to see how severe the wounds are, in order to handle the worst ones first. Those who don't need further attention are carried right on through to the ward tents to wait for the next ambulance on back to a hospital.

Those who have graver wounds are carried into the operating room. Two big army trunks sit up-ended there on the dirt floor. The trunks contain all kinds of surgical supplies, in drawers. On top of each trunk is fastened a steel rod which curves up at each end. The wounded man is carried in his litter and set on these two trunks. The curved rods keep him from sliding off. His litter thus forms his operating table.

A portable surgical lamp stands in a tripod over the wounded man. A little motor and generator outside the tent furnish power, but usually they just use flashlights. One or two surgeons in coveralls or ordinary uniforms bend over the man and remove his dressings. Medical-aid men crowd around behind them, handing them compresses or bandages with steel forceps from a sterile cabinet. Other aid men give the patient another shot of morphine or inject blood plasma or give him a drink of water from a tin cup through a rubber tube they put in his mouth.

Incidentally, one of the duties of the surgical ward boys is to keep the sweat wiped off the surgeon's face so it won't drop down onto the wound.

*

Just outside the surgical tent is a small trench filled with bloody shirt sleeves and pant legs the surgeons have snipped off wounded men in order to get at the wounds more quickly. The surgeons redress the wounds, and sprinkle on sulfanilamide as though it were ant powder. Sometimes they poke for buried shrapnel, or recompress broken arteries to stop the flow of blood, or inject plasma if the patient is turning pale.

They don't give general anesthetics here. Occasionally they give a local, but usually the wounded man is so doped up with morphine by the time he reaches here he doesn't feel much pain. The surgeons believe in using lots of morphine. It spares a man so much pain and consequently relieves the general shock to his system.

On my third day at the clearing station, when I was beginning to feel better, I spent most of my time around this operating table. As they would undress each new wound, I held firmly to a lamp bracket above my head, for I was still weak and I didn't want to disgrace myself by suddenly keeling over at the sight of a bad wound.

Many of the wounds were hard to look at, and yet Lt. Michael de Giorgio said he had never seen a human body as badly smashed up here as he had in traffic accidents back in New York, where he practiced.

One stalwart fellow had caught a machine-gun bullet right alongside his nose. It had made a small clean hole and gone clear through his cheek, leaving a larger hole just beneath his ear as it came out. It gave you the willies to look at it, yet the doctors said it wasn't serious at all and would heal with no bad effects.

The nerviest fellow I saw had two big holes in his back. You could have put your whole hand in either one of them. As the surgeons worked on him he lay on his stomach and talked a blue streak.

"I killed five of the sonsabitches with a hand grenade just before they got me," he said. "What made me so damn mad was that I was just out of reach of my rifle and couldn't crawl over to it, or I'd a got five more of them. Jeez, I'm hungry! I ain't had nothing to eat since yesterday morning."

*

But most of the wounded say nothing at all when brought in—either because they see no acquaintances to talk to, or because they're too weak from their wounds or too dopey from morphine. Of the hundreds that passed through while I was there, I never heard but one man groaning with pain.

Another thing that struck me as the wounded came through in a ceaseless stream on their stretchers was how dirt and exhaustion reduce human faces to such a common denominator. It got so everybody they carried in looked alike. The only break in the procession of tired and dirty men who all looked exactly alike would be when an extreme blond would be carried in. His light hair would seem like a flower in a row of weeds.

August 13, 1943—Every day at the front produces its quota of freak wounds and hairbreadth escapes. Almost any wounded man has missed death only by a matter of inches. Sometimes a bullet can go clear through a man and not hurt him much, while at other times an infinitesimal fragment of a shell can pick out one tiny vital spot and kill him.

Bullets and fragments do crazy things. Our surgeons picked out more than two hundred pieces of shrapnel from one fellow. There was hardly a square inch of him, from head to toe, that wasn't touched. Yet none of them made a vital hit, and the soldier will live.

I remember one soldier who had a hole in the front of his leg just below the hip. It was about the size of a half dollar. It didn't look bad at all, yet beneath that little wound the leg bone was shattered and arteries were severed, and the surgeons were working hard to get the arteries closed so he wouldn't bleed to death.

Another fellow I saw caught a small shell fragment in the wrist. It had entered at a shallow angle and gone clear up the arm to the elbow, and remained buried there. The skin wasn't even broken at the elbow, but right over the spot where the fragment stopped was a blister as big as a pigeon egg. The blister had been generated by the terrific heat of that tiny piece of metal. . . .

August 14, 1943—The doctors asked me at least a dozen times to write about plasma.* "Write lots about it, go clear overboard for it, say that plasma is the outstanding medical discovery of this war," they said.

So I beg you folks back home to give and keep on giving your blood. We've got plenty on hand here now, but if we ever run into mass casualties such as they have on the Russian front, we will need untold amounts of it.

They say plasma is absolutely magical. They say scores of thousands who died in the last war could have been saved by it. Thousands have already been saved by it in this war.

They cite case after case where a wounded man was all but dead and within a few minutes after a plasma injection would be sitting up and talking, with all the life and color back in his face.

The doctors asked me to repeat what you have been told so many times already—that it doesn't make any difference what type your blood is, and that the normal person has no ill or weakening effects from giving his blood. . . .

*Blood plasma, derived from the separations of red and white blood cells in a centrifuge, can be frozen or dried for storage or transport. American physicians developed the process in the early 1930's, thus making possible blood transfusions for the severely injured.

"What Is These Barons, Anyway?"

SOMEWHERE IN SICILY, *August 20, 1943*—At one time in central Sicily we correspondents were camped in a peach orchard behind the country home of an Italian baron. Apparently the baron had skadoodled, as royalty is wont to do, before the fighting started, because German and Italian troops had been occupying the place before we came.

The baron had built himself a big stone house that was pink and palatial with a marvelous view over miles of rolling country. It had the usual royal peacocks strutting around but not a bath in the place. The dining-room ceiling was hand-painted and the staircase gigantic, yet the royal family used porcelain washbowls and old-fashioned thundermugs [chamber pots]. It was the perfect shabby rococo domicile of what H. R. Knickerbocker calls the "wretched aristocracy of Europe."

While the baron lived in this comparative luxury, his employees lived in sheds and even caves in the big rocky hill just back of the house. They looked like gypsies.

When we arrived the interior of the castle was a wreck. I've never seen such a complete shambles. Every room was knee-deep in debris. The enemy had thoroughly looted the place before fleeing. And servants gave us the shameful news that most of the looting and destruction was done by Italian soldiers rather than German.

They'd gone through the house shelf by shelf, drawer by drawer. Expensive dishes were thrown on the tile floor, antique vases shattered, women's clothes dumped in jumbled heaps, pictures torn down, medicine cabinets dashed against walls, dressers broken up, wine bottles dropped on the floor, their contents turning the trash heap into a gooey mass as it dried.

It was truly the work of beasts. We tiptoed into the place gingerly, suspecting booby-traps, but finally decided it had not been fixed up. Then some of us rummaged around the debris seeing if anything left was worth taking as souvenirs. As far as I have seen, Americans have been good about not looting. Usually they take only what is left from the Germans' and Italians' destruction or what the inhabitants voluntarily give them. All I could salvage were a few pieces of lace from the baroness's sewing-room floor.

Then we decided the dining room was the least messy place in the building so we set to with grass brooms and shovels and water and cleaned it up. Thus it became our press room. The Signal Corps ran wires from a portable generator and gave us light so we could work by night.

One day I was writing while all the other correspondents were away, and a stray soldier peered in after having wandered in astonishment through the jumbled house.

He asked, "What is this place?"

I told him it was the former home of an Italian baron. His next question was so typically American you had to laugh despite a little shame at the average soldier's bad grammar and lack of learning.

He said, "What is these barons, anyway? Is they something like lords in England?"

To avoid a technical discussion, I told him that for all practical purposes they were somewhat along the same line. He went away apparently satisfied.

*

Our orchard bivouac behind the castle was fine except for one thing. That was the barnyard collection which surrounded us. About an hour before dawn we were always awakened by the most startling orchestra of weird and ghoulish noises ever put together. Guinea hens would cackle, ducks would quack, calves bawl, babies cry, men shout, peacocks jabber and turkeys gobble. And to cap it all, a lone donkey at just the right dramatic moment in this hideous cacophony would let loose a long sardonic hee-haw that turned your exasperation into outlandish laughter.

The baron's servants were a poor-looking lot, yet they seemed very nice. Their kids hung around our camp all day, very quiet and meek. They looked at us so hungrily we couldn't resist giving them cans of food. We tried to teach them to say *grazie*, or thanks in Italian, but with no success. One day some of us correspondents were doing our washing when one of the Sicilian women came up and took it away from us and washed it herself. When she finished we asked her "How much?"

She said, "Nothing at all." We said, well, then, we'd give her some food. She said she didn't expect any food, that she was just doing it for us free but we gave her some food anyway.

Stories like that are countless. The Army engineers tell me how the Sicilians would come up where they were working, grab shovels and start digging themselves and refuse to take anything for it. Whatever else you can say about them, the Sicilians don't seem lazy. One soldier summed it up when he said: "After living nine months with Arabs, the sight of somebody working voluntarily is almost too much for me."

One Dull, Dead Pattern

SOMEWHERE IN SICILY, *August 25, 1943*—Outside of the occasional peaks of bitter fighting and heavy casualties that highlight military operations, I believe the outstanding trait in any campaign is the terrible weariness that gradually comes over everybody.

Soldiers become exhausted in mind and in soul as well as physically. They acquire a weariness that is mixed up with boredom and lack of all gaiety. To lump them all together, you just get damn sick of it all.

The infantry reaches a stage of exhaustion that is incomprehensible to you folks back home. The men in the 1st Division, for instance, were in the lines twenty-eight days—walking and fighting all that time, day and night.

After a few days of such activity, soldiers pass the point of known human weariness. From then on they go into a sort of second-wind daze. They keep going largely because the other fellow does and because you can't really do anything else.

Have you ever in your life worked so hard and so long that you didn't remember how many days it was since you ate last, or didn't recognize your friends when you saw them? I never have either, but in the 1st Division, during that long, hard fight around Troina, a company runner one day came slogging up to a certain captain and said, excitedly, "I've got to find Captain Blank right away. Important message."

The Captain said, "But I am Captain Blank. Don't you recognize me?"

And the runner said, "I've got to find Captain Blank right away." And he went dashing off. They had to run to catch him.

*

Men in battle reach that stage and still go on and on. As for the rest of the Army—supply troops, truck drivers, hospital men, engineers—they too become exhausted but not so inhumanly. With them and with us correspondents it's the ceaselessness, the endlessness of everything that finally worms its way through you and gradually starts to devour you.

It's the perpetual dust choking you, the hard ground wracking your muscles, the snatched food sitting ill on your stomach, the heat and the flies and dirty feet and the constant roar of engines and the perpetual moving and the never settling down and the go, go, go, night and day, and on through the night again. Eventually it all works itself into an emotional tapestry of one dull, dead pattern—

yesterday is tomorrow and Troina is Randazzo and when will we ever stop and, God, I'm so tired.

I've noticed this feeling has begun to overtake the war correspondents themselves. It is true that we don't fight on and on like the infantry, that we are usually under fire only briefly and that, indeed, we live better than the average soldier. Yet our lives are strangely consuming in that we do live primitively and at the same time must delve into ourselves and do creative writing.

That statement may lay me open to wisecracks, but however it may seem to you, writing is an exhausting and tearing thing. Most of the correspondents work like slaves. Especially is this true of the press-association men. A great part of the time they go from dawn till midnight or two A.M.

I'm sure they turn in as much toil in a week as any newspaperman at home does in two weeks. We travel continuously, move camp every few days, eat out, sleep out, write wherever we can and just never catch up on sleep, rest, cleanliness, or anything else normal.

The result is that all of us who have been with the thing for more than a year have finally grown befogged. We are grimy, mentally as well as physically. We've drained our emotions until they cringe from being called out from hiding. We look at bravery and death and battlefield waste and new countries almost as blind men, seeing only faintly and not really wanting to see at all.

Just in the past month the old-timers among the correspondents have been talking for the first time about wanting to go home for a while. They want a change, something to freshen their outlook. They feel they have lost their perspective by being too close for too long.

I am not writing this to make heroes of the correspondents, because only a few look upon themselves in any dramatic light whatever. I am writing it merely to let you know that correspondents too can get damn sick of war—and deadly tired.

August 27, 1943— . . . Scores of times during the Sicilian fighting I heard the expression voiced by everybody from generals to privates that "This is certainly an engineer's war." And indeed it was.

Every foot of our advance upon the gradually withdrawing enemy was tempoed by the speed with which our engineers could open the highways, clear the mines and by-pass the blown bridges.

In northeast Sicily, where the mountains are close together and the valleys are steep and narrow, it was an ideal country for withdrawing and the Germans made full use of it.

They blew almost every bridge they crossed. In the American area alone they destroyed around one hundred sixty bridges. They mined the by-passes around the bridges, they mined the beaches, they even mined orchards and groves of trees that would be a logical bivouac for our troops.

They didn't fatally delay us, but they did give themselves time for considerable escaping. The average blown bridge was fairly easy to by-pass and we'd have the mines cleared and a rough trail gouged out by a bulldozer within a couple of hours but, now and then, they'd pick a lulu of a spot which would take anywhere up to twenty-four hours to get around.

And in reading of the work of these engineers you must understand that a twenty-four-hour job over here would take many days in normal construction practice. The mine detector and the bulldozer are the two magic instruments of our engineering. As one sergeant said, "This has been a bulldozer campaign."

In Sicily, our Army would have been as helpless without the bulldozer as it would have been without the jeep. The bridges in Sicily were blown much more completely than they were in Tunisia. Back there they'd just drop one span with explosives. But over here they'd blow down the whole damn bridge, from abutment to abutment. They used as high as a thousand pounds of explosives to a bridge and on one long, seven-span bridge they blew all seven spans. It was really senseless and the pure waste of the thing outraged our engineers. Knocking down one or two spans would have delayed us just as much as destroying all of them. . . .

August 30, 1943—Each infantry division has a battalion of engineers which is actually part of that division and works and suffers with it. The battalion consists of four companies totaling around eight hundred men.

Sometimes all the companies are working in separate places with various infantry regiments. At other times, in mountainous country, when the whole division is strung out in a single line twenty miles or more long, the engineer companies keep leapfrogging each other, letting one company go into twenty-four-hour reserve about every three days for a much needed rest.

*

Behind these division engineers are what are called corps engineers. They are under control of the 2nd Army Corps and can be shifted anywhere at the Corps' command. Corps engineers follow up the division engineers, strengthening and smoothing the necessarily makeshift work of the division engineers.

Capt. Ben Billups of Alamogordo, New Mexico, put it this way: "Our job is to clear the way for our division of roughly two thousand vehicles to move ahead just as quickly as possible. We are interested only in the division. If we were to build a temporary span across a blown bridge, and that span were to collapse one second after the last division truck had crossed, we would have done the theoretically perfect job. For we would have cleared the division, yet not wasted a minute of time doing more than we needed to do when we passed.

"Then it is the corps engineers' job to create a more permanent bridge for the supply convoys that will be following for days and weeks afterward."

Often there is jealousy and contempt between groups of similar types working under divisions and corps. But in the engineers it is a sort of mutual-esteem society. Each respects and is proud of the other. . . .

*

At first, particularly, all the officers of the engineers battalion were graduate engineers in civil life, but with the Army expanding so rapidly and professional experience running so thin, some younger officers now assigned to the engineers have just come out of officers' school and have little or no engineering experience.

Of the enlisted men only a handful in each company ever had any construction experience. The rest are just run of the mine—onetime clerks, butchers, cow punchers. That little handful of experienced enlisted men carries the load and they are as vital as anything I know of in the Army.

Practically every man in an engineering company has to double in half a dozen jobs. Today he'll be running a mine detector, tomorrow he'll be a stone mason, next day a carpenter and the day after a plain pick-and-shovel man. But unlike the common laborer at home, he's picking and shoveling under fire about half the time.

August 31, 1943—. . . It falls to the engieers to provide water for the Army. Engineer officers scout the country right behind the retiring enemy, looking for watering places.

They always keep three water points set up constantly for each division—one for each three regiments, usually a couple of extra ones. When a water point is found, the engineers wheel in their portable purifying unit. This consists of a motorized pump, a sand filter, chlorinating machine and a collapsible three-thousand-gallon canvas tank which stands about shoulder-high when put up.

Purified water is pumped into this canvas tank. Then all day and all night vehicles of the regiment from miles around line up and fill their cans, tanks, and motors by a hose out of this tank.

Painted signs saying "Water Point," with an arrow pointing the direction, are staked along the roads for miles around.

The sources of our water in Sicily were mainly wells, mountain springs, little streams, shell craters, and irrigation ditches. The engineers of the 45th Division found one shell crater that contained a broken town-water main, and the seepage into this crater provided water for days. They also discovered some of Sicily's dry riverbeds had underground streams flowing beneath and by drilling down a few feet they could pump all they needed.

Another time they put pumps into a tiny little irrigation ditch only four inches deep and a foot wide. You wouldn't think it would furnish enough water for a mule, yet it kept flowing and carried them safely through.

In their municipal water systems the Sicilians use everything from modern twenty-inch cast-iron pipe down to primitive earthen aqueducts still there from the Roman days.

Our engineers made it a practice not to tap the local water supplies. We made a good many friends that way, for the Sicilians said the Germans used no such delicacy. In fact, we leaned over the other way, and furnished water to scores of thousands of Sicilians whose water supply had been shattered by bombing. . . .

September 1, 1943—One of the outfits with which I lived for a while on the Sicilian front was the 120th Engineers Battalion, attached to the 45th Division.

The bulk of the 120th hail from my adopted state of New Mexico. They are part of the old New Mexico outfit, most of which was lost on Bataan.* It was good to get back to these slow-talking, wide and easy people of the desert, and good to speak of places like Las Cruces, Socorro, and Santa Rosa. It was good to find somebody who lives within sight of my own picket fence on the mesa.

The 120th is made up of Spanish-Americans, Indians, straight New Mexicans, and a smattering of men from the East. It is com-

*The Bataan Peninsula in the Philippines, where American and Filipino troops endured a three-month siege against Japanese invaders in early 1942. When the Americans surrendered in April 1942, survivors, starved and diseased, were forced to walk to prison camps—the so-called Bataan Death March.

manded by Lt. Col. Lewis Frantz, who was superintendent of the Las Vegas, New Mexico, Light and Power Co., before entering the service. . . .

SOMEWHERE IN SICILY *September 2, 1943*—You may never have seen it mentioned, but a map is as common a piece of equipment among front-line officers as a steel helmet. A combat officer would be perfectly useless without his map.

It is the job of the engineers to handle the maps for each division. Just as soon as a division advances to the edge of the territory covered by its maps, the map officer has to dig into his portable warehouse and fish out thousands of new maps.

The immensity of the map program would amaze you. When it came from America, the 45th Division brought with it eighty-three tons of Sicilian maps! I forgot to ask how many individual maps that would be, but it would surely run close to half a million.

The 45th's maps were far superior to any we'd been using and here's the reason: Our maps were based fundamentally on old Italian maps. Then for months ahead of the invasion our reconnaissance planes flew over Sicily taking photographs. These photos immediately were flown across the Atlantic to Washington. There, if anything new was discovered in the photographs, it was superimposed on the maps.

They kept this process of correction open right up to the last minute. The 45th sailed from America only a short time before we invaded Sicily, and in the last week before it sailed the Map Section in Washington printed, placed in waterproofed cases, and delivered to the boats those eighty-three tons of maps, hot off the presses.

*

The 120th Engineers went back into antiquity for one of their recent jobs. They were scouting for a by-pass around a blown bridge when they stumbled onto a Roman stone road, centuries old and now unused and nearly covered with sand grass. They cleaned up the old highway, and used it for a mile and a half. If it hadn't been for this antique road, it would have taken four hundred men twelve hours to build a by-pass. By using it, the job was done in four hours by one hundred fifty men.

The engineers were very careful throughout the campaign about tearing up native property. They used much extra labor and time to avoid damaging orchards, buildings, or vineyards. Sometimes they'd build a road clear around an orchard rather than through it.

This consideration helped make us many friends here.

I met a bulldozer driver who operates his huge, clumsy machine with such utter skill that it is like watching a magician do card tricks. The driver is Joseph Campagnone of Newton, Massachusetts. He is an Italian who came to America several years ago, when he was sixteen. He is all American now. He has a brother in the Italian army who was captured by the British in Egypt.

His mother and sisters live near Naples, and he hopes to see them before this is over. I asked Joe if he had a funny feeling about fighting his own people and he said, "No, I guess we've got to fight somebody and it might as well be them as anybody else."

Campagnone has been a cat [caterpillar tractor] driver ever since he started working. I sat and watched him for two hours one afternoon while he ate away a rocky bank overhanging a blown road, and worked it into a huge hole until it was ready for traffic. He is so astonishingly adept at manipulating the big machine that groups of soldiers and officers gathered at the crater's edge to admire and comment.

Joe has had one close shave. He was bulldozing a by-pass around a blown bridge when the blade of his machine hit a mine. The explosion blew him off and stunned him, but he was not wounded. The driverless dozer continued to run and drove itself over a fifty-foot cliff and turned a somersault as it fell. It landed right side up with the engine still going.

*

Our troops along the coast occasionally got a chance to bathe in the Mediterranean. As an incidental statistic, the engineers during the campaign cleared mines off a total of seven miles of beaches just so the soldiers could get down to the water to swim.

Up in the mountains you'd see hundreds of soldiers, stark naked, bathing in Sicilian horse troughs, or out of their steel helmets. The American soldier has a fundamental phobia about bodily cleanliness that is considered all nonesense by philosophers of the Great Unwashed, which includes Arabs, Sicilians and me.

A Spectacular Engineering Job

SOMEWHERE IN SICILY, *September 3, 1943*—When the 45th Division went into reserve along the north coast of Sicily after several weeks of hard fighting, I moved on with the 3rd Division, which took up the ax and drove the enemy on to Messina. It was on my very first day with the 3rd that we hit the most difficult and spectacular enginering job of the Sicilian campaign.

You've doubtless noticed Point Calavà* on your maps. It is a great stub of rock that sticks out into the sea, forming a high ridge running back into the interior. The coast highway is tunneled through this big rock, and on either side of the tunnel the road sticks out of the sheer rock wall like a shelf.

Our engineers figured the Germans would blow the tunnel entrance to seal it up. But they didn't. They had an even better idea. They picked out a spot about fifty feet beyond the tunnel mouth and blew a hole one hundred fifty feet long in the road shelf. They blew it so deeply and thoroughly that if you dropped a rock into it the rock would never stop rolling until it bounced into the sea a couple of hundred feet below.

We were beautifully bottlenecked. You couldn't by-pass around the rock, for it dropped sheer into the sea. You couldn't by-pass up over the mountain, for it would take weeks. You couldn't fill the hole, for it would keep sliding off into the water.

All you could do was bridge it, and that was a hell of a job. But bridge it they did, and in only twenty-four hours.

*

When the first engineer officers went up to inspect the tunnel, I went with them. We had to leave the jeep at a blown bridge and walk the last four miles uphill. We went with an infantry battalion that was following the retreating Germans.

When we got there we found the tunnel floor mined. But each spot where they'd dug into the hard rock floor left its telltale mark, so it was no job for the engineers to uncover and unscrew the detonators of scores of mines. Then we went on through to the vast hole beyond, and the engineering officers began making their calculations.

As we did so, the regiment of infantry crawled across the chasm, one man at a time. You could just barely make it on foot by holding on to the rock juttings and practically crawling.

Another regiment went up over the ridge and took out after the evacuating enemy with only what weapons and provisions they could carry on their backs. Before another twenty-four hours, they'd be twenty miles ahead of us and in contact with the enemy, so getting this hole bridged and supplies and supporting guns to them was indeed a matter of life and death.

*

*In Italian, Cap Calavà. Located in northeastern Sicily overlooking the Mediterranean, its coastal highway serves as the most direct route between Messina and Cefalù.

It was around two P.M. when we got there, and in two hours the little platform of highway at the crater mouth resembled a littered street in front of a burning building. Air hoses covered the ground, serpentined over each other. Three big air compressors were parked side by side, their engines cutting off and on in that erratically deliberate manner of air compressors, and jackhammers clattered their nerve-shattering din.

Bulldozers came to clear off the stone-blocked highway at the crater edge. Trucks, with long trailers bearing railroad irons and huge timbers, came and unloaded. Steel cable was brought up. And kegs of spikes and all kinds of crowbars and sledges.

The thousands of vehicles of the division were halted some ten miles back in order to keep the highway clear for the engineers. One platoon of men worked at a time in the hole. There was no use of throwing in the whole company, for there was room for only so many.

At suppertime, hot rations were brought up by truck. The 3rd Division engineers go on K-rations at noon, but morning and evening they get hot food up to them, regardless of the job.

If you could see how they toil, you would know how important this hot food is. By dusk the work was in full swing and half the men were stripped to the waist.

The night air of the Mediterranean was tropical. The moon came out at twilight and extended our light for a little while. The moon was new and pale, and transient high-flying night clouds brushed it and scattered shadows down on us.

Then its frail light went out, and the blinding night-long darkness settled over the insidious abyss. But the work never slowed nor halted, throughout the night.

September 4, 1943—. . . It took our engineers twenty-four hours to bridge this enormous gap, but the men of the 3rd Division didn't just sit and twiddle their thumbs during that time.

The infantry was sent across on foot and continued after the Germans. Some supplies and guns were sent around the roadblock by boat, and even the engineers themselves continued on ahead by boat. They had discovered other craters blown in the road several miles ahead. These were smaller ones that could be filled in by a bulldozer except that you couldn't get a bulldozer across that vast hole they were trying to bridge.

So the engineers commandeered two little Sicilian fishing boats about twice the size of rowboats. They lashed them together, nailed planking across them and ran the bulldozer up onto this improvised barge. They tied an amphibious jeep in front of it, and went chugging around Point Calava at about one mile an hour.

As we looked down at them laboring along so slowly, Lieut. Col. Leonard Bingham, commanding officer of the 3rd Division's 10th Engineers, grinned and said, "There goes the engineers' homemade Navy." . . .

During the night Maj. Gen. Lucian Truscott, commanding the 3rd Division, came up to see how the work was coming along. Bridging that hole was his main interest in life that night. He couldn't help any, of course, but somehow he couldn't bear to leave. He stood around and talked to officers, and after a while he went off a few feet to one side and sat down on the ground and lit a cigaret.

A moment later, a passing soldier saw the glow and leaned over and said, "Hey, gimme a light, will you?" The General did and the soldier never knew he had been ordering the General around.

Gen. Truscott, like many men of great action, has the ability to refresh himself by tiny catnaps of five or ten minutes. So instead of going back to his command post and going to bed he stretched out there against some rocks and dozed off. One of the working engineers came past, dragging some air hose. It got tangled up in the General's feet. The tired soldier was annoyed, and he said crossly to the dark, anonymous figure on the ground, "If you're not working, get the hell out of the way."

The General got up and moved farther back without saying a word. . . .

September 5, 1943—. . . On the Point Calavà road crater job, there were two men I couldn't take my eyes off of. They worked like demons. Both were corporals and had little to gain by their extraordinary labors, except maybe some slight future promotion. And I doubt that's what drove them. Such men must be driven by the natures they're born with—by pride in their jobs, by that mystic spark which forces some men to give all they've got, all the time.

These two men were Gordon Uttech of Merrill, Wisconsin, and Alvin Tolliver of Alamosa, Colorado. Both were air-compressor operators and rock drillers. Uttech worked all night and when the night shift was relieved for breakfast, he refused to go. He worked on throughout the day without sleep and in the final hours of the job, he went down under the frail bridge to check the sag and strain, as heavier and heavier vehicles passed over it.

Tolliver, too, worked without ceasing, never resting, never stopping, even to wipe off the sweat that made his stripped body look as though it were coated with olive oil. I never saw him stop once throughout the day. He seemed to work without instruction from anybody, knowing what jobs to do and doing them alone. He rassled the great chattering jackhammers into the rock. He spread and rewound his airhose. He changed drills. He regulated his compressor. He drove eye-hooks into the rock, chopped down big plants to fit the rocky ledges he'd created.

Always he worked as though the outcome of the war depended on him alone. I couldn't help being proud of these men, who gave more than was asked. . . .

The Kind of Bridge That Wins Wars

SOMEWHERE IN SICILY, *September 6, 1943*—It was an hour after daylight when I returned to the German-blown highway crater which our 3rd Division engineers had been working on all night.

It really didn't look as though they'd accomplished much, but an engineer's eye would have seen that the groundwork was all laid. They had drilled and blasted two holes far down the jagged slope. These were to set upright timbers into so they wouldn't slide downhill when weight was applied.

The far side of the crater had been blasted out and leveled off so it formed a road across about one-third of the hole. Small ledges had been jackhammered at each end of the crater and timber bolted into them, forming abutments of the bridge that was to come.

Steel hooks had been imbedded deep into the rock to hold wire cables. At the tunnel mouth lay great timbers, two feet square, and other long pieces of timber bolted together in the middle to make them long enough to span the hole.

*

At about ten A.M., the huge uprights were slid down the bank, caught by a group of men clinging to the steep slope below, and their ends worked into the blasted holes. Then they were brought upright by men on the banks, pulling on ropes tied to them. Similar heavy timbers were slowly and cautiously worked out from the bank until their tops rested on the uprights.

A half-naked soldier, doing practically a wire-walking act, edged out over the timber and bored a long hole down through two timbers with an air-driven bit. Then he hammered a steel rod into it, tying them together.

Others added more bracing, nailing them together with huge spikes driven in by sledge hammers. Then they slung steel cable from one end of the crater to the other, wrapped it around the upright stanchions and drew it tight with a winch mounted on a truck.

*

Now came the coolie scene as twenty shirtless, sweating soldiers to each of the long-spliced timbers carried and slid them out across the chasm, resting them on the two wooden spans just erected. They sagged in the middle, but still the cable beneath took most of the strain. They laid ten of those across and the bridge began to take shape. Big stringers were bolted down, heavy flooring was carried on and nailed to the stringers. Men built up the approaches with stones. The bridge was almost ready.

Around eleven A.M., jeeps had begun to line up at the far end of the tunnel. They carried reconnaissance platoons, machine gunners and boxes of ammunition. They'd been given Number One Priority to cross the bridge.

First, Maj. Gen. Truscott arrived again and sat on a log talking with the engineering officers, waiting patiently. Around dusk of the day before, the engineers had told me they'd have jeeps across the crater by noon of the next day. It didn't seem possible at the time, but they knew whereof they spoke.

But even they will have to admit it was pure coincidence that the first jeep rolled cautiously across the miracle bridge at high noon, to the very second.

In that first jeep was Gen. Truscott and his driver, facing a two-hundred-foot tumble into the sea if the bridge gave way. The engineers had insisted they send a test jeep across first. It wasn't done dramatically but it was a sort of dramatic thing. It showed that the "Old Man" had complete faith in his engineers. I heard soldiers speak of it appreciatively for an hour.

*

Jeeps snaked across the rickety bridge behind the General while the engineers kept stations beneath the bridge to watch and measure the sag under each load. The bridge squeaked and bent as the jeeps crept over. But it held, and nothing else matters. When the vital spearhead of the division got across, traffic was halted again and the engineers were given three hours to strengthen the bridge for heavier traffic by inserting a third heavy upright in the middle.

That, too, was a terrific job, but at exactly four P.M. the first three-quarter-ton truck rolled across, and they kept putting over heavier and heavier loads until before dark a giant bulldozer was sent across, and after that, everything could follow.

The tired men began to pack their tools into trucks. Engineer officers who hadn't been to sleep in thirty-six hours went back to their olive orchard to clean up. They had built a jerry bridge, a comical bridge, a proud bridge, but above all the kind of bridge that wins wars. And they had built it in one night and half a day. The General was mighty pleased.*

Operation Husky ended on August 17, 1943, with the Allied capture of Messina, on Sicily's northeastern coast, just two miles across the Strait of Messina from the Italian mainland. The Germans and Italians sustained heavy loses, mostly in prisoners, but thirty-nine thousand German soldiers were evacuated across the strait to the mainland under cover of darkness.

September 8, 1943—As the Sicilian campaign drew to an end some weeks ago and we went into our rest bivouac, rumors by the score popped up out of thin air and swept through the troops like a forest fire.

Number One rumor in every outfit, of course, was that ships already were waiting to take them back to the States. That one was so old I don't think half the men will believe it's true when the war ends, and they actually do start back.

Other rumors had them staying in Sicily as occupation troops, going to England, going to China, and—ugly thought—going right on as the spearhead of the next invasion.

Some people worry about such rumors that constantly sweep our armies, but personally I think they are harmless. When the Army doesn't have women, liberty, ice cream, beer or clean clothes, it certainly has to have something to look forward to, even if only a faint hope for some kind of change that lies buried in an illogical rumor.

In fact, I don't know how we would endure without our rumors. . . .

During the first week of September 1943 Pyle left Sicily and flew to the United States, via North Africa, for a vacation.

*The Army Corps of Engineers asked that Pyle's client papers run this appeal with the foregoing column: "HELP WANTED: One hundred thousand men with construction skills are needed urgently for overseas service with the Corps of Engineers, U.S. Army, to do the kind of work being described by Ernie Pyle in his current series on the work of the engineers. Construction men who want to build and fight with the Army Engineers should go to any Army Recruiting Station or to any office of the Corps of Engineers."

Fed Up and Bogged Down

WASHINGTON, *September 11, 1943*—How should a war correspondent who has been away a long time begin his first column after he returns to his homeland?

Frankly, I don't know. I can't truthfully say, "My, it's wonderful to be back," because I haven't had a moment to sense whether it's wonderful or not. In my first forty-eight hours in America I got two hours' sleep, said "no" three hundred twenty-four times, lost my pocketbook and caught a bad cold.

That pocketbook business, incidentally, is sort of disheartening to a guy who returns full of eagerness for his own people. The wallet contained about a hundred dollars and all my War Department credentials and private papers. It had my name and address in it at least a dozen times, but it has not yet been returned.

Whoever got it, if he had a crumb of decency, could certainly send back the papers even if he kept the money. Anybody who wouldn't do that, it seems to me, would make a fine client for some oil-boilers. This thing happened in New York on my first day home. And here I've been ranting for a year about the lowly Arab!*

*

Perhaps you who read this column wonder why I came home just at this special time, when events are boiling over in Italy.

Well, I might as well tell you truthfully. I knew, of course, that the Italian invasion was coming up, but I chose to skip it. I made that decision because I realized, in the middle of Sicily, that I had been too close to the war for too long.

I was fed up, and bogged down. Of course you say other people are too, and they keep going on. But if your job is to write about the war, you're very apt to begin writing unconscious distortions and unwarranted pessimisms when you get too tired.

I had come to despise and be revolted by war clear out of any logical proportion. I couldn't find the Four Freedoms† among the dead men. Personal weariness became a forest that shut off my view of events about me. I was no longer seeing the little things that you at home want to know about the soldiers.

When we fought through Sicily, it was to many of us like seeing

*The wallet was returned a few days later, in a neatly wrapped packaged postmarked Wilmington, Delaware. Pyle's personal papers were intact, but the money was missing. "I'm grateful beyond words for the return of the wallet and the credentials," Pyle wrote. "And it's comforting to know that our thieves are honest thieves."

†A reference to one of President Roosevelt's most celebrated speeches (January 6, 1941), in which he declared that all people the world over should enjoy freedom of speech, freedom of worship, freedom from want, and freedom from fear.

the same movie for the fourth time. Battles differ from one another only in their physical environment—the emotions of fear and exhaustion and exaltation and hatred are about the same in all of them. Through repetition, I had worn clear down to the nub my ability to weight and describe. You can't do a painting when your oils have turned to water.

There is, in the months and years ahead, still a lot of war to be written about. So I decided, all of a sudden one day in Sicily, that you who read and I who write would both benefit in the long run if I came home to refreshen my sagging brain and drooping frame. To put it bluntly, I just got too tired in the head. So here I am.

*

It has been fifteen months since I left America. Things at home have changed a lot in that time, I'm sure. But at first glance there doesn't seem to be much change.

When I rode in from the airport in New York, and checked into the hotel, everything was so perfectly natural that it truly seemed as though I had never been away at all. It was all so normal, so exactly like what it had been on other returns, that I couldn't realize that now I was going through that beautiful hour that millions of our men overseas spend a good part of their waking hours yearning for and dreaming about. I do hope that when their hour comes, they'll find themselves more capable of enthrallment by it.

*

On the whole, the few little things that struck me the most were normal things that I had thought would be gone by now. I was surprised to find sugar bowls on the table. We have plenty of sugar in the Army overseas, but we had figured you were very short over here.

And I was astonished at finding the store windows of New York looking so full and so beautiful. I'd like to take a pocketful of money and just go on a spree, buying everything that was smart and pretty whether I really wanted it or not.

We've had nothing to spend money on for so long, over on the other side. The countries we've been in were so denuded; why, England was shorter of everything after one year of war than we are after nearly two.

The decline of traffic on the streets was noticeable; and how much nicer it is too, isn't it? In fact, it's too nice, and I propose to recreate some of our old congestion by getting out my own jalopy and dashing nonessentially around the streets for a month or so.

Well, anyway, on second thought, it's wonderful to be home.

ITALY:

December 1943—May 1944

ARMY SIGNAL CORPS

Before leaving the United States for Italy in late November 1943, Pyle commented on his popularity, telling readers that "the most sincere plaudits of people, when multiplied and piled too high, can become something obsessing you, claiming your life away." At home, Pyle felt "like a deserter and a heel—not so much to the war effort, but to your friends who are still over there freezing and getting shot at."

Nonetheless, he didn't want to go back. "It is one of our popular heroic myths that anybody who comes back from the combat zone begins to itch after a few weeks, and finally get so homesick for the front he can hardly stand it." Nonsense, Pyle wrote. "I've never hated to do anything as badly in my life as I hate to go back to the front. I dread it and I'm afraid of it. But what can a guy do? I know millions of others who are reluctant too, and they can't even get home."

He commented, too, on the American homefront. "With us so big and scattered, and the enemy so far away, the war is bound to seem academic to most of us. Only those who have received the dreaded telegram from the War Department feel it really.

"Materially, it seems to me we have been hardly touched by war here at home. . . . Our little annoying restrictions and shortages are so puny compared to those of other countries. We are still so rich and so well fed and so plentiful." And, citing suffering as the antecedent to character, he added, "We haven't had anything yet, on a national scale, to burn and crucify us into anything greater than we were to begin with."

The Italians, whose homeland was now host to two occupying armies, had seen plenty of fighting; war was anything but academic to them. Mussolini had resigned and the country's new government had broken with the Nazis when the Allies invaded southern Italy in early September 1943. The Germans, however, stiffly opposed the Allies, absorbing many Italian troops into their own units. Like the Sicilians, many mainland Italians had tired of life under a fascist regime and welcomed the Allies as liberators. Despite severe reprisals, many engaged in covert action against the Germans.

By early October, the Allies had impounded most of the Italian navy, occupied several important cities, including Naples, and secured the air base at Foggia, from which Allied planes could bomb targets in the Balkans and central and southern Europe.

By the time Pyle arrived in Italy, the war had bogged down in winter mud. Snow and freezing rain inflicted hardships on both sides. Depressed about returning to war, burdened with recurring colds, and drinking heavily, he settled in with other correspondents in a drafty castle at Caserta, north of Naples. "The long winter misery has started," he wrote his wife. "By this time tomorrow night I will be in the lines. Sometimes I've felt that I couldn't make myself go, but now that I'm here I want to take the plunge and . . . get the first return over with. . . ."

The Way Is Cruel

AT THE FRONT LINE IN ITALY, *December 14, 1943*—The war in Italy is tough. The land and the weather are both against us.

It rains and it rains. Vehicles bog down and temporary bridges wash out. The country is shockingly beautiful, and just as shockingly hard to capture from the enemy. The hills rise to high ridges of almost solid rock. You can't go around them through the flat peaceful valleys, because the Germans look down upon you and would let you have it.

So you have to go up and over. A mere platoon of Germans, well dug in on a high, rock-spined hill, can hold out for a long time against tremendous onslaughts.

Having come from home so recently, I know you folks back there are disappointed and puzzled by the slow progress in Italy. You wonder why we move northward so imperceptibly. You are impatient for us to get to Rome.

Well, I can tell you this—our troops are just as impatient for Rome as you. But they all say such things as this: "It never was this bad in Tunisia." "We ran into a new brand of Krauts over here." "If it would only stop raining." "Every day we don't advance is one day longer before we get home."

*

Our troops are living in a way almost inconceivable to you in the States. The fertile black valleys are knee-deep in mud. Thousands of the men have not been dry for weeks. Other thousands lie at night in the high mountains with the temperature below freezing and the thin snow sifting over them.

They dig into the stones and sleep in little chasms and behind rocks and in half caves. They live like men of prehistoric times, and a club would become them more than a machine gun. How they survive the winter misery at all is beyond us who have the opportunity of drier beds in the warmer valleys.

It is not the fault of our troops, nor of their direction, that the northward path is a tedious one. It is the weather and the terrain and the weather.

If there were no German fighting troops in Italy, if there were merely German engineers to blow the bridges in the passes, if never a shot were fired at all, our northward march would still be slow.

The country over here is so difficult we've created a great deal of cavalry for use in the mountains. Each division has hundreds of horses and mules to carry it beyond the point where vehicles can go no farther. On beyond the mules' ability, mere men—American men—take it on their backs.

Here is a little clue to the war over here. I flew across the Mediterranean in a cargo plane weighted down with more than a thousand pounds beyond the normal load. The cabin was filled with big pasteboard boxes which had been given priority above all other freight.

In those boxes were packboards, hundreds of them, for husky men to pack—one hundred, even one hundred fifty, pounds of food and ammunition on their backs—to comrades high in the miserable mountains.

*

But we can take consolation from many things. The air is almost wholly ours. All day long Spitfires patrol above our fighting troops like a half-dozen policemen running up and down the street watching for bandits. During my four days in the lines, just ended, I saw German planes only twice, then just two at a time, and they skedaddled in a hurry.

Further, our artillery prevails and how! We are prodigal with ammunition against these rocky crags, and well we should be, for a fifty-dollar shell can often save ten lives in country like this. Little by little, the fiendish rain of explosives upon the hillsides softens the Germans. They've always been impressed by, and afraid of, our artillery and we have concentrations of it here that are demoralizing.

And lastly, no matter how cold the mountains, or how wet the snow, or how sticky the mud, it's just as miserable for the German soldier as for the American.

Our men will get to Rome all right. There's no question about that. But the way is cruel. Right this minute some of them are fighting hand-to-hand up there in fog and clouds so dense they can barely see each other—one man against another.

No one who has not seen this mud, these dark skies, these forbidding ridges and ghostlike clouds that unveil and then quickly hide your killer, has the right to be impatient with the progress along the road to Rome.

December 15, 1943— . . . It had been my intention to work back into the war gradually by doing maybe a couple of weeks' columns about how things were in Naples, what Italian women looked like, and whether the Island of Capri was as pretty as they say.

But I don't know what happened. Something happened. I hadn't been in Naples two hours before I felt I couldn't stand it, and by the next evening there I was—up in the mud again, sleeping on some straw and awakening throughout the night with the old familiar crash and thunder of the big guns in my reluctant ears.

It was the artillery for me this time. I went with an outfit I had known in England a year ago last fall, made up largely of men from the Carolinas and eastern Tennessee.

This regiment shoots 155-mm howitzers. They are terrifically big guns and, Lordy, do they make a noise! The gun weighs six tons, and the shell itself is so big it's all an ammunition carrier can do to lug one up to the gun pit.

Thc regiment has all new guns now. I can't tell you how far they shoot, but as the Carolina boys said, "It's awful fur." . . .

. . . Our artillery has played a huge part all through the Mediterranean fighting. It was good even last spring, and it has grown better all the time. The Germans fear it almost more than anything we have.

We've got plenty of it, and plenty of ammunition too. The artillery is usually a few miles back of the front-line infantry, although there have been cases right here in Italy where artillerymen have actually been under machine-gun fire.

In ninety-nine cases out of a hundred an artilleryman never sees what he's shooting at, and in nine cases out of ten he never knows what he's shooting at. Somebody just gives him a set of figures over his telephone. He sets his gun by those figures, rams in a shell, pulls the lanyard and gets ready for the next one.

He usually shoots over a hill, and here in Italy the men say they're getting sick of going around one hill and always finding another one just like it ahead of them. They sure wish they could get out in the open country and shoot at something just once that didn't have a hill in front of it. . . .

On my first night at the front I slept only fitfully—never very wide awake, never deeply asleep. It seemed almost impossible to make the transition from a place like America to the depth of war-strewn Italy. All night long the valley beside us, and the mountains and the valleys over the hill, were dotted and punctured with the great blasts of the guns.

You could hear the shells chase each other through the sky across the mountains ahead, making a sound like cold wind through the leaves on a winter night. Then the concussion of the blasts of a dozen guns firing at once would strike the far mountains across the valley and rebound in a great mass sound that was prolonged with the immensity and the fury of an approaching sandstorm.

Then the nearer guns would fire and the ground under your bedroll would tremble and you could feel the awful breath of the blast push the tent walls and nudge your whole body ever so slightly. And through the darkened hodgepodge of noise you could occasionally pick out, through experience, the slightly different tone of German shells bursting in our valley.

It didn't really seem true. Three weeks ago I was in Miami, eating fried chicken, sleeping in deep beds with white sheets, taking hot baths and hearing no sound more vicious than the laughing ocean waves and the laughter of friends. One world was a beautiful dream and the other a horrible nightmare, and I was still a little bit in each of them.

As I lay on the straw in the darkness they became mixed up, and I was confused and not quite sure which was which.

December 17, 1943— . . . Our four guns are set in and around a grape arbor. On one side a ridge rises steeply four or five hundred feet. A broad valley spreads out below us. It is very pretty where we are.

The four guns form a rough square about the size of a city block, and they are so close under the brow of a hill that it's almost impossible for the German artillery to reach us. Each gun is planted in a pit about three feet deep, and the front of the pit is lined, shoulder-high, with sandbags.

Over the entire pit is stretched a camouflage net on poles. The net, just head-high, gives you the sense of having a roof over you. When the guns are quiet you can yell from one gun pit to another.

A few feet on one side of the gun pit is a stack of black cases about three feet long, clipped together in triple clusters. These are the powder charges.

On the other side of the pit lies a double row of rust-colored shells. The ammunition carriers keep a supply of ten or twelve shells inside the pit, but the powder charges are brought in one at a time, just before the shooting, because of the danger of fire.

The floor of the gun pit is muddy and you have to move carefully to stay on your feet. One day one of the ammunition carriers, a slight fellow, slipped with his heavy shell and let out an irritated

"Goddamit!" Whereupon the sergeant said sarcastically, "Hush. The devil will get you for talking like that." . . .

*

Several times a day an ammunition truck comes plowing through the muddy field, backs up to the gun pit and unloads another truckload of shells. It's a game with the gun crew to try to get the truckers to carry the shells inside the pit instead of stacking them outside, and sometimes, when in good humor, they'll do it.

All four guns are connected to the battery's executive post by telephone, and the chief of each crew wears a headphone all the time he's in the pit. An executive post may be anything from a telephone lying on the ground under a tree, clear up to the luxury of an abandoned cowshed. But it is always within a few yards of the battery.

An officer in the executive post gives the firing directions to the four guns of his battery. He gets his instructions from the regimental command post half a mile or so to the rear, which in turn receives its firing orders from the division command posts and from its own observers far ahead in the mountains.

The men of a gun crew live in pup tents a few feet from the gun pit. Since an artillery unit usually stays in one place for several days, the men have time to pitch their tents securely and dig little irrigation ditches around them.

They cover the floors of the tents with straw and make themselves dry inside the tents, at least. For each two gun crews, there is also a larger pyramidal tent, empty except for the straw on the ground. Nobody lives in here, but the ground crews use it for a loafing place in the daytime when they aren't firing, and for playing poker at night by candlelight. They just sit or lie on the ground while they play, since there is no furniture.

*

There is a kitchen truck for each battery. Our truck is full of battle scars. There are holes in the walls and roof from bomb fragments, and the stove itself has a huge gash in it, yet nobody in the kitchen has ever been hurt.

The battery's three officers eat standing up at a bench inside the truck while the men eat outside, either sitting on their steel helmets in the mud or standing up with their mess kits resting on a farmer's stone wall. They don't all eat at once. Three go at a time from each crew, since the guns are never left, day or night, without enough men to fire them. Our crew claims it can fire faster with three men than the others can with ten, but of course all crews say that. The crews don't actually stay at the alert inside the gun pit all the time. But they are always close enough to get there in a few seconds when the whistle blows.

Supper is at four-thirty, and by five-thirty it is dark. There is nothing to do, no place to go, and even inside the big tents the candlelight isn't conducive to much fun, so usually the crews are asleep by eight-thirty. Some take off their pants, but most of the men just remove their shoes and leggings. Each crew posts a guard, which is changed every two hours throughout the night, to stand by the field telephone and listen for firing orders.

Most of the cannoneers have got so they can sleep through anything. Steady firing, even fairly close, doesn't keep you awake after you're used to it. It's the lone battery that suddenly whams away after hours of complete silence that brings you awake practically jumping out of your skin.

December 18, 1943— . . . Most of the men are from small towns or farms.* They are mostly hill people. As I wrote of them more than a year ago in England, there is something fundamentally fine and sound about their character that must have been put there by a closeness to their hills and their trees and their soil.

They are natively courteous. Most of them have little education, and their grammar is atrocious, but their thinking is clear and they seem to have a friendliness toward all people that much of America doesn't have. They have an acceptance of their miserable fate and a sense of gaiety and good humor, despite their hardships, that you seldom find in other Army outfits.

The artillery lives tough, but it, too, like nearly every other branch of the Army, bows in sympathy and admiration to the infantry. One day we were sitting on our steel hats, planted in the mud around a bonfire made of empty pasteboard powder cases, when one member of the gun crew said, "We live like kings in comparison to the infantry."

"What's that you say?" burst in another cannoneer. The sentence was repeated.

*Pyle wrote about the following men in passages I've deleted: Lieut. Col. Ansel Godfrey of Clinton, South Carolina; PFC Lloyd Lewman of Ottumwa, Iowa; PFC Frank Helms of Newburg, West Virginia; PFC Raymond Wilson of North Pittsburgh; Capt. Robert Perrin of Union, South Carolina; Lt. Heath Stewart of Columbia, South Carolina; Corp. James Smith of Dogwood, Tennessee; PFC Roy Christmas and PFC Oscar Smith of Marion, South Carolina; Pvt. Wayne Aedden of Hawarden, Iowa; Pvt. John Borrego (address unknown); and Pvt. Charles Hook of St. Joseph, Missouri.

"Oh, I thought you said we live like kings," the questioner said. "I thought you must be crazy in the head. But if you compare us with the infantry, that's all right. Those poor guys really have to take it." . . .

*

. . . Tragedy has struck twice in my battery of four guns since it came to Italy only a few weeks ago. Number two gun blew up from a premature explosion as they were putting in a shell. Three men were killed and half a dozen wounded.

Not long before that, some German raiders did get through and a bomb explosion killed three men and wounded nearly a dozen others. I was told over and over the story of one of the three who died. His legs were blown off clear up to his body. He stayed conscious, but couldn't possibly live long.

When the medical man went to help him, he raised what was left of himself up on his elbows and said:

"I'm done for, so don't waste time on me. Go help the other boys."

He lived seven minutes, conscious all the time.

Things like that knock the boys down for a few days. But if they don't come too often, they can take it without serious damage to their fighting spirit.

It's when casualties become so great that those who remain feel they have no chance to live, if they must go on and on, that morale in an army gets low.

The morale is excellent in this battery I've been living with. They gripe, of course, but they are never grim or even mad about the toughness of their life. The only thing is they're impatient for movement—they'd fire all day and move all night every day and every night if they could only keep going forward swiftly.

Because everywhere in our army, "forward," no matter what direction, is toward home.

December 20, 1943— . . . Although profanity is a normal part of their language, the boys in the artillery seem to be less profane than the infantry. The rougher a man lives the rougher he talks, and nothing can touch the infantry for rough and horrible living.

The impending arrival of galoshes forms a good part of the conversation in our howitzer crew. Galoshes have been promised for weeks, actually from day to day, but the rains are two months old and galoshes aren't here yet.

"I'd give my payroll for a pair of galoshes," one soldier said.

"They're supposed to be on a ship already in the harbor," another cannoneer said. "And sure as hell the Jerries will sink it before they get them unloaded."

Dozens of times a day the subject of galoshes comes up.

"My feet haven't been dry for six weeks," one soldier said. And another one spoke up:

"If you take a shot of that lousy cognac they sell in Naples, it will dry your socks as soon as it hits bottom." . . .

*

Like soldiers everywhere, the gun crews kill time by gambling. Our battery got paid for the first time in two months while I was with them, and immediately a poker game started in every crew.

Our crew even brought a shelter half and spread it on the floor of the gun pit and played right there while waiting for further firing orders. As Sgt. Jack McCray said, the best way to bring on a firing mission is to start a hand of poker. And sure enough, they hadn't played five minutes till the firing order came and everybody grabbed his cards and money and scrambled for the shells.

While they were playing, one of the boys said, "I wonder if the Germans got paid today." And another one said, "Do you suppose the Germans play poker too?" To which another answered, "Hell no, them guys ain't got enough money to play poker," which was probably a little misconception on his part, since most of the prisoners I've seen had money in their pockets.

The boys will bet on anything. I've heard of one bet on whether I would come back to this theater or go to the Pacific. They've got bets on when we'll get to Rome, and when the war will be over, and a couple of them were betting on whether Schlitz beer was sometimes put in green bottles instead of brown. They came to me to settle this but I didn't know.

This is the regiment, incidentally, that had a payday just before leaving America more than a year ago. They left the States with around fifty-two thousand dollars and when they arrived in England and turned in their money for foreign exchange, they had fifteen thousand dollars more than they started with. They had taken it away from other outfits on the ship at poker.

Dumb, these hillbillies.

December 21, 1943— . . . One night about eight of our crew were lying or kneeling around a blanket in a big tent playing poker by the light of two candles. Our battery wasn't firing, but the valley and the mountains all around us were full of the dreadful noise of cannon.

There was a lull in the talk among the players, and then out of the clear sky one of the boys, almost as though talking in his sleep, said: "World war, my friends, is a silly business. War is the craziest thing I ever heard of."

And another one said also, mainly to himself, "I wish there wasn't no blankety-blank war no more at all."

Then complete silence, as though nobody had heard. And when words were spoken it was something about the game and no one talked about war. Weird little snatches like that stand out in your mind for a long time. . . .

*

The powder charges for our guns come in white sacks about the size of two-pound sugar sacks. Three of them tied together make one charge, and that is the way they arrive in their cases. The type and number of each charge are printed on the bag.

One day the sergeant in calling out his instructions asked for a charge of a certain size. When the powderman brought it, it was only half as big as it should be.

The whole crew gathered around and studied it. They read the printing, and there it was in black and white just as it should be, and yet it was obviously a short charge. So the boys just threw it aside and got another, and that started a long run of conversation and wisecracks along this line:

"Some defense worker who had to work on Sunday made that one," they'd say. "He was too tired to fill it up, the poor fellow."

"If we'd shot that little one the shell would have landed on the battery just ahead."

"Guess somebody had worked eight hours already that day and made twenty or thirty dollars for it and had to work overtime at time-and-a-half and was just worn out."

"Or somebody who had to drive all of three or four miles after work to a cocktail bar and he was in too big a hurry to finish this one. It sure is tough on the poor defense workers."

The boys were more taken with their own humor than by any bitterness. It's as Corp. John C. "Peewee" Graham says:

"You can't stand around all day with your trap hanging open, so you got to talk about something. And practically anything new for a subject is mighty welcome."

December 22, 1943— . . . One night in the tent a soldier brought out a box from home and passed around some pecans that had been sent from his own farm.

"Just think," he said. "Three years ago I had my hands on the very trees these nuts came from."

"If you're lucky," another one said, "you can have your hands on them again in another three years—maybe."

That's the way conversation at the front goes all the time. Ten minutes hardly ever goes by without some nostalgic reference to home, how long you've been away, how long before you get back, what you'll do first when you hit the States, what your chances are for returning before the war is over.

*

In one gun crew I ran onto, there is a cannoneer who used to be a photographer for Harris & Ewing in Washington, back in the days when I worked in Washington. He is Pvt. Francis J. Hoffman. He has just been in the Army since March, and overseas only two months. He is a perfect example of the queer things the Army can do.

Hoffman had eighteen years' experience as a photographer, yet they listed him as a cook at first and then changed their minds and made him a cannoneer. He doesn't think he's a very good cannoneer, but if they want him to be a round peg in a square hole he'll do the best he can at it. . . .

December 23, 1943—Our artillerymen in the front lines don't try to keep themselves looking very pretty. As they say, "There ain't nobody going to see you that amounts to a damn unless the colonel should happen to come around.

Their clothes are muddy and greasy and often torn. Some of them wear coveralls, but most of them wear regular O.D. pants, jackets and leggings.

It's funny to see them when they're routed out just before dawn on a firing mission. They jerk on their shoes and wade through the mud to their guns. Naturally they don't take time to put on their leggings. Then when it gets light and the firing mission is over they sit around scraping the mud off their shoes and putting on their leggings.

It is a very strict military regulation in the combat zones that everybody must wear leggings, but the average soldier, just like myself, is careless about it. Along this line one of the boys said the worst trouble they had was with new officers.

"One morning we were firing," he said, "and one of them asked over the telephone if we had our leggings on. It made me so damn mad that I just called this gun out of commission while we all sat down and put on our leggings." . . .

December 24, 1943— . . . The commanding officer of this artillery regiment did what seems to me a pretty smart thing. Since most of the boys can't get to a city to buy souvenirs, he had a Special Service officer go to Capri and buy souvenirs for anybody who wanted them.

Lt. Don H. Poston of Logan, Ohio, who used to be a theater manager in Columbus, is the Special Service officer. He was helped out by Pvt. Joe Pacucci of South Philadelphia. Joe lived for seven years in Naples and didn't go to America until he was twenty, so he knows all the ins and outs over here.

They made two trips to Capri, and they spent over three thousand dollars. They bought seven hundred ladies' cigarette boxes, five hundred cameo brooches, nearly one hundred vivid little paintings on wood, and scores of rings, bracelets, necklaces and other gadgets. These will be wrapped individually and shipped home at the direction of the individual soldier.

Prices went up more than one hundred percent between their first and second trips. This was partly due to inflation induced by the American soldiers' willingness to pay practically any amount for practically anything. Also they've had some sounder justifications—the electric current was off in the cities and Italian craftsmen had to run their jigsaws and do their welding by hand, thus cutting down on production.

All this in the heart of a bitter war. It's a funny world. As one of our gun crew remarked, "The Germans fight for glory, their cities, and their homes, and the Americans fight for souvenirs." . . .

*

This regiment has a lottery on. The grand prize is one bottle of Coca-Cola.

It seems that a few weeks ago Master Sgt. Woodrow Daniel of Jacksonville, Florida, got a bottle of Coke in a package from home. He toyed with the bottle awhile and then decided he had a better idea than the obvious one of drinking it. He'd raffle it off and give the proceeds to some worthy cause. So he started selling chances at two bits apiece.

From there on the thing got big. They decided to adopt an orphan with the money, the orphan to be called the child of some man in this regiment killed in combat. The recipient hasn't been picked yet, but the money is still rolling in.

The receipts have already passed a thousand dollars. Some soldiers are giving as high as ten dollars for a two-bit chance, and practically everybody throws in more than the necessary quarter.

The raffle comes off January 1, and the boys hope the Coca-Cola company will match whatever amount they raise over here. I have no doubt they will. You'll probably be hearing about it in January. . . .*

December 27, 1943—Shells and big guns cost money, but it's better to spend money than lives.

Along that line a bunch of us were sitting around conjecturing, the other day, on how much it costs to kill one German with our artillery.

When you count the great cost of the big modern guns, training the men, all the shipping to get everything over here, and the big shells at fifty dollars each, it surely would cost twenty-five thousand dollars for every German we kill with our shelling.

"Why wouldn't it be better," one fellow said, "just to offer the Germans twenty-five thousand dollars apiece to surrender, and save all the in-between process and the killing? I bet they'd accept it too."

It's a novel theory, but personally I bet they wouldn't. . . .

December 30, 1943— . . . One night we were routed out of our blankets an hour before dawn to put down a barrage preceding an infantry attack.

Every battery for miles around was firing. Batteries were dug in close together and you could get the blasts and concussions from other guns as well as your own. Every gun threw up a fiendish flame when it went off, and the black night was pierced like a sieve with the flashes of hundreds of big guns.

Standing there in the midst of it all, it seemed the most violent and terrifying thing I'd ever been through. Just being on the sending end of it was staggering. I don't know how human sanity could survive the receiving end.

When it was all over and daylight came with a calm and unnatural quiet, a rainbow formed over the mountain ahead of us. It stood out

*By the time Sgt. William de Schneider of Hackensack, New Jersey, won the raffle, the brigade had raised four thousand dollars. The Coca-Cola people didn't match the kitty, but they did kick in another two thousand dollars.

spectacularly against the moist green hillsides and drifting whitish-gray clouds. One end of it was anchored on the mountain slope on our side of the valley, while the other disappeared behind a hill on the German side.

And, as we watched, that latter end of the rainbow became gradually framed by a rising plume of white smoke—set by the shells we had just sent over. The smoke didn't obscure the rainbow. Rather it seemed to rise enfoldingly around it, like honeysuckle climbing a porch column.

Men newly dead lay at the foot of that smoke. We couldn't help thinking what a strange pot of gold such a beautiful rainbow was pointing to.

Notes from a Battered Country

IN ITALY, *December 28, 1943*—The little towns of Italy that have been in the path of this war from Salerno northward are nothing more than great rubble heaps. There is hardly enough left of most of them to form a framework for rebuilding.

When the Germans occupied the towns, we rained artillery on them for days and weeks at a time. Then after we captured a town, the Germans would shell it heavily. They got it from both sides.

Along the road for twenty or thirty miles behind the fighting front, you pass through one demolished town after another. Most of the inhabitants take to the hills after the first shelling. At least they did up here. Some go to live in caves; some go to relatives in the country. A few in every town refuse to leave no matter what happens, and many of them have been killed by the shelling and bombing from both sides.

A countryside is harder to disfigure than a town. You have to look closely, and study in detail, to find the carnage wrought upon the green fields and the rocky hillside. It is there, but it is temporary—like a skinned finger—and time and the rains will heal it. Another year and the countryside will cover its own scars.

If you wander on foot and look closely you will see the signs—the limb of an olive tree broken off, six swollen dead horses in the corner of a field, a strawstack burned down, a chestnut tree blown clear out with its roots by a German bomb, little gray patches of powder burns on the hillside, snatches of broken and abandoned rifles and grenades in the bushes, grain fields patterned with a million crisscrossing ruts from the great trucks crawling frame-deep through the mud, empty gun pits, and countless foxholes, and rubbish-heap stacks of empty C-ration cans, and now and then the lone grave of a German soldier.

These are all there, clear across the country, and yet they are hard to see unless you look closely. A countryside is big, and nature helps fight for it.

*

The apple season is on now, and in the cities and those towns that still exist there are hundreds of little curbside stands selling apples, oranges, and hazelnuts. The apples are to us here what the tangerines were in North Africa a year ago, and the tomatoes and grapes in Sicily last summer.

I haven't been in Italy long enough to really know much about the people, but I do know that the average soldier likes Italy a great deal better than he did Africa. As one soldier said, "They seem more civilized."

Our soldiers are a little contemptuous of the Italians and don't fully trust them, and yet with the typical American tenderheartedness they feel sorry for them, and little by little they are becoming sort of fond of them. They seem to us a pathetic people, not very strong in character but fundamentally kind-hearted and friendly.

A lot of our American-Italian soldiers are taking to the land of their fathers like ducks to water, but not all of them. The other night I was riding in a jeep with an officer and an enlisted man of Italian extraction, both from New York. The officer was talking about the plentitude of girls in Naples, and he said most of the soldiers there had girls.

"Not me," said the driver. "I won't have anything to do with them. The minute they find out I speak Italian they start giving me a sob story about how poor and starved they are and why don't the Americans feed them faster.

"I look at it this way—they've been poor for a long time and it wasn't us that made them poor. They started this war and they've killed plenty of our soldiers, and now that they're whipped they expect us to take care of them. That kind of talk gives me a pain. I tell them to go to hell. I don't like 'em."

*

But our average soldier can't seem to hold animosity very long. And you can't help liking a lot of the Italians. For instance, when I pull back to write for a few days, I stay in a bare, cold room of a huge empty house out in the country. My roommates are Reynolds Packard of the United Press, and Clark Lee of the International News Service.

We have an Italian boy twenty-four years old who takes care of the room. I don't know whether the Army hired him or whether he just walked in and went to work. At any rate, he's there all day and he can't do enough for us. He sweeps the room six times and mops it twice every day.

He boards up blown-out windows, does our washing, and even picks up the scraps of wood and builds a little fire to take the chill off. When he runs out of anything to do he just sits around, always in sight awaiting our pleasure.

His name is Angelo. He smiles every time you look at him. We talk to each other all the time without knowing what we're saying. He admires my two-fingered speed on the typewriter. He comes and looks over my shoulder while I'm writing, which drives me crazy, but he's so eager and kind I can't tell him to go away. It's hard to hate a guy like that.

December 30, 1943—As far as we can observe, the Italian people have more to eat, and more goods, than the French did when we hit North Africa.

There is more in the shops to buy, and the better-off people seem to have a greater variety of food. Of course the poorest people of both countries are pretty close to starvation, but that's not a new experience for them.

The first American troops to hit Naples could buy fine watches and sweaters and carpenter's tools and real silk stockings—I know of one officer who bought fifty pairs for a dollar and a half a pair. Good liquor is now almost exhausted and there is considerable bootlegging of very dangerous booze in the cities. But as time goes on other types of merchandise come out of hiding and go on sale.

It seems the Italians hid a great deal of stuff while the Germans were here. Not that the Germans would steal it, but the German army regulates prices strictly and the German price standard was below what the Italians wanted. So they waited until we came.

They say the Germans didn't go in much for buying souvenirs and jewelry, as we do, but instead bought clothing and food to send home to their families.

Out of their fear of the Germans these people hid strange things in strange places. The other day I talked with a soldier who said he had helped clean out the sewing machine an Italian family had buried in the bottom of the manure pile in their barnyard.

*

Some of our front-line troops, for the first time in many months, are not getting enough cigarets.

In the middle and latter days of Tunisia we were issued up to five or seven packs a week. One outfit I've been with recently said that since hitting Italy they've been averaging only three and a half packs per man per week. Another unit not five miles away was getting more than a carton a week. Nobody seems to know the reason for it.

And speaking of cigarets, the boys wonder why after all these months they must still be cursed with those three obscure brands that nobody likes. Washington could do several million soldiers a favor by either cutting them out entirely or else explaining why they have to be included. . . .

Soldiers of the Super Race

IN ITALY, *January 4, 1944*—The other day I dropped into one of our prisoners-of-war collecting points and picked up a little lore on the super race.

German prisoners these days are on the whole a fairly crummy-looking lot. Most of them are very young. A great many are still in summer uniform and wearing light underwear, although I believe they all have winter overcoats by now.

The German winter uniform is grayish green, similar to the Italian and not nearly as military and snappy-looking as their khaki summer clothes.

The prisoners are much more talkative now than they used to be. It's only the dyed-in-the-wool Nazis who get on their high horse and refuse to talk. The others seem so relieved to be out of the war that they just open their traps and let it run.

Lots of the prisoners are Poles and Austrians, and many who aren't Poles insist they are. They figure they'll get better treatment if we think they are Poles. But they can't fool the examiners, because most of our Army men who examine prisoners can speak German like a native and can tell an accent a mile away. The German officers know we treat prisoners well, but apparently they feed their troops some horror stories to discourage desertion. Many prisoners come in obviously fearful about what we may do to them.

*

It may interest our optimists at home to know that a great many German soldiers captured in Italy still feel that Germany will win the war. That is, they thought so up until the time they were captured. But as they are brought to rear areas they are astounded at the amount of Allied equipment and supplies that they see along the roads and in the fields.

Some of the more sensitive ones have actually been crying when brought to collecting points—overwhelmed by the sudden realization that we've got enough stuff to beat them.

The examiners say that by the time the prisoners reach the rear areas, seventy-five percent of them are doubtful of Germany winning. But that percentage has grown by leaps and bounds on the way back. While they are still in the German lines they are confident.

The examiners often ask prisoners what makes them think they are going to win. Some of them say they'll win because the Allies will collapse. Some think Germany will soon sweep back over Russia. Some talk wishfully about a new secret weapon, due out in the spring, which will bring quick victory.

Others, almost in desperation, say some miracle will happen—they say Germany just can't, just doesn't dare lose the war, and so they won't let themselves think of defeat. As far as I could gather, the German soldiers in Italy are aware of what is happening in Russia and on the bombing front at home. I was surprised that the German censors allowed so much gloom to seep through in soldiers' letters from home. I have heard of a good many letters found on German soldiers from their families in Germany. Some had fright in them, some bitterness. All of them carried an air of war weariness and of devout hope for quick victory.

But I can't honestly say that on the whole the letters showed any general tendency to give up. Some of them rang with the same wordy confidence in victory that our own family letters and editorials carry.

In other words, the Germans don't admit yet that they are whipped.

*

Our prisoner collecting points are staffed, of course, with American soldiers who speak perfect German. Mostly these are men born in Germany who emigrated and became American citizens. They say that often when a prisoner is brought in and hears nothing but good old German flying around the place he is utterly bewildered, and can hardly be made to believe he is in American hands.

I had a talk with two of these examiners of enemy personnel, as they are called. Both had worked all through the previous day and all night too, examining a steady flow of prisoners. It was then three o'clock in the afternoon and they hadn't slept since the morning before.

One of them, a sergeant, was a short, slight man of scholarly appearance who seemed out of place in uniform. He had been a student most of his life. He went to America nine years ago because he sensed that he would likely get into trouble with the Nazis. He lived in America by tutoring.

The other, also a sergeant, was a real-estate man in private life. He was born near Hamburg and went to America when he was twenty-one, which was seventeen years ago. He still talks English with a slight accent—says *v* for *w*. He has just passed his thirty-eighth birthday, and says he doesn't know whether to apply for a discharge or not, but guesses he won't, since his work is pretty important.

He says it's almost impossible for a German prisoner to lie to him, because he knows so much about the German army from having examined thousands of prisoners. He knows every unit, where it is, and who commands it. If a prisoner lies and tells him his company commander is so-and-so, the sergeant says, "Oh no he isn't," and then gives the right name. Which is disconcerting to the prisoner, to say the least.

"Actually I know a great deal more about the German Army than I do about the American Army," he says, "for all I do all day long is sit here behind this desk in this battered old building, talking to Germans, and I never get out to see the American Army."

Mule Packing

AT THE FRONT LINES IN ITALY, *January 5, 1944*—You have been reading in the papers for weeks about the mountain fighting in Italy, and how some of the troops are so high and remote that they have to be supplied by pack mule.

Well, for the last few days I have been hanging around with one of these mule outfits.

There is an average of one mule-packing outfit for every infantry battalion in the mountains. Some are run by Americans, some by Italian soldiers.

The pack outfit I was with supplied a battalion that was fighting on a bald, rocky ridge nearly four thousand feet high. It fought constantly for ten days and nights, and when it finally came down, less than a third of the original men were left.

All through those bitter days every ounce of their supplies had to go up to them on the backs of mules and men. Mules took it the first third of the way. Men took it the last bitter two-thirds, because the trail was too steep even for mules.

The mule skinners of my outfit were Italian soldiers. The human packers were mostly American soldiers.

The Italian mule skinners were from Sardinia. They belonged to a mountain artillery regiment, and thus were experienced in climbing and in handling mules. They were bivouacked in an olive grove alongside a highway at the foot of the mountain.

They made no trips in the daytime, except in emergencies, because most of the trail was exposed to artillery fire. Supplies were brought into the olive grove by truck during the day, and stacked under trees. Just before dusk they would start loading the stuff onto mules.

The Americans who actually managed the supply chain liked to get the mules loaded by dark, because if there was any shelling the Italians instantly disappeared and you never could find them.

There were one hundred fifty-five skinners in this outfit and usually about eighty mules were used each night. Every mule had a man to lead it, and about ten extra men went along to help get mules up if they fell, and to repack any loads that came loose, and to unpack at the top. They could be up and back in less than three hours.

Usually a skinner made just one trip a night, but sometimes in an emergency they made two.

*

On an average night the supplies would run something like this— eighty-five cans of water, one hundred cases of K-ration, ten cases of D-ration, ten miles of telephone wire, twenty-five cases of grenades and rifle and machine-gun ammunition, about one hundred rounds of heavy mortar shells, one radio, two telephones, and four cases of first-aid packets and sulfa drugs.

In addition, the packers would load their pockets with cigarets for the boys on top— also cans of Sterno, so they could heat some coffee once in a while.

Also, during that period, they took up more than five hundred of the heavy combat suits we are issuing to the troops to help keep them warm. They carried up cellophane gas capes for some of the men to use as sleeping bags, and took extra socks for the boys too.

Mail was their most tragic cargo. Every night they would take up sacks of mail, and every night bring a large portion of it back down

—the recipients would have been killed or wounded the day their letters came.

On the long man-killing climb above the end of the mule trail they used anywhere from twenty to three hundred men a night. They rang in cooks, truck drivers, clerks, and anybody else they could lay their hands on.

A lot of stuff was packed up by the fighting soldiers themselves. On the biggest night, when they were building up supplies for an attack, another battalion which was in reserve sent three hundred first-line combat troops to do the packing.

*

The mules again would leave the olive grove in bunches of twenty, starting just after dark. American soldiers were posted within shouting distance of each other all along the trail, to keep the Italians from getting lost in the dark.

Those guides form a little sidelight that I wish everybody in America who thinks he's having a tough time in this war could know about.

The guides were men who had fought all through a long and bitter battle at the top of the mountain. For more than a week they had been far up there, perched behind rocks in the rain and cold, eating cold K-rations, sleeping without blankets, scourged constantly with artillery and mortar shells, fighting and ducking and growing more and more weary, seeing their comrades wounded one by one and taken down the mountain.

Finally sickness and exhaustion overtook many of those who were left, so they were sent back down the mountain under their own power to report to the medics at the bottom and be sent back to a rest camp. It took most of them the better part of a day to get two-thirds of the way down, so sore were their feet and so weary their muscles.

And then—when actually in sight of their haven of rest and peace —they were stopped and pressed into this guide service, because there just wasn't anybody else to do it.

So there they stayed, right on the mountainside, for at least three additional days and nights that I know of, just lying miserably alongside the trail to shout in the darkness and guide the mules.

They still had no blankets to keep them warm, no beds but the rocks. And they did it without complaining. The human spirit is an astounding thing.

Human Supply Trains

AT THE FRONT LINES IN ITALY, *January 7, 1944*—The human packers of supplies to our group high in the Italian mountains interested me much more than the mule trains, partly because their job was much harder and partly because they talk instead of heehawing.

You can get an idea of the magnitude of this human freight service when you realize that in one ten-day period American soldiers packed up this one mountain nearly one hundred thousand pounds of supplies for their battalion. That was just one outfit. The same thing was being duplicated in a dozen or more places during the same time, and it continues to be.

More than half the trail was out in the open, across bare rocks, all under German artillery fire. The top part of the trail was so steep they anchored weights alongside the path for the men to pull themselves upward with.

We tried to hire Italians to do the packing, but after the first day they were never seen again. I heard a report that on one mountain Italian women had volunteered and were carrying up five-gallon cans balanced on their heads, but I was never able to verify this story. I think it's a myth.

Some of the soldiers carry the water cans on their shoulders while others lash them onto packboards. At first some of the packers would cheat a little and pour out some of the precious water when the can became too heavy. But the laws of physics soon stopped this, for with the can only partly filled, the water would slosh around inside and throw the packers off balance and make it doubly hard to walk.

*

From the bottom of the mountain to the top a good walker carrying nothing whatever could make it in three hours. Carrying a heavy load it took longer than that, and yet there were some fantastic exhibitions of human strength on that mountain.

The champion packer in our outfit was Pfc. Lester Scarborough, but he had left the area when I was there and I never did get to see him. He was from somewhere in West Virginia, and he was a miniature Paul Bunyan.

He had been sick and was supposed to be convalescing, yet he could take a full can of water to the top and be clear back down again in two and a half hours, where others took three hours and longer just to get up.

He didn't do this just once, but day after day. He reached the climax of his carrying career when he made four round trips in one day—the fourth one being an emergency dash to the mountaintop to help beat off a German counterattack.

Scarborough is no giant. He is eighteen years old, stands only five feet seven-and-a-half inches, and weighs only one hundred thirty-five pounds. I have never heard of so much strength in such a small package.

*

When I went up the trail my guard was Pfc. Fred Ford of East St. Louis, Illinois. He is a tall, rugged fellow, and he had two weeks of whiskers and grime on his face. He looked sort of ferocious but turned out to be pleasant and friendly.

Like practically all of the regular packers, Ford was a line soldier who had fought for weeks on top and was supposed to be down for a rest. He was a Browning automatic rifleman in an infantry company. And there's a funny thing about that.

"I threw dozens of hand grenades, and even rocks, and I guess I killed plenty of Germans," Ford said. "But I never had a single chance to shoot that automatic rifle."

On the back of his jacket, Ford has printed in purple ink his serial number, the name "Betty," and underneath that "East St. Louis, Ill." Betty is his wife, and she is a chemist in a defense plant.

Ford's feet were all taped up because of blisters, and he walked on his toes to save his heels from rubbing. "Sometimes going up the mountain you get to the point where you know you can't make it," he said, "but somehow you always do." Actually some of them don't. I saw packer after packer report back in at the bottom of the trail saying he "couldn't make her." He's dumped his load and come back down.

A few of these may have been malingerers, but most of them were genuine. The men were exhausted, and their feet were broken out, and infirmities such as arthritis, hernia or heart weakness would leap to the fore on those man-killing climbs.

*

When we started back down, German shells began dropping quite a ways behind us.

"If I get to going too fast for you, just yell," Ford said. "When they start shelling we practically fly down the mountain. We don't stop for nothing."

But I didn't have any pressing business engagements along the way to detain us, so Ford and I flew down the mountainside together, going so fast the rocks we kicked loose couldn't even keep up with us.

January 8, 1944—You've heard of trench mouth and athlete's foot, but now another occupational disease of warfare has sprung up on both sides here in the Italian war. It is called "trench foot." The Germans as well as the Americans have it. It was well known in the last war.

Trench foot comes from a man's feet being wet and cold for long periods and from his not taking off his shoes often enough. In the mountains the soldiers sometimes go for two weeks and longer without ever having their shoes off and without ever being dry.

With trench foot the tissues gradually seem to go dead, and sores break out. It is almost the same as the circulation being stopped and the flesh dying. In extreme cases gangrene occurs. We have had cases where amputation was necessary. And in other cases the soldier won't be able to walk again for six months. . . .

*

The fighting on the mountaintop sometimes almost reaches the caveman stage. The Americans and Germans are frequently so close that they actually throw rocks at each other.

They use up many times as many hand grenades as we have had in any other phase of the Mediterranean war. And you have to be pretty close when you throw hand grenades.

Rocks play a big part in the mountain war. You hid behind rocks, you throw rocks, you sleep in rock crevices, and you even get killed by flying rocks.

When an artillery shell bursts on a loose rock surface, rock fragments are thrown for many yards. In one battalion fifteen percent of the casualties are from flying rocks.

Also, now and then an artillery burst from a steep hillside will loosen big boulders which go leaping and bounding down the mountainside for thousands of yards. The boys say such a rock sounds like a windstorm coming down the mountainside. . . .

*

When soldiers come down the mountain out of battle they are dirty, grimy, unshaven and weary. They look ten years older than they are. They don't smile much.

But the human body and mind recover rapidly. A couple of days down below and they begin to pick up. It's funny to see a bunch of combat soldiers after they've shaved and washed up. As one said: "We all look sick after we've cleaned up, we're so white."

It's funny to hear them talk. One night in our cowshed I heard one of them say how he was going to keep his son out of the next war.

"As soon as I get home I'm going to put ten-pound weights in his hands and make him jump off the garage roof, to break down his arches," he said. "I'm going to feed him a little ground glass to give him a bad stomach, and I'm going to make him read by candlelight all the time to ruin his eyes. When I get through with him he'll be double-4 double-F."

Another favorite expression of soldiers just out of combat runs like this:

"Well, let's go down to Naples and start a second draft." Meaning let's conscript all the clerks, drivers, waiters, M.P.'s, office workers and so on who flood any big city near a fighting area, and send them up in the mountains to fight.

The funny thing is they wouldn't have to draft many soldiers down there. A simple call for volunteers would be enough, I really believe. One of the paradoxes of war is that those in the rear want to get up into the fight, while those in the lines want to get out.

The following is the most anthologized of Pyle's war pieces. It stands among a handful of classic World War II newspaper articles. Its terse expression of emotion and repetition of descriptive detail recall some of Ernest Hemingway's World War I pieces.

The Death of Captain Waskow

AT THE FRONT LINES IN ITALY, *January 10, 1944*—In this war I have known a lot of officers who were loved and respected by the soldiers under them. But never have I crossed the trail of any man as beloved as Capt. Henry T. Waskow of Belton, Texas.

Capt. Waskow was a company commander in the 36th Division. He had led his company since long before it left the States. He was very young, only in his middle twenties, but he carried in him a sincerity and gentleness that made people want to be guided by him.

"After my own father, he came next," a sergeant told me.

"He always looked after us," a soldier said. "He'd go to bat for us every time."

"I've never knowed him to do anything unfair," another one said.

I was at the foot of the mule trail the night they brought Capt. Waskow's body down. The moon was nearly full at the time, and you could see far up the trail, and even part way across the valley below. Soldiers made shadows in the moonlight as they walked.

Dead men had been coming down the mountain all evening, lashed onto the backs of mules. They came lying belly-down across the wooden pack-saddles, their heads hanging down on the left side of the mule, their stiffened legs sticking out awkwardly from the other side, bobbing up and down as the mule walked.

The Italian mule-skinners were afraid to walk beside dead men, so Americans had to lead the mules down that night. Even the Americans were reluctant to unlash and lift off the bodies at the bottom, so an officer had to do it himself, and ask others to help.

The first one came early in the morning. They slid him down from the mule and stood him on his feet for a moment, while they got a new grip. In the half light he might have been merely a sick man standing there, leaning on the others. Then they laid him on the ground in the shadow of the low stone wall alongside the road.

I don't know who that first one was. You feel small in the presence of dead men, and ashamed at being alive, and you don't ask silly questions.

We left him there beside the road, that first one, and we all went back into the cowshed and sat on water cans or lay on the straw, waiting for the next batch of mules.

Somebody said the dead soldier had been dead for four days, and then nobody said anything more about it. We talked soldier talk for an hour or more. The dead man lay all alone outside in the shadow of the low stone wall.

Then a soldier came into the cowshed and said there were some more bodies outside. We went out into the road. Four mules stood there, in the moonlight, in the road where the trail came down off the mountain. The soldiers who led them stood there waiting. "This one is Captain Waskow," one of them said quietly.

Two men unlashed his body from the mule and lifted it off and laid it in the shadow beside the low stone wall. Other men took the other bodies off. Finally there were five lying end to end in a long row, alongside the road. You don't cover up dead men in the combat zone. They just lie there in the shadows until somebody else comes after them.

The unburdened mules moved off to their olive orchard. The men in the road seemed reluctant to leave. They stood around, and gradually one by one I could sense them moving close to Capt. Waskow's body. Not so much to look, I think, as to say something in finality to him, and to themselves. I stood close by and I could hear.

One soldier came and looked down, and he said out loud, "God damn it." That's all he said, and then he walked away. Another one came. He said, "God damn it to hell anyway." He looked down for a few last moments, and then he turned and left.

Another man came; I think he was an officer. It was hard to tell officers from men in the half light, for all were bearded and grimy dirty. The man looked down into the dead captain's face, and then he spoke directly to him, as though he were alive. He said: "I'm sorry, old man."

Then a soldier came and stood beside the officer, and bent over, and he too spoke to his dead captain, not in a whisper but awfully tenderly, and he said:

"I sure am sorry, sir."

Then the first man squatted down, and he reached down and took the dead hand, and he sat there for a full five minutes, holding the dead hand in his own and looking intently into the dead face, and he never uttered a sound all the time he sat there.

And finally he put the hand down, and then reached up and gently straightened the points of the captain's shirt collar, and then he sort of rearranged the tattered edges of his uniform around the wound. And then he got up and walked away down the road in the moonlight, all alone.

After that the rest of us went back into the cowshed, leaving the five dead men lying in a line, end to end, in the shadow of the low stone wall. We lay down on the straw in the cowshed, and pretty soon we were all asleep.

Pyle's profile of cartoonist Bill Mauldin called the young artist's work to the attention of Pyle's editor, Lee Miller, who helped arrange for its syndication stateside through United Feature, which distributed Pyle's column.

Bill Mauldin, Cartoonist

IN ITALY, *January 15, 1944*—Sgt. Bill Mauldin appears to us over here to be the finest cartoonist the war has produced. And that's not merely because his cartoons are funny, but because they are also terribly grim and real.

Mauldin's cartoons aren't about training-camp life, which you at home are best acquainted with. They are about the men in the line —the tiny percentage of our vast army who are actually up there in that other world doing the dying. His cartoons are about the war.

Mauldin's central cartoon character* is a soldier, unshaven, unwashed, unsmiling. He looks more like a hobo than like your son. He looks, in fact, exactly like a doughfoot who has been in the lines for two months. And that isn't pretty.†

Mauldin's cartoons in a way are bitter. His work is so mature that I had pictured him as a man approaching middle age. Yet he is only twenty-two, and he looks even younger. He himself could never have raised the heavy black beard of his cartoon dogface. His whiskers are soft and scant, his nose is upturned good-naturedly, and his eyes have a twinkle.

His maturity comes simply from a native understanding of things, and from being a soldier himself for a long time. He has been in the Army three and a half years.

*

Bill Mauldin was born in Mountain Park, New Mexico. He now calls Phoenix home base, but we of New Mexico could claim him without much resistance on his part.

Bill has drawn ever since he was a child. He always drew pictures of the things he wanted to grow up to be, such as cowboys and soldiers, not realizing that what he really wanted to become was a man who draws pictures.

He graduated from high school in Phoenix at seventeen, took a year at the Academy of Fine Arts in Chicago, and at eighteen was in the Army. He did sixty-four days on KP duty in his first four months. That fairly cured him of a lifelong worship of uniforms.

Mauldin belongs to the 45th Division. Their record has been a fine one, and their losses have been heavy. Mauldin's typical grim cartoon soldier is really a 45th Division infantryman, and he is one who has truly been through the mill.

Mauldin was detached from straight soldier duty after a year in the infantry, and put to work on the division's weekly paper. His true war cartoons started in Sicily and have continued on through Italy, gradually gaining recognition. Capt. Bob Neville, *Stars and Stripes* editor, shakes his head with a veteran's admiration and says of Mauldin: "He's got it. Already he's the outstanding cartoonist of the war."

*

*There were two central characters in Mauldin's cartoons, Willie and Joe.

†When Mauldin's cartoons were first syndicated stateside, some readers objected to the scruffy appearance of Willie and Joe. Mauldin, however, continued his realistic portrayal of men in the lines.

Mauldin works in a cold, dark little studio in the back of *Stars and Stripes'* Naples office. He wears silver-rimmed glasses when he works. His eyes used to be good, but he damaged them in his early Army days by drawing for too many hours at night with poor light.

He averages about three days out of ten at the front, then comes back and draws up a large batch of cartoons. If the weather is good he sketches a few details at the front. But the weather is usually lousy.

"You don't need to sketch details anyhow," he says. "You come back with a picture of misery and cold and danger in your mind and you don't need any more details than that."

His cartoon in *Stars and Stripes* is headed "Up Front . . . By Mauldin." The other day some soldier wrote in a nasty letter asking what the hell did Mauldin know about the front.

Stars and Stripes printed the letter. Beneath it in italics they printed a short editor's note: "Sgt. Bill Mauldin received the Purple Heart for wounds received while serving in Italy with Pvt. Blank's own regiment."

That's known as telling 'em.

*

Bill Mauldin is a rather quiet fellow, a little above medium size. He smokes and swears a little and talks frankly and pleasantly. He is not eccentric in any way.

Even though he's just a kid he's a husband and father. He married in 1942 while in camp in Texas, and his son was born last August 20 while Bill was in Sicily. His wife and child are living in Phoenix now. Bill carries pictures of them in his pocketbook.

Unfortunately for you and Mauldin both, the American public has no opportunity to see his daily drawings. But that isn't worrying him. He realizes this is his big chance.

After the war he wants to settle again in the Southwest, which he and I love. He wants to go on doing cartoons of these same guys who are now fighting in the Italian hills, except that by then they'll be in civilian clothes and living as they should be.

Pyle moved from the ground forces to the Air Corps, which afforded him respite from the rigors of front-line infantry life. Much as he enjoyed the break, Pyle told his editor that the Corps was "colorless and anticlimactic" compared with the infantry.

WITH THE AIR FORCE
IN ITALY, *January 18, 1944*—It has been more than a year since I last spent any time with our Air Forces overseas. So now for a little while I'll try to tell you what a gigantic thing our "air" has become in this theater.

In the past year I have written so much about the ground forces that they have become an obsession with me. They live and die so miserably and they do it with such determined acceptance that your admiration for them blinds you to the rest of the war.

To any individual the war is seldom any bigger than the space of a few hundred yards on each side of him. All the war in the world is concentrated down into his own personal fight. To me all the war of the world has seemed to be borne by the few thousand front-line soldiers here, destined merely by chance to suffer and die for the rest of us.

All over the world other millions are fighting too, many of them under conditions as wretched as our infantry faces in Italy. But it is easy to forget them in your intentness upon your own hundred yards.

But now, remembering once again, this column will do its stuff with the Air Forces. We may break it up with a short nostalgic jump back to the infantry now and then, but on the whole for the next few weeks we'll be learning about the flying men.

*

You have to make some psychological adjustments when you switch from the infantry to the Air Forces. The association with death is on a different basis. You approach death rather decently in the Air Forces.

You die well-fed and clean-shaven, if that's any comfort. You're at the front only a few hours of the day, instead of day and night for months on end. In the evening you come back to something approximating a home and fireside.

In the Air Forces you still have some semblance of an orderly life, even though you may be living in tents. But in the infantry you must become half beast in order to survive.

Here is the subtle difference between the two: when I'm with the infantry I never shave, for anyone clean-shaven is an obvious outsider and apt to be abused. But in the Air Forces if you go for three days without shaving you get to feeling self-conscious, like a bum among nice people, so you shave in order to conform.

*

I'm now with a dive-bomber squadron of the 12th Air Force Command. There are about fifty officers and two hundred fifty enlisted men in a squadron.

They all live, officers and men too, in a big apartment house that the Italian government built to house war workers and their families. It looks like one of our own government housing projects.

It is out in the country at the edge of a small town. The Germans demolished the big nearby factories beyond, but left the homes intact. When our squadron moved into this building it was their first time under a roof in six months of combat.

Now our airmen have wood stoves in their rooms, they sleep in sleeping bags on folding cots, they have shelves to put their things on, they have electric light, they eat at tables, sitting on stools, and have an Italian boy to clear the dishes away.

They have an Italian barber, and their clothes are clean and pressed. They have a small recreation room with soldier-drawn murals on the walls. They can go to a nearby town of an evening and see American movies, in theaters taken over by the Army. They can have dates with nurses. They can play cards. They can read by good light in a warm room.

Don't get the wrong impression. Their life is not luxurious. At home we wouldn't consider it adequate. It has the security of walls and doors, but it is a dog's life at that.

The toilets don't work, so you have to flush them with a tin hat full of water dipped out of an always filled bathtub. The lights go out frequently and you have to use candles.

It's tough getting up two hours before daylight for a dawn mission. The floors are cold, hard tile. There are no rugs. Some of the windows are still blown out.

*

And yet, as the airmen unblushingly admit, their life is paradise compared with the infantry. They are fully appreciative of what the infantry goes through. There has recently been a program of sending pilots up to the front as liaison officers for a few days at a time. They come back and tell the others, so that the whole Air Corps may know the ground problem and how their brothers are living up there in the mud.

It has resulted in an eagerness to help out those ground kids that is actually touching. On days when the squadron dive-bombs the Germans just ahead of our own lines it isn't as academic to them as it used to be. Now the pilots are thinking of how much that special bomb may help the American boys down below them.

It is teamwork with a soul in it, and we're fighting better than ever before.

Dive Bombing

IN ITALY, *January 19, 1944*—The dive bomber has never been fully accepted by the Allied armies. The British have always been against it—they call the German Stuka a vastly overrated instrument of war—and America has more or less followed suit.

Our Navy has used the dive bomber to good effect in the Pacific. But in the Mediterranean this weapon didn't show up until the beginning of Sicily, and it has never been built up in great numbers.

In the dive-bomber groups over here we have several hundred pilots and mechanics who believe with a fanatical enthusiasm that the dive bomber is the most wonderful machine produced in this war. I don't want to enter into the argument, when I'm in no position to know, but regardless I'm going to write a little about these dive-bomber boys. For they are probably the most spectacular part of our Air Forces.

The function of the dive bomber is to work in extremely close support of our own infantry. For instance, suppose there is a German gun position just over a hill which our troops cannot get at with our guns and which is holding us up.

They call on the dive bombers and give them the location. Within an hour, and sometimes much quicker, they come screaming out of the sky right on top of that gun and blow it up.

They can do the same to bunched enemy troops, bridges, tank columns, convoys, or ammunition dumps. Because of their great accuracy they can bomb much closer to our own troops than other planes would dare. Most of the time they work less than a thousand yards ahead of our front lines, and they have had missions much closer than that.

*

The group I am with has been in combat six months. During that time they have flown ten thousand sorties, fired more than a million rounds of fifty-caliber ammunition, and dropped three million pounds of bombs. That's more than the entire 8th Air Force in England dropped in its first year of operation.

Our dive bombers are known as A-36 Invaders. Actually they are nothing more than the famous P-51 Mustang equipped with diving brakes. For a long time they didn't have any name at all, and then one day in Sicily one of the pilots of the squadron said:

"Why don't we call them Invaders, since we're invading?"

The name was carried home in newspaper dispatches, and today even the company that makes them calls them Invaders.

The pilot who originated the name was Lt. Robert B. Welsh of Felt, Idaho. He has since completed his allotted missions and gone back to the States. His younger brother is now in the same squadron as a replacement pilot.

The P-51 Mustang is a wonderful fighter. But when you transform it into an A-36 by the addition of diving brakes it becomes a grand dive bomber as well.

The brakes are necessary because of the long straight-down dive on the target. A regular fighter would get to going too fast. The controls would become rigid, and the pilot would have to start pulling out of his dive so early that he'd have to drop his bombs from too great a height.

These boys dive about eight thousand feet before dropping their bombs. Without brakes they would ordinarily build up to around seven hundred miles an hour in such a dive, but the brakes hold them to about three hundred ninety. The brakes are nothing but metal flaps in the form of griddles about two feet long and eight or ten inches high. They lie flat on the wings during ordinary flights.

*

The dive bombers approach their target in formation. When the leader has made sure he has spotted the target he wiggles his wings, raises his diving brakes, rolls on his back, then noses over and down he goes. The next man behind follows almost instantly.

They follow one right after the other, not more than one hundred fifty feet apart. There's no danger of their running over the next one ahead, for the brakes hold them all at the same speed.

They're so close together that as many as twenty dive bombers have been seen in a dive all at once, making a straight line up into the sky like a gigantic stream of water.

At about four thousand feet the pilot releases his bombs. Then he starts his pull-out. The strain is terrific, and all the pilots "blackout" a little bit. It lasts only four or five seconds, and is not a complete blackout. It is more a heaviness in the head and a darkness before the eyes, the pilots say.

Once straightened out of the dive, they go right on down to "the deck," which means flying close to the ground. For by this time everything in the vicinity that can shoot has opened up, and the safest place to be is right down close, streaking for home as fast as they can go.

January 20, 1944— . . . Maj. Ed Bland, a squadron leader, was telling me about coming suddenly over a hilltop one day and finding a German truck right in his gunsights.

Now it's the natural human impulse, when you see a plane come upon you, to dive for the ditch. But the German gunner in this truck swung a gun around and started shooting at Bland. German and American tracer bullets were streaming back and forth in the same groove in opposite directions, almost hitting each other. The German never stopped firing until Bland's six machine guns suddenly chewed the truck into complete disintegration. . . .

January 21, 1944— . . . The planes have to fly in constant "evasive action," which means going right, going left, going up, going down, all the time they are over enemy territory. If they flew in a straight line for as long as fifteen seconds, the Germans would pick them off.

A pilot sits up there and figures this way: "Right now they've got a bearing on me. In a certain number of seconds they'll shoot and in a few more seconds the shell will be up here. It's up to me to be somewhere else then."

But he also knows that the Germans know he will turn, and that consequently they will send up shells to one side or the other or above or below his present position.

Thus he must never make exactly the same move two days in a row. By constantly turning, climbing, ducking, he makes a calculated hit almost impossible. His worst danger is just flying by chance right into a shell burst.

I asked one of the pilots, "Why wouldn't it be a good idea to fool them about once every two weeks by just flying straight ahead for a while?"

He said, "Because they've got that figured out too. They always keep the air dead ahead of you full of shells, just in case." . . .

*

It isn't the heavy flak up above or the medium flak on the way down that worries the pilots as much as the small-arms fire from the ground after they've finished their dive.

If you'd ever been in a raid on either side, you'd understand. I know that when German planes come over our lines the whole valley for miles and miles becomes one vast fountain of flying lead with bullets going up by the thousands. It's actually like a water spray, filling the air as far as you can see.

Our dive-bomber pilots have to fly through this every day. They "hit the deck" the minute they've pulled out of their bombing dive, for it's harder to see a plane that is close to the ground. Also, when they're almost down to earth the Germans firing at them may shoot their own troops—but even that doesn't stop them, they keep banging away.

The pilots say it's the accidental bullet they're most afraid of. They say that nine times out of ten it's some goof standing out in the field shooting wildly into the air who gets a hit.

When a big push is on, our dive-bomber pilots sometimes have to go through this sort of thing three times in a single day. So you see that, although they live well when at home base, they aren't on any picnic when they go out to work.

January 25, 1944— . . . The turnover of pilots is high in any combat outfit—partly due to casualties but mainly due to the system of relieving pilots after a certain number of missions. It would be unusual for a combat airman to be overseas more than a year, at the present rate.

Take this squadron of Invader dive bombers, for instance. They came into combat just six months ago, yet today only three of the original fifty pilots are left. Twelve have been casualties, and the rest have finished their missions and gone home. The three originals will be homeward bound in a few days.

These dive-bomber boys have compiled some statistics about their operations. They find that a new pilot, starting in to build up the required missions for going home, has about a seventy-five percent chance of coming through safely, and if shot down he has almost a fifty-fifty chance of becoming a prisoner. . . .

January 27, 1944— . . . One night I went into a little Italian town with some pilots to see the movie *This Is the Army.* The Air Forces had taken over a local theater, and as long as you were in uniform all you had to do was to walk in and sit down. About a third of the audience were pilots and the rest mechanics. I couldn't help but be interested in their reaction to the picture. On the whole they applauded, but every time the action got a little gooey or mushily patriotic, you could hear a combination boo and groan go through the audience. Soldiers at the front can't stomach flag-waving back home. . . .

February 1, 1944—One night I was gossiping in a tent with a bunch of dive-bomber pilots, and one of them who was sitting next to me said in a sudden offhand way:

"I wonder what those Germans in that truck are doing tonight?"

He was referring to a truck he had strafed and blown up the afternoon before. Such things sometimes sort of get under their skins. The pilots like to go on a hunt, and it's thrilling to sweep down and shoot hell out of something, the same as it is to shoot a running deer, but underneath they don't relish the idea of killing people who aren't trying to kill them.

The pilot said to himself, "Some of them aren't doing anything tonight," and then the subject was changed. . . .

*

The other night I was talking with a very swell lieutenant who said frankly that although he liked planes and liked to fly, he was scared of combat. He admitted that he had balled up a good many missions, and he said he was absolutely no good as a combat pilot.

If all this gives you the impression that pilots are worried to death and go around with long faces, then I've committed a crime. The pilot I've just spoken of is one of the happy-go-lucky type. I suppose pilots as a class are the gayest people in the Army. When they come back from a mission they're usually full of high spirits. And when they sit around together of an evening nine-tenths of their conversation is exuberant and full of howling jokes. There is nothing whatsoever of the grimness in their conduct that you get in the infantry while it is in the line. . . .

Back to the 34th Division

IN ITALY, *February 14, 1944*—For several days I've been living with an infantry company* of the 34th Division. The 34th is the oldest division on this side of the Atlantic. It has been away from home two full years.

Two years is a long time overseas, even if you do nothing but travel around and work hard. But when in addition you fill two years with campaign after bitter campaign, a division of men becomes eventually wise and worn and old, like a much-read book or a cottage that wears its aging stone stoutly, ignoring the patchwork of new concrete that holds it together.

*Company E, 168th Infantry. Because of censorship, Pyle refers to it as "X" company in later columns.

Today out of any front-line rifle company of around two hundred men in the 34th, you find usually fewer than a dozen men who came overseas with the division originally. In one battalion not a single one of the original officers is left.

That doesn't mean they've all been killed, but it does mean that through casualties of all sorts, plus sickness and transfer and some small rotation back to the States, a division has almost a complete turnover in two years of fighting. Only its number remains the same. But even a number can come to have character and life, to those who are intimate with its heritage. I was with the 34th as long ago as June of 1942, in Ireland, and I have a feeling about it.

*

I came to the regimental command post in a jeep after dark one night.

Regimental handed me down to battalion, and battalion on down to the company I was to stay with. They were bivouacked for the moment in an olive grove, with their company command post in a stone Italian farmhouse—the first time their CP had been inside walls since they hit Italy five months ago.

The company commander is Lt. John J. Sheehy of New York City. The division was originally all Iowa and Minnesota men, but now you'll find men from everywhere. The Iowans are the veterans, however, and they still stand out.

Jack Sheehy is tall and thin and quite young, and of course he's Irish. In the regiment he is considered pretty remarkable. Any time you mention him among higher officers, they nod and say, "Yes, Sheehy is a case."

I don't know exactly what causes this, but I gather from innuendo that he is addicted to using his noggin in spectacular ways in the pinches, and that he fears neither German soldiers nor American brass hats. He is an extremely likable and respected company commander.

Lt. Sheehy used to be a clerk for American Airlines in New York. He says that after the war he's going into salesmanship of some kind, because he figures his gift of gab will carry him through—which surprised me, because during all the time I was with him he was far from garrulous, but actually very kind and reserved.

I've never seen a man prouder of his company than Lt. Sheehy, and the men in it are proud, too. I've been around war long enough to know that nine-tenths of morale is pride in your outfit and confidence in your leaders and fellow fighters.

A lot of people have morale confused with the desire to fight. I don't know of one soldier out of ten thousand who wants to fight. They certainly don't in my company. The old-timers are sick to death of battle, and the new replacements are scared to death of it. And yet the company goes on into battle, and it is a proud company.

A Lull in the Lines

IN ITALY, *February 16, 1944*—When I joined "X" company it was in one of those lulls that sometimes come in war. The company was still "in the lines," as you say, but not actually fighting.

They had taken a town a few days before, and since then had been merely waiting for the next attack. We moved forward twice while I was with them, always in night marches, and on the last move the company went into battle again. These intervals give the soldiers time to restore their gear and recuperate their spirits. Usually they come weeks apart.

A regiment will be bivouacked over an area a mile or more square, with the men in foxholes under olive trees, and the company, battalion and regimental command posts set up in farmhouses.

*

In areas recently passed over by battles the towns have been largely evacuated—in fact, practically all of them are mere heaps of rubble from bombing and shelling—and no stores are open. There is little chance of buying wine.

But this regiment had gone sniffing into cellars in a depopulated town and turned up with all kinds of exotic liquors which they dug out of the rubble.

The result was that you could make a tour on foot of a dozen company and battalion command posts around the perimeter of the town and in nearly every one discover a shelf full of the finest stuff imaginable.

It was ironic to walk into a half-demolished building and find a command post set up in the remaining rooms, with soldiers sitting in front of a crackling fireplace, and at ten o'clock in the morning, with enemy shell bursts making the old building tremble, be offered your choice of cherry, peach, apricot and half a dozen other varieties of fine brandy out of fancy bottles. But I must say a windfall like that doesn't come often.

*

Our company command post consisted of one table, one chair and one telephone, in a second-story room of a stone farmhouse. In most of these two-story farmhouses the stairway goes up the outside. You hang blankets at the door for blackout, and burn candles.

Five platoons of the company were bivouacked in olive orchards in a circle around the farmhouse, the farthest foxhole being not more than two hundred yards away. Some soldiers just dug regular foxholes and put their blankets at the bottom. During the day they would sit at the edge of the hole cleaning guns, writing letters or just talking, and at night they would sleep at the bottom of the foxhole. Others dug more elaborate places.

I've always been struck by the work some men will put into a home as temporary as a foxhole. I've been with men in this company who would arrive at a new bivouac at midnight, dig a hole just big enough to sleep in the rest of the night, then work all the next day on a deep, elaborate, roofed-over foxhole, even though they knew they had to leave the same evening and never see that hole again.

In the olive groves throughout this bitter Cassino area there are pitiful testimonials to close-up warfare. In our grove I don't believe there was a single one of the thousands of old trees that hadn't at least one bullet scar in it. Knocked-off branches littered the ground. Some trees were cut clear down by shells. The stone walls had shell gaps every so often, and every standing thing was bullet-pocked.

You couldn't walk fifty feet without hitting a shell or bomb crater. Every house and shed had at least a corner knocked off.

*

Some soldiers were sleeping in the haymow of a stone barn. They had to get up into it via a stepladder they had pieced together, because the steps had been blown away. Between the house and the barn ran a footpath on a sort of ledge. Our men had been caught there that first night by a tank in the valley below firing at them point-blank. One soldier had been instantly killed, and as we walked along the path a few days later his steel helmet was still lying there, bloody and riddled with holes. Another soldier had a leg blown off, but lived.

The men were telling me of a replacement—a green soldier—who joined the company the day after, when this soldier's leg was still lying in the path. The new soldier stopped and stared at it and kept on staring.

The other boys watched him from a distance. They said that when anyone came along the path the new man would move off to one side so as not to be seen. But as soon as they would pass, he would come back and stare, sort of hypnotized. He never said anything about it afterwards, and nobody said anything to him. Somebody buried the leg the next day.

More Soldier Than Civilian

IN ITALY, *February 17, 1944*—Of the nearly two hundred men who came overseas in the company I'm with now, only eight are left. In those eight men you will find everything a military man would like to have in a soldier.

They have all been in the Army nearly three years. They have been away from America two years. They have served in Northern Ireland, Scotland, England, Algeria, Tunisia and Italy. They have been at it so long they have become truly more soldier than civilian.

Their life consists wholly and only of war, for they are and always have been front-line infantrymen. They have survived because the fates have been kind to them, certainly, but also because they have become hard and immensely wise in the animal-like ways of self-preservation.

None of them likes war. They all want go home, but they have been at it so long they know how to take care of themselves and to lead others. Every company is built around a little group like them.

I wouldn't go so far as to say these boys haven't changed since they left America. Of course they have changed—they have had to. And yet when I sit and talk with them they seem just like ordinary humans back home.

*

Take Sgt. Paul Allumbaugh, for instance. He's an Iowa boy and a great soldier, yet so quiet, kind and good-natured you can't imagine him ever killing anybody. He's only twenty-one, after these years of fighting, and when shaved and cleaned up after battle he doesn't look a bit older. At first he looks too small to be a soldier, but then you realize how well built he is.

He is good-looking, and his face is the kind you instinctively like.

Sgt. Allumbaugh's nickname is Tag. He has gone through the whole thing so far without a wound, although narrow escapes have been countless. He had one bullet scratch across his hand and another across a foot. These are not counted as wounds.

Tag served for three months in the British Commandos when volunteers were asked for out of his company in Scotland. He fought with them in Africa too, then came back with his buddies—and his relatives. At one time this outfit was practically the Allumbaugh family, with Tag and his brother and five cousins in it, all from Shenandoah, Iowa. All seven of them are still alive, but their fates have been varied.

Tag's brother Donald was captured a year ago and is still a German prisoner. Two cousins were captured also, but one of these has escaped. Of the remaining three, one is soon going home on rotation, one is in the engineers and one is still in this division.

While my company was in its brief olive-grove bivouac, Tag was living in a captured German dugout with his close buddy, Sgt. William Knobbs of Keokuk, Iowa. They had such a battle getting the place that they decided to live in it for a while.

Sgt. Knobbs' nickname is Knobby, and he too has had some close shaves. Once a bullet went right through his helmet, across the top of his head. It burned the hair off in a groove just as though you had shaved it, yet it never broke the skin. Knobby said his wife has never known he has been in combat. Then he corrected himself. He said actually she did know, through friends, but not from him. He has never once written her of any of his experiences or said he was in battle.

*

Some of the remarks the men recount in fun are pathetically revealing and touching. Take the thing Sgt. Jack Pierson said one day in battle. Jack Pierson is a wonderful guy. He was in the Commandos with Tag. He's almost a Sgt. Quirt,* except that he's good-looking, smart and friendly. But he is tough. As the other men say, "Jack is really a rough man. He would be rough even back home."

He comes from Sidney, Iowa. He is older than most of the others. For many years he ran a pile-driver doing construction work along the Missouri and Mississippi rivers. He calls himself a river rat. The boys here call him a "one-man Army." He has been wounded once.

Jack is married and has three children. He has a girl nine, a boy seven, and then he has Junior, who is going on two and whom Jack has never seen. Jack pretty much dotes on Junior, and everybody in the company knows about Junior and knows how badly Jack wants to see him.

Well, one day in battle they were having it tough. There were rifle fire, mortars and hand grenades all around, and soldiers on both sides getting knocked off like flies. Tag Allumbaugh was lying within shouting distance of where Jack was pinned down, and he yelled over:

*Slang for an excessively hard-driving leader.

"How you doin', Jack."

And then this man who was hard in peacetime and is hard in war called back a resigned answer that expresses in a general way every combat soldier's pathetic reason for wanting to live and hating to die.

He called back—and he wasn't joking—and he said:

"It don't look like I'm gonna get to see Junior."

BUCK EVERSOLE: ONE OF THE GREAT MEN OF THE WAR

IN ITALY, *February 21, 1944*—The company commander said to me, "Every man in this company deserves the Silver Star."

We walked around in the olive grove where the men of the company were sitting on the edges of their foxholes, talking or cleaning their gear.

"Let's go over here," he said. "I want to introduce you to my personal hero."

I figured that the lieutenant's own "personal hero," out of a whole company of men who deserved the Silver Star, must be a real soldier indeed.

Then the company commander introduced me to Sgt. Frank Eversole, who shook hands sort of timidly and said, "Pleased to meet you," and then didn't say any more.

I could tell by his eyes and by his slow and courteous speech when he did talk that he was a Westerner. Conversation with him was sort of hard, but I didn't mind his reticence for I know how Westerners like to size people up first.

The sergeant wore a brown stocking cap on the back of his head. His eyes were the piercing kind. I noticed his hands—they were outdoor hands, strong and rough.

Later in the afternoon I came past his foxhole again, and we sat and talked a little while alone. We didn't talk about the war, but mainly about our West, and just sat and made figures on the ground with sticks as we talked.

We got started that way, and in the days that followed I came to know him well. He is to me, and to all those with whom he serves, one of the great men of the war.

*

Frank Eversole's nickname is "Buck." The other boys in the company sometimes call him "Buck Overshoes," simply because Eversole sounds a bit like "overshoes."

Buck was a cowboy before the war. He was born in the little town of Missouri Valley, Iowa, and his mother still lives there. But Buck went West on his own before he was sixteen, and ever since has worked as a ranch hand. He is twenty-eight, and unmarried.

He worked a long time around Twin Falls, Idaho, and then later down in Nevada. Like so many cowboys, he made the rodeos in season. He was never a star or anything. Usually he just rode the broncs out of the chute for pay—seven-fifty a ride. Once he did win a fine saddle. He has ridden at Cheyenne and the other big rodeos.

Like any cowboy, he loves animals. Here in Italy one afternoon Buck and some other boys were pinned down inside a one-room stone shed by terrific German shellfire. As they sat there, a frightened mule came charging through the door. There simply wasn't room inside for men and mule both, so Buck got up and shooed him out the door. Thirty feet from the door a direct hit killed the mule. Buck has always felt guilty about it.

Another time Buck ran onto a mule that was down and crying in pain from a bad shell wound. Buck took his .45 and put a bullet through its head. "I wouldn't have shot him except he was hurtin' so," Buck says.

*

Buck Eversole has the Purple Heart and two Silver Stars for bravery. He is cold and deliberate in battle. His commanders depend more on him than on any other man. He has been wounded once, and had countless narrow escapes. He has killed many Germans.

He is the kind of man you instinctively feel safer with than with other people. He is not helpless like most of us. He is practical. He can improvise, patch things, fix things.

His grammar is the unschooled grammar of the plains and the soil. He uses profanity, but never violently. Even in the familiarity of his own group his voice is always low. He is such a confirmed soldier by now that he always says "sir" to any stranger. It is impossible to conceive of his doing anything dishonest.

After the war Buck will go back West to the land he loves. He wants to get a little place and feed a few head of cattle, and be independent.

"I don't want to be just a ranch hand no more," he says. "It's all right and I like it all right, but it's a rough life and it don't get you nowhere. When you get a little older you kinda like a place of your own."

Buck Eversole has no hatred for Germans. He kills because he's trying to keep alive himself. The years roll over him and the war becomes his only world, and battle his only profession. He armors himself with a philosophy of acceptance of what may happen.

"I'm mighty sick of it all," he says very quietly, "but there ain't no use to complain. I just figured it this way, that I've been given a job to do and I've got to do it. And if I don't live through it, there's nothing I can do about it."

IN ITALY, *February 22, 1944*—Buck Eversole is a plattoon sergeant in an infantry company. That means he has charge of about forty front-line fighting men.

He has been at the front for more than a year. War is old to him and he has become almost the master of it. He is a senior partner now in the institution of death.

His platoon has turned over many times as battle whittles down the old ones and the replacement system brings up the new ones. Only a handful now are veterans.

"It gets so it kinda gets you, seein' these new kids come up," Buck told me one night in his slow, barely audible Western voice, so full of honesty and sincerity.

"Some of them have just got fuzz on their faces, and don't know what it's all about, and they're scared to death. No matter what, some of them are bound to get killed."

We talked about some of the other old-time noncoms who could take battle themselves, but had gradually grown morose under the responsibility of leading green boys to their slaughter. Buck spoke of one sergeant especially, a brave and hardened man, who went to his captain and asked him to be reduced to a private in the lines.

"I know it ain't my fault that they get killed," Buck finally said. "And I do the best I can for them, but I've got so I feel like it's me killin' 'em instead of a German. I've got so I feel like a murderer. I hate to look at them when the new ones come in."

*

Buck himself has been fortunate. Once he was shot through the arm. His own skill and wisdom have saved him many times. But luck has saved him countless other times.

One night Buck and an officer took refuge from shelling in a two-room Italian stone house. As they sat there, a shell came through the wall of the far room, crossed the room and buried itself in the middle wall with its nose pointing upward. It didn't go off.

Another time Buck was leading his platoon on a night attack. They were walking in Indian file. Suddenly a mine went off, and killed the entire squad following Buck. He himself had miraculously walked through the mine field without hitting a one.

One day Buck went stalking a German officer in close combat, and wound up with the German on one side of a farmhouse and Buck on the other. They kept throwing grenades over the house at each other without success. Finally Buck stepped around one corner of the house, and came face to face with the German, who'd had the same idea.

Buck was ready and pulled the trigger first. His slug hit the German just above the heart. The German had a wonderful pair of binoculars slung over his shoulders, and the bullet smashed them to bits. Buck had wanted some German binoculars for a long time.

*

The ties that grow up between men who live savagely and die relentlessly together are ties of great strength. There is a sense of fidelity to each other among little corps of men who have endured so long and whose hope in the end can be but so small.

One afternoon while I was with the company, Sgt. Buck Eversole's turn came to go back to rest camp for five days. The company was due to attack that night.

Buck went to his company commander and said. "Lieutenant, I don't think I better go. I'll stay if you need me."

The lieutenant said, "Of course I need you, Buck, I always need you. But it's your turn and I want you to go. In fact, you're ordered to go."

The truck taking the few boys away to rest camp left just at dusk. It was drizzling and the valleys were swathed in a dismal mist. Artillery of both sides flashed and rumbled around the horizon. The encroaching darkness was heavy and foreboding.

Buck came to the little group of old-timers in the company with whom I was standing, to say goodbye. You'd have thought he was leaving forever. He shook hands all around, and his smile seemed sick and vulnerable. He was a man stalling off his departure.

He said, "Well, good luck to you all." And then he said, "I'll be back in just five days." He said goodbye all around and slowly started away. But he stopped and said goodbye all around again, and he said, "Well, good luck to you all."

I walked with him toward the truck in the dusk. He kept his eyes on the ground, and I think he would have cried if he knew how, and he said to me very quietly:

"This is the first battle I've ever missed that this battalion has been in. Even when I was in the hospital with my arm they were in bivouac. This will be the first one I've ever missed. I sure do hope they have good luck."

And then he said:

"I feel like a deserter."

He climbed in, and the truck dissolved in the the blackness. I went back and lay down on the ground among my other friends, waiting for the night orders to march. I lay there in the darkness thinking —terribly touched by the great simple devotion of this soldier who was a cowboy—and thinking of the millions far away at home who must remain forever unaware of the powerful fraternalism in the ghastly brotherhood of war.

Swallowed in a Great Blackness

IN ITALY, *February 23, 1944*—Our company was alerted for its night march just before suppertime. We got the word about four in the afternoon, and we ate at four-thirty. Word was passed around to collect twenty-four hours' field rations at suppertime and a full supply of ammunition.

At chow time the soldiers all held their tin hats crooked in their left arms while holding their mess kits in their right. At the end of the mess line the soldiers put five C-ration cans into each man's hat and one bar of D-ration.

After supper, the men rolled their one blanket inside their one shelter half while there was still light. Early darkness had come before five-thirty. It was chilly. A misty rain began to fall. The men just lay or sat in their foxholes under the doubtful shelter of the olive trees.

Full darkness came over the olive grove, the artillery raged and flashed around half the horizon, and the concussion crashed and ran across the sky along the sounding board of the low clouds. We of our little company were swallowed in a great blackness.

We were connected to the war by one field telephone which ran to the battalion command post a quarter mile away. Nobody knew when the marching order would come. We just had to sit there and wait.

*

There were only two places to get out of the rain. Both were pig sheds dug into the side of a bank by an Italian farmer and stacked over with straw.

Lt. Jack Sheehy, the company commander, and four enlisted men and I crawled into one and dragged the phone in after us. A few sergeants went into the other.

We lay down on the ground there in the pig shed. We had on our heavy coats but the chill came through like anything. The lieutenant had an extra blanket which he carried unrolled when not actually in battle, so he spread it out and he and I both sat under it. We huddled against each other and became a little warmer.

The lieutenant said, "I used to read your column back home, and I never supposed we'd ever meet. Imagine us lying together here on the ground in Italy."

Then we talked a little while in low tones, but pretty soon somebody started to snore and before long all of us were asleep although it still was only seven o'clock.

Every now and then the lieutenant would phone battalion to see if any orders had come yet. Finally he was told the line to regiment was out.

Linemen were out in the darkness feeling with their hands, tracing the entire length of the line trying to find the break. Around nine o'clock it was open again. Still no marching orders came.

A dark form appeared fairly silhouetted in the open end of the shed and asked if Lt. Sheehy was there. The lieutenant answered yes.

"Can the men unroll their blankets?" the form asked. "They're wet and cold."

The lieutenant thought a moment and then he said, "No, better not. We should get the word to go any minute now, certainly within half an hour. They better keep them rolled." The form said, "Yes, sir," and merged back into the darkness.

By ten, everybody in the shed had awakened from their nap. Our grove was deathly still, as though no one existed in it, for the night was full of distant warfare.

Now and then we'd get clear under the blanket and light a cigaret and hide it under the blanket when we puffed it. Over on the far hillside where the Germans were we could see a distant light. We finally decided it was probably a lamp in some unwitting Italian farmhouse.

*

For a little while there was a sudden splurge of flares in the distance. The first was orange and then came some in green, and then a white and then some more orange ones. Our soldiers couldn't tell whether they were German or ours.

Between flashes of artillery we could hear quite loud blasts of machine guns. Even I can distinguish between a German machine gun and ours, for theirs is much faster.

Machine guns are rarely fired except in flashes, so the barrel won't get too hot, but once some jerry just held the trigger down and let her roll for about fifteen seconds. "Boy, he'll have to put on a new barrel after that one," a soldier said.

The time dragged on and we grew colder and stiffer. At last, nearly at midnight, the phone rang in the stillness of our pig shed. It was the order to go.

One of the boys said, "It's going to be a bitch of a thing to move. The ground is slick and you can't see your hand in front of you."

One sergeant went out to start the word for the company to assemble. Another disconnected the field telephone and carried it under his arm. Everybody wrestled into the harness of his heavy packs.

"Assemble down by the kitchen tent," the lieutenant told the first sergeant. "Platoons will form in this order—headquarters, third, first, second, and heavy weapons. Let's go." The first sergeant moved off. I moved after him. The first two steps were fine. On the third step I went down into a ditch and said a bad word. That's the way it was with everybody all the rest of the night.

IN ITALY, *February 24, 1944*—After the marching order came it took our company about fifteen minutes to get itself together, with the head of the line assembled at the appointed place in front of the kitchen tent at the edge of the olive grove.

It was midnight. The night was utterly black. It was the dark of the moon, and thick, low clouds further darkened the sky. "In two years overseas, this is the blackest night we've ever moved," one soldier said.

With a couple of others, I felt my way from our pig shed down to where we thought the kitchen tent was. We knew we were near it, but we couldn't see it.

"It's up ahead about fifty feet," one soldier said.

I butted in and said, "No, it's over to the right about thirty feet."

Just at that moment a flash of fire from one of our nearby cannon brightened the countryside for a split second, and we saw the tent. It was six feet in front of us. That's how dark it was.

*

One by one the platoon leaders felt their way up to the head of the column, reported their platoons ready in line, and felt their way back. Finally the lieutenant said, "Let's go."

There's no military formality about a night movement of infantry. You don't try to keep step. Nobody says "Forward march," or any of that parade-ground stuff. After a rest the lieutenant says, "All right, let's get along." And everybody gets up and starts.

In trying to get out of the orchard we lost our various places. Finally everybody stopped and called each other's name in order to get reassembled. The lieutenant and the sergeant would call for me occasionally to make sure I was still along.

When we fell in again, I was marching behind Sgt. Vincent Conners of Imogene, Iowa. His nickname is "Pete." We hadn't gone far before I realized that the place behind Pete was the best spot in the column for me, for I had found a little secret.

He had a rolled-up map about two feet long stuck horizontally through the pack harness on his back. By keeping close to it, I could just barely make out the vague white shape of this map. And that was my beacon throughout the night.

It was amazing how you could read the terrain ahead of you by the movement of that thin white line. If it went down a couple of inches, I knew Pete had stepped into a hole. If it went down fast, I knew he had struck a slope. If it went down sideways, I knew his feet were sliding on a slippery slope.

In that split second before my own step followed his, I could correct for whatever had happened to him. As a result I was down only once the whole night.

*

We were startled to hear some magnificent cussing down at one side, and recognized the company commander's voice. He had stepped right off into a narrow ditch about two feet deep and gone down on his back. Bundled as he was with pack-sacks, he couldn't get out of the ditch. He finally made it on about the third try.

The thing that always amazes me about these inhuman night movements of troops in war areas is how good-natured the men are about it. A certain fundamental appreciation for the ridiculous carries them through. As we slogged along, slipping and crawling and getting muddier and muddier, the soldier behind me said:

"I'm going to write my congressman about this."

Another soldier answered:

"Hell, I don't even know who my congressman is. I did three years ago, but I don't now."

The first voice was that of Pfc. Eddie Young of Pontiac, Michigan, the company's runner and message carrier. You get to know voices very quickly. Even though I was a newcomer to the company, there were a dozen men I could name in the blackness by their voices.

Eddie Young's voice especially haunted me. It was fast, and there was a tolerant and gentle humor in it. It was a perfect duplicate of the voice of my friend Ben Robertson, the correspondent who was killed in the Clipper crash at Lisbon a year ago. Whenever Eddie spoke, I could not help feeling that Ben was marching behind me.

The company's first sergeant is Bill Wood of Council Bluffs, Iowa, a tall man who carried a heavy pack, and when he fell there was a lot of him to go down. Whenever Bill would fall we'd hear him and stop. And then we could hear him clawing with his feet and getting partway up and then hitting the mud again, and cussing more eloquently with each attempt.

It really was so funny we all had to laugh. When Bill finally got back in line he was good and mad, and he said he couldn't see anything funny about it.

It took us half an hour to feel our way out of the big orchard and down a few feet onto the so-called road, which was actually not much more than a furrow worn by Italian mule carts. There were knee-deep ruts and bucket-sized rocks.

Once on the road, the column halted to let a train of pack mules pass. As we stood there, the thought occurred to all of us: "It's bad enough to be floundering around on the ground and mud, but now it'll be like groveling in a barnyard."

IN ITALY, *February 25, 1944*—At long last our company was really under way on its night movement up into the line. It was just past midnight, and very black. The trail was never straight. It went up and down, across streams, and almost constantly around trees.

How the leaders ever followed it is beyond me. The trees on each side had been marked previously with white tape or toilet paper, but even so we did get lost a couple of times and had to backtrack.

Our pace was miserably slow. The rain had stopped, but the mud was thick. You literally felt each step out with the toes of your boots. Every half hour or so we'd stop and send runners back to see how the tail end of the column was doing. Word came back that they were doing fine, and that we could step up the pace if we wanted to.

Somewhere in the night, both ahead of us and strung out behind us in files, was the rest of our battalion. In fact, the whole regiment of more than three thousand men was moving that night. But we knew nothing about the rest.

Throughout the night the artillery of both sides kept up a steady pounding. When we started, our own guns were loud in our ears. Gradually we drew away from them, and finally the explosion of their shells on German soil was louder than the blast of the guns.

The German shells traveled off at a tangent from us, and we were in no danger. The machine-gun and rifle fire grew louder as our slow procession came nearer the lines. Now and then a front-line flare would light up the sky, and we could see red bullets ricocheting.

The gun blasts made a continuous crashing in the night, yet they were always so brief they didn't give you a revealing view of the trail ahead.

The nagging of artillery eventually gets plain aggravating. It's always worse on a cloudy night, for the sounds crash and reverberate against the low ceiling. One gun blast alone can set off a continuous rebounding of sound against clouds and rocky slopes that will keep going for ten seconds and more.

And on cloudy nights you can hear shells tearing above your head more loudly than on a clear night. In fact, that night the rustle was so magnified that when we stopped to rest and tried to talk you couldn't hear what the other fellow said if a shell was passing overhead. And they were passing almost constantly.

*

At last we passed through a village and stopped on the far edge to rest while the column leader went into a house for further directions. We had caught up with the mules and drawn alongside them.

One of the muleskinners out in the darkness kept up a long monologue on the subject of the mules being completely done in. Nobody would answer him, and he would go on: "They're plumb done in. They can't go another foot. If we try to go on, they'll fall down and die."

Finally, some soldier in the darkness told him to shut up. We all privately endorsed his suggestion. But the monologist got huffy and wanted to know who that was. The voice said it wasn't anybody, just a new replacement soldier.

Then the muleskinner waxed sarcastic and louder. He had an objectionable manner, even in the dark. "Oh, oh!" he said. "So we've got a baby right from the States telling me how to run mules! A tenderfoot, huh? Trying to talk to us veterans! A hero right from the States, huh?"

Whereupon one of the real veterans in our company called out to the gabby skinner: "Aw, shut up! You probably haven't been overseas two months yourself."

He must have hit the nail on the head, or else his voice carried command, for that's the last we heard of the muleskinner.

*

It was almost midnight when the company reached its bivouac area and dug its foxholes into the mud. Always that's the first thing to do. It becomes pure instinct. The drippy, misty dawn found our men dispersed and hidden in the bottom of shallow, muddy depressions of their own digging, eating cold hash from C-ration cans.

They attacked just after dawn. The Germans were only a short distance away. I stayed behind when the company went forward.

In the continuously circulating nature of my job, I may never again see the men in this outfit. But to me they will always be "my" company.

February 28, 1944—When soldiers sit around during lull periods at the front, they talk about everything under the sun. Out of my recent times with front-line outfits I've tried to remember some of the things they talked about.

Two things eventually come up in every extended conversation: the latest rumor about the outfit, and discussions of what home is like and when we'll get home.

The latest rumor was that my outfit was to get no more replacements for men lost in battle, which led inevitably to a belief that they were to be withdrawn and sent home. Nobody really believed it, but everybody wanted to believe it. There were also rumors that the outfit was going to England and to India.

Memories of what America was like are actually getting pretty dim to men who have been overseas two years. As one Iowa boy said, "Why, even England is dim in my memory now, and we were there long after we were in the States." . . .

*

The soldiers talk about the Italian people, and on the whole the average soldier doesn't dislike the Italians too much. Nine out of ten much prefer Italy to Africa. And the sight of the poor children always gets them.

At an Army chow line near a village or close to farms, you see a few solemn and patient children with tin buckets waiting to get what is left over.

One soldier said to me: "I just can't bear to eat when they stand and look at me like they do. Lots of times I've filled my mess kit and just walked over and dumped it in their buckets and gone back to my foxhole. I wasn't hungry." . . .

February 29, 1944— . . . Somebody in our army must have been a roadside advertising man before the war, for we have all kinds of signs along the highways in addition to the direction signs. They are tacked onto trees, telephone poles and posts.

There are many in the Burma Shave poetic style, the several phrases being on separate boards about fifty yards apart, such as this one: "If you leave — good clothes behind — you may need them — some other time." That's an admonition against the American soldier's habit of abandoning gear when he gets more than he can carry.

Another one in Burma Shave fashion, and of dubious rhyme, says, "Some like gold — some like silver — we like salvage — bring it, will you?"

There are also frequent warnings against venereal disease, and one sign way out in the country says, "Is your tent clean?" A lot of front-line soldiers who haven't even been in a pup tent for months would get a laugh out of that one. . . .

*

As we advance mile by slow mile across the Italian mountains and valleys, our many command posts are set up wherever possible in Italian farm or village houses.

The houses are mostly all alike. They are very old and substantial-looking, yet they shake all over from the blast of our nearby guns.

Sometimes the Italian family still lives in one room of the house while the Americans occupy the rest. At other times the family has gone—nobody knows where—and taken with it everything but the heaviest furniture.

Faded pictures still hang on the walls—wedding-group pictures of forty years ago, and a full-face picture of some mustachioed young buck in the uniform of the last war, and old, old pictures of grandpa and grandma, and always a number of pictures of Christ and various religious scenes and mottoes.

I've billeted in dozens of Italian homes on the farms and little towns of our front lines, and invariably the faded pictures on the walls are of the same sort.

In one house nothing was left inside except the heavy cupboards and two heavy suitcases stored on top of the cupboards. We didn't nose into the suitcases, but I noticed that one bore the label of a big Italian steamship line and underneath the label it said, in English, "Steerage Passenger." Somebody in that poor family had been to America and back. . . .

Throughout his time in Italy, Pyle used his considerable influence to improve the men's lot and morale, particularly that of the infantry. Early on, he had scolded Washington for cigarette shortages at the front. Later, he had urged officials to adopt "wound and foreign-service" stripes for front-line soldiers. But the following was by far Pyle's strongest intercessory statement.

Going to Bat for the Boys

IN ITALY, *March 1, 1944*—In my usual role of running other people's business, I've been thrashing around with an idea—honest. It's to give the combat soldier some little form of recognition more than he is getting now.

Everybody who serves overseas, no matter where or what he's doing, gets extra pay. Enlisted men get twenty percent additional and officers ten percent.

Airmen get an extra fifty percent above this for flight pay. As a result, officer-fliers get sixty percent above their normal base pay and enlisted-fliers such as gunners and radio operators get seventy percent.

All that is fine and as it should be, but the idea I was toying with is why not give your genuine combat ground soldier something corresponding to flight pay? Maybe a good phrase for it would be "fight pay."

Of any one million men overseas, probably no more than one hundred thousand are in actual combat with the enemy. But as it is now, there is no official distinction between the dogface lying for days and nights under constant mortar fire on an Italian hill, and the headquarters clerk living comfortably in a hotel in Rio de Janeiro.

Their two worlds are so far apart the human mind can barely grasp the magnitude of the difference. One lives like a beast and dies in great numbers. The other is merely working away from home. Both are doing necessary jobs, but it seems to me the actual warrior deserves something to set him apart. And medals are not enough.

When I was at the front the last time several infantry officers brought up this same suggestion. They say combat pay would mean a lot to the fighting man. It would put him into a proud category and make him feel that somebody appreciates what he endures.

Obviously no soldier would ever go into combat just to get extra "fight pay." That isn't the point. There is not enough money in the world to pay any single individual his due for battle suffering.

But it would put a mark of distinction on him, a recognition that his miserable job was a royal one and that the rest of us were aware of it.*

*

One of the meanest stunts I've heard of was a Christmas envelope full of clippings that a practical joker back home sent a soldier over here.

The clippings consisted of colored ads cut out of magazines—and they showed every luscious American thing from huge platters of ham and eggs on up to vacationists lolling in bright bathing robes on the sand, surrounded by beautiful babes. There ought to be a law.

On second thought, I know even a meaner trick than that one. In fact, this one would take first prize in an orneriness contest at any season, Christmas or otherwise. The worst is that it happened to a front-line infantryman.

Some of his friends back home sent him three bottles of whiskey for Christmas. They came separately, were wonderfully packed, and the bottles came through without a break.

The first bottle tasted fine to the cold kids at the front, but when the second and third ones came the boys found they had been opened and drained along the way, then carefully resealed and continued on their journey.

Of course, mailing them in the first place was illegal, but that's beside the point. The point is that somewhere in the world there is a louse of a man with two quarts of whiskey inside him who should have his neck wrung off.

LIGHT-BOMBER GROUP

IN ITALY, *March 3, 1944*—The Mediterranean Allied Air Force, under the command of Lt. Gen. Ira Eaker,† covers everything in this whole Mediterranean theater all the way from Casablanca on the Atlantic almost to Cairo at the edge of Asia.

It is a gigantic force. Although there are many British planes and pilots in it, and even a few squadrons of Frenchmen, still it is predominantly an American air theater.

The main geographical objective of our push into Italy was to get heavy-bomber bases near enough to start pounding Germany from the south. The great plains around Foggia are capable, they say, of basing all the air forces in the world.

*Congress quickly acted on Pyle's suggestion. It granted fifty percent extra pay for combat service the week of May 8, 1944. The legislation was nicknamed "the Ernie Pyle bill."
†Pyle had known Eaker since Pyle's aviation-reporting days in Washington.

Our heavy-bomber force is still being built up, and has not yet really begun its program of blasting Germany proper, but planes have been flowing across the South Atlantic all winter.

Soon good weather will be here, and then woe upon Germany from south as well as west.

*

In the meantime, the 12th Air Support Command bears the burden of the close-in fighting here in Italy, and that's what I'm dealing with now. The 12th Air Support command is composed of fighters, dive bombers and light bombers, which work over the front line, helping our ground troops, bombing supply dumps and strafing roads just back of the enemy lines. Right now I'm living with a light-bomber group—the 47th—which flies the fast twin-engined Douglas-built plane known as the A-20 Boston.

The 47th is a veteran outfit. It fought through Tunisia. It helped beat the Germans back at Kasserine a year ago. It flew from Souk-El-Arba [Algeria] and Cap Bon [Tunisia] and Malta and Sicily, and now it is on the front in Italy.

Like most air groups of long service, it has almost no flying personnel left who came overseas with it. Its casualty rate has been low, but the crew men have all reached or passed their allotted number of missions and gone home.

In fact, some of its members went home so long ago that they are now back overseas on their second tour of combat duty, fighting out of England or in the South Pacific. The ground-crew men get letters from them sometimes.

I've been living with a certain squadron of the 47th. It has changed commanders while I've been with it. The previous commander was Maj. Cy Stafford, a brilliant young pilot-engineer from Oak Park, Illinois.

Maj. Stafford has been promoted to the group staff, and his place as squadron commander has been taken by Maj. Reginald Clizbe of Centralia, Washington.

Maj. Clizbe is a veteran in combat, but for several months has been on staff duty. He is pleased to get back to the small and intimate familiarity of a squadron. As he says: "Squadron commander is the best job in the Air Corps."

On his first day, Major Clizbe got a plane and went out and practiced while the rest went on their mission. I was staying in the same tent with him, and although at that time I didn't know him very well I could tell he was worried and preoccupied.

He wasn't afraid. Everybody knew that. But he was rusty, everybody's eyes were on him, and he was scared to death he would foul up on his first mission.

*

He flew the morning mission on his second day in command. He flew a wing position, and he did all right. He was in good spirits when they came back before lunch.

There was another mission that afternoon. Instead of resting, Maj. Clizbe put himself on the board for that one too, this time leading a flight of three. I was at his revetment when the planes came back just before dusk. When they got out, Maj. Clizbe was a changed man. He was just like a football player after winning a game.

It had been a perfect mission. The bomb pattern had smothered the target. They'd started fires. Their break-out from the bomb run was just right, and the planes got only a little flak. The new man had his teeth into the game again, and he was over the hump. He was all elation and enthusiasm.

"We'll give 'em hell from now on," he said.

All evening he kept smiling to himself, and he was like somebody released from a great oppression. That night he went to bed around nine o'clock, for he was tired, and he had assigned himself to lead the mission early next morning. Just before he went to sleep, he happened to think of something. He raised up and said: "Say, this is my birthday! I'd forgotten about it. Boy, I couldn't have had a better birthday present than those two missions today." And he really meant it.

The major was back in the war. He was doing a job again in person, with his own hands and brain, and he went to sleep with a fine satisfaction.

March 9, 1944— . . . Most of my time with the 47th Group of A-20 Boston light bombers has been spent with the gunners. All the gunners are sergeants. Each plane carries two. They ride in the rear compartment of the plane.

The top gunner sits in a glass-enclosed bubble rising above the fuselage. The bottom gunner sits on the floor during takeoff, and after they're in the air he opens a trap door, and swivels his machine gun down into the open hole.

Due to the nature of their missions and to the inferiority of German fighter strength in Italy, the A-20 gunners seldom have a battle in the air. Their main worry is flak, and that's plenty to worry about.

*

The gunners live in pyramidal tents, four and five to a tent. Some of their tents are fixed up inside even nicer than the officers'. Others are bare.

The gunners have to stand in chow line the same as other soldiers, and eat out of mess kits. Now and then they even have to go on clean-up detail and help pick up trash throughout their area. They must keep their own tents clean, and stand frequent inspection.

I found them a high-class and sincere bunch of boys. Those who really love to fly in combat are the exceptions. Most of them take it in workaday fashion, but they keep a fanatical count on the number of missions flown, each one of which takes them a little nearer to the final goal—the end of their tour of duty.

Ordinarily a gunner goes on only one mission a day, but with the increased air activity of late they sometimes go both morning and afternoon, day after day. There are boys here who arrived only in December and are already almost finished with their missions, whereas it used to take six months and more to run up the allotted total.

Flying in Combat

IN ITALY, *March 14, 1944*—As I got to know the A-20 gunners better and better, they gradually began to tell me their inner feelings about a life of flying in combat.

Several had just about completed their missions, yet they said they were willing to stay if needed and fly extra missions.

In any squadron you'll find many men willing to fly beyond the stated missions if it's put up to them, but you'll average only about one who is actually eager to go on. In our squadron I found such a gunner in Sgt. John D. Baker of Indianapolis.

Sgt. Baker is twenty-one. He has flown more missions than anybody in the squadron, men or officers. He says it is his ambition to fly a hundred.

Many in our squadron have gone beyond the required goal. Some are still flying, and others have gone on to the breaking point and had to be grounded. The flight surgeons try to sense when the strain is beginning to get a man.

Some of them seem to have nerves that are untouchable. One of my pilot friends told me that on a mission earlier in the day, when the flak was breaking all around, he didn't think much of the danger but kept thinking that if a fragment should break the Plexiglas globe, and let the below-zero air rush through the plane, he would be one mad pilot.

Another one told of the funny reflexes you have up there. For example, every combat airman knows you needn't worry about the flak you see, for if you see it the danger is over and you haven't been hit. Yet this pilot, after a harmless puff of smoke appears ahead of him, goes around it.

*

One of the gunners—a man with a fine record—told me he had not only become terrified of combat but had actually become afraid to fly at all.

He said that when the generators came on that morning, and the radio in their tent started crackling, it made him dream they were being attacked in the air. He dreamed that a bullet came up through the fuselage and hit him in the throat.

Another one told me he felt he just couldn't go on. He had completed his allotted missions, and nobody could doubt his courage. He wanted to go and ask to be grounded, but just couldn't bring himself to do it.

So I urged him to go ahead. Afterwards I got both sides of the story.

The officers told me later that they were kicking themselves for not noticing the gunner's nervousness in time and for letting it go until he had to hurt his pride by asking to be grounded.

But those are men's innermost feelings. They don't express them very often. They don't spend much time sitting around glooming to each other about their chances.

Their outlook and conversation is just as normal as that of a man in no danger at all. They play jokes, and write letters, and listen to the radio, and send gifts home, and drink a little vino and carry on just like anybody else.

It's only when a man "has had it"—the combat expression for anyone who has had more than he can take—that he sits alone and doesn't say much, and begins to stare.

*

Sgt. Alban J. Petchal of Steubenville, Ohio, and Sgt. Charles Ramseur of Gold Hill, North Carolina, both have flown their allotted missions, both have been wounded, both are true veterans, quiet and kind and efficient.

Sgt. Petchal, although an Easterner, is in a way something of the same kind of man as my cowboy friend Sgt. Buck Eversole. He doesn't like any part of war, but he has done his job and done it well.

Sgt. Petchal never heard of Buck Eversole, and yet the morning I left he spoke about his place in the war with the same sort of sadly restrained philosophy and even in almost the same words that Buck Eversole had used at the front. He said, "The job has to be done, and somebody has to do it, and we happen to be the ones that were picked to do it, so we'll go on doing it the best we can."

And Sgt. Ramseur said, "I don't ever want to fly again, but if they tell me to keep on flying then I'll just keep on flying, that's all. You can't do anything else."

Rudolf Charles Von Ripper, Soldier-Artist

IN ITALY, *March 18, 1944*—One of the most fabulous characters in this war theater is Lt. Rudolf Charles Von Ripper. He is so fabulous you might be justified in thinking him a phony until you got to know him.

I've known him since last summer in Algeria. Most of the other correspondents know him. One whole fighting infantry division knows him. He's no phony.

Von Ripper is the kind they write books about. He was born in Austria. His father was a general in the Imperial Austrian army, his mother a baroness. They had money. He could have had a rich, formal, royal type of existence.

Instead he ran away from home at fifteen, worked in the sawmills, collected garbage, was a coal miner for a while, and then a clown in a small traveling circus.

At nineteen he went into the French Foreign Legion, served two years, and was wounded in action. After that he went back to Europe and studied art. He is fundamentally an artist.

He traveled continuously. He lived in London and Paris. He lived in Shanghai during 1928. Then he returned to Berlin, joined liberal groups, and did occasional cartoons. Because he helped friends hiding from the Nazis, he was arrested in 1933, accused of high treason, and sent to a concentration camp.

Dollfuss of Austria* got him out after seven months. Then he went to the Balearic Islands off the coast of Spain and hibernated for a year, doing political, satirical drawing.

*

*Engelbert Dollfuss, anti-Nazi Austrian chancellor killed by Austrian Nazi rebels on July 25, 1934.

All his life has been a fluctuation between these violent extremes of salon intellectualism and the hard, steady reality of personal participation in war. You don't think of an artist as being tough or worldly, yet Von Ripper has been shot in battle more than twenty times.

In 1936 he went to Spain as an aerial gunner in the Loyalist air force. He got sixteen slugs in his leg during that adventure, and barely came out alive.

Back in Austria in 1938, he saw there was no possibility of organizing even a token resistance against Hitler, so he left for America. He became an American citizen five years later. By that time he was a private in the United States Army.

His Army career has been a curious one. At first he was a hospital laboratory technician. Then he was transferred to the newly formed Army Arts Corps, and left for North Africa last May to paint battle pictures for the War Department.

*

I happened to meet him a few days after he arrived on this side. He had hardly got started on his art work when Congress abolished the whole program. So he went back to being a regular soldier again, this time an infantryman. He was transferred to the 34th Division.

Last fall he was put in a front-line regiment, and in October he was wounded by shell splinters. He doesn't seem to mind being shot at all. A month later, while leading a night patrol, he got four machine-pistol slugs in him.

One slug split his upper lip just where it joins his nose. Another ripped a deep groove in the back of his hand. Another shot one finger clear off at the first joint. The fourth went through his shoulder. Before all his bandages were off he was back patrolling again.

All this time overseas he had been a sergeant, but after his November wounding he was given a battlefield commission as second lieutenant, and transferred to the division's engineers. Later it was possible for him to resume his art work in his spare time. Right now Lt. Von Ripper has a nice little room on the top floor of an apartment building in Naples taken over by the Army. Here he works at a huge drawing board, doing water colors and pen-and-ink sketches of war. He sleeps on a cot in the same room. Around the walls are tacked dozens of his sketches.

Now and then he returns to the front with his old outfit. Whenever he does, he's out in front getting shot at before you can say scat. He's quite a guy.

IN ITALY, *March 20, 1944*—Lt. Rudolf C. Von Ripper, the soldier-artist, is a soldier of fortune, in a way, yet he doesn't look or act like one. He is intelligent, and his approach is simple rather than adventurous. He is thirty-nine, but seems younger. He is medium tall, slightly stooped, and one eye has a cast that makes it appear to be looking beyond you. His face is long and thin, and his teeth are prominent. His knowledge of the English language is profound and his grammar perfect, but he still pronounces his words with a hissing imperfection. He swears lustily in English.

Von Ripper is as much at home discussing philosophy or political idealism as he is in describing the best way to take cover from a machine gun.

He is meticulous in his personal appearance, yet doesn't seem to care whether he sleeps between satin sheets or in the freezing mud of the battlefield.

*

It is hard to reconcile the artist with the soldier in Von Ripper, yet he is obviously professional at both. It may be that being a fine soldier makes him a better artist.

His long experience at warfare has made him as cunning as a fox. You can't conceive of his being rattled in a tight spot, and he seems to have been born without the normal sense of fear that inhibits most of mankind.

Von Ripper is so calm and so bold in battle that he has become a legend at the front. High officers ask his advice in planning attacks. He will volunteer for anything.

Being wounded four times hasn't touched his nerve in the slightest. In fact, he became so notorious as an audacious patrol leader that his division finally forbade his going on patrol unless by specific permission.

One night Von Ripper was returning from patrol and was stopped by an itchy-fingered sentry who called, "Who goes there?" The answer came back in a heavily German accent: "Lieutenant Von Ripper." He was wearing lieutenant bars, but his dog tag showed him to be a sergeant. It took an hour to get it straightened out.

Some sentries would have shot first and then investigated.

*

Out of this background as a proven fighting man, Von Ripper is painting the war. He has produced more than a hundred pictures already. His work goes to the War Department in Washington, but he hopes an arrangement might be made whereby a book of his war drawings could be published.

I believe that Von Ripper, like most of us over here, has finally become more interested in the personal, human side of war than in the abstract ideals for which wars are fought.

He says that in his paintings he is trying to take the applesauce out of war, trying to eliminate the heroics with which war is too often presented. From what I've seen of the work of other artists, Von Ripper is not alone in this sincerity. It's hard to be close enough to war to paint it, and still consider it heroic.

Von Ripper's dead men look awful, as dead men do. Live soldiers in foxholes have that spooky stare of exhaustion. His landscapes are sad and pitifully torn.

His sketches aren't photographic at all. They are sometimes distorted and grotesque, and often he goes into pen-and-ink fantasy.

He has given me one of these, labeled "Self-Portrait in Italy," which shows himself and another wounded man, against a background of wrecked walls and starving children, being led downhill by the bony arms of a chortling skeleton representing ultimate and inevitable death.

You get to seeing things like that when you're a soldier for a long time.

Pyle decided to travel to the beachhead at Anzio, about one hundred sixty miles up the coast from Naples. British and American troops, hoping to break the winter deadlock during which Allied progress toward Rome had been virtually stalled at the German-held Gustav Line, had made an end run around German defenses, landing at Anzio on January 22, 1944.

The well-planned mission faltered when the Allies delayed pushing inland, thus allowing the Germans to consolidate their defenses. For four months, Allied troops were pinned on the flat, rocky beaches, suffering heavy casualties to German bombing and shelling.

Daily ship convoys supplied and replaced troops on the beachhead, and it was on one of these convoys that Pyle took passage. Near Naples, he boarded an LST (landing ship, tank), "a great big thing, big as an ocean freighter. The engines and crew's quarters and bridges are all on the back end. All the rest of the ship is just a big empty warehouse sort of thing, much like a long, rectangular garage without any pillars in it.

"Two huge swinging doors open in the bow, and then a heavy steel ramp comes down so that trucks and tanks and jeeps can drive in. It can land at a beach for loading and unloading, or run nose first to a dock." The LST's skipper was Captain Joseph Kahrs of Newark, New Jersey, a thirty-seven-year-old lawyer whom Pyle had met in Bizerte Habor before the invasion of Sicily.

"Long lines of soldiers loaded down with gear marched along the dock to enter adjoining ships," Pyle wrote. "They were replacements to bolster the fighters at Anzio. You could tell from their faces that they were brand-new from America."

"Hey, Joe, Bis-ueet"

WITH THE ALLIED BEACHHEAD FORCES IN ITALY, *March 22, 1944*—We were due to sail for the Anzio beachhead a few hours after I got aboard our LST. But at the last minute came a warning of a storm of gale force brewing in the Mediterranean, so we laid over for twenty-four hours.

Some of the sailors took the opportunity next day to go ashore, and asked if I didn't want to go along. But I said, "What for? I've been ashore for three months already." So I stayed aboard, and just killed a full day with doing nothing.

We were tied up along the waterfront street of a small port city near Naples. All day long the dock was a riot of Italians grouped down below to catch cookies and chocolates and knickknacks the sailors and soldiers would throw down to them.

There must have been two hundred people on the dock, either participating in the long-shot chance of actually catching something, or there just to look on.

Most of them were children, boys and girls both. Mostly they were ragged and dirty. Yet they were good-natured.

Every time a package of crackers went down from above, humanity fought and stamped over it like a bunch of football players. Now and then some youngster would get hurt, and make a terrible face and cry. But mostly they'd laugh and look a little sheepish, and dash back in again after the next one.

All Italian children call all American soldiers "Hey, Joe," and all along the dock was a chicken-yard bedlam of "Hey, Joe, bis-ueet."* Each one crying at the top of his lungs to call attention to himself, and holding up his hands.

*

The soldier's favorite was a stocky little fellow of about eight, with coal-black hair and a constant good humor. He was about the only one of them who wasn't ragged, the reason being that he was entirely clad in military garb.

He had on a blue Navy sweater. Then for pants he had the biggest

*Italian mispronunciation of American "biscuit."

pair of British tropical shorts you ever saw, which came clear below his knees.

His legs were bare. He had on gray Army socks rolled down to his shoetops. And on his feet were a pair of brand-new American GI shoes, which must have been at least size eight. To top it all off, he had a beguiling grin with a tooth out in the middle of it.

This youngster was adept at walking on his hands. He spent hours walking around the muddy stone street on his hands, with his feet sticking straight up in the air.

The soldiers and sailors were crazy about him, and every time he finished his little performance he'd get a flood of crackers. I finally figured out that he was walking on his hands so much because it was easier than walking in those gigantic shoes.

Pretty teenage Italian girls in red sweaters would come and stand at the edge of the throng watching the fun. But the sailors and soldiers at the rail would soon spot them, and the play for them would start. Reluctant and timid at first, they would finally obey the sailors' demand that they try to catch something too, and pretty soon would be in there battling for broken crackers.

Most Americans are touched by the raggedness and apparent hunger of the children over here. But it was hard to feel sorry for these kids, for although maybe some of them were really hungry, the rest of them were just having a wonderful mob-scene sort of good time.

It was the old women in the crowd whom I could hardly bear to look at. Throughout the day there must have been a couple of dozen who came, tried for half an hour to catch something, and finally went dejectedly away.

They were horrible specimens of poverty and insanitation. They were old and pitiful, and repulsive. But their hunger most surely was genuine.

*

One elderly woman, dressed in tattered black and carrying a thin old shopping bag on her arm, stood at the far edge of the crowd, vainly beseeching a toss in her direction. Finally one sailor, who had just started on a large box of Nabiscos piece by piece, changed his mind and threw the entire box toward the old woman.

It was a good throw and a good catch. She got it like an outfielder. But no sooner did she have it in her arms than the crowd was upon her. Kids and adults both tore at the box, scratched and yelled and grabbed, and in five seconds the box was empty and torn.

The poor old woman never let go. She clung to it as though it were something human. And when the last cracker was gone she walked sort of blindly away, her head back and her eyes toward the sky, weeping with a hideous face just like that of a heartbroken child, still gripping the empty box.

It was a lot of fun watching this foreign riot of childish emotions and adult greed that day. But some of it was too real—greed born of too great a necessity—and I was glad when word came that we would sail that night.

The convoy set sail after dark. By dawn the next day, Pyle could see Anzio. The day was gray with clouds, so German bombers couldn't attack. Shells, however, landed in the water nearby, making the passage into Anzio harbor precarious. As Capt. Kahrs maneuvered the LST into the harbor, Pyle "couldn't help but admire this new skill of a man whose profession was so alien to the sea.

"Here he stood in tennis shoes, far from home, worming his ship into a half-wrecked harbor with shells passing a few feet over his head. And he did it with complete absorption and confidence. Men can do strange and great things when they have to do them."

No Area Is Immune

WITH THE ALLIED BEACHHEAD FORCES IN ITALY, *March 28, 1944*—When you get to Anzio you waste no time getting off the boat, for you have been feeling pretty much like a clay pigeon in a shooting gallery. But after a few hours in Anzio you wish you were back on the boat, for you could hardly describe being ashore as any haven of peacefulness.

As we came into the harbor, shells skipped the water within a hundred yards of us.

In our first day ashore, a bomb exploded so close to the place where I was sitting that it almost knocked us down with fright. It smacked into the trees a short distance away.

And on the third day ashore, an 88 went off within twenty yards of us.

I wished I was in New York.

*

When I write about my own occasional association with shells and bombs, there is one thing I want you folks at home to be sure to get straight. And that is that the other correspondents are in the same boat—many of them much more so. You know about my own small experiences, because it's my job to write about how these things sound and feel. But you don't know what the other reporters go through, because it usually isn't their job to write about themselves.

There are correspondents here on the beachhead, and on the Cassino front also, who have had dozens of close shaves. I know of one correspondent who was knocked down four times by near misses on his first day here.

Two correspondents, Reynolds Packer of the United Press and Homer Bigart of the *New York Herald-Tribune,* have been on the beachhead since D-day without a moment's respite. They've become so veteran that they don't even mention a shell striking twenty yards away.

*

On this beachhead every inch of our territory is under German artillery fire. There is no rear area that is immune, as in most battle zones. They can reach us with their 88's, and they use everything from that on up.

I don't mean to suggest that they keep every foot of our territory drenched with shells all the time, for they certainly don't. They are short of ammunition, for one thing. But they can reach us, and you never know where they'll shoot next. You're just as liable to get hit standing in the doorway of the villa where you sleep at night, as you are in a command post five miles out in the field.

Some days they shell us hard, and some days hours will go by without a single shell coming over. Yet nobody is wholly safe, and anybody who says he has been around Anzio two days without ever having a shell hit within a hundred yards of him is just bragging.

*

People who know the sounds of warfare intimately are puzzled and irritated by the sounds up here. For some reason, you can't tell anything about anything.

The Germans shoot shells of half a dozen sizes, each of which makes a different sound of explosion. You can't gauge distance at all. One shell may land within your block and sound not much louder than a shotgun. Another landing a quarter mile away makes the earth tremble as in an earthquake, and starts your heart to pounding.

You can't gauge direction, either. The 88 that hit within twenty yards of us didn't make so much noise. I would have sworn it was two hundred yards away and in the opposite direction.

Sometimes you hear them coming, and sometimes you don't. Sometimes you hear the shell whine after you've heard it explode.

Sometimes you hear it whine and it never explodes. Sometimes the house trembles and shakes and you hear no explosion at all.

But I've found out one thing here that's just the same as anywhere else—and that's that old weakness in the joints when they get to landing close. I've been weak all over Tunisia and Sicily, and in parts of Italy, and I get weaker than ever up here.

When the German raiders come over at night, and the sky lights up bright as day with flares, and ack-ack guns set up a turmoil and pretty soon you hear and feel that terrible power of exploding bombs—well, your elbows get flabby and you breathe in little short jerks, and your chest feels empty, and you're too excited to do anything but hope.

"I Thought It Was the End"

WITH THE FIFTH ARMY BEACHHEAD FORCES IN ITALY, *March 20, 1944*—We correspondents stay in a villa run by the 5th Army's Public Relations Section. In that house live five officers, twelve enlisted men and a dozen correspondents, both American and British.

The house is on the waterfront. The current sometimes washes over our back steps. The house is a huge, rambling affair with four stories down on the beach and then another complete section of three stories just above it in the bluff, all connected by a series of interior stairways.

For weeks long-range artillery shells had been hitting in the water or on shore within a couple of hundred yards of us. Raiders came over nightly, yet ever since D-day this villa had seemed to be charmed.

The night before our bombing Sgt. Slim Aarons of *Yank* magazine said, "Those shells are so close that if the German gunner had just hiccuped when he fired, *bang* would have gone our house."

And I said, "It seems to me we've about used up our luck. It's inevitable that this house will be hit before we leave here."

Most of the correspondents and staff lived in the part of the house down by the water, it being considered safer because it was lower down. But I had been sleeping alone in the room in the top part because it was a lighter place to work in the daytime. We called it "Shell Alley" up there because the Anzio-bound shells seemed to come in a groove right past our eaves day and night.

*

On this certain morning I had awakened early and was just lying there for a few minutes before getting up. It was just seven and the sun was out bright.

Suddenly the anti-aircraft guns let loose. Ordinarily I don't get out of bed during a raid, but I did get up this one morning. I was sleeping in long underwear and shirt so I just put on my steel helmet, slipped on some wool-lined slippers and went to the window for a look at the shooting.

I had just reached the window when a terrible blast swirled me around and threw me into the middle of my room. I don't remember whether I heard any noise or not.

The half of the window that was shut was ripped out and hurled across the room. The glass was blown into thousands of little pieces. Why the splinters or the window frame itself didn't hit me I don't know.

From the moment of the first blast until it was over probably not more than fifteen seconds passed. Those fifteen seconds were so fast and confusing that I truly can't say what took place, and the other correspondents reported the same.

There was debris flying back and forth all over the room. One gigantic explosion came after another. The concussion was terrific. It was like a great blast of air in which your body felt as light and as helpless as a leaf tossed in a whirlwind.

I jumped into one corner of the room and squatted down and sat cowered there. I definitely thought it was the end. Outside of that I don't remember what my emotions were.

*

Suddenly one whole wall of my room flew in, burying the bed where I'd been a few seconds before under hundreds of pounds of brick, stone and mortar. Later when we dug out my sleeping bag we found the steel frame of the bed broken and twisted. If I hadn't gone to the window I would have two broken legs and a crushed chest today.

Then the wooden doors were ripped off their hinges and crashed into the room. Another wall started to tumble, but caught only partway down. The French doors leading to the balcony blew out and one of my chairs was upended through the open door. As I sat cowering in the corner, I remember fretting because my steel hat had blown off with the first blast and I couldn't find it. Later I found it right beside me.

I was astonished at feeling no pain, for debris went tearing around every inch of the room and I couldn't believe I hadn't been hit. But the only wound I got was a tiny cut on my right cheek from flying glass, and I didn't even know when that happened. The first time I knew of it was when blood ran down my chin and dropped onto my hat.

I had several unfinished columns lying on my table and the continuing blasts scattered them helter-skelter over the room and holes were punched in the paper. I remember thinking, "Well, it won't make any difference now anyhow."

Finally the terrible nearby explosions ceased and gradually the ack-ack died down and at last I began to have some feeling of relief that it was over and I was still alive. But I stayed crouched in the corner until the last shot was fired.

WITH THE FIFTH ARMY BEACHHEAD FORCES IN ITALY, *March 21, 1944*—When our bombing was over, my room was a shambles. It was the sort of thing you see only in the movies.

More than half the room was knee-deep with broken brick and tiles and mortar. The other half was a disarray all covered with plaster dust and broken glass. My typewriter was full of mortar and broken glass, but was not damaged.

My pants had been lying on the chair that went through the door, so I dug them out from under the debris, put them on and started down to the other half of the house.

Down below everything was a mess. The ceilings had come down upon men still in bed. Some beds were a foot deep in debris. That nobody was killed was a pure miracle.

Bill Strand of the *Chicago Tribune* was out in the littered hallway in his underwear, holding his left arm. Maj. Jay Vessels of Duluth, Minnesota, was running around without a stitch of clothing. We checked rapidly and found that everybody was still alive.

The boys couldn't believe it when they saw me coming in. Wick Fowler of the *Dallas News* had thought the bombs had made direct hits on the upper part of the house. He had just said to George Tucker of the Associated Press, "Well, they got Ernie."

But after they saw I was all right they began to laugh and called me "Old Indestructible." I guess I was the luckiest man in the house, at that, although Old Dame Fortune was certainly riding with all of us that morning.

*

The German raiders had dropped a whole stick of bombs right across our area. They were apparently five-hundred-pounders, and they hit within thirty feet of our house.

Many odd things happened, as they do in all bombings. Truthfully, I don't remember my walls coming down at all, though I must have been looking at them when they fell.

Oddly, the wall that fell on my bed was across the room from where the bomb hit. In other words, it fell toward the bomb. That is caused by the bomb's terrific blast creating a vacuum; when air rushes back to the center of that vacuum, its power is as great as the original rush of air outward.

When I went to put on my boots there was broken glass clear up into the toes of them. My mackinaw had been lying on the foot of the bed and was covered with hundreds of pounds of debris, yet my goggles in the pocket were unbroken.

At night I always put a pack of cigarets on the floor beside my bed. When I went to get a cigaret after the bombing, I found they'd all been blown out of the pack.

The cot occupied by Bob Vermillion of the United Press was covered a foot deep with broken tile and plaster. When it was all over somebody heard him call out plaintively, "Will somebody come and take this stuff off of me?"

*

After seeing the other correspondents, I went back to my shattered room to look around again, and in came Sgt. Bob Geake of Fort Wayne, Indiana, the first sergeant of our outfit. He had some iodine, and was going around painting up those who had been scratched.

Bob took out a dirty handkerchief, spit on it two or three times, then washed the blood off my face before putting on the iodine, which could hardly be called the last word in sterilization.

Three of the other boys were rushed off to the tent hospital. After an hour or so, five of us drove out to the hospital in a jeep to see how they were.

We found them not in bad shape, and then we sat around a stove in one of the tents and drank coffee and talked with some of the officers.

By now my head and ears had started to ache from the concussion blasts, and several of the others were feeling the same, so the doctors gave us codeine and aspirin.

Much to my surprise, I wasn't weak or shaky after it was all over. In fact I felt fine—partly buoyed up by elation over still being alive, I suppose. But by noon I was starting to get jumpy, and by midafternoon I felt very old and "beat up," as they say, and the passage of the afternoon shells over our house really gave me the willies.

We got Italian workmen in to clean up the debris, and by evening all the rooms had been cleared, shaky walls knocked down, and blankets hung at the windows for blackout.

All except my room. It was so bad they decided it wasn't worth cleaning up, so we dug out my sleeping bag, gathered up my scattered stuff, and I moved to another room.

The hospital has invited Wick Fowler and me to move out with them, saying they'd put up a tent for us, and I wouldn't be surprised if we took them up on it. There's such a thing as pressing your luck too far in one spot.

Anzio-Nettuno Described

WITH THE ALLIED BEACHHEAD FORCES IN ITALY, *March 29, 1944*—Anzio and Nettuno run together along the coast of our beachhead, forming practically one city. There is really only one main street, which runs along the low blocks just back of the first row of waterfront buildings.

The two cities stretch for about three miles, but extend only a few blocks back from the waterfront. A low hill covered thick with tall cedar trees rises just back of them, and along some of the streets there are palm trees.

I had supposed these two places were just ancient little fishing villages. Well, they are old, but not in their present form.

Anzio is where Nero is supposed to have fiddled while Rome burned, but in more recent years he would doubtless have been sprawling in a deck chair on the patio of his seaside villa, drinking cognac.

For these two towns are now (or rather, were until recently) high-class seaside resorts. They've been built up in the modern manner within the last twenty years. They are much bigger and much more modern than I had supposed.

When you look at them from a certain place, they extend two hundred yards from the water's edge, forming a solid flank of fine stone buildings four and five stories high. Most of these are apartment houses, business buildings, and rich people's villas.

Today there is no civilian life in Anzio-Nettuno. The Germans had evacuated everybody before we came, and we found the place deserted. A few Italians have straggled back in, but they are few indeed.

*

In the path of warfare over here, "business as usual" seems to have been the motto of the natives. Adult civilians have stayed in some places despite the fall of heaven and earth upon them. They'd stay and deal with the Germans while we were blasting their towns to bits, and those who survived would stay and deal with us when the town changed hands and the Germans began showering the same death and destruction back upon us. The ties of a man's home are sinewy and strong, and something that even war can hardly break.

But in Anzio and Nettuno the expensive villas are deserted—the swanky furniture wrapped in burlap and stored all in one room or two. The little hovels are empty also, and so are the stores. Scarcely a door or a window with whole shutters remains. There is no such thing as a store or shop in business today in these two towns.

When our troops first came they found things intact and undamaged, but the Germans changed that. Little by little, day by day, these cities have become eroded and torn from the shells and bombs of the enemy.

It has happened slowly. The Germans shell spasmodically. Hours will go by without a single shell coming in, and then all of a sudden a couple of shells will smack the water just offshore.

A few buildings will go down, or the corners fly off some of them. One day's damage is almost negligible. But it is cumulative, and after a couple of weeks you realize that less of the city is left whole than two weeks previously.

Today you can't walk half a block without finding a building half crumpled to the ground. Between breakfast and lunch the building next to the mess where we eat was demolished. One man was killed, and our cook got a broken arm.

The sidewalks have shell holes in them. Engineers repair new holes in the streets. Military police who direct auto traffic occasionally are killed at their posts.

Broken steel girders lie across the sidewalks. Marble statues fall in littered patios. Trees are uprooted, and the splattered mud upon them dries and turns to gray. Wreckage is washed up on shore. Everywhere there is rubble and mud and broken wire.

Yet this German shelling and bombing has had only the tiniest percentage of effect on our movement of supplies and troops into the beachhead. One day of bad weather actually harms us more than a month of German shelling.

It is a thrilling thing to see an LST pull anchor when its turn comes, and drive right into the harbor despite shells all around. And it is thrilling, too, to see the incessant hurry-hurry-hurry of the supply trucks through the streets all day and all night despite anything and everything.

From all indications we are supplying our troops even better by sea than the Germans are supplying theirs by land.

A Flat, Lethal Beachhead

WITH THE 5TH ARMY BEACHHEAD FORCES IN ITALY, *March 30, 1944*—You've heard how flat the land of the Anzio beachhead is. You've heard how strange and naked our soldiers feel with no rocks to take cover behind, no mountains to provide slopes for protection.

This is a new kind of warfare for us. Here distances are short, and space is confined. The whole beachhead is the front line. The beachhead is so small that you can stand on high ground in the middle of it and see clear around the thing. That's the truth, and it ain't no picnic feeling either.

I remember back in the days of desert fighting around Tébessa more than a year ago, when the forward echelons of the corps staff and most of the hospitals were usually more than eighty miles back of the fighting. But here everybody is right in it together. You can drive from the rear to the front in less than half an hour, and often you'll find the front quieter than the rear.

Hospitals are not immune from shellfire and bombing. The unromantic finance officer counting out his money in a requisitioned building is hardly more safe than the company commander ten miles ahead of him. And the table waiter in the rear echelon mess gets blown off his feet in a manner quite contrary to the Hoyle rules of warfare.*

*

It's true that the beachhead land is flat, but it does have some rise and fall to it. It's flat in a western Indiana way, not in the billiard-table flatness of the country around Amarillo, Texas, for example.

You have to go halfway across the beachhead area from the sea before the other half of it comes into view. There are general rises of a few score feet, and little mounds and gulleys, and there are groves of trees to cut up the land.

There are a lot of little places where a few individuals can take

*A jocular take-off on the eighteenth-century Englishman Edmond Hoyle's rule manuals for games of chance.

cover from fire. The point is that the generalized flatness forbids whole armies taking cover.

Several main roads—quite good macadam roads—run in wagon-spoke fashion out through the beachhead area. A few smaller gravel roads branch off from them.

In addition, our engineers have bulldozed miles of road across the fields. The longest of these "quickie" roads is named after the commanding general here, whose name is still withheld from publication. A painted sign at one end says "Blank Boulevard," and everybody calls it that. It's such a super-boulevard that you have to travel over it in super-low gear with mud above your hubcaps, but still you do travel.

*

Space is at a premium on the beachhead. Never have I seen a war zone so crowded. Of course, men aren't standing shoulder to shoulder, but I suppose the most indiscriminate shell dropped at any point in the beachhead would land not more than two hundred yards from somebody. And the average shell finds thousands within hearing distance of its explosion. If a plane goes down in No-Man's Land, more than half the troops on the beachhead can see it fall.

New units in the fighting, or old units wishing to change positions, have great difficulty in finding a place. The "already spoken for" sign covers practically all the land in the beachhead. The space problem is almost as bad as in Washington.

Because of the extreme susceptibility to shelling, our army has moved underground. At Youkous and Thélepte and Biskra, in Africa a year ago, our Air Forces lived underground. But this is the first time our entire ground force has had to burrow beneath the surface.

Around the outside perimeter line, where the infantry lie facing the Germans a few hundred yards away, the soldiers lie in open foxholes devoid of all comfort. But everywhere back of that the men have dug underground and built themselves homes. Here on this beachhead the dugouts, housing from two to half a dozen men each, will surely run into the tens of thousands.

As a result of this, our losses from shelling and bombing are small. It's only the first shell after a lull that gets many casualties. After the first one, all the men are in their dugouts. And you should see how fast they can get there when a shell whines.

In addition to safety, these dugouts provide two other comforts our troops have not always had—warmth and dryness.

A dugout is a wonderful place to sleep. In our Anzio-Nettuno sector a whole night's sleep is as rare as January sun in sunny Italy. But for the last three nights I've slept in various dugouts at the front, and slept soundly. The last two nights I've slept in a grove which was both bombed and shelled, and in which men were killed each night, and yet I never even woke up. That's what the combination of warmth, insulation against sound, and the sense of underground security can do for you.

In Shallow Foxholes

WITH FIFTH ARMY BEACHHEAD FORCES IN ITALY, *April 1, 1944*—The American infantry fighters on the 5th Army beachhead were having a welcome breathing spell when I dropped around to leave my calling card.

There's nothing that suits me better than a breathing spell, so I stayed and passed the time of day. My hosts were a company of the 179th Infantry. They had just come out of the lines that morning, and had dug in on a little slope three miles back of the perimeter. The sun shone for a change, and we lay around on the ground talking and soaking up the warmth.

Every few minutes a shell would smack a few hundred yards away. Our own heavy artillery made such a booming that once in a while we had to wait a few seconds in order to be heard. Planes were high overhead constantly, and now and then you could hear the ratta-ta-tat-tat of machine-gunning up there out of sight in the blue, and see thin white vapor trails from the planes.

That scene may sound very warlike to you, but so great is the contrast between the actual lines and even a little way back, that it was actually a setting of great calm.

*

This company had been in the front lines for more than a week. They were back to rest for a few days. There hadn't been any real attacks from either side during their latest stay in the lines, and yet there wasn't a moment of the day or night when they were not in great danger.

Up there in the front our men lie in shallow foxholes. The Germans are a few hundred yards on beyond them, also dug into foxholes, and buttressed in every farmhouse with machine-gun nests. The ground on the perimeter line slopes slightly down toward us—just enough to give the Germans the advantage of observation.

There are no trees or hillocks or anything up there for protection. You just lie in your foxhole from dawn till dark. If you raise your head a few feet, you get a rain of machine-gun bullets.

During these periods of comparative quiet on the front, it's mostly a matter of watchful waiting on both sides. That doesn't mean that nothing happens, for at night we send out patrols to feel out the German positions, and the Germans try to get behind our lines. And day and night the men on both sides are splattered with artillery, although we splatter a great deal more of it nowadays than the Germans do.

Back on the lines, where the ground is a little higher, men can dig deep into the ground and make comfortable dugouts which also give protection from shell fragments. But on the perimeter line the ground is so marshy that water rises in the bottom of a hole only eighteen inches deep. Hence there are many artillery wounds.

When a man is wounded, he just has to lie there and suffer till dark. Occasionally, when one is wounded badly, he'll call out and the word is passed back and the medics will make a dash for him. But usually he just has to treat himself and wait till dark.

For more than a week these boys lay in water in their foxholes, able to move or stretch themselves only at night. In addition to water seeping up from below, it rained from above all the time. It was cold, too, and of a morning new snow would glisten on the hills ahead.

Dry socks were sent up about every other day, but that didn't mean much. Dry socks are wet in five minutes after you put them on.

Wet feet and cold feet together eventually result in that hideous wartime occupational disease known as trench foot. Both sides have it up here, as well as in the mountains around Cassino.

The boys have learned to change their socks very quickly, and get their shoes back on, because once your feet are freed of shoes they swell so much in five minutes you can't get the shoes back on.

Extreme cases were evacuated at night. But only the worst ones. When the company came out of the lines some of the men could barely walk, but they had stayed it out.

*

Living like this, it is almost impossible to sleep. You finally get to the point where you can't stay awake, and yet you can't sleep lying in cold water. It's like the irresistible force meeting the immovable object.

I heard of one boy who tried to sleep sitting up in his foxhole, but kept falling over into the water and waking up. He finally solved his dilemma. There was a fallen tree alongside his foxhole, so he tied some rope around his chest and tied the other end to the tree trunk, so that it held him up while he slept.

Living as these boys do, it seems to me they should all be down with pneumonia inside of a week. But cases of serious illness are fairly rare.

Maybe the answer lies in mind over matter. I asked one sergeant if a lot of men didn't get sick from exposure up there and have to be sent back. I'll always remember his answer.

He said, "No, not many. You just don't get sick—that's all."

April 4, 1944— . . . As tiny and shell-raked as our Anzio beachhead is, life in some respects is astonishingly normal. For example, the 5th Army runs a daily movie here. It started less than a month after our troops first landed.

They put on two shows a day, and we've had such recent pictures as Abbott and Costello in *Hit the Ice*, Jean Arthur in *The More the Merrier*, and Rosalind Russell in *What a Woman!*

I go occasionally, just to kill time at night, since the place where I write has no electricity, and I haven't got enough Abe Lincoln in me to do my work by candlelight. . . .

*

Also, our beachhead has a rest camp for infantry troops. The camp is under artillery fire, as is everything else on the beachhead.

But still it serves its purpose by getting the men out of the foxholes, and as somebody said, "There's a hell of a lot of difference getting shells spasmodically at long range, and in being right up under Jerry's nose where he's aiming at you personally."

Furthermore, our beachhead has a big modern bakery, which has been working under fire for weeks, turning out luscious, crisp loaves of white bread from its portable ovens at a pace of around twenty-seven thousand pounds a day.

More than eighty soldiers work in this bakery. It is the first draftee baking outfit in our Army, and the company will be three years old in June. They've been overseas a year and a half, and have baked through half a dozen bitter campaigns.

They've had casualties right here on the beachhead, both physical and mental, from too much shelling. Their orders are to keep right on baking through an artillery barrage, but when air-raiders come over, they turn out the fires and go to the air-raid shelter. . . .

"They Don't Have That Stare"

WITH 5TH ARMY BEACHHEAD FORCES IN ITALY, *April 5, 1944**—One day I was driving on a muddy lane alongside a woods, with an officer friend of mine who has been wounded twice and who has been at war a long time.

On both sides of the lane were soldiers walking, returning to the rear. It was the typical movement of troops being relieved after a siege in the front line. Their clothes were muddy, and they were heavily laden. They looked rough, and any parade ground officer would have been shocked by their appearance. And yet I said: "I'll bet those troops haven't been in the line three days."

My friend thought a minute, looked more closely as they passed, and then said: "I'll bet they haven't been in the line at all. I'll bet they've just been up in reserve and weren't used, and now they're being pulled back for a while."

How can you tell things like that? Well, I made my deduction on the fact that their beards weren't very long, and although they were tired and dirty, they didn't look tired and dirty enough.

My friend based his on that, too, but more so on the look in their eyes.

"They don't have that stare," he said.

A soldier who has been a long time in the line does have a "look" in his eyes that anyone with practice can discern.

It's a look of dullness, eyes that look without seeing, eyes that see without transferring any response to the mind. It's a look that is the display room for the thoughts that lie behind it—exhaustion, lack of sleep, tension for too long, weariness that is too great, fear beyond fear, misery to the point of numbness, a look of surpassing indifference to anything anybody can do to you. It's a look I dread to see on men.

*

And yet it's one of the perpetual astonishments of war life to me that humans recover as quickly as they do. You can take a unit that is pretty well exhausted, and if they are lucky enough to be blessed with some sunshine and warmth, they'll begin to be normal after two days out of the line. The human spirit is just like a cork.

When companies like this are pulled out for a rest, they spend the first day getting dug into their new position, for safety against occasional shellings or bombings. Usually they've slept little during

*Pyle left Italy on April 5. This column—and those that follow—were part of a backlog Pyle had filed during March.

their time in the line, so on their first night they're asleep early and boy, how they sleep.

Next day they get themselves cleaned up as best they can. They shave, and wash, and get on some fresh clothes if their barracks bags have been brought up. They get mail and they write letters, and they just loaf around most of the day.

On both the second and third days, they take on replacements and begin getting acquainted with them. All over the bush slope where they're bivouacked, you see little groups of men squatting in tight circles. These are machine-gun classes. The classes are for the new men, to make sure they haven't forgotten what they learned in training, and to get them accustomed to the great necessity of knowing their guns and depending on them.

Replacements arrive in many different stages of warfare. The best method is for replacements to come when a whole regiment is out of the line for a long rest. Then the new men can get acquainted with the older ones, they can form their natural friendships, and go into their first battle with a feeling of comradeship.

Others arrive during these very short rest periods, and have only a day or so to fit themselves into the unit before going on into the great adventure.

The worst of all is when men have to join an outfit while it's right in the line. That has happened here on the 5th Army beachhead.

*

There have been cases here where a company had to have replacements immediately. It was in circumstances where no front-line movement whatever in daytime was possible. Hence the new men would have to be guided up at night, establish themselves in their foxholes in darkness, and inhabit that foxhole until it was all over.

I feel sorry for men who have to do that. All of us who have had any association at all with the possibility of death know that the main thing you want is not to be alone. You want company, and preferably somebody you know.

It must be an awful thing to go up to the brink of possible death in the nighttime in a faraway land, puzzled and afraid, knowing no one and facing the worst moment of your life totally alone. That takes strength.

Tunisian Reunion

WITH FIFTH ARMY BEACHHEAD FORCES IN ITALY, *April 8, 1944*—About thirteen months ago I struggled one forenoon into a cactus patch about halfway between Sbeïtla and Faïd Pass, in Tunisia.

Hidden in that patch was all that was left of an armored combat team which had been overrun the day before, when the Germans made the famous surprise breakthrough which led finally to our retreat through Kasserine Pass.

A few of you more tenacious readers may remember my writing about this bunch at the time. I found them almost in a daze—and a very justifiable one, too, for they had been fleeing and groping their way across the desert for a day and a night, cut to pieces, and with the swarming Germans relentlessly upon them.

The few who escaped had never expected to survive at all, and on that weary morning they were hardly able to comprehend that they were still alive.

I had good friends in that gang, and I've just seen them again after thirteen months. Talk about your family reunions! It was like Old Home Week for a while.

I stayed with them two days, and we fought the Tunisian wars over and over again. I can just visualize us on some far day when we cross each other's paths back in America, boring our families and friends to distraction with our long-winded recountings and arguments about some afternoon in Tunisia.

*

Maj. Ronald Elkins, sometimes known in fact as R. Lafayette Elkins, used to be a professor at Texas A&M, College Station, Texas. He is one of this old gang. His nickname is "Satch," and he goes around in the green two-piece coverall of the infantry. Everybody loves him.

That memorable night in Tunisia I excitedly went away and left my helmet and shovel lying under a half-track in which Maj. Elkins was sleeping, and never saw them again. In our reminiscing I told the major how last fall, when I was home, several people told me that this steel helmet was now in somebody's house out on Long Island. How it got there I haven't the remotest idea.

But I've got another helmet now, and Satch Elkins has another half-track, *Bird Dog the Second*, to replace the old one that was shot out from under him that awful Tunisian afternoon.

I saw Sgt. Pat Donadeo of Allison Park, a suburb of Pittsburgh, who is one of the best mess sergeants overseas. He has lived in the field for nearly two years, cooking in a truck on his portable kitchen, turning out excellent meals, and always having a snack for a correspondent, no matter what hour you show up.

Sgt. Donadeo looks a little thinner than he used to, but he's still all right. He speaks good Italian, and since hitting Italy he has come into his own. He makes little foraging trips and comes back with such delicacies as fresh eggs, chicken, olive oil and cows.

And there's Lt. Col. Daniel Talbot, who owns a big cattle ranch outside of Fort Worth, Texas. His nickname is "Pinky," and he doesn't look like a warrior at all, but he is.

Col. Talbot used to have a driver named Manuel Gomez, from Laredo, Texas. One afternoon beyond Sidi-Bou-Zid, a year ago, the three of us drove up to the foothills so we could look down over the valley where the Germans were. Shells were falling in the valley, and every time we'd hear one we'd ditch the jeep and start for the gulleys, although they'd actually be landing a mile away from us.

Pvt. Gomez is still driving for the colonel, and the three of us laughed today at our inexperience and nervousness so long ago. None of us has got brave in the meantime, but all of us have enriched our knowledge of shell sounds. Today we think it's far away when a shell misses by two hundred yards.

*

Our tanks haven't had much chance to do their stuff in the Italian war, because of the mountainous terrain and the incessant rains. But the tankers are ready, and they're hoping. They know that sooner or later their big battle here on the beachhead will come. When I walked in, they laughed and said: "This must be it. Every time you'd show up in Tunisia, we'd have a battle. This must be the sign."

So you see I have my life work cut out for me. I just go around the country starting battles, like a nasty little boy, and then immediately run back and hide.

WITH FIFTH ARMY BEACHHEAD FORCES IN ITALY, *April 10, 1944*—In our old gang of Tunisian tankmen of a year and more ago there was Capt. Jed Dailey, who comes from Sharon, Massachusetts, near Boston. Jed was through that battle at Sidi-Bou-Zid, and it was he who was so furious about losing his camera and his bedroll and all his films to the Germans.

I wrote about him at the time, saying he bet the Germans would develop those films eagerly, thinking they'd reveal some military secrets, but all they'd find would be a picture of a man in a silly pose with Tunisian flowers stuck behind his ears.

Jed says that after that column he got dozens of letters kidding him about putting flowers behind his ears, but he didn't care.

He has avenged the loss of his camera, too. Since then he has personally captured from the Germans an even better one to replace it, and has added a Luger and a fine pair of binoculars for good measure.

*

Jed Dailey is an unusual person. I think I like him about as much as anybody I know. He is a pure Bostonian. He talks with a Harvard broad A. He is a far cry from the farm boy of the Kentucky hills, yet he commands a company of such boys and they love him.

Following the battle at Kasserine, Jed Dailey was switched from a desk job to the command of a company of tanks. The job of company commander, whether it's infantry or tanks or what, is the greatest job in the Army—the greatest and the toughest.

The boys themselves have told me what they think of Jed Dailey. When he first arrived, they were contemptuous of that cultured accent and had little faith in him. They laugh now and tell how he tries to speak in a flat accent whenever he gives them a talk, but without realizing it lapses back into his broad A.

But he has lived that down, and all their other jokes about him. They'd go anywhere with him now, or for him. He has proved himself in many ways.

Whenever there is a battle he is in his own tank, directing his company. I just had the pleasure of seeing him get the Silver Star for gallantry in action. He has been wounded twice since I saw him in Tunisia.

Whenever his company pulls back from battle, Jed Dailey throws the small details of Army discipline out the back door and the men really get a rest. As they say, "He fights hard and he rests hard." That's the way the boys get the most out of it, and they appreciate it.

*

Capt. Dailey is tall and his black hair stands up and roaches back and you'd have to call him good-looking. He nearly always goes bare-headed even in the danger zone. It is not an affectation; he simply likes to go bare-headed. He usually wears an Air Corps fleece-lined leather jacket that he once haggled out of some flier friend.

At the left shoulder of the jacket are two holes—one in front of the shoulder, one in back. The first hole is where a piece of shell fragment went in. The back hole is where it came out after going through his arm. They took a piece out of his leg to patch up his wounded shoulder.

The other officers laugh and say, "Jed wouldn't sew those holes up for ten thousand dollars." And another one says, "Not only that, but you can see where he has taken his knife and made them bigger."

You don't talk like that in front of a man when you mean it. Jed just grins and says, "Sure."

Before that he was wounded in the face from an air burst. When he got out of the hospital from his second wound he had a week's leave at Sorrento, the beautiful resort city below Naples. He stayed one night and then returned to his company. Everybody at the rest camp thought he was crazy.

"It isn't that I am anxious to fight," Jed said, "but when you are commanding a combat outfit your place is with your outfit. You feel like a heel if you are able to be there and aren't. I feel lots better since I got back."

Tankers

WITH 5TH ARMY ALLIED BEACHHEAD FORCES IN ITALY, *April 13, 1944*—One day I sat around with a tank crew, in emergency position just behind our front-line infantry. They had been there for eight days.

They hadn't done anything. They were there just to help repel any attacks that might be coming. We keep lots of tanks located thus at all times.

This crew had its metal behemoth hidden behind a small rise, half obscured by oak bushes. The men were cooking a pot of dried beans when I got there in mid-forenoon. They had coffee boiling as usual, and we drank coffee as we talked.

When tank men are out like this, ten-in-one rations and C-rations are brought up to them at night by jeeps. They do all their own cooking, and sleep in the tank for safety. They aren't supposed to smoke inside the tanks, but everybody does. Some crews even burn their little cookstoves right in the driver's compartment.

A tank and the territory around it are a mess after five men have lived in it for eight days. The ground is strewn with boxes and tin cans and mess gear. The inside of the tank looks as though a hurricane had hit it.

This tank had everything in it from much-handled comic books to a pocket edition of the Bible. You found old socks, empty tobacco cans, half cups of cold coffee. The boys used the top of the tank for table and shelves, and this too was littered.

But all this disarray doesn't keep it from being a good tank, because this crew holds the battalion record for firing its entire ammunition load in the shortest time.

Sleeping five nights in a tank isn't too comfortable, for space is very limited. They spread their blankets around the interior, sleep in their clothes, and nobody gets completely stretched out. The worst spot is around the gunner's seat, where the man really has to sleep halfway sitting up, so they take turns sleeping in this uncomfortable spot.

After they've stayed at the front eight to ten days, another company relieves them, and they move back a couple of miles, dig in, then clean up and relax for a few days.

*

These medium tanks carry a five-man crew. This one was commanded by Sgt. Speros Bakalos, a short, nice-looking ex-truck-driver from Boston. Once the tank he was serving in was hit, and his tank commander's head was shot clear off.

The driver is Sgt. Oscar Stewart of Bristol, Virginia. They call him "Pop," because he is in his middle thirties. He used to work for the State Highway Department.

His assistant driver is Pvt. Donald Victorine of Crystal Lake, Illinois. He, incidentally, is a friend of Capt. Max Kuehnert, whom I knew in Tunisia and whose baby I had the honor of naming Sandra, though Lord knows how I ever thought of that one.

The gunner is Corp. Bud Carmichael of Monterey, California, and his assistant is Pvt. George Everhart from Thomasville, North Carolina.

Carmichael's nickname is "Hoagy," after the famous composer of "Stardust." This Carmichael used to be a pipefitter for the gas company in Monterey. When I saw him he hadn't shaved or washed for a week. He wore a brown muffler around his neck, a roll stocking cap on his head, unbuckled overshoes, and was altogether the toughest-looking soldier I ever laid eyes on. But he belied his looks, for he was full of good nature and dry wit.

*

A few days later I saw the same gang again, and the other boys were saying that after I left that day they talked about me. I'd remarked, upon meeting them, that I'd gone to college with the real Hoagy Carmichael, so this "Hoagy" told the boys that if he'd been thinking fast he would have replied, "That's funny, Ernie. I don't remember you. What seat did you sit in?"

The men cook in a big aluminum pot they took out of an abandoned house, and on a huge iron skillet that Carmichael got in barter for the equivalent of twenty dollars. They call it their "twenty-dollar skillet," and are careful of it, even washing it sometimes.

Carmichael has a photo pasted on the barrel of his gun inside the turret—a dancing picture of Carmen Miranda and Cesar Romero. He says it gives him inspiration in battle, and then grins until his eyes squint.*

April 14, 1944— . . . I found that tankers, like everybody else, take their hats off to the infantry.

The average doughfoot or airman says you'd never get him shut up in a tank. Once in a while you do get a tank man who has a feeling of claustrophobia about being cooped up in there, but it's very seldom.

The boys say that more than half of them get safely out of damaged tanks, even the ones that catch fire. They tell funny stories about how four and five men come out of a burning tank all at once, when it isn't actually possible for more than two to get through the door at the same time.

They hate snipers worse than anything else. That is because visibility is pretty poor in a tank and the commander usually rides with his door open and his head sticking out. Unseen snipers are always shooting at them.

The boys showed me all the little improvements that have come out on recent tanks. And they also wondered why tank designers haven't thought of some of the simplest things for making tank life more practical—such as putting racks for water cans on the rear, and a bracket where you could tie your bedding roll. The men have welded on these necessary racks for their gear.

An armored unit's fighting usually comes in spurts, with long intervals between. When the tank boys are in a lull they are used for emergency jobs. This is very unusual, but here on the beachhead everybody has to do a little of everything.

Nearly every day the men of the tank crews back in bivouac have a detail starting just at dawn. They carry mines and barbed wire up to the front for the engineers to put in place. They pack the stuff on their backs, and they don't like it, but they do it without grumbling.

*This was no *ordinary* photo of Carmen Miranda. It seems Miss Miranda never wore any underwear when she danced, and this picture, taken on the set of one of her films, shows her skirts swirling high in the air as Cesar Romero lifts her. Much to 20th Century-Fox's consternation, someone had slipped the photo out of the publicity department. The picture was duplicated and distributed abroad during the war and has since been published in books like *Hollywood Babylon*.

April 17, 1944— . . . Here is a sad story. It concerns a tank driver named Corp. Donald Vore, a farm boy from Auxvasse, Missouri.

The corporal had a girl back home he was crazy about. After he came to Italy she sent a beautiful new big photograph of herself. Like most tank men, he carried it with him in his tank.

The other day a shell hit the tank. It caught fire, and the whole crew piled out and ran as fast as they could. Corp. Vore had gone a little way when he suddenly stopped, turned, and went dashing back to the tank.

Flames were shooting out of it, and its heavy ammunition was beginning to go off. But he went right into the flaming tank, disappeared a moment, and came climbing out—with his girl's picture safely in his hand.

A few hours later the crew came trudging back to home base. Mail had arrived during their absence. There was a letter for Corp. Vore from his girl. He tore it open. The letter was merely to tell him she had married somebody else.

They said that if it hadn't been such a long walk back, and he hadn't been so tired, Corp. Vore would have returned to his tank and deposited the picture in the flames. . . .

Supplying the Beachhead

WITH FIFTH ARMY BEACHHEAD FORCES IN ITALY, *April 18, 1944*—The real drama of this Anzio beachhead campaign is the supply system. I'd almost like to write that sentence twice—to make sure you get it. The supplying of this 5th Army beachhead has been one of the superlative chapters of our Mediterranean war.

The beachhead is really like a little island. Everything has to come by water. Without a steady flow of food and ammunition, the beachhead would perish.

All this concentration of shelling and bombing against the Anzio-Nettuno area is for the purpose of hindering our movement of supplies. They have hindered it some. I can't give you the percentage, but you'd be surprised how low it really is. They certainly haven't hindered us enough. For the supplies keep coming, and the stockpiles have now grown so great and so numerous that we've almost run out of room for establishing new dumps.

*

Many branches of the service deserve credit for the supply miracle —the Navy, the Merchant Marine, the Combat Engineers, the

Quartermaster Corps. And again let me remind you that the British are always there, too. You don't hear much about them from me, because my job is to write about the Americans. But in all our Allied work down here the British do their part too (and in the case of shipping to Anzio, the Greeks and Poles as well).

American Army Engineers are in command of all port facilities at the beachhead.

The city of Anzio is a mess today. Just off the waterfront, there is absolutely nothing but wreckage. And the wreckage grows day by day under German shelling and bombing. We call Anzio a "potential Bizerte," for soon it may be in as complete a state of wreckage as was that thoroughly wrecked city in Tunisia.

Yet our soldiers and sailors continue to live and work in Anzio. There isn't a man in town who hasn't had dozens of "experiences." If you try to tell a bomb story, anybody in Anzio can top it. Casualties occur daily. But the men go on and on.

The American soldier's irrepressible sense of humor still displays itself in Anzio. Down on the dock is a big, boxlike cart in which they pick up slop buckets and trash that gets in the way on the dock front. The cart is freshly painted snow-white, and printed in neat blue letters on each side is "Anzio Harbor Department of Sanitation." You'd have to see the bedlam of wreckage to get the full irony of the "Sanitation" part.

At a corner in Anzio some soldiers have set up a broken statue of a woman (the place is lousy with statues), and put a sign under it saying, "Anzio Annie." If somebody would write a poem about her, she might become as famous as "Dirty Gertie."*

I noticed another sign—this one not funny—along the waterfront. This sign said, "No Parking—For Ambulances Only."

*

Everybody jokes about the perilous life in the Anzio-Nettuno area. I've been with it long enough myself to appreciate the humor of nervousness. Some people have had to leave because of nerves, and those who stay like to make fun of their own shakes.

The jitters are known as "Anzio anxiety" and "Nettuno neurosis." A lieutenant will hold out his hand and purposely make it tremble, and say, "See, I'm not nervous."

Then there is "Anzio foot," where your feet are pointing in one direction and your face in another—the position sometimes momen-

*Dirty Gertie from Bizerte, the subject of a bawdy soldier limerick.

tarily assumed when you're going somewhere and the scream of a shell suddenly turns you on another course.

Also, we have the "Anzio walk," a new dance in which the performer jumps, jerks, cowers, cringes and twitches his head this way and that, something halfway between the process of dodging shells and just going plain nuts.

You wouldn't imagine people could joke about the proximity of death; but you sometimes have to joke about it—or else.

And through all this, men keep working and supplies keep coming in. I can't, of course, tell you in figures the total of this magnificent job they've done. But I can say that today this beachhead is receiving nine times as many supplies daily as they figured in the beginning was possible. It has been a thrilling privilege to be here and see them do it.

WITH FIFTH ARMY BEACHHEAD FORCES IN ITALY, *April 19, 1944*—The mechanics of supplying the 5th Army forces on the Anzio beachhead are undeniably beautiful in execution.

We have taken a port full of sunken ships and jumbled streets and wrecked buildings and cleared enough paths through it for the movement of our ships and vehicles.

Once our supplies reach the vicinity of beachhead waters they are under shellfire and bombing raids that may come any moment of the day or night. In addition, German E-boats and destroyers lurk on the edge of our concentration of ships, and naval forces must be always on the lookout for them.

Our supplies are unloaded in many ways. Some few ships can go right up to a dock. Others go to nearby beaches. The bigger freight ships have to lie off the harbor and be unloaded into smaller boats which in turn unload onto the docks or beaches.

All day long the waters in a great semicircle around Anzio, reaching to the horizon, are churned by big and little ships moving constantly back and forth. It resembles the hustle and bustle of New York Harbor.

On the far edges lie cruisers and other battle craft. In the vicinity there is always a white hospital ship to evacuate our wounded and sick from the beachhead.

Along toward dusk small, fast craft shoot in and out of the great flock of ships, laying smoke screens, while smoke pots ashore put out their blinding cloud of fog.

At night when the raiders come over, a mightly bedlam of ack-ack crushes all thought on shore and far out to sea as the ships themselves let go at the groan and grind of German motors in the sky.

Sometimes the raiders drop flares, and then the universe is lighted with a glare more cruel and penetrating than the brightest day, and every human on the beachhead feels that the Germans are looking down at him individually with their evil eyes.

When the moon is full it throws its swath of gold across the lovely Mediterranean, and sometimes the nights are so calm and moon-tinged and gentle that you cannot remember or believe that the purpose of everything around you is death.

When there is no moon it is so black you have to grope your way about, and even the ominous split-second flashes from our own big guns do not help you to see.

Sometimes the shelling and the raiding are furious and frenzied. At other times, hour after quiet hour goes by without a single crack of an exploding shell. But always the possibility and the anticipation are there.

All these things you can see from the window of the house where we live. There are times when you stand with your elbows on the windowsill and your chin in your hand, and see right before you a battlefield in action in the three dimensions of land, sea and air, all so spectacular that even Hollywood might well bow in deference to a drama beyond its own powers of creation.

*

The streets and roads around Anzio are under a steady thundering flow of heavy war traffic. The movement is endlessly fascinating. One day I stood by the road just to watch for a while, and of the first twelve vehicles that passed, each was something different.

There was a tank, and a great machine shop on heavy tractor treads that shook the earth as it passed, and the jeep of a one-star general, and a "duck," and a high-wheeled British truck, and a famous American six-by-six, and a prime mover trundling the great "Long Tom" gun with its slim, graceful barrel pointing rearward.

Then came a command car, and a stubby new gun covered with canvas, on four rubber-tired wheels, and an ambulance, and a crew of wire stringers, and a weapon carrier. Then a big self-propelled gun on tractor treads, and finally another "duck" to start the heterogeneous cycle over again.

Everywhere there is activity. Soldier-workmen saw down trees and cut down concrete lampposts so that trucks may use the sidewalks of the narrow streets. Huge shovels mounted on truck chassis stand amid the wreckage of buildings scooping up brick and stone to be hauled away in trucks for repairing damaged roads.

Allied military police stand on every corner and crossroads to highball traffic on through, and believe me, it's highballed.

Everything moves with a great urgency, a great vitality. The less hesitation the better in this land where shells whistle and groan. There is little hesitation anywhere around Anzio.

Anzio Greeter

WITH FIFTH ARMY BEACHHEAD FORCES IN ITALY, *April 21, 1944*—Lt. Eugene Tousineau of Detroit is the official greeter for the new Anzio Chamber of Commerce. He visits every ship as soon as it drops anchor in Anzio waters, and "extends the key to the city." Most of his guests would prefer being ridden out of town on a rail.

He's the guy who checks the cargo of every incoming ship and checks daily on the progress and the quality of their unloading.

All day long he rides around in an LCVP* climbing rope ladders up the sides of ships, snaking back down on single ropes—just holding on with his hands while his bouncing steel boat below tries to crush him. "I've got ten thousand dollars' insurance," he laughs.

All day he is out there on the water with shells speckling the whole area. I wouldn't have his job for a million dollars. But he enjoys it.

*

I rode around with him one day seeing how the ships unload, seeing how it feels to be sitting there at anchor aboard a ship full of explosives within range of enemy artillery. It doesn't feel too good.

Lt. Tousineau has been on this job for six weeks. He is an ebullient fellow who insists on enjoying whatever he does regardless, because he gets a great kick out of it.

He goes aboard ships and serves notice to ships' officers. He bawls out some people even though he's only a second lieutenant, and commiserates with others who have been bawled out by somebody who matters.

If things aren't going well enough on a certain ship, he'll say to the Army officer in charge, "No excuse for this, sir," and never bat an eye. But that's the way wars are won.

Riding around with us that day was Lt. John Coyle of Philadelphia, who is learning the game. Our supply shipping has become so

*Landing craft, vehicles and personnel.

thick that the checking job is too much for one man, so the two will divide it between them in the future.

Lt. Tousineau has had dozens of Hairbreadth Harry escapes. Shells explode in the water, bombs drop beside his house at night. He has even climbed off a ship just a few minutes before it was hit.

Before the war, Lt. Tousineau was a nightclub manager, a sandhog and numerous other things. He is tall and dark, has a very long and narrow face and a little pencil mustache, and looks like the Anzio edition of Cesar Romero.

He calls himself the "bad boy" of his regiment. "I get a commendation one day and a reprimand the next," he says. "The colonel will commend me for good work under dangerous conditions and then I'll go to Naples and get ticketed for having my hands in my pockets." But that's the Army, and Tousineau can take it.

*

The lieutenant has a crew of four soldiers who run his boat. The former crew, according to the lieutenant, got "Anzio anxiety" and took off, so he picked his own men.

Volunteers for the boat job were called for. Nobody volunteered. So four men were assigned. Now that they've got the hang of it, everybody else in the company is mad at himself for not volunteering, for it's a soft job. All they do all day long is ride around in this boat and dodge a shell now and then.

None of them knew anything about boats before Anzio. They learned by trying. "We didn't know nothin' from sour apples about a boat," said Pvt. James Davis, a farm boy from Covert, Michigan, "but we went along."

Later, as we lay alongside a British ship, I heard Davis say, "Let's go ashore onto that boat." Such nautical sabotage as that would turn Admiral Dewey over in his grave.

The coxswain of the boat (the guy who drives it) is Pfc. Arthur Handy of Fellows, California, down in the oil-field district near Taft. Handy spent years learning how to be a sailor by driving a truck in the oil fields.

One of the "seamen" is Pfc. Nicholas Kardos of Chicago. His nickname is "Rabbit" and he used to be a punch-press operator.

The other is Pfc. William Lipiczky of Cleveland. His ancestry is a combination of Russian and Hungarian, and the others call him "Hunky." He was a welder.

When these soldiers first started learning how to run a boat they sometimes got seasick, but they don't anymore. And they have become fairly indifferent to shells too.

They don't even wear their steel helmets half the time. When shells begin coming too close, Pvt. Davis will remark: "For a month I've been telling that fellow to take a furlough and go to Rome and have himself a time. But he doesn't seem to get my message."

April 22, 1944— . . . The bigger ships are unloaded just as they would be at a dock, with winches hoisting out big netfuls of cargo from the deep holds and swinging them over the sides and letting them down—not onto a dock, however, but into flat-bottomed LCT's which carry the stuff to the beaches.

Each hold has a dozen or more men working down below, plus the winch crews and signal men. They are all soldiers. They work in twelve-hour shifts, but they get intervals of rest.

I was aboard one Liberty Ship about ten A.M. All five hatches were bringing up stuff. You could lean over and watch the men down below piling up ration boxes. And on the deck immediately below us you could see scores of other soldiers trying to sleep, the deafening noise of the winches making no difference to them. They were the night shift. They slept on folding cots between blankets, with their clothes on.

One crew boss was Sgt. Sam Lynch of Wilmington, Delaware. He is a veteran soldier, having served four months in the Arctic and fourteen months on this side. Before the war he was a fireman on the Pennsylvania Railroad and later a railway mail clerk. He is married and has one child.

I asked him how he liked coming up to Anzio on a ship and he said he didn't like it any too well. "The trouble is," he said, "that you feel so darned defenseless. If you could just man a gun and shoot back it wouldn't be so bad."

But the Navy operates the gun crews aboard all these freight ships and the soldiers can only sit there idle and sweat it out when bombs or shells start flying. . . .

The Quartermaster Corps

WITH FIFTH ARMY BEACHHEAD FORCES IN ITALY, *April 24, 1944*—Once on shore, our supplies for the Anzio beachhead are taken over by the Quartermaster Corps (food and clothing) and the Ordnance Department (ammunition).

The Quartermaster Corps is traditionally seldom in great danger. Up here on the beachhead they are blowing that tradition all to hell.

The Quartermaster Corps has been under fire ever since the

beachhead was established, and still is. Its casualties from enemy action have been relatively high.

Around seventy percent of the Quartermaster troops on the beachhead are colored boys. They help unload ships right at the dock. They drive trucks. They man the supply dumps. Hardly a day goes by without casualties among them. But they take this bombing and shelling bravely. They make an awful lot of funny remarks about it, but they take it.

*

We drove out to one of the ration dumps where wooden boxes of rations are stacked head-high in piles for hundreds of yards, as in a lumber yard. Trucks from the waterfront add continually to the stock, and other trucks from the various outfits continually haul it away.

Our ration dumps are not at all immune from shellfire. This single one has had more than a hundred shells in it. Many of the soldier workmen have been killed or wounded.

Ration dumps seldom burn, because you can't burn C-rations. But early in the beachhead's existence they hit a dump of cigarets and millions of them went up in smoke.

Our local dumps of ammunition, food, and equipment of a thousand kinds are now so numerous that a German artilleryman could shut his eyes and fire in our general direction and be almost bound to hit something.

Our dumps do get hit; but the fires are put out quickly, the losses are immediately replaced, and the reserve grows bigger and bigger.

*

The boss of the Quartermaster troops is a former newspaper man —Lt. Col. Cornelius Holcomb of Seattle. He worked on the *Seattle Times* for twelve years before going into the Army. He is a heavily built, smiling, fast-talking, cigar-smoking man who takes terrific pride in the job his colored boys have done. He said there's one thing about having colored troops—you always eat like a king. If you need a cook you just say, "Company, halt! Any cooks in this outfit?" And then pick out whoever looks best.

The colonel himself has had many close squeaks up here. Just before I saw him, a bomb had landed outside his bivouac door. It blew in one wall, and hurt several men.

Another time he was standing in a doorway on the Anzio waterfront talking to a lieutenant. Stone steps led from the doorway down into a basement behind him.

As they talked, the colonel heard a bomb whistle. He dropped down on the steps and yelled to the lieutenant, "Hit the deck!"

The bomb hit smack in front of the door and the lieutenant came tumbling down on top of him. "Are you hurt?" Colonel Holcomb asked. The lieutenant didn't answer. Holcomb nosed back to see what was the matter. The lieutenant's head was lying over in a corner.

Soon a medical man came and asked the blood-covered colonel if he was hurt. Colonel Holcomb said no. "Are you sure?" the doctor asked. "I don't think I am," the colonel said.

"Well, you better drink this anyway," the doctor said. And poured him a water glass full of rum which had him in the clouds all day.

*

In the Quartermaster Corps they've begun a system of sending the key men away after about six weeks on the beachhead and giving them a week's rest at some nice place like Sorrento.

A man who goes day and night on an urgent job under the constant strain of danger finally begins to feel a little punchy or "slugbutt," as the saying goes. In other words, he has the beginnings of "Anzio anxiety," without even knowing it.

But after a week's rest he comes back to the job in high gear, full of good spirits, and big and brave. It's too bad all forms of war can't be fought that way.

April 25, 1944—In addition to its regular job of furnishing food and clothing to the troops, the Quartermaster Corps of the 5th Army beachhead runs the bakery, a laundry for the hospitals, a big salvage depot of old equipment, and the military cemetery.

Hospital pillows and sheets are the only laundry done on the beachhead by the Army. Everything else the individual soldiers either wash themselves or hire Italian farm women to do. People like me just go dirty and enjoy it.

The Army laundry is on several big mobile trucks hidden under the sharp slope of a low hill. They are so well camouflaged that a photographer who went out to take some pictures came away without any—he said the pictures wouldn't show anything.

This laundry can turn out three thousand pieces in ten hours of work. About eighty men are in the laundry platoon. They are dug in and live fairly nicely. . . .

*

Our salvage dump is a touching place. Every day five or six truckloads of assorted personal stuff are dumped on the ground in an open space near town. It is mostly the clothing of soldiers who have been killed or wounded. It is mud-caked and often bloody.

Negro soldiers sort it out and classify it for cleaning. They poke through the great heap, picking out shoes of the same size to put together, picking out knives and forks and leggings and underwear and cans of C-ration and goggles and canteens and sorting them into different piles.

Everything that can be used again is returned to the issue bins as it is or sent to Naples for repair.

They find many odd things in the pockets of the discarded clothing. And they have to watch out, for pockets sometimes carry hand grenades.

You feel sad and tight-lipped when you look closely through the great pile. Inanimate things can sometimes speak so forcefully—a helmet with a bullet hole in the front, one overshoe all ripped with shrapnel, a portable typewriter pitifully and irreparably smashed, a pair of muddy pants, bloody and with one leg gone.

*

The cemetery is neat and its rows of wooden crosses are very white—and it is very big. All the American dead of the beachhead are buried in one cemetery.

Trucks bring the bodies in daily. Italian civilians and American soldiers dig the graves. They try to keep ahead by fifty graves or so. Only once or twice have they been swamped. Each man is buried in a white mattress cover.

The graves are five feet deep and close together. A little separate section is for the Germans, and there are more than three hundred in it. We have only a few American dead who are unidentified. Meticulous records are kept on everything.

They had to hunt quite a while to find a knoll high enough on this Anzio beachhead so that they wouldn't hit water five feet down. The men who keep the graves live beneath ground themselves, in nearby dugouts.

Even the dead are not safe on the beachhead, nor the living who care for the dead. Many times German shells have landed in the cemetery. Men have been wounded as they dug graves. Once a body was uprooted and had to be reburied.

The inevitable pet dog barks and scampers around the area, not realizing where he is. The soldiers say at times he has kept them from going nuts.

Pyle left Anzio on a Naples-bound hospital ship carrying five hundred wounded men from the beachhead.

Hospital Ship

NAPLES, *April 28, 1944*—On the hospital ship which I rode back from Anzio, part of two decks remained just about as they were when the vessel was a luxury cruise ship in the Caribbean. In this part the permanent staff of doctors and nurses live, and also the officers of the ship.

But the rest has been altered just as liners are altered when made into troop ships. Cabin walls have been cut out to form big wards. Double-deck steel beds have been installed. The whole thing is fitted like a hospital operating room and wards.

The wounded men get beautiful treatment. They lie on mattresses and have clean white sheets—the first time since coming overseas for most of them.

There is a nurse to each ward, and the bigger wards have more than one. Enlisted men serve the meals and help the nurses.

The doctors have little to do. On this run the wounded are on the ship less than twenty-four hours. Their wounds have been thoroughly attended before they are brought aboard, and it's seldom that anything drastic develops on the short voyage.

*

One of the doctors took me in tow and showed me the entire ship after supper. He was Capt. Benjamin Halporn of Harrisburg, Pennsylvania. Captain Halporn's wife is also a doctor back in Harrisburg, practicing under her own name, Dr. Miriam R. Polk.

"We really have so little to do we almost forget how," Capt. Halporn said. "My wife back home does more work in one day than I do in a month." But that's nobody's fault. The doctors must be on the ship for advice and emergencies.

As we went around the ship our trip turned into a kind of personal-appearance tour. When we left one ward, the nurse came running after us and said to me, "Do you mind coming back? The boys want to talk to you."

And while I stood beside the bunk gabbing with a couple of wounded men, another one across the ward yelled, "Hey, Ernie, come over here. We want to see what you look like." If this keeps up I'll have to have my face lifted. Nobody with a mug like mine has a right to go around scaring wounded men.

The boys had read about the proposal in Congress to give "fight pay" to combat troops* and they were for it. Most of them said it wasn't so much the money as to give them some recognition and distinction, and money seemed the only way to do it.

As we went around, some of the wounded would call to the doctor and he would have a nurse attend to them. One boy with an arm wound was bleeding too much, and needed a new bandage. Another one in a shoulder cast said good-naturedly that he couldn't tell by the feel whether he was bleeding or just sweating under his cast.

A colored boy with a shattered leg said his cast was too tight and hurt his instep. So the doctor drew a curved line on it with his pencil and ordered the cast sawed off there. Each cast has written on it the type of wound beneath it.

We stopped behind one man whose right leg was in a cast. The writing on it revealed that he was a British commando. The doctor asked him if he were in pain, and he smiled and said with some effort, "Quite a bit, sir, but not too much."

When you ask a wounded man how he got hit, the majority of them are eager to tell you in great detail just how it happened. But those in the most pain are listless and uninterested in what goes on around them.

When the ship is overcrowded there aren't bunks enough for everybody. So those who aren't in bad shape—merely sick or with slight wounds—sleep on mattresses on the floor of what used to be the salon. Everybody does have a mattress, which is just so much velvet to any soldier.

*

Down below in smaller wards were the shock cases. Actually most of them were what doctors call "exhaustion" cases and would be all right after a few days' rest. Their wards had heavy screen doors that could be locked, but not a single door was closed, which showed that the boys weren't in too bad shape.

In addition the ship has four padded cells for extreme shock cases. The steel door to each one has a little sliding-panel peephole. Only one cell was occupied. This was a boy who refused to keep his clothes on. We peeked in and he was lying on his mattress on the floor, stark naked and asleep.

*Pyle's proposal. See pp. 224–25.

So Little Like War

NAPLES, *April 29, 1944*—A Red Cross worker rides each hospital ship, not only to do anything for the wounded she can, but also to help keep the ship's staff and crew happy.

On our ship the Red Cross girl was Percy Gill of Palo Alto, California. She used to teach physical education at Castilleja School for Girls.

After supper she passed out a bottle of Coca-Cola to every man on the ship. It was the first time most of the boys had had one since leaving America. The merchant-marine seamen in the crew always help her pass the Cokes around.

Miss Gill has a tiny office filled with books, toilet supplies, musical instruments and magazines. As soon as the wounded men are brought aboard she gives every one a pack of cigarets and a toothbrush, for most of them have lost their gear.

*

As they are swung aboard, you see some completely empty-handed and others carrying their pitiful little possessions in their tin hats, balanced on their stomachs. Some have on hospital pajamas, some just O.D. shirts, some only their dirty gray underwear.

Miss Gill does not intrude herself on the men, for she knows that the most badly wounded want to be left alone. Now and then she'll give a boy a book and discover that he's still looking at the same page three hours later. Another boy used his as a fan all afternoon.

Miss Gill has books in French, and in German too. Every shipload has a few wounded prisoners. We had two on my trip. One was a startled-looking German kid whose card showed him to be only seventeen. The prisoners are treated just the same as anybody else.

Miss Gill's musical warehouse includes an accordion, four guitars, a violin, two banjos, two saxophones, a clarinet, a trombone, and two dozen harmonicas. She doesn't have many requests for either the musical instruments or the books on these short trips between the beachhead and Naples, for there's hardly time. But on the long trip back to America they are a godsend, for the men are feeling better by then and time goes slowly. On one sixteen-day trip across the ocean the men read three thousand books—an average of six to a man.

It is a relief and a comfort for men to be on a hospital ship after their months of mud and misery and danger and finally the agony of their wounding. It is a relief because the hospital ship is so little like war, and because those who operate it are in a world apart from the world these men have known.

There's no blackout at all. Nobody is ever dirty or cold. Cabin windows have no shutters. You can smoke on the deck. Big spotlights slung on brackets point their dazzling beams at the big red cross painted on the ship's sides.

The ship takes its course far outside the channels of regular war shipping, and instead of keeping radio secrecy, we broadcast our position every fifteen minutes. The hospital ship wants the enemy to know where it is so no mistake can be made.

Our ship has had several "incidents." It has been stopped by surfaced submarines and has been circled by enemy planes. But the enemy has always respected it. The greatest danger is going to such places as Anzio, or standing in ports during air raids.

*

Usually the ward lights are left on until ten-thirty P.M. But on our trip they were turned off at nine-thirty, for we were to dock very early next morning and the men had to be wakened by five A.M. to give the nurses time to get the wounded all washed and fed.

By ten o'clock the inside of the ship was dim and quiet. Nurses went about softly in the faint glow of the blue night-light. The doctors, all through, were playing chess and solitaire in their small salon on the top deck. A few soldiers strolled on deck or hung over the rail. It was warm and gentle outside. The washing of the water seemed like a purring against the ship's sides.

It was wonderful to be going away from war instead of toward it. For the badly wounded there was a sense of completion of a task, for others a sense of respite. And the sheets and the soft beds and the security of walls lent a confidence in things present and to come.

There was intense suffering aboard that ship. But by ten-thirty you could somehow feel the quiet, masked composure that comes to men of turmoil when they settle down for the night in the clasp of a strange new safety.

And early next morning we were [at Naples].

Pyle was set to leave Italy for England, where he would await the invasion of Western Europe. But first he had to say farewell to the troops with whom he had spent a bitter winter and spring.

May 4, 1944— . . . I do hate to leave now that the time has come. I've been in this war theater so long that I think of myself as a part of it. I'm not in the Army, but I feel sort of like a deserter at leaving.

There has been some exhilaration here and some fun, along with the misery and the sadness, but on the whole it has been bitter. Few of us can ever conjure up any truly fond memories of the Italian campaign.

The enemy has been hard, and so have the elements. Men have had to stay too long in the lines. A few men have borne a burden they felt should have been shared by many more.

There is little solace for those who have suffered, and none at all for those who have died, in trying to rationalize about why things in the past were as they were.

I look at it this way—if by having only a small army in Italy we have been able to build up more powerful forces in England, and if by sacrificing a few thousand lives here this winter we can save half a million lives in Europe this summer—if these things are true, then it was best as it was.

I'm not saying they are true. I'm only saying you've got to look at it that way or else you can't bear to think of it at all. Personally, I think they are true. . . .

*

To all . . . of you in this Mediterranean army of ours—it has been wonderful in a grim, homesick, miserable sort of way to have been with you.

In two years of living with the Army there has not been one single instance from private to general when you have not been good to me. I want to thank you for that.

I've hated the whole damn business just as much as you do who have suffered more. I often wonder why I'm here at all, since I don't have to be, but I've found no answer anywhere short of insanity, so I've quit thinking about it. But I'm glad to have been here.

So this is farewell, I guess, for me. I'll probably spend the rest of the war in England and upper Europe. And then—maybe I'll see you in India.

Until then, goodbye, good luck and—as the Scottish say—God bless.

Pyle flew from Naples to Algiers and Casablanca, and from there to London.

May 5, 1944— . . . We flew most of the day and far into the night. Crossing the Mediterranean I knotted myself up on top of a pile of mail sacks and slept half the trip away.

And then, in a different plane, over western Algeria and Morocco, I got myself a blanket, stretched out on the floor and slept for hours. The sun was just setting when I woke up.

I've written many times that war isn't romantic to the people in it. Seldom have I ever felt any drama about the war or about myself in two years overseas. But here in that plane all of a sudden things did seem romantic.

A heavy darkness had come inside the cabin. Passengers were indistinct shapes, kneeling at the windows to absorb the spell of the hour. The remnants of the sun streaked the cloud-banked horizon ahead, making it vividly red and savagely beautiful.

We were high, and the motors throbbed in a timeless rhythm. Below us were the green peaks of the Atlas Mountains, lovely in the softening shroud of the dusk. Villages with red roofs nestled on the peak tops. Down there lived sheep men—obscure mountain men who had never heard of a *nebelwerfer** or a bazooka. Men at home at the end of the day in the poor, narrow, beautiful security of their own walls.

And there high in the sky above and yet part of it all were plain Americans incongruously away from home. For a moment it seemed terribly dramatic that we should be there at all amid that darkening beauty so far away and so foreign and so old.

It was one of those moments impossible to transmit to another mind. A moment of overpowering beauty, of the surge of a marching world, of the relentlessness of our own fate. It made you want to cry.

*A smoke-shell projector the Germans used to screen their positions.

FRANCE:

June 1944—September 1944

UPI

Pyle spent nearly two months in England before the invasion. He wrote a few columns to maintain his circulation, had his innoculations brought up-to-date, and attended briefings on invasion plans. London, crowded and bustling with military personnel, bothered him. "Being so close for so long to the high tension and fantastic massed suffering and tragedy of war seems to have robbed me of all ability to adjust myself to normal people," he wrote a friend. He added: "I'm no longer content unless I am with soldiers in the field." Proximity to war had fostered in him a mounting sense of his own mortality, and by the time he arrived at Falmouth, England, from London in early June 1944, he had what he called a bad case of "nerves."

Assembled along the southern English seacoast was the biggest invasion force ever. This was to be the cross-channel attack on Fortress Europe's western flank the Allies had been planning since the Casablanca Conference in early 1943. Honored that he was one of twenty-eight correspondents chosen to land in France during the first phase of the invasion, Pyle felt compelled to do so, though he had planned to go ashore only after a beachhead had been secured. General Omar Bradley, who was to command all American forces in the Normandy landings, invited Pyle to travel with him, but Pyle declined, preferring to be with the GIs. He left Falmouth aboard an LST on June 4, the same day Allied soldiers liberated Rome.

Pyle's nervousness was well-founded. He went ashore on June 7, the day after D-day, at Omaha Beach, which, along with Utah Beach, was the most heavily defended of the Allied invasion points. Ten days later he wrote a friend, "I'm sick of living in misery and fright." By that time, almost half a million Allied soldiers were ashore in France, and the breakout from the beachheads was well under way.

The Ocean Was Infested With Ships

NORMANDY BEACHHEAD, *June 15, 1944**—The ship on which I rode to the invasion of the Continent brought certain components of the second wave of assault troops. We arrived in the congested waters of the beachhead shortly after dawn on D-One Day.

We aboard this ship had secretly dreaded the trip, for we had

*Pyle wrote this column from the beachhead. Though it appears here out of chronological order, it is better suited as a prelude to his going ashore.

expected attacks from U-boats, E-boats, and at nighttime from aircraft. Yet nothing whatever happened.

We were at sea for a much longer time than it would ordinarily take to make a beeline journey from England to France. The convoy we sailed in was one of several which comprised what is known as a "force."

As we came down, the English Channel was crammed with forces going both ways, and as I write it still is. Minesweepers had swept wide channels for us, all the way from England to France. These were marked with buoys. Each channel was miles wide.

We surely saw there before us more ships than any human had ever seen before at one glance. And going north were other vast convoys, some composed of fast liners speeding back to England for new loads of troops and equipment.

As far as you could see in every direction, the ocean was infested with ships. There must have been every type of oceangoing vessel in the world. I even thought I saw a paddle-wheel steamer in the distance, but that was probably an illusion.

There were battleships and all other kinds of warships clear down to patrol boats. There were great fleets of Liberty ships. There were fleets of luxury liners turned into troop transports, and fleets of big landing craft and tank carriers and tankers. And in and out through it all were nondescript ships—converted yachts, riverboats, tugs, and barges.

The best way I can describe this vast armada and the frantic urgency of the traffic is to suggest that you visualize New York Harbor on its busiest day of the year and then just enlarge that scene until it takes in all the ocean the human eye can reach, clear around the horizon. And over the horizon there are dozens of times that many.

We were not able to go ashore immediately after arriving off the invasion coast amidst the great pool of ships in what was known as the "transport area."

*

Everything is highly organized in an invasion, and every ship, even the tiniest one, is always under exact orders timed to the minute. But at one time our convoy was so pushed along by the wind and the currents that we were five hours ahead of schedule, despite the fact that our engines had been stopped half the time. We lost this by circling.

Although we arrived just on time, they weren't ready for us on the beaches and we spent several hours weaving in and out among the multitude of ships just off the beachhead, and finally just settled down to await our turn.

That was when the most incongruous—to us—part of the invasion came. Here we were in a front-row seat at a great military epic. Shells from battleships were whamming over our heads, and occasionally a dead man floated face downward past us. Hundreds and hundreds of ships laden with death milled around us. We could stand at the rail and see both our shells and German shells exploding on the beaches, where struggling men were leaping ashore, desperately hauling guns and equipment in through the water.

We were in the very vortex of the war—and yet, as we sat there waiting, Lt. Chuck Conick and I played gin rummy in the wardroom and Bing Crosby sang "Sweet Leilani" over the ship's phonograph.

Angry shells hitting near us would make heavy thuds as the concussion carried through the water and struck the hull of our ship. But in our wardroom men in gas-impregnated uniforms and wearing lifebelts sat reading *Life* and listening to the BBC telling us how the war before our eyes was going.

But it wasn't like that ashore. No, it wasn't like that ashore.

A Pure Miracle

NORMANDY BEACHHEAD, *June 12, 1944*—Due to a last-minute alteration in the arrangements, I didn't arrive on the beachhead until the morning after D-day, after our first wave of assault troops had hit the shore.

By the time we got here the beaches had been taken and the fighting had moved a couple of miles inland. All that remained on the beach was some sniping and artillery fire, and the occasional startling blast of a mine geysering brown sand into the air. That plus a gigantic and pitiful litter of wreckage along miles of shoreline.

Submerged tanks and overturned boats and burned trucks and shell-shattered jeeps and sad little personal belongings were strewn all over these bitter sands. That plus the bodies of soldiers lying in rows covered with blankets, the toes of their shoes sticking up in a line as though on drill. And other bodies, uncollected, still sprawling grotesquely in the sand or half hidden by the high grass beyond the beach.

That plus an intense, grim determination of work-weary men to get this chaotic beach organized and get all the vital supplies and the reinforcements moving more rapidly over it from the stacked-up ships standing in droves out to sea.

*

Now that it is over it seems to me a pure miracle that we ever took the beach at all. For some of our units it was easy, but in this special sector where I am now our troops faced such odds that our getting ashore was like my whipping Joe Louis down to a pulp.

In this column I want to tell you what the opening of the second front in this one sector entailed, so that you can know and appreciate and forever be humbly grateful to those both dead and alive who did it for you.

Ashore, facing us, were more enemy troops than we had in our assault waves. The advantages were all theirs, the disadvantages all ours. The Germans were dug into positions that they had been working on for months, although these were not yet all complete. A one-hundred-foot bluff a couple of hundred yards back from the beach had great concrete gun emplacements built right into the hilltop. These opened to the sides instead of to the front, thus making it very hard for naval fire from the sea to reach them. They could shoot parallel with the beach and cover every foot of it for miles with artillery fire.

Then they had hidden machine-gun nests on the forward slopes, with crossfire taking in every inch of the beach. These nests were connected by networks of trenches, so that the German gunners could move about without exposing themselves.

Throughout the length of the beach, running zigzag a couple of hundred yards back from the shoreline, was an immmense V-shaped ditch fifteen feet deep. Nothing could cross it, not even men on foot, until fills had been made. And in other places at the far end of the beach, where the ground is flatter, they had great concrete walls. These were blasted by our naval gunfire or by explosives set by hand after we got ashore.

Our only exits from the beach were several swales or valleys, each about one hundred yards wide. The Germans made the most of these funnel-like traps, sowing them with buried mines. They contained, also, barbed-wire entanglements with mines attached, hidden ditches, and machine guns firing from the slopes.

This is what was on the shore. But our men had to go through a maze nearly as deadly as this before they even got ashore. Underwater obstacles were terrific. The Germans had whole fields of evil devices under the water to catch our boats. Even now, several days after the landing, we have cleared only channels through them and cannot yet approach the whole length of the beach with our ships. Even now some ship or boat hits one of these mines every day and is knocked out of commission.

The Germans had masses of those great six-pronged spiders, made of railroad iron and standing shoulder-high, just beneath the surface of the water for our landing craft to run into. They also had huge logs buried in the sand, pointing upward and outward, their tops just below the water. Attached to these logs were mines.

In addition to these obstacles they had floating mines offshore, land mines buried in the sand of the beach, and more mines in checkerboard rows in the tall grass beyond the sand. And the enemy had four men on shore for every three men we had approaching the shore.

And yet we got on.

*

Beach landings are planned to a schedule that is set far ahead of time. They all have to be timed, in order for everything to mesh and for the following waves of troops to be standing off the beach and ready to land at the right moment.

As the landings are planned, some elements of the assault force are to break through quickly, push on inland, and attack the most obvious enemy strong points. It is usually the plan for units to be inland, attacking gun positions from behind, within a matter of minutes after the first men hit the beach.

I have always been amazed at the speed called for in these plans. You'll have schedules calling for engineers to land at H-hour plus two minutes, and service troops at H-hour plus thirty minutes, and even for press censors to land at H-hour plus seventy-five minutes. But in the attack on this special portion of the beach where I am—the worst we had, incidentally—the schedule didn't hold.

Our men simply could not get past the beach. They were pinned down right on the water's edge by an inhuman wall of fire from the bluff. Our first waves were on that beach for hours, instead of a few minutes, before they could begin working inland.

You can still see the foxholes they dug at the very edge of the water, in the sand and the small, jumbled rocks that form parts of the beach.

Medical corpsmen attended the wounded as best they could. Men were killed as they stepped out of landing craft. An officer whom I knew got a bullet through the head just as the door of his landing craft was let down. Some men were drowned.

The first crack in the beach defenses was finally accomplished by terrific and wonderful naval gunfire, which knocked out the big emplacements. They tell epic stories of destroyers that ran right up into shallow water and had it out point-blank with the big guns in those concrete emplacements ashore.

When the heavy fire stopped, our men were organized by their officers and pushed on inland, circling machine-gun nests and taking them from the rear.

As one officer said, the only way to take a beach is to face it and keep going. It is costly at first, but it's the only way. If the men are pinned down on the beach, dug in and out of action, they might as well not be there at all. They hold up the waves behind them, and nothing is being gained.

Our men were pinned down for a while, but finally they stood up and went through, and so we took that beach and accomplished our landing. We did it with every advantage on the enemy's side and every disadvantage on ours. In the light of a couple of days of retrospection, we sit and talk and call it a miracle that our men ever got on at all or were able to stay on.

Before long it will be permitted to name the units that did it. Then you will know to whom this glory should go. They suffered casualties. And yet if you take the entire beachhead assault, including other units that had a much easier time, our total casualties in driving this wedge into the continent of Europe were remarkably low—only a fraction, in fact, of what our commanders had been prepared to accept.

And these units that were so battered and went through such hell are still, right at this moment, pushing on inland without rest, their spirits high, their egotism in victory almost reaching the smart-alecky stage.

Their tails are up. "We've done it again," they say. They figure that the rest of the army isn't needed at all. Which proves that, while their judgment in this regard is bad, they certainly have the spirit that wins battles and eventually wars.

The Horrible Waste of War

NORMANDY BEACHHEAD, *June 16, 1944*—I took a walk along the historic coast of Normandy in the country of France.

It was a lovely day for strolling along the seashore. Men were sleeping on the sand, some of them sleeping forever. Men were floating in the water, but they didn't know they were in the water, for they were dead.

The water was full of squishy little jellyfish about the size of your hand. Millions of them. In the center each of them had a green design exactly like a four-leaf clover. The good-luck emblem. Sure. Hell yes.

I walked for a mile and a half along the water's edge of our many-miled invasion beach. You wanted to walk slowly, for the detail on that beach was infinite.

The wreckage was vast and startling. The awful waste and destruction of war, even aside from the loss of human life, has always been one of its outstanding features to those who are in it. Anything and everything is expendable. And we did expend on our beachhead in Normandy during those first few hours.

*

For a mile out from the beach there were scores of tanks and trucks and boats that you could no longer see, for they were at the bottom of the water—swamped by overloading, or hit by shells, or sunk by mines. Most of their crews were lost.

You could see trucks tipped half over and swamped. You could see partly sunken barges, and the angled-up corners of jeeps, and small landing craft half submerged. And at low tide you could still see those vicious six-pronged iron snares that helped snag and wreck them.

On the beach itself, high and dry, were all kinds of wrecked vehicles. There were tanks that had only just made the beach before being knocked out. There were jeeps that had burned to a dull gray. There were big derricks on caterpillar treads that didn't quite make it. There were half-tracks carrying office equipment that had been made into a shambles by a single shell hit, their interiors still holding their useless equipage of smashed typewriters, telephones, office files.

There were LCT's turned completely upside down, and lying on their backs, and how they got that way I don't know. There were boats stacked on top of each other, their sides caved in, their suspension doors knocked off.

In this shoreline museum of carnage there were abandoned rolls of barbed wire and smashed bulldozers and big stacks of thrown-away lifebelts and piles of shells still waiting to be moved.

In the water floated empty life rafts and soldiers' packs and ration boxes, and mysterious oranges.

On the beach lay snarled rolls of telephone wire and big rolls of steel matting and stacks of broken, rusting rifles.

On the beach lay, expended, sufficient men and mechanism for a small war. They were gone forever now. And yet we could afford it.

We could afford it because we were on, we had our toehold, and behind us there were such enormous replacements for this wreckage on the beach that you could hardly conceive of their sum total. Men and equipment were flowing from England in such a gigantic stream that it made the waste on the beachhead seem like nothing at all, really nothing at all.

*

A few hundred yards back on the beach is a high bluff. Up there we had a tent hospital, and a barbed-wire enclosure for prisoners of war. From up there you could see far up and down the beach, in a spectacular crow's-nest view, and far out to sea.

And standing out there on the water beyond all this wreckage was the greatest armada man has ever seen. You simply could not believe the gigantic collection of ships that lay out there waiting to unload.

Looking from the bluff, it lay thick and clear to the far horizon of the sea and on beyond, and it spread out to the sides and was miles wide. Its utter enormity would move the hardest man.

As I stood up there I noticed a group of freshly taken German prisoners standing nearby. They had not yet been put in the prison cage. They were just standing there, a couple of doughboys leisurely guarding them with tommy guns.

The prisoners too were looking out to sea—the same bit of sea that for months and years had been so safely empty before their gaze. Now they stood staring almost as if in a trance.

They didn't say a word to each other. They didn't need to. The expression on their faces was something forever unforgettable. In it was the final horrified acceptance of their doom.

If only all Germans could have had the rich experience of standing on the bluff and looking out across the water and seeing what their compatriots saw.

A Long Thin Line of Personal Anguish

NORMANDY BEACHHEAD, *June 17, 1944*—In the preceding column we told about the D-day wreckage among our machines of war that were expended in taking one of the Normandy beaches.

But there is another and more human litter. It extends in a thin little line, just like a high-water mark, for miles along the beach. This is the strewn personal gear, gear that will never be needed again, of those who fought and died to give us our entrance into Europe.

Here in a jumbled row for mile on mile are soldiers' packs. Here are socks and shoe polish, sewing kits, diaries, Bibles and hand grenades. Here are the latest letters from home, with the address on each one neatly razored out—one of the security precautions enforced before the boys embarked.

Here are toothbrushes and razors, and snapshots of families back home staring up at you from the sand. Here are pocketbooks, metal mirrors, extra trousers, and bloody, abandoned shoes. Here are broken-handled shovels, and portable radios smashed almost beyond recognition, and mine detectors twisted and ruined.

Here are torn pistol belts and canvas water buckets, first-aid kits and jumbled heaps of lifebelts. I picked up a pocket Bible with a soldier's name in it, and put it in my jacket. I carried it half a mile or so and then put it back down on the beach. I don't know why I picked it up, or why I put it back down.

Soldiers carry strange things ashore with them. In every invasion you'll find at least one soldier hitting the beach at H-hour with a banjo slung over his shoulder. The most ironic piece of equipment marking our beach—this beach of first despair, then victory—is a tennis racket that some soldier had brought along. It lies lonesomely on the sand, clamped in its rack, not a string broken.

Two of the most dominant items in the beach refuse are cigarets and writing paper. Each soldier was issued a carton of cigarets just before he started. Today these cartons by the thousand, water-soaked and spilled out, mark the line of our first savage blow.

Writing paper and air-mail envelopes come second. The boys had intended to do a lot of writing in France. Letters that would have filled those blank, abandoned pages.

Always there are dogs in every invasion. There is a dog still on the beach today, still pitifully looking for his masters.

He stays at the water's edge, near a boat that lies twisted and half sunk at the water line. He barks appealingly to every soldier who approaches, trots eagerly along with him for a few feet, and then, sensing himself unwanted in all this haste, runs back to wait in vain for his own people at his own empty boat.

*

Over and around this long thin line of personal anguish, fresh men today are rushing vast supplies to keep our armies pushing on into France. Other squads of men pick amidst the wreckage to salvage ammunition and equipment that are still usable.

Men worked and slept on the beach for days before the last D-day victim was taken away for burial.

I stepped over the form of one youngster whom I thought dead. But when I looked down I saw he was only sleeping. He was very young, and very tired. He lay on one elbow, his hand suspended in the air about six inches from the ground. And in the palm of his hand he held a large, smooth rock.

I stood and looked at him a long time. He seemed in his sleep to hold that rock lovingly, as though it were his last link with a vanishing world. I have no idea at all why he went to sleep with the rock in his hand, or what kept him from dropping it once he was asleep. It was just one of those little things without explanation that a person remembers for a long time.

*

The strong, swirling tides of the Normandy coastline shift the contours of the sandy beach as they move in and out. They carry soldiers' bodies out to sea, and later they return them. They cover the corpses of heroes with sand, and then in their whims they uncover them.

As I plowed out over the wet sand of the beach on that first day ashore, I walked around what seemed to be a couple of pieces of driftwood sticking out of the sand. But they weren't driftwood.

They were a soldier's two feet. He was completely covered by the shifting sands except for his feet. The toes of his GI shoes pointed toward the land he had come so far to see, and which he saw so briefly.

Pyle spent his first night ashore in an apple orchard, his head beneath a jeep fender for protection from shell fragments. "Sometimes planes would come in low, and we would lie there scrunched up in that knotty tenseness you get when waiting to be hit."

On the Lighter Side

SOMEWHERE IN FRANCE, *June 21, 1944*—The war is constantly producing funny things as well as tragic things, so I might as well tell you some of our lighter incidents.

For example, the first night we spent in France one of the colonels who slept with us under an apple tree was an Army observer from Washington. Usually we don't care for observers from Washington, but this colonel was a very nice guy and a good field soldier too, and everybody liked him.

While we were eating our K-rations next morning he said he had slept fine for the first hour, before we had moved in under our jeep for protection from the flak. He said that before we moved he had found a nice little mound of earth to put his head on for a pillow. He said that all his life he had had to have a pillow of some kind. After moving under the jeep he couldn't find anything to put his head on.

With that he walked over a few feet to show us the nice mound of earth. When he looked down he started laughing. His excellent pillow of the night before had turned out in the light of day to be a pile of horse manure.

*

Another story concerns a masterful piece of wartime understatement by one of our truck drivers, Pvt. Carl Vonhorn of rural Cooperstown, New York. He had pulled into an apple orchard adjoining ours the night before, parked his truck in the darkness, spread his blankets on the ground in front of the truck, and gone to sleep.

When he woke up at daylight Vonhorn looked about him sleepily. And there on the ground right beside him, within arm's reach, was a dead German soldier. And when he looked on the other side, there, equally close, were two potato-mashers [hand grenades]. Pvt. Vonhorn got up very quickly.

Later he was telling his officers about his startling experience, and he ended his description with this philosophical remark: "It was very distasteful."

Everybody thought that was so funny it spread around the camp like fire, and now the phrase "It's very distasteful" has become practically a byword.

*

After breakfast that first morning we had to round up about fifty dead Germans and Americans in the series of orchards where we were camping, and carry them to a central spot in a pasture and bury them.

I helped carry one corpse across a couple of fields. I did it partly because the group needed an extra man, and partly because I was forcing myself to get used to it, for you can't hide from death when you're in a war.

This German was just a kid, surely not over fifteen. His face had already turned black, but you could sense his youth through the death-distorted features.

The boys spread a blanket on the ground beside him. Then we lifted him over onto it. One soldier and I each took hold of a foot, and two others took his arms. One of the two soldiers in front was hesitant about touching the corpse. Whereupon the other soldier said to him:

"Go on, take hold of him, dammit. You might as well get used to it now, for you'll be carrying plenty of dead ones from now on. Hell, you may even be carrying me one of these days."

So we carried him across two fields, each of us holding a corner of the blanket. Our burden got pretty heavy, and we rested a couple of times. The boys made wisecracks along the way to cover up their distaste for the job.

When we got to the field we weren't sure just where the lieutenant wanted the cemetery started. So we put our man down on the ground and went back for instructions. And as we walked away the funny guy of the group turned and shook a finger at the dead German and said: "Now don't you run away while we're gone."

*

The Germans leave snipers behind when they retreat, so all American bivouac areas are heavily guarded by sentries at night. And the sentries really mean business.

The other night a pretty important general whom I know was working late, as all our staff officers do these days. About midnight he left his tent to go to another general's tent and talk something over.

He had gone only about twenty feet when a sentry challenged him. And just at that moment the general, groping around in the dark, fell headlong into a deep slit trench.

It was funny, even to the general, but there was nothing humorous about it to the sentry. He suspected monkey business. He rushed up to the trench, pointed his gun at the general, and in a tone that was a mixture of terror and intent to kill, he yelled: "Git out of there and git recognized, you!"

The European Campaign Clarified

SOMEWHERE IN FRANCE, *June 22, 1944*—Folks newly arrived from America say that you people at home are grave and eager about this, our greatest operation of the war so far.

But they say also that you are giving the landings themselves an importance out of proportion to what must follow before the war can end. They say you feel that now that we are on the soil of France we will just sweep rapidly ahead and the Germans will soon crumble.

It is natural for you to feel that, and nobody is blaming you. But I thought maybe in this column I could help your understanding of things if we sort of charted this European campaign. This is no attempt to predict—it is just an effort to clarify.

*

On the German side in Western Europe we face an opponent who has been building his defenses and his forces for four years. A great army of men was here waiting for us, well prepared and well equipped.

On the English side of the Channel, we and the British spent more than two years building up to equality in men and arms with this opponent. Finally we reached that equality, and I am sure considerably more than equality.

Then—on June 6—came the invasion we had awaited for so long. The big show has begun. So let's divide the remainder of this campaign into phases.

*

Phase Number One was the highly vital task of getting ashore at all. That phase could not last long. We either had to break a hole in the beach defenses and have our men flowing through that hole within a few hours, or the jig was up. Phase Number One came out all in our favor.

We planned Phase Number Two so that we could throw in our first follow-up waves without casualties or delay. That also was a phase we didn't dare to dilly-dally about. The beaches were fairly clear of shellfire within two days.

*

Phase Number Three is what we are in right now. And that is to build a wall of troops around the outer rim of our beachhead that will hold off any German counterattacks.

The whole split-second question of the first few days was whether we could get troops and supplies through our little needle's-eye of a beachhead faster than the Germans could bring theirs from all over Europe.

As this is written, no important counterattack has developed. The Germans are having plenty of trouble moving their stuff up, because of our savage air activity. Every day that passes adds to our forces and gives us greater security.

If we can hold that outer line against all attack for a short while yet, then we will have won Phase Number Three. And right now it certainly seems that we are winning it.

*

Phases One, Two and Three were all preliminary ones. It took three of them merely to get us a place in Europe from which to begin. The three of them merely give us the corner lot on which we are going to build our house.

Phase Number Four is the house-building phase. This is the phase you folks at home have been working so hard to make possible.

In England and America we've got the men and machines and supplies and munitions to overbalance the great stockpile Germany has built up in Western Europe. But we've got to get it over here into France before we go on.

You may have imagined that we would hit the beach and go right on, advancing thirty miles a day till we reached the German border. We could no more do that than a baby, after taking its first step, could run a hundred-yard dash. You have to wait until your strength is built up before you can run.

That is Phase Number Four. It will go on for some time yet. Don't be impatient. The wall in front of us will hold while we gradually pile this beachhead to the saturation point with extra men, guns, trucks, food, ammunition, gasoline, telephone wire, repair shops, hospitals, airfields, and thousands of other items—pack it until we have more than the Germans have, and with lots of reserves in addition.

*

Then, and not until then, will Phase Number Five start. Phase Number Five is the real war—big-scale war. How long we will have to wait between now and the beginning of Phase Number Five I don't know. But my guess is that it will take months rather than weeks.

Naturally there will be fighting during that time. The Germans will try to crush us back onto the beaches. We at the same time will try to extend our holdings enough to protect our accumulating men and supplies.

But Phase Number Five will be the final one. How long it will last I also don't know—and in that ignorance I have a great deal of company. I doubt if anyone in the world knows. All we do know is that things look good and that it will definitely end in our favor.

So don't be impatient if we seem to go slowly for a while. You can't lay the foundation of a house in the forenoon and move into the house that evening. We are just now laying the foundation of our house of war in Europe. It will take a while to build the walls and get the roof on. And then . . .

A Tour of the Peninsula

ON THE CHERBOURG PENINSULA, *June 23, 1944*—The day after troops of our 9th Division pushed through and cut off this peninsula I went touring in a jeep over the country they had just taken.

This Norman country is truly lovely in many places. Here in the western part of the peninsula the ground becomes hilly and rolling. Everything is a vivid green, there are trees everywhere, and the view across the fields from a rise looks exactly like the rich, gentle land of eastern Pennsylvania. It is too wonderfully beautiful to be the scene of war, and yet so were parts of Tunisia and Sicily and Italy. Someday I would like to cover a war in a country that is as ugly as war itself.

Our ride was a sort of spooky one. The American troops had started north and were driving on Cherbourg. This was possible because the Germans in that section were thoroughly disorganized, and by now capable of nothing more than trying to escape.

There was no traffic whatever on the roads. You could drive for miles without seeing a soul. We had been told that the country was still full of snipers, and we knew there were batches of Germans in the woods waiting to surrender. And yet we saw nothing. The beautiful, tree-bordered lanes were empty. Cattle grazed contentedly in the fields. It was as though life had taken a holiday and death was in hiding. It gave you the willies.

Finally we came to a stone schoolhouse which was being used as a prisoner-of-war collection point, so we stopped for a look. Here groups of prisoners were constantly being brought in. And here individual American soldiers who had been cut off behind the lines for days came wearily to rest for a while in the courtyard before going on back to hunt up their outfits.

Most of the prisoners coming in at the time were from a captured German hospital. German doctors had set up shop in a shed adjoining the school and were treating their prisoners, who had slight wounds. At the moment I walked up, one soldier had his pants down and a doctor was probing for a fragment in his hip.

Two or three of the German officers spoke some English. They were in a very good humor. One of them, a doctor, said to me: "I've been in the Army four years, and today is the best day I have spent in the Army."

*

In this courtyard I ran onto two boys who had just walked back after losing their jeep and being surrounded for hours that morning by Germans.

They were Pfc. Arthur MacDonald of Portsmouth, New Hampshire, and Pvt. T. C. McFarland of Southern Pines, North Carolina. They were forward observers for the 9th Division's artillery.

They had bunked down the night before in a pasture. When they woke up they could hear voices all around, and they weren't American voices. They peeked out and saw a German at a latrine not thirty feet away.

So they started crawling. They crawled for hours. Finally they got out of the danger zone, and they started walking. They met a French farmer along the road, and took him in tow.

"We sure captured that Frenchman," they said. "He was so scared he could hardly talk. We used high-school French and a dictionary and finally got it through his head that all we wanted was something to eat. So he took us to his house. He fried eggs and pork and made coffee for us.

"Our morale sure was low this morning, but that Frenchman we captured fixed it up."

The boys pulled out a couple of snapshots of the Frenchman, and they were so grateful that I imagine they will carry those pictures the rest of their lives.

At this time the French in that vicinity had been "liberated" less than twelve hours, and they could hardly encompass it in their minds. They were relieved, but they hardly knew what to do.

As we left the prison enclosure and got into our jeep we noticed four or five French country people—young farmers in their twenties, I would take them to be—leaning against a nearby house.

As we sat in the jeep getting our gear adjusted, one of the farmers walked toward us, rather hesitantly and timidly. But finally he came up and smilingly handed me a rose.

I couldn't go around carrying a rose in my hand all afternoon, so I threw it away around the next bend. But little things like that do sort of make you feel good about the human race.

Good-Will-Towards-Men Rang Through the Air

BARNEVILLE, NORMANDY, *June 24, 1944*—From this picturesque little town you can look down upon the western sea. In the center of Barneville is a sloping, paved court, a sort of public square except that it is rectangular instead of square.

At one end of the square an Army truck was parked. Scattered around the square were half a dozen American soldiers standing in doorways with their rifles at the ready. There were a few French people on the streets.

We went to the far end of the square, where three local French policemen were standing in front of the mayor's office.

They couldn't speak any English, but they said there was one woman in town who did, and a little boy was sent running for her. Gradually a crowd of eager and curious people crushed in upon us, until there must have been two hundred of them, from babies to old women.

Finally the woman arrived—a little dark woman with graying hair, and spectacles, and a big smile. Her English was quite good, and we asked her if there were any Germans in the town. She turned and asked the policemen.

Instantly everybody in the crowd started talking at once. The sound was like that of a machine that increases in speed until its noise drowns out all else.

Finally the policeman had to shush the crowd so the woman could answer us.

She said there were Germans all around, in the woods, but none whatsoever left in the town. Just then a German stuck his head out of a nearby second-story window. Somebody saw him, and an American soldier was dispatched to get him.

Barneville is a fortunate place, because not a shell was fired into it by either side. The lieutenant with us told the woman we were glad nobody had been hurt. When she translated this for the crowd, there was much nodding in approval of our good wishes.

*

We must have stood and talked for an hour and a half. It was a kind of holiday for the local people. They were relieved but still not quite sure the Germans wouldn't be back. They were still under a restraint that wouldn't let them open up riotously. But you could sense from little things that they were glad to have us.

A little French shopkeeper came along with a spool of red, white and blue ribbon from his store. He cut off pieces about six inches long for all hands, both American and French. In a few minutes everybody was going around with a French tricolor in his buttonhole.

Then a ruddy-faced man of middle age, who looked like a gentleman farmer, drove up in one of those one-horse, high-wheeled work carts that the French use.

He had a German prisoner in uniform standing behind him, and another one, who was sick, lying on a stretcher. The farmer had captured these guys himself, and he looked so pleased with himself that I expected him to take a bow at any moment.

French people kept coming up and asking us for instructions. A man who looked as if he might be the town banker asked what he was supposed to do with prisoners.

We told him to bring them to the truck, and asked how many he had. To our astonishment he said he had seventy in the woods a couple of miles away, a hundred twenty in a nearby town, and forty in another town.

As far as I could figure it out he had captured them all himself.

Another worried-looking Frenchman came up. He was a doctor. He said he had twenty-six badly wounded Germans down at the railroad station and desperately needed medical supplies. He wanted chloroform and sulfa drugs. We told him we would have some sent.

One character in the crowd looked as if he belonged in a novel of bohemian life on the Left Bank in Paris. He couldn't possibly have been anything but a poet. He wore loose, floppy clothes that made him look like a woman. His glasses were thick, and hair about a foot long curled around his ears. I wish you could have seen the expressions of our tough, dirty soldiers when they looked at him.

*

When we finally started away from the crowd, a little old fellow in faded blue overalls ran up and asked us, in sign language, to come to his café for a drink. Since we didn't dare violate the spirit of hands-across-the-sea that was then wafting about the town, we had to sacrifice ourselves and accept.

So we sat on wooden benches at a long bare table while the little Frenchman puttered and sputtered around. He let two policemen and his own family in, and then took the handle out of the front door so nobody else could get in.

The Germans had drunk up all his stock except for some wine and some *eau de vie.* In case you don't know, *eau de vie* is a savage liquid made by boiling barbed wire, soapsuds, watch springs and old tent pegs together. The better brands have a touch of nitroglycerine for flavor.

So the little Frenchman filled our tiny glasses. We raised them, touched glasses all around, and *vived la France* all over the place, and good-will-towards-men rang out through the air and tears ran down our cheeks.

In this case, however, the tears were largely induced by our violent efforts to refrain from clutching at our throats and crying out in anguish. This good-will business is a tough life, and I think every

American who connects with a glass of *eau de vie* should get a Purple Heart.

Hedgerow Sniping

SOMEWHERE IN FRANCE, *June 26, 1944*—Sniping, as far as I know, is recognized as a legitimate means of warfare. And yet there is something sneaking about it that outrages the American sense of fairness.

I had never sensed this before we landed in France and began pushing the Germans back. We have had snipers before—in Bizerte and Cassino and lots of other places. But always on a small scale.

Here in Normandy the Germans have gone in for sniping in a wholesale manner. There are snipers everywhere. There are snipers in trees, in buildings, in piles of wreckage, in the grass. But mainly they are in the high, bushy hedgerows that form the fences of all the Norman fields and line every roadside and lane.

It is perfect sniping country. A man can hide himself in the thick fence-row shrubbery with several days' rations, and it's like hunting a needle in a haystack to find him.

Every mile we advance there are dozens of snipers left behind us. They pick off our soldiers one by one as they walk down the roads or across the fields.

It isn't safe to move into a new bivouac area until the snipers have been cleaned out. The first bivouac I moved into had shots ringing through it for a full day before all the hidden gunmen were rounded up. It gives you the same spooky feeling that you get on moving into a place you suspect of being sown with mines.

*

In past campaigns our soldiers would talk about the occasional snipers with contempt and disgust. But here sniping has become more important, and taking precautions against it is something we have had to learn and learn fast.

One officer friend of mine said: "Individual soldiers have become sniper-wise before, but now we're sniper-conscious as whole units."

Snipers kill as many Americans as they can, and then when their food and ammunition run out they surrender. To an American, that isn't quite ethical. The average American soldier has little feeling against the average German soldier who has fought an open fight and lost. But his feelings about the sneaking snipers can't very well be put into print. He is learning how to kill the snipers before the time comes for them to surrender.

As a matter of fact this part of France is very difficult for anything but fighting between small groups. It is a country of little fields, every one bordered by a thick hedge and a high fence of trees. There is hardly anyplace where you can see beyond the field ahead of you. Most of the time a soldier doesn't see more than a hundred yards in any direction.

In other places the ground is flooded and swampy with a growth of high, junglelike grass. In this kind of stuff it is almost man-to-man warfare. One officer who had served a long time in the Pacific says this fighting is the nearest thing to Guadalcanal that he has seen since.

*

Thousands of little personal stories will dribble out of D-day on the Normandy beachhead. A few that I pick up from time to time I will pass along to you.

The freakiest story I've heard is of an officer who was shot through the face. He had his mouth wide open at the time, yelling at somebody. The bullet went in one cheek and right through his mouth without touching a thing, not even his teeth, and out the other cheek. That sounds dreadful, but actually the wound is a fairly slight one and the officer will be in action again before very long.

June 28, 1944— . . . Some . . . German officers are pleased at being captured, but your dyed-in-the-wool Nazi is not. They brought in a young one the other day who was furious. He considered it thoroughly unethical that we fought so hard.

The Americans had attacked all night, and the Germans don't like night attacks. When this special fellow was brought in he protested in rage.

"You Americans! The way you fight! This is not war! This is madness!"

The German was so outraged he never even got the irony of his own remarks—that madness though it be, it works.

*

Another high-ranking officer was brought in and the first thing he asked was the whereabouts of his personal orderly. When told that his orderly was deader than a mackerel, he flew off the handle and accused us of depriving him of his personal comfort.

"Who's going to dig my foxhole for me?" he demanded. . . .

June 29, 1944—All the American soldiers here are impressed by the loveliness of the Normandy countryside. Except for swampy places it is almost a dreamland of beauty. Everything is so green and rich and natural looking.

There are no fences as such. All the little fields are bordered either by high trees or by earthen ridges built up about waist-high and now after many centuries completely covered with grass, shrubbery, ferns and flowers.

Normandy differs from the English landscape mainly in that rural England is fastidiously trimmed and cropped like a Venetian garden, while in Normandy the grass needs cutting and the hedgerows are wild, and everything has less of neatness and more of the way nature makes it.

The main roads in Normandy are macadam and the side roads gravel. The roads are winding, narrow, and difficult for heavy military traffic. In many places we've made roads one-way for miles at a stretch.

The average American finds the climate of Normandy abominable, even in June. We have about one nice day for three bad days. On nice days the sky is clear blue and the sun is out and everything seems wonderful except that there is still a hidden chill in the air, and even in your tent or under a shade tree you're cold.

And on the bad days the whole universe is dark and you need lights in your tent at noontime, and it drizzles or sprinkles, and often a cold wind blows, and your bones and your heart, too, are miserable.

Most everybody has on his long underwear. I wear four sweaters in addition to my regular uniform. Overcoats were taken away from our troops before we left England, and there are a lot of our boys not too warmly clad.

There is a constant dampness in the air. At night you put your clothes under your bedroll or they're wet in the morning. All this dampness makes for ruddy cheeks and green grass. But ruddy cheeks are for girls and green grass for cows, and personally I find the ordinary American is happiest when he's good and stinking hot. . . .

June 30, 1944—One of the most vital responsibilities during these opening weeks of our war on the Continent of Europe has been the protection of our unloading beaches and ports.

For over and through them must pass, without interruption, and in great masses, our build-up of men and material in sufficient masses to roll the Germans clear back out of France.

Nothing must be allowed to interfere with that unloading. Everything we can lay our hands on is thrown into the guarding of those beaches and ports. Allied ground troops police them from the land side. Our two navies protect them from sneak attacks by sea. Our great air supremacy makes daytime air assaults rare and costly.

It is only at night that the Germans have a chance. They do keep pecking away at us with night bombers, but their main success in this so far has been in keeping us awake and making us dig our foxholes deeper.

The job of protecting the beaches at night has been given over to the anti-aircraft artillery, or ack-ack. I read recently that we have here on the beachhead the greatest concentration of anti-aircraft guns ever assembled in an equivalent space. After three solid weeks of being kept awake all night long by the guns, and having to snatch your little sleep in odd moments during the daytime, that is not hard to believe.

Ack-Ack on the Beachhead

IN NORMANDY, *July 1, 1944*—American anti-aircraft gunners began playing their important part in the Battle of Normandy right on D-day and shortly after H-hour.

Ordinarily you wouldn't think of the anti-aircraft coming ashore with the infantry, but a little bit of everything came ashore on that memorable day—from riflemen to press censors, from combat engineers to chaplains—and everybody had a hand in it.

The ack-ack was given a place in the very early waves because the general in command felt that the Germans would throw what air strength they had onto the beaches that day and he wanted his men there to repel it.

As it turned out, the Germans didn't use their planes at all and the ack-ack wasn't needed to protect the landings from air attack. So, like many other units, they turned themselves into infantry or artillery and helped win the battle of the beaches.

They took infantry-like casualties, too. One unit lost half of its men and guns.

When I started rounding up material for this ack-ack series I ran onto the story of one crew of ack-ackers who had knocked out a German 88 deeply ensconced in a thick concrete emplacement—and did it with a tiny 37-mm gun, which is somewhat akin to David slaying Goliath.

So I hunted up this crew to see how they did it. By that time they had moved several miles inland. I found them at the edge of a small open field far out in the country.

Their gun had been dug into the ground. Two men sat constantly in their bucket seats behind the gun, keeping watch on the sky even in the daytime. The others slept in their pup tents under the bushes, or just loafed around and brewed an occasional cup of coffee.

The commander of this gun is Sgt. Hyman Haas of Brooklyn. Sgt. Haas is an enthusiastic and flattering young man who was practically beside himself with delight when I showed up at their remote position, for he had read this column back in New York but hadn't supposed our trails would ever cross in an army this big. When I told him I wanted to write a little about his crew he beamed and said:

"Oh boy! Wait till Flatbush Avenue hears about this!"

Their story is this:

They came ashore behind the first wave of infantry. A narrow valley leading away from the beach at that point was blocked by the German 88, which stopped everything in front of it. So driver Bill Hendrix from Shreveport, Louisiana, turned their half-track around and drove the front end back into the water so the gun would be pointing in the right direction.

Then the boys poured twenty-three rounds into the pillbox. Some of their shells hit the small gun slits and went inside. At the end of their firing, what Germans were left came out with their hands up.

The boys were very proud of their achievement, but I was kind of amused at their modesty. One of them said: "The credit should go to Lt. Gibbs, because he gave us the order to fire."

The lieutenant is Wallace Gibbs of rural Charlotte, North Carolina. The other members of the crew are Corp. John Jourdain of New Orleans; Pvt. Frank Bartolomeo of Ulevi, Pennsylvania; Pvt. Joseph Sharpe of Clover, South Carolina; Pfc. Frank Furey of Brooklyn; Corp. Austin Laurent, Jr., of New Orleans; and Pvt. Raymond Bullock of Coello, Illinois.

Their gun is named "BLIP," which represents the first letters of Brooklyn, Louisiana, Illinois and Pennsylvania, where most of the crew come from.

*

Our ack-ack on the Normandy beachhead can be divided into three categories. First are the machine guns, both 50-caliber and 20-mm. Airplanes have to be fairly low for these to be effective.

The ack-ack branch has thousands of such guns, and so does every other fighting unit. When a low-flying strafer comes in, everybody who has anything bigger than a rifle shoots at him, whether he is an ack-ack man or not.

The second big category of ack-ack is the Bofors, a 40-mm long-barreled gun which can fire rapidly and with great accuracy at medium altitudes.

Our ack-ack is equipped with thousands of these, and although they can't see their targets at night they put a lot of shells into the sky anyhow.

The big gun, and the elite of our ack-ack, is the 90-mm. This is for high-altitude shooting. It is the gun which keeps most of the planes away, and which has such a high score of planes shot down. I spent two days and nights with one of these crews, and I will try to tell you what life is like for them.

July 3, 1944— . . . My crew consists of thirteen men. Some of them operate the dials on the gun, others load and fire it, others lug the big shells from a storage pit a few feet away.

These big 90-mm guns usually operate in batteries, and a battery consists of four guns and the family of technicians necessary to operate the many scientific devices that control the guns.

The four guns of this particular battery are dug into the ground in a small open field, about fifty yards apart. The gunners sleep in pup tents or under half-tracks hidden under trees and camouflage nets.

The boys work all night and sleep in the daytime. They haven't dug foxholes, for the only danger is at night and they are up firing all night.

The guns require a great deal of daytime work to keep them in shape, so half of the boys sleep in the forenoon and half in the afternoon while the other half work.

Their life is rugged, but they don't see the seamiest side of the war. They stay quite a while in one place, which makes for comfort, and they are beyond enemy artillery range. Their only danger is from bombing or strafing, and that is not too great. They are so new at war that they still try to keep themselves clean. They shave and wash their clothes regularly.

Their service section has not come over yet from England, so they have to cook their own meals. They're pretty sick of this and will be glad when the service boys and the field kitchens catch up with them. They eat ten-in-one rations, heating them over a fire of wooden sticks sunk into a shallow hole in the ground.

The sergeant who is commander of my gun is a farm boy from Iowa, and none of the crew are past their middle twenties. Only two of the thirteen are married. They have been overseas more than six months, and like everybody else they are terribly anxious to go home. They like to think in terms of anniversaries, and much of their conversation is given to remembering what they were doing a year ago today when they were in camp back in America. They all hope they won't have to go to the Pacific when the European war is over.

My crew are a swell bunch of boys. They all work hard and they work well together. There are no gold-brickers in the crew. As in any group of a dozen men, some are talkative and some are quiet. There are no smart-alecks among them. . . .

My boys are very proud of their first night on the soil of France. They began firing immediately from a field not far from the beach. The snipers were still thick in the surrounding hedges, and bullets were singing around them all night. The boys like to tell over and over how the infantry all around them were crouching and crawling along while they had to stand straight up and dig their guns in.

It takes about twelve hours of good hard work to dig in the guns when they move to a new position. They dig in one gun at a time while the three others are firing. My gun is dug into a circular pit about four feet deep and twenty feet across. This has been rimmed with a parapet of sandbags and dirt, until when you stand on the floor of the pit you can just see over the top. The boys are safe down there from anything but a direct hit.

Their gun is covered in the daytime by a large camouflage net. My crew fires anywhere from ten to one hundred fifty shells a night. In the very early days on the beachhead they kept firing one night until they had only half a dozen shells left. But the supply has been built up now, and there is no danger of their running short again.

The first night I was with them was a slow night and they fired only nine shells. The boys were terribly disappointed. They said it would have to turn out that the night I was with them would be the quietest and also the coldest they had ever had.

So just because of that I stayed a second night with them. And that time we fired all night long. It was indicated that we had brought down seven of the fifteen planes we fired at, and the boys were elated.

July 5, 1944—The Germans are methodical in their night air attacks on our positions in Normandy, as they are in everything else. You begin to hear the faint, faraway drone of the first bomber around eleven-twenty every night.

Our own planes patrol above us until darkness. It gets dusk

around eleven o'clock, and you are suddenly aware that the skies which have been roaring all day with our own fighters and bombers are now strangely silent. Nothing is in the air.

The ack-ack gunners, who have been loafing near their pup tents or sleeping or telling stories, now go to their guns. They bring blankets from the pup tents and pile them up against the wall of the gun pit, for the nights get very cold and they will wrap up during long lulls in the shooting.

The gunners merely loaf in the gun pit as the dusk deepens into darkness, waiting for the first telephoned order to start shooting. They smoke a few last-minute cigarets. Once it is dark they can't smoke except by draping blankets over themselves for blackout. They do smoke some that way during the night, but not much.

*

In four or five places in the wall of the circular pit, shelves have been dug and wooden shell boxes inserted to hold reserve shells. It is just like pigeonholes in a filing cabinet.

When the firing starts, two ammunition carriers bring new shells from a dump a few feet away up to the rim of the gun pit and hand them down to a carrier waiting below, who keeps the pigeonholes filled. The gun is constantly turning in the pit and there is always a pigeonhole of fresh shells right behind it.

The shells are as long as your arm and they weigh better than forty pounds. After each salvo the empty shell case kicks out onto the floor of the pit. These lie there until there is a lull in the firing, when the boys toss them over the rim of the pit. Next morning they are gathered up and put in boxes for eventual shipment back to America, where they are retooled for further use.

Each gun is connected by telephone to the battery command post, in a dugout. At all times one member of each gun crew has a phone to his ear. When a plane is picked up within range the battery commander gives a telephonic order, "Stand by!" Each gun commander shouts the order to his crew, and the boys all jump to their positions. . . .

Night in a Gun Pit

IN NORMANDY, *July 6, 1944*—It is eleven-fifteen at night. The sky darkens into an indistinct dusk, but it is not yet fully dark. You can make out the high hedgerow surrounding our field and the seven long barrels of the other ack-ack guns of our battery poking upwards.

We all lean against the wall of our gun pit, just waiting for our night's work to start. We have plenty of time yet. The Germans won't be here for ten or fifteen minutes.

But no. Suddenly the gun commander, who is at the phone, yells: "Stand by!"

The men jump to their positions. The plane is invisible, but you can hear the distant motors throbbing in the sky. Somehow you can always sense, just from the tempo in which things start, when it is going to be a heavy night. You feel now that this will be one.

*

One of the gunners turns a switch on the side of the gun, and it goes into remote control. From now on a mystic machine at the far end of the field handles the pointing of the gun, through electrical cables. It is all automatic. The long snout of the barrel begins weaving in the air and the mechanism that directed it makes a buzzing noise. The barrel goes up and down, to the right and back to the left, grinding and whining and jerking. It is like a giant cobra, maddened and with its head raised, weaving back and forth before striking.

Finally the gun settles rigidly in one spot and the gun commander calls out: "On target! Three rounds! Commence firing!"

The gun blasts forth with sickening force. A brief sheet of flame shoots from the muzzle. Dense, sickening smoke boils around in the gun pit. You hear the empty shell case clank to the ground.

Darkly silhouetted figures move silently, reloading. In a few seconds the gun blasts again. And once again. The smoke is stifling now. You feel the blast sweep over you and set you back a little.

The salvo is fired. The men step back. You take your fingers from your ears. The smoke gradually clears. And now once more the gun is intently weaving about, grinding and whining and seeking for a new prey.

That's the way it is all night. You never see a thing. You only hear the thrump, thrump of motors in the sky and see the flash of guns and the streaking of red tracers far away. You never see the plane you're shooting at, unless it goes down in flames, and "flamers" are rare.

I found out one thing by being with the ack-ack at night. And that is that you're much less nervous when you're out in the open with a gun in front of you than when you're doubled up under blankets in your tent, coiled and intent for every little change of sound, doubtful and imagining and terrified.

*

We shoot off and on, with "rest" periods of only a few minutes, for a couple of hours. The Germans are busy boys tonight.

Then suddenly a flare pops in the sky, out to sea, in front of us. Gradually the night brightens until the whole universe is alight and we can easily make each other out in the gun pit and see everything around us in the field.

Now everybody is tense and staring. We all dread flares. Planes are throbbing and droning all around in the sky above the light. Surely the Germans will go for the ships that are standing off the beach, or they may even pick out the gun batteries and come for us in the brightness.

The red tracers of the machine guns begin arching toward the flares but can't reach them. Then our own "Stand by!" order comes, and the gun whines and swings and feels its way into the sky until it is dead on the high flare.

Yes, we are shooting at the flare. And our showering bursts of flak hit it, too.

You don't completely shoot out a flare. But you break it up into small pieces, and the light is dimmed, and the pieces come floating down more rapidly and the whole thing is over sooner.

Flares in the sky are always frightening. They strip you naked, and make you want to cower and hide and peek out from behind an elbow. You feel a great, welcome privacy when the last piece flickers to the ground and you can go back to shooting at the darkness from out of the dark.

Catnap and Fire

IN NORMANDY, *July 7, 1944*—The six hours of nighttime go swiftly for our ack-ack battery, which is a blessing. Time races when you are firing. And in the long lulls between the waves of enemy planes you doze and catnap and the time gets away.

Once, during a lull long after midnight, half a dozen of the boys in our gunpit start singing softly. Their voices are excellent. Very low and sweetly they sing in perfect harmony such songs as "I've Been Workin' on the Railroad" and "Tipperary."

There isn't anything forced, or dramatic, about it. It's just half a dozen young fellows singing because they like to sing—and the fact that they are in a gunpit in France shooting at people, trying to kill them, is just a circumstance.

*

The night grows bitterly chill. Between firings every man drapes an army blanket around his shoulders, and sometimes up over his head, capelike. In the darkness they are just silhouettes, looking strange and foreign like Arabs.

After two o'clock there is a long lull. Gradually the boys wrap up in their blankets and lie down on the floor of the pit and fall asleep. Pretty soon you hear them snoring. I talk with the gun commander for a few minutes, in low tones. Then my eyes get heavy too.

I wrap a blanket around me and sit down on the floor of the pit, leaning against the wall. The night is now as silent as a grave. Not a shot, not a movement anywhere.

My head slacks over to one side. But I can't relax enough to sleep in that position. And it is so cold. I am so sleepy I hurt, and I berate myself because I can't go to sleep like the others.

But I'm asleep all the time. For suddenly a voice shouts "Stand by!"—and it is as shocking as a bucket of cold water in your face. You look quickly at your watch and realize that an hour has passed. All the silent forms come frantically to life. Blankets fly. Men bump into each other.

"Commence firing!" rings out above the confusion, and immediately the great gun is blasting away, and smoke again fills the gunpit.

Sleep and rouse up. Catnap and fire. The night wears on. Sometimes a passing truck sounds exactly like a faraway plane. Frightened French dogs bark in distant barnyards.

Things are always confusing and mysterious in war. Just before dawn an airplane draws nearer and nearer, lower and lower, yet we get no order to shoot and we wonder why. But machine guns and Bofors guns for miles around go after it.

The plane comes booming on in, in a long dive. He seems to be heading right at us. We feel like ducking low in the pit. He actually crosses the end of our field less than a hundred yards from us, and only two or three hundred feet up. Our hearts are pounding.

We don't know who he is or what he is doing. Our own planes are not supposed to be in the air. Yet if this is a German why doesn't he bomb or strafe us? We never find out.

*

The first hint of dawn comes. Most of us are asleep again. Suddenly one of the boys calls out, "Look! What's that?"

We stare into the faint light, and there just above us goes a great, silent, grotesque shape, floating slowly through the air. It is a ghostly sight.

Then we recognize it, and all of us feel a sense of relief. It is one of our barrage balloons which has broken loose and is drifting to earth. Something snags it in the next field, and it hangs there poised above the apple trees until somebody comes and gets it long after daylight.

As fuller light comes we start lighting cigarets in the open. The battery commander asks over the phone how many shells were fired, and tells us our tentative score for the night is seven planes shot down. The crew is proud and pleased.

Dawn brings an imagined warmth and we throw off our blankets. Our eyes feel gravelly and our heads groggy. The blast of the gun has kicked up so much dirt that our faces are as grimy as though we had driven all night in a dust storm. The green Norman countryside is wet and glistening with dew.

Then we hear our own planes drumming in the distance. Suddenly they pop out of a cloud bank and are over us. Security for another day has come, and we surrender willingly the burden of protecting the beaches. The last "Rest!" is given and we put the gun away until another darkness comes.

Pyle spent nine days with the 9th Infantry Division during its assault on the port city of Cherbourg, north of the Normandy beachheads. The 9th, though it had served in Tunisia and Sicily, had received scant press attention, an oversight Pyle sought to remedy. Here he describes an infantry attack on German positions on the city's outskirts, during which the 9th "kept tenaciously on the enemy's neck."

Anticipation is the Worst

IN NORMANDY, *July 13, 1944*—Lt. Orion Shockley came over with a map and explained to us just what his company was going to do.

There was a German strong point of pillboxes and machine-gun nests about half a mile down the street ahead of us.

Our troops had made wedges into the city on both sides of us, but nobody had yet been up this street where we were going. The street, they thought, was almost certainly under rifle fire.

"This is how we'll do it," the lieutenant said. "A rifle platoon goes first. Right behind them will go part of a heavy-weapons platoon, with machine guns to cover the first platoon.

"Then comes another rifle platoon. Then a small section with mortars, in case they run into something pretty heavy. Then another rifle platoon. And bringing up the rear, the rest of the heavy-weapons outfit to protect us from behind.

"We don't know what we'll run into, and I don't want to stick you right out in front, so why don't you come along with me? We'll go in the middle of the company."

I said, "Okay." By this time I wasn't scared. You seldom are once you're into something. Anticipation is the worst. Fortunately this little foray came up so suddenly there wasn't time for much anticipation.

*

The rain kept on coming down, and you could sense that it had set in for the afternoon. None of us had raincoats, and by evening there wasn't a dry thread on any of us. I could go back to a tent for the night but the soldiers would have to sleep the way they were.

We were just ready to start when all of a sudden bullets came whipping savagely right above our heads.

"It's those damn twenty-millimeters again," the lieutenant said. "Better hold it up a minute."

The soldiers all crouched lower behind the wall. The vicious little shells whanged into a grassy hillside just beyond us. A French suburban farmer was hitching up his horses in a barnyard on the hillside. He ran into the house. Shells struck all around it.

Two dead Germans and a dead American still lay in his driveway. We could see them when we moved up a few feet.

The shells stopped, and finally the order to start was given. As we left the protection of the high wall we had to cross a little culvert right out in the open and then make a turn in the road.

The men went forward one at a time. They crouched and ran, apelike, across this dangerous space. Then, beyond the culvert, they filtered to either side of the road, stopping and squatting down every now and then to wait a few moments.

The lieutenant kept yelling at them as they started: "Spread it out now. Do you want to draw fire on yourselves? Don't bunch up like that. Keep five yards apart. Spread it out, dammit."

There is an almost irresistible pull to get close to somebody when you are in danger. In spite of themselves, the men would run up close to the fellow ahead for company.

The other lieutenant now called out: "Now you on the right watch the left side of the street for snipers, and you on the left watch the right side. Cover each other that way."

And a first sergeant said to a passing soldier: "Get that grenade out of its case. It won't do you no good in the case. Throw the case away. That's right."

*

Some of the men carried grenades already fixed in the ends of their rifles. All of them had hand grenades. Some had big Browning automatic rifles. One carried a bazooka. Interspersed in the thin line of men every now and then was a medic, with his bags of bandages and a Red Cross arm band on the left arm. The men didn't talk any. They just went.

They weren't heroic figures as they moved forward one at a time, a few seconds apart. You think of attackers as being savage and bold. These men were hesitant and cautious. They were really the hunters, but they looked like the hunted. There was a confused excitement and a grim anxiety on their faces.

They seemed terribly pathetic to me. They weren't warriors. They were American boys who by mere chance of fate had wound up with guns in their hands sneaking up a death-laden street in a strange and shattered city in a faraway country in a driving rain. They were afraid, but it was beyond their power to quit. They had no choice.

They were good boys. I talked with them all afternoon as we sneaked slowly forward along the mysterious and rubbled street, and I know they were good boys.

And even though they aren't warriors born to the kill, they win their battles. That's the point.

You Feel Lonely Out There

IN NORMANDY, *July 14, 1944*—It was about time for me to go—out alone into that empty expanse of fifteen feet—as the infantry company I was with began its move into the street that led to what we did not know.

One of the soldiers asked if I didn't have a rifle. Every time you're really in the battle lines they'll ask you that. I said no, correspondents weren't allowed to carry weapons; it was against international law. The soldiers thought that didn't seem right.

Finally the sergeant motioned—it was my turn. I ran with bent knees, shoulders hunched, out across the culvert and across the open space. Lord, but you felt lonely out there.

I had to stop right in the middle of the open space, to keep my distance behind the man ahead. I got down behind a little bush, as though that would have stopped anything.

*

Just before starting I had got into a conversation with a group of soldiers who were to go right behind me. I was just starting to put down the boys' names when my turn came to go. So it wasn't till an hour or more later, during one of our long waits as we sat crouching against some buildings, that I worked my way back along the line and took down their names.

*

It was pouring rain, and as we squatted down for me to write on my knee each soldier would have to hold my helmet over my notebook to keep it from being soaked. Here are the names of just a few of my "company mates" in that little escapade that afternoon:

Sgt. Joseph Palajsa of Pittsburgh.

Pfc. Arthur Greene of Auburn, Massachusetts. His New England accent was so broad I had to have him spell out "Arthur" and "Auburn" before I could catch what he said.

Pfc. Dick Medici of Detroit.

Lt. James Giles, a platoon leader, from Athens, Tennessee. He was so wet, so worn, so soldier-looking that I was startled when he said "lieutenant," for I thought he was a GI.

Pfc. Arthur Slageter of Cincinnati. He was an old reader of this column back home, and therefore obviously a fine fellow.

Pfc. Robert Edie of New Philadelphia, Pennsylvania. Edie is thirty, he is married, and he used to work in a brewery back home. He is a bazooka man, but his bazooka was broken that day so he was just carrying a rifle.

Pfc. Ben Rienzi of New York.

Sgt. Robert Hamilton of Philadelphia, who was wounded in Africa.

And Sgt. Joe Netscavge of Shenandoah, Pennsylvania, who sports two souvenirs of the Normandy campaign—a deep dent in his helmet, where a sniper's bullet glanced off, and a leather cigaret case he got from a German prisoner.

These boys were 9th Division veterans, most of whom had fought in Tunisia and Sicily too.

*

Gradually we moved on, a few feet at a time. The soldiers hugged the walls on both sides of the street, crouching all the time. The city around us was still full of sound and fury. You couldn't tell where anything was coming from or going to.

The houses had not been blown down along this street. But now and then a wall would have a round hole through it, and the windows had all been knocked out by concussion and shattered glass littered the pavements. Gnarled telephone wire was lying everywhere.

It was a poor district. Most of the people had left the city. Shots, incidentally, always sound louder and distorted in the vacuumlike emptiness of a nearly deserted city. Lonely doors and shutters banged noisily back and forth.

All of a sudden a bunch of dogs came yowling down the street, chasing each other. Apparently their owners had left without them, and they were running wild. They made such a noise that we shooed them on in the erroneous fear that they would attract the Germans' attention.

The street was a winding one and we couldn't see as far ahead as our forward platoon. But soon we could hear rifle shots not far ahead, and the rat-tat-tat of our machine guns, and the quick blirp-blirp of German machine pistols.

For a long time we didn't move at all. While we were waiting the lieutenant decided to go into the house we were in front of. A middle-aged Frenchman and his wife were in the kitchen. They were poor people.

The woman was holding a terrier dog in her arms, belly up, the way you cuddle a baby, and soothing it by rubbing her cheek against its head. The dog was trembling with fear from the noise.

Pretty soon the word was passed back down the line that the street had been cleared as far as a German hospital about a quarter of a mile ahead. There were lots of our wounded in that hospital and they were now being liberated.

So Lt. Shockley and [Charles] Wertenbaker and [Robert] Capa* and myself got up and went up the street, still keeping close to the walls. I lost the others before I had gone far. For as I would pass doorways soldiers would call out to me and I would duck in and talk for a moment and put down a name or two.

By now the boys along the line were feeling cheerier, for no word of casualties had been passed back. And up here the city was built up enough so that the waiting riflemen had the protection of doorways. It took me half an hour to work my way up to the hospital —and then the excitement began.

IN NORMANDY, *July 15, 1944*—The hospital was in our hands, but just barely. On up the street a block, there seemed to be fighting. I say

*Charles Wertenbaker, head of the London bureau of *Time* and *Life*, had come to France to cover the Normandy invasion. Robert Capa was the celebrated war photographer.

seemed to be, because actually you can't always tell. Street fighting is just as confusing as field fighting.

One side will bang away for a while, then the other side. Between these sallies there are long lulls, with only stray and isolated shots. Just an occasional soldier is sneaking about, and you don't see anything of the enemy at all. You can't tell half the time just what the situation is, and neither can the soldiers.

About a block beyond the hospital entrance two American tanks were sitting in the middle of the street, one about fifty yards ahead of the other. I walked toward them. Our infantrymen were in doorways along the street.

I got within about fifty feet of our front tank when it let go its seventy-five-mm gun. The blast was terrific there in the narrow street. Glass came tinkling down from nearby windows, smoke puffed around the tank, and the empty street was shaking and trembling with the concussion.

As the tank continued to shoot I ducked into a doorway, because I figured the Germans would shoot back. Inside the doorway there was a sort of street-level cellar, dirt-floored. Apparently there was a wine shop above, for the cellar was stacked with wire crates for holding wine bottles on their sides. There were lots of bottles, but they were all empty.

*

I went back to the doorway and stood peeking out at the tank. It started backing up. Then suddenly a yellow flame pierced the bottom of the tank and there was a crash of such intensity that I automatically blinked my eyes. The tank, hardly fifty feet from where I was standing, had been hit by an enemy shell.

A second shot ripped the pavement at the side of the tank. There was smoke all around, but the tank didn't catch fire. In a moment the crew came boiling out of the turret.

Grim as it was, I almost had to laugh as they ran toward us. I have never seen men run so violently. They ran all over, with arms and heads going up and down and with marathon-race grimaces. They plunged into my doorway.

I spent the next excited hour with them. We changed to another doorway and sat on boxes in the empty hallway. The floor and steps were thick with blood where a soldier had been treated within the hour.

What had happened to the tank was this:

They had been firing away at a pillbox ahead when their 75 backfired, filling the tank with smoke and blinding them.

They decided to back up in order to get their bearings, but after backing a few yards the driver was so blinded that he stopped. Unfortunately he stopped exactly at the foot of a side street. More unfortunately there was another German pillbox up the side street. All the Germans had to do was take easy aim and let go at the sitting duck.

The first shot hit a tread, so the tank couldn't move. That was when the boys got out. I don't know why the Germans didn't fire at them as they poured out.

The escaped tankers naturally were excited, but they were as jubilant as June bugs and ready for more. They had never been in combat before the invasion of Normandy, yet in three weeks their tank had been shot up three times. Each time it was repaired and put back in action. And it can be repaired again this time. The name of their tank, appropriately, is *Be Back Soon.*

*

The main worry of these boys was the fact that they had left the engine running. We could hear it chugging away. It's bad for a tank motor to idle very long. But now they were afraid to go back and turn the motor off, for the tank was still right in line with the hidden German gun.

Also, they had come out wearing their leather crash helmets. Their steel helmets were still inside the tank, and so were their rifles.

"We'll be a lot of good without helmets or rifles!" one of them said.

The crew consisted of Corp. Martin Kennelly of Chicago, the tank commander; Sgt. L. Wortham of Leeds, Alabama, driver; Pvt. Ralph Ogren of Minneapolis, assistant driver; Corp. Albin Stoops of Marshalltown, Delaware, gunner; and Pvt. Charles Rains of Kansas City, the loader.

Private Rains was the oldest of the bunch, and the only married one. He used to work as a guard at the Sears, Roebuck plant in Kansas City.

"I was M.P. to fifteen hundred women," he said with a grin, "and how I'd like to be back doing that!"

The other tankers all expressed loud approval of this sentiment.

IN NORMANDY, *July 17, 1944*—Tank Commander Martin Kennelly wanted to show me just where his tank had been hit. As a matter of fact he hadn't seen it for himself yet, for he came running up the street the moment he jumped out of the tank.

So when the firing died down a little we sneaked up the street until we were almost even with the disabled tank. But we were careful not to get our heads around the corner of the side street, for that was where the Germans had fired from.

The first shell had hit the heavy steel brace that the tread runs on, and then plunged on through the side of the tank, very low.

"Say!" Kennelly said in amazement. "It went right through our lower ammunition storage box! I don't know what kept the ammunition from going off. We'd have been a mess if it had. Boy, it sure would have got hot in there in a hurry!"

The street was still empty. Beyond the tank about two blocks was a German truck, sitting all alone in the middle of the street. It had been blown up, and its tires had burned off. This truck was the only thing you could see. There wasn't a human being in sight anywhere.

Then an American soldier came running up the street shouting for somebody to send up a medic. He said a man was badly wounded just ahead. He was extremely excited, yelling, and getting madder because there was no medic in sight.

Word was passed down the line, and pretty soon a medic came out of a doorway and started up the street. The excited soldier yelled at him and began cussing, and the medic broke into a run. They ran past the tanks together, and up the street a way they ducked into a doorway.

*

On the corner just across the street from where we were standing was a smashed pillbox. It was in a cut-away corner like the entrances to some of our corner drugstores at home, except that instead of there being a door there was a pillbox of reinforced concrete, with gun slits.

The tank boys had shot it to extinction and then moved their tank up even with it to get the range of the next pillbox. That one was about a block ahead, set in a niche in the wall of a building. That's what the boys had been shooting at when their tank was hit. They knocked it out, however, before being knocked out themselves.

For an hour there was a lull in the fighting. Nobody did anything about a third pillbox, around the corner. Our second tank pulled back a little and just waited. Infantrymen worked their way up to second-story windows and fired their rifles up the side street without actually seeing anything to shoot at.

Now and then blasts from a 20-mm gun would splatter the buildings around us. Then our second tank would blast back in that general direction, over the low roofs, with its machine gun. There was a lot of dangerous-sounding noise, but I don't think anybody on either side got hit.

Then we saw coming up the street, past the wrecked German

truck I spoke of, a group of German soldiers. An officer walked in front, carrying a Red Cross flag on a stick. Bob Capa, the photographer, braved the dangerous funnel at the end of the side street where the damaged tank stood, leapfrogging past it and on down the street to meet the Germans.

First he snapped some pictures of them. Then, since he speaks German, he led them on back to our side of the invisible fence of battle. Eight of them were carrying two litters bearing two wounded German soldiers. The others walked behind with their hands up. They went on past us to the hospital. We assumed they were from the second knocked-out pillbox.

*

I didn't stay to see how the remaining pillbox was knocked out. But I suppose our second tank eventually pulled up to the corner, turned, and let the pillbox have it. After that the area would be clear of everything but snipers.

The infantry, who up till then had been forced to keep in doorways, would now continue up the street and poke into the side streets and into the houses until everything was clear.

That's how a strong point in a city is taken. At least that's how ours was taken. You don't always have tanks to help, and you don't always do it with so little shedding of blood.

But the city was already crumbling when we started in on this strong point, which was one of the last, and they didn't hold on too bitterly. But we didn't know that when we started.

I hope this has given you a faint idea of what street fighting is like. If you got out of it much more than a headful of confusion, then you've got out of it exactly the same thing as the soldiers who do it.

July 20, 1944—Capt. John Jackson is an unusual fellow with an unusual job. It has fallen to his lot to be the guy who goes in and brings out German generals who think maybe they would like to surrender.

This happens because he speaks German, and because he is on the staff of the 9th Division, which captured the German generals commanding the Cherbourg area.*

Capt. Jackson goes by the nickname of "Brinck." He is a bachelor, thirty-two years old. It is quite a coincidence that he was born in the town of Dinard, about thirty miles from Cherbourg. But he is straight American, for generations back. His folks just happened to be traveling over here at the time he showed up.

*The Germans surrendered Cherbourg on June 26, 1944.

Capt. Jackson's mother lives in New Canaan, Connecticut, but he likes to think of New Mexico as home. For several years he has been a rancher out there, and he loves it. His place is near Wagon Mound and Klines Corners, about forty miles east of Santa Fe. The war has played hob with his business. Both he and his partner are overseas, and there's nobody left to look after the business. They lost money last year for the first time.

Capt. Jackson is a short, dark man with a thin face. He wears a long trench coat with a pack harness, and his helmet comes down over his ears, giving him the appearance of a Russian soldier rather than an American.

He speaks perfect French, but he says his German is only so-so. He says it is actually better in his job not to speak flawless German, for then the German officers would think he was a German-turned-American and would be so contemptuous they wouldn't talk to him.

*

Another remarkable character is Pfc. Ivan Sanders.

Sanders is the "Mister Fixit" of the 9th Division. His actual job is that of electrician, but his native knack for fixing things has led him into a sort of haloed status that keeps him working like a dog twenty-four hours a day, doing things for other people.

No matter what gets out of fix, Sanders can fix it. Without previous experience he now repairs fountain pens, radios, electric razors, typewriters, broken knives, stoves and watches. He has become an institution. Everybody from the commanding general on down depends on him and yells for him whenever anything goes wrong.

There is just one thing about Sanders. Nobody can get him to clean up. He is a sight to behold.

Even the commanding general just threw up his hands about a year ago and gave up. When distinguished visitors come, they try to hide Sanders.

But the funny part about Sanders' deplorable condition is that he is eager to be clean. They just never give him time to wash. They keep him too busy fixing things.

In civilian life Sanders was an auto mechanic. He comes from Vinton, Iowa. After the war he guesses he will set up another auto-repair shop. He figures there will be enough veterans with cars to keep him busy.

Another unusual thing about Sanders is that he doesn't have to be over here at all. He is forty-three, and he has had three chances to go home. And do you know why he turned them down? It's because he's so conscientious he figures they couldn't get anybody else to do his work properly! . . .

July 21, 1944—When the now-famous Gen. Carl Wilhelm von Schlieben was captured I happened to be at the 9th Division command post to which he was first brought.

Maj. Gen. Manton S. Eddy, division commander, had a long interview with him in his trailer. When he was about finished and ready to send the captured general on to higher headquarters, General Eddy sent word that the photographers could come and take pictures.

So they stood in a group in an orchard while the photographers snapped away. Von Schlieben was obviously sourpuss about being captured, and even more sourpuss at having his picture taken. He made no effort to look other than sullenly displeased.

General Eddy was trying to be decent about it. He had an interpreter tell the prisoner that this was the price of being a general. Von Schlieben just snorted. And then General Eddy said to the interpreter: "Tell the general that our country is a democracy and therefore I don't have authority to forbid these photographers to take pictures."

Von Schlieben snorted again. And we chuckled behind our beards at one of the slickest examples of working democracy we had ever seen. And General Eddy had the appearance of the traditional cat that swallowed something wonderful. . . .

Much as he favored the infantry, Pyle also wrote about soldiers whose behind-the-lines labors made the infantry's work possible. This distribution of credit was a great morale builder.

In Praise of Ordnance

IN NORMANDY, *July 25, 1944*—One of the things the layman doesn't hear much about is the Ordnance Department. In fact it is one of the branches that even the average soldier is little aware of except in a vague way.

And yet the war couldn't keep going without it. For ordnance repairs all the vehicles of an army and furnishes all the ammunition for its guns.

Today there are more vehicles in the American sector of our beachhead than in the average-sized American city. And our big guns on an average heavy day are shooting up more than ten million dollars worth of ammunition. So you see ordnance has a man-sized job.

Ordnance personnel is usually about six or seven percent of the total men of an army. That means we have many thousands of ordnancemen in Normandy. Their insignia is a flame coming out of a retort—nicknamed in the Army "the flaming onion."

Ordnance operates the ammunition dumps we have scattered about the beachhead. But much bigger than its ammunition mission is ordnance's job of repair. Ordnance has two hundred seventy-five thousand items in its catalog of parts, and the mere catalog itself covers a twenty-foot shelf.

In a central headquarters here on the beachhead a modern filing system housed in big tents keeps records on the number and condition of five hundred major items in actual use on the beachhead, from tanks to pistols.

We have scores and scores of separate ordnance companies at work on the beachhead—each of them a complete firm within itself, able to repair anything the Army uses.

Ordnance can lift a thirty-ton tank as easily as it can a bicycle. It can repair a blown-up jeep or the intricate breech of a mammoth gun.

*

Some of its highly specialized repair companies are made up largely of men who were craftsmen in the same line in civil life. In these companies you will find the average age is much above the army average. You will find craftsmen in their late forties, you'll find men with their own established businesses who were making thirty to forty thousand dollars a year back home and who are now wearing sergeant's stripes. You'll find great soberness and sincerity, plus the normal satisfaction that comes from making things whole again instead of destroying them.

You will find an IQ far above the average for the Army. It has to be that way or the work would not get done.

You'll find mechanical work being done under a tree that would be housed in a fifty-thousand-dollar shop back in America. You'll find men working sixteen hours a day, then sleeping on the ground, who because of their age don't even have to be here at all.

Ordnance is one of the undramatic branches of the Army. They are the mechanics and the craftsmen, the fixers and the suppliers. But their job is vital. Ordinarily they are not in a great deal of danger. There are times on newly won and congested beachheads when their casualty rate is high, but once the war settles down and there is room for movement and dispersal it is not necessary or desirable for them to do their basic work within gun range.

Our ordnance branch in Normandy has had casualties. It has two small branches which will continue to have casualties—its bomb-disposal squads and its retriever companies that go up to pull out crippled tanks under fire.

But outside of those two sections, if your son or husband is in ordnance in France you can feel fairly easy about his returning to you. I don't say that to belittle ordnance in any way, but to ease your worries if you have someone in this branch of the service overseas.

*

Ordnance is set up in a vast structure of organization the same as any other Army command. The farther back you go the bigger become the outfits and the more elaborately equipped and more capable of doing heavy, long-term work.

Every infantry or armored division has an ordnance company with it all the time. This company does quick repair jobs. What it hasn't time or facilities for doing it hands on back to the next echelon in the rear.

The division ordnance companies hit the beach on D-day. The next echelon back began coming on D-day plus four. The great heavy outfits arrived somewhat later.

Today the wreckage of seven weeks of war is all in hand, and in one great depot after another it is being worked on—repaired or rebuilt or sent back for salvage until everything possible is made available again to our men who do the fighting. In later columns I'll take you along to some of these repair companies that do the vital work.

Mobile Maintenance

SOMEWHERE IN NORMANDY, *July 26, 1944*—Let's go to what the ordnance branch calls one of its "mobile maintenance companies."

This type company repairs jeeps, light trucks, small arms and light artillery. It does not take tanks, heavy trucks or big guns.

The company is bivouacked around the hedgerows of a large, grassy, L-shaped pasture. There are no trees in the pasture. There is nothing in the center except some grazing horses. No man or vehicle walks or drives across the pasture. Always they stick to the tree-high hedgerows.

It is hard to conceive that here in the thin, invisible line around the edges of this empty pasture there is a great machine shop with nearly two hundred men working with wrenches and welding torches, that six teams of auto mechanics are busy, that the buzz of urgent labor goes on through all the daylight hours.

Actually there is little need for such perfect camouflage for this company is perhaps ten miles behind the lines, and German planes never appear in the daytime. But it's a good policy to keep in practice on camouflage.

*

This is a proud company. It was the first one to land in France —first, that is, behind the companies actually attached to divisions. It landed on D-day plus two and lost three men killed and seven wounded when a shell hit their ship as they were unloading.

For five days it was the only ordnance company of its type ashore. Its small complement, whose job in theory is to back up only one division in medium repair work, carried all repair work for four divisions until help arrived.

The company had a proud record in the last war, being in nine major engagements. And it has a sentimental little coincidence in its history, too. In 1917 and in 1943 it left America for France on the same date, December 12.

*

In one corner of the pasture is the command post tent where two sergeants and two officers work at folding tables and keep the records so necessary in ordnance.

A first lieutenant is in command of the company, assisted by five other lieutenants. Their standby is Warrant Officer Ernest Pike of Savoy, Texas, who has been in the Army fifteen years, thirteen of them with this very company. What he doesn't know about practical ordnance you could put in a dead German's eye.

In another corner of the pasture is a mess truck with its field kitchens under some trees. Here the men of the company line up for meals with mess kits, officers as well as men, and eat sitting on the grass.

The officers lounge on the grass in a little group apart and when they finish eating they light cigarets and play awhile with some cute little French puppies they found in German strong points, or traded soap and cigarets for. The officers know the men intimately and if they are in a hurry and have left their mess kits behind, they just borrow one from some soldier who has finished eating.

*

A company of this kind is highly mobile. It can pack up and be underway in probably less than an hour.

Yet ordnance figures as a basic policy that its companies must not move oftener than every six days if they are to work successfully. They figure one day for moving, one for settling down and four days of full-time work, then move forward again.

If at any time the fighting army ahead of them gets rolling faster than this rate, the ordnance companies begin leapfrogging each other, one working while another of the same type moves around it and sets up.

Their equipment is moved in trucks and trailers. Some trucks are machine shops, others are supply stores. Some plain trucks are for hauling miscellaneous stuff.

Once set up, the men sleep on the ground in pup tents along the hedge with foxholes dug deep and handy. But usually their greatest enemy is the hordes of mosquitoes that infest the hedgerows at night.

The more skilled men work at their benches and instruments inside the shop trucks. The bulk of the work outside is done under dark-green canvas canopies stretched outward from the hedgerows and held taut on upright poles, their walls formed of camouflage nets.

Nothing but a vague blur is visible from a couple of hundred yards away. You have to make a long tour clear around the big pasture, nosing in under the hedge and camouflage nets to realize anything is going on at all.

In the far distance you can hear a faint rumble of big guns, and overhead all day our own planes roar comfortingly.

But outside those fringes of war it is as peaceful in this Normandy field as it would be in a pasture in Ohio. Why, even the three liberated horses graze contentedly on the ankle-high grass, quite indifferent to the fact that this peaceful field is a part of the great war machine that will destroy their recent masters.

Small-Arms Repair

SOMEWHERE IN NORMANDY, *July 27, 1944*—At the edge of a pasture, sitting cross-legged on the grass or on low boxes as though they were at a picnic, are thirteen men in greasy soldiers' coveralls.

Near them on one side is a shop truck with a canvas canopy stretched out from it, making a sort of patio alongside the truck. And under this canopy and all over the ground are rifles—rusty and muddy and broken rifles.

This is the small-arms section of our medium ordnance company. To this company comes daily in trucks the picked-up rusting rifles of men killed or wounded, and rifles broken in ordinary service. There are dozens of such companies.

This company turns back around a hundred rifles a day to its division, all shiny and oily and ready to shoot again.

They work on the simple salvage system of taking good parts off one gun and placing them on another. To do this they work like a small assembly plant.

The first few hours of the morning are given to taking broken rifles apart. They don't try to keep the parts of each gun together. All parts are alike and transferable, hence they throw each type into a big steel pan full of similar parts. At the end of the job they have a dozen or so pans, each filled with the same kind of part.

Then the whole gang shifts over and scrubs the parts. They scrub in gasoline, using sandpaper for guns in bad condition after lying out in the rain and mud.

When everything is clean they take the good parts and start putting them back together and making guns out of them again.

When all the pans are empty they have a stack of rifles—good rifles, all ready to be taken back to the front.

Of the parts left over some are thrown away, quite beyond repair. But others are repairable and go into the section's shop truck for working on with lathes and welding torches. Thus the division gets one hundred reclaimed rifles a day, in addition to the brand new ones issued to it.

And believe me, during the first few days of our invasion men at the front desperately needed these rifles. Repairmen tell you how our paratroopers and infantrymen would straggle back, dirty and hazy-eyed with fatigue, and plead like a child for a new rifle immediately so they could get back to the front and "get at them sonsabitches."

One paratrooper brought in a German horse he had captured and offered to trade it for a new rifle, he needed it so badly. During those days the men in our little repair shop worked all hours trying to fill the need.

I sat around on the grass and talked to these rifle repairmen most of one forenoon. They weren't working so frenziedly then for the urgency was not so dire, but they kept steadily at it as we talked.

The head of the section is Sgt. Edward Welch of Watts, Oklahoma, who used to work in the oil fields. Just since the invasion he's invented a gadget that cleans rust out of a rifle barrel in a few seconds whereas it used to take a man about twenty minutes.

Sgt. Watts did it merely by rigging up a swivel shaft on the end of an electric drill and attaching a cylindrical wire brush to the end. So now you just stick the brush in the gun barrel and press the button on the drill. It whirls and in a few seconds all rust is ground out. The idea has been turned over to other ordnance companies.

The soldiers do a lot of kidding as they sit around taking rusted guns apart. Like soldiers everywhere they razz each other constantly about their home states. A couple were from Arkansas, and of course they took a lot of hillbilly razzing about not wearing shoes till they got in the Army and so on.

One of them was Corp. Herschel Grimsley of Springdale, Arkansas. He jokingly asked if I'd put his name in the paper. So I took a chance and joked back. "Sure," I said, "except I didn't know anybody in Arkansas could read."

Everybody laughed loudly at this scintillating wit, most of all Corp. Grimsley, who can stand anything.

Later Grimsley was telling me how paratroopers used to come in and just beg for another rifle. And he expressed the sincere feeling of the men throughout ordnance, the balance weighing of their own fairly safe job, when he said: "Them old boys at the front have sure got my sympathy. Least we can do is work our fingers off to give them the stuff."

*

The original stack of muddy, rusted rifles is a touching pile. As gun after gun comes off the stack, you look to see what is the matter with it:

Rifle butt split by fragments; barrel dented by bullet; trigger knocked off; whole barrel splattered with shrapnel marks; gun gray from the slime of weeks in swamp mud, faint dark splotches of blood still showing.

You wonder what became of each owner; you pretty well know.

Infantrymen, like soldiers everywhere, like to put names on their equipment. Just as a driver paints a name on his truck, so does a doughboy carve his name or initials on his rifle butt.

You get crude whittlings of initials in the hard walnut stocks and unbelievably craftsmanlike carvings of soldiers' names, and many, many names of girls.

The boys said the most heart-breaking rifle they'd found was one of a soldier who had carved a hole about silver-dollar size and put his wife's or girl's picture in it, and sealed it over with a crystal of Plexiglas.

They don't, of course, know who he was or what had happened

to him. They only know the rifle was repaired and somebody else was carrying it now, picture and all.

July 28, 1944— . . . I moved over to an ordnance evacuation company.

These men handle the gigantic trucks, the long, low trailers and the heavy wreckers that go out to haul back crippled tanks and wrecked anti-tank guns from the battlefield.

The ordnance branch's policy on these wrecking companies is that if they don't have a casualty now and then, or collect a few shrapnel marks on their vehicles, then they're not doing their job efficiently.

Tanks must be retrieved just as quickly as possible after they have been shot up. In the first place, we don't want the Germans to get them; secondly, we want to get them repaired and back in action for ourselves right away. . . .

Tank Retrieval

SOMEWHERE IN NORMANDY, *July 29, 1944*—It was just beginning dusk when the order came. A soldier came running up the pasture and said there was a call for our ordnance evacuation company to pull out some crippled tanks.

We had been sitting on the grass and we jumped up and ran down the slope. Waiting at the gate stood an M-19 truck and behind it a big wrecker with a crane.

The day had been warm but dusk was bringing a chill, as always. One of the soldiers loaned me his mackinaw.

Soldiers stood atop their big machine with a stance of impatience, like firemen waiting to start. We pulled out through the hedgerow gate onto the main macadam highway. It was about ten miles to the front lines.

"We should make it before full darkness," one of the officers said.

We went through shattered Carentan and on beyond for miles. Then we turned off at an angle in the road. "This is Purple Heart Corner," the officer said.

Beyond there the roadside soldiers thinned out. Traffic ceased altogether. With an increasing tempo, the big guns crashed around us. Hedges began to make weird shadows. You peered closely at sentries in every open hedge-gate just out of nervous alertness.

The smell of death washed past us in waves as we drove on. There is nothing worse in war than the foul odor of death. There is no last vestige of dignity in it.

We turned up a gravel lane, and drove slowly. The dusk was deepening. A gray stone farmhouse sat dimly off the road. A little yard and driveway semicircled in front of it. Against the front of the house stood five German soldiers, facing inward, their hands above their heads. An American doughboy stood in the driveway with a tommy gun pointed at them. We drove on for about fifty yards and stopped. The drivers shut off their diesel motors.

One officer went into an orchard to try to find where the tanks were. In wartime nobody ever knows where anything is. The rest of us waited along the road beside an old stone barn. Three jeeps were parked beside it. The dusk was deeper now.

Out of the orchards around us roared and thundered our own artillery. An officer lit a cigaret. A sergeant with a rifle slung on his shoulder walked up and said, "You better put that out, sir. There's snipers all around and they'll shoot at a cigaret."

The officer crushed the cigaret in his fingers, not waiting to drop it to the ground, and said, "Thanks."

"It's for your own good," the sergeant said, apologetically.

The only traffic past us was an occasional jeep rigged up with a steel framework above to carry two stretcher cases. Every few minutes a jeep would pass with its patient burdens, slowly and silently and almost as though it were feeling its way.

Somehow as darkness comes down in a land of great danger you want things hushed. People begin to talk in low voices and feet on jeep throttles tread less heavily.

An early German plane droned overhead, passed, turned, dived —and his white tracers came slanting down out of the sky. We crouched behind a stone wall. He was half a mile away, but the night is big and bullets can go anywhere and you are nervous.

An armored car pulled around us, pulled into a ditch ahead and shut off its motor. They said it was there in case the German night patrols tried to filter through.

On ahead there were single rifle shots and the give and take of machine-gun rattles—one fast and one slow, one German and one American. You wondered after each blast if somebody who was whole a moment ago, some utter stranger, was now lying in sudden new anguish up there ahead in the illimitable darkness.

A shell whined that old familiar wail and hit in the orchard ahead with a crash. I moved quickly around behind the barn.

"You don't like that?" inquired a soldier out of the dusk.

I said, "No, do you?"

And he replied as honestly, "I sure as hell don't."

A sergeant came up the road and said, "You can stay here if you want to, but they shell this barn every hour on the hour. They're zeroed in on it."

We looked at our watches. It was five minutes till midnight. Some of our soldiers stood boldly out in the middle of the road talking. But you could sense some of us, who were less composed, easing close to the stone wall, even close to the motherhood of the big silent trucks. Then an officer came out of the orchard. He had the directions. We all gathered around and listened. We had to back up, cross two pastures, turn down another lane and go forward from there.

We were to drag back two German tanks for fear the Germans might retrieve them during the night. We backed ponderously up the road, our powerful exhaust blowing up dust as we moved.

As we passed the gray stone farmhouse we could see five silhouettes, very faintly through the now almost complete night—five Germans still facing the gray farmhouse.

We came to a lane, and pulled forward into the orchard very slowly, for you could barely see now. Even in the lightning flashes of the big guns you could barely see.

SOMEWHERE IN NORMANDY, *July 30, 1944*—We drove slowly across the two pastures in the big M-19 retriever truck with which our ordnance evacuation company was to pick up two crippled German tanks. The wrecker truck followed us. It was just after midnight.

We came to a lane at the far side of the pasture. Nobody was there to direct us. The officers had gone on ahead. We asked a sentry if he knew where the German tanks were. He had never heard of them. We shut off the motors and waited.

I think everybody was a little on edge. We certainly had American troops ahead of us, but we didn't know how far. When things are tense like that you get impatient of monkeying around. You want to get the job done and get the hell out of there.

We waited about ten minutes, and finally a sergeant came back and said for us to drive on up the road about half a mile. He climbed on to direct us. Finally we came to a barnyard, pulled in, turned around and then very slowly backed on up the road toward the enemy lines. I stood on the steel platform behind the driver so I could see.

It was very dark and you could only make out vague shapes. You could see dark walls of hedges and between them lighter strips of gravel road. Finally a huge black shape took form at one side of the road. It was the first of the German tanks. Just before we got to it we could make out two dark stripes on either side of the road on the ground. They were the size and shape of dead men, but they were only forms and I couldn't tell for sure.

Being tense and anxious to get finished, I hoped our truck would take the first tank. But no. We passed by, of course, and went backing on up the road.

When you're nervous you feel even twelve inches closer to the front is too much and the noise of your motor sounds like all the clanging of hell, directing the Germans to you.

I knew it was foolish to be nervous. I knew there was plenty of protection ahead. And yet there are times when you don't feel good to start with, you're uncomposed and the framework of your character is off balance, and you are weak inside. That's the way I was that night. Fortunately I'm not always that way.

Finally the dark shape of the second tank loomed up. Our officers and some of the men were standing in the road beside it. We backed to within about five feet of it, and the driver shut off his motor and we climbed down.

A layman would think all you have to do is to hook a chain to the tank and pull it out of the ditch. But we were there half an hour. It seemed like all night to me.

First it had to be gone over for booby traps. I couldn't help but admire our mechanics. They know these foreign tanks as well as our own.

One of them climbed down the hatch into the driver's seat and there in the dark, completely by feel, investigated the intricate gadgets of the cockpit and found just what shape it was in and told us the trouble.

It seemed that on this tank two levers at the driver's seat had been left in gear and they were so bent there was not room to shift them out of gear.

One man was sent back up the road to get a hacksaw from the wrecker truck so they could saw off the handles. After five minutes he came back and said there wasn't any hacksaw. Then they sent him back after a crowbar and that finally did the trick.

During this time we stood in a group around the tank, about a dozen of us, just talking. Shells still roamed the dark sky but they weren't coming as near as before.

There would be lulls of many minutes when there was hardly a sound but our own voices. Most everybody talked in low tones, yet in any group there's always somebody who can't bear to speak in anything less than foghorn proportions.

And now and then when they'd have to hammer on the tank it sounded as though a boiler factory had collapsed. I tried to counteract this by not talking at all.

An officer asked if anybody had inspected the breech of the tank's 88 gun. It seems the Germans sometimes leave a shell in the gun rigged up so it goes off when the tank is moved. Another officer said the breech was empty. So we started.

Slowly we ground back down the road in low gear with our great, black, massive load rolling behind us. One soldier rode in the tank to steer it.

We'd planned to pull it a long way back. Actually we pulled it only about half a mile, then decided to put it in a field for the night.

When we pulled into a likely pasture the sentry at the hedgerow-gate wanted to know what we were doing and we told him, "leaving a German tank for the night."

And the sentry, in a horrified voice, said, "Good God, don't leave it here. They might come after it." But leave it there we did, and damn glad to get rid of it, I assure you.

We drove home in the blackout, watching the tall hedgerows against the lighter sky for guidance. For miles the roads were as empty and silent as the farthest corner of a desert. The crash of the guns grew welcomely dimmer and dimmer until finally everything was nearly silent and it seemed there could be only peace in Normandy.

At last we came to our own hedgerow-gate. As we drove in the sentry said, "Coffee's waiting at the mess tent." They feed twenty-four hours a day in these outfits that work like firemen.

But my sleeping bag lay unrolled and waiting on the ground in a nearby tent. It was three A.M. With an almost childish gratitude at being there at all I went right to bed.

The Fixers

SOMEWHERE IN NORMANDY, *August 1, 1944*—I know of nothing in civilian life at home by which you can even remotely compare the contribution to his country made by the infantry soldier with his life of bestiality, suffering and death.

But I've just been with an outfit whose war work is similar enough to yours that I believe you can see the difference between life overseas and in America.

This is the heavy ordnance company which repairs shot-up tanks, wrecked artillery, and heavy trucks.

These men are not in much danger. They work at shop benches with tools. Compared with the infantry, their life is velvet and they know it and appreciate it. But compared with them your life is velvet. That's what I'd like for you to appreciate.

These men are skilled craftsmen. Many of them are above military age. Back home they made big money. Their jobs here are fundamentally the same as those of you at home who work in war plants. It's only the environment that is different.

These men don't work seven, eight or nine hours a day. They work from seven in the morning until darkness comes at night. They work from twelve to sixteen hours a day.

You have beds and bathrooms. These men sleep on the ground, and dig a trench for their toilets.

You have meals at the table. These men eat from mess kits, sitting on the grass. You have pajamas, and places to go on Sunday. These men sleep in their underwear, and they don't even know when Sunday comes. They have not sat in a chair for weeks. They live always outdoors, rain and shine.

In the War World, their life is not bad. By peacetime standards it is outrageous. But they don't complain—because they are close enough to the front to see and appreciate the desperate need of the men they are trying to help. They work with an eagerness and an intensity that is thrilling to see.

*

This company works under a half-acre grove of trees and along the hedgerows of a couple of adjoining pastures. Their shops are in the trucks or out in the open under camouflage nets.

Most of their work seems unspectacular to describe. It just consists of welding steel plates into the sides of tanks, of changing the front end of a truck blown up by a mine, or repairing the barrel of a big gun hit by a bazooka, of rewinding the coils of a radio, of welding new teeth in a gear.

It's the sincere way they go at it and their appreciation of its need that impressed me.

*

Corp. Richard Kelso is in this company. His home is in Chicago.

He is an Irishman from the Old Sod. He apprenticed in Belfast as a machinist nearly thirty years ago. He went to America when he was twenty-five and now he is forty-five.

He still has folks in Ireland, but he didn't have a chance to get over there when he was stationed in England. He is thin and a little stooped, and the others call him "Pop." He is quiet and intent and very courteous. He never did get married.

Kelso operates the milling machine in a shop truck. His truck is covered deep with extra strips of steel, for these boys pick up and hoard steel as some people might hoard money.

When I stopped to chat, Kelso had his machine grinding away on the rough tooth of the gearwheel of a tank.

The part that did the cutting was one he had improvised himself. In this business of war so much is unforeseen, so much is missing at the right moment that were it not for improvisation, wars would be lost.

Take these gearwheels, for instance. Suppose a tank strips three teeth off some gear. The entire tank is helpless and out of action. They have no replacement wheels in stock. They have to repair the broken one.

So they take it to their outdoor foundry, make a form, heat up some steel till it is molten, pour it in the form and mold a rough geartooth which is then welded onto the stub of the broken-off tooth.

Now this rough tooth has to be ground down to the fine dimensions of the other teeth and that is an exact job. At first they didn't have the tools to do it with.

But that didn't stop them. They hacked those teeth down with cold chisels and hand files. They put back into action twenty tanks by this primitive method. Then Kelso and Warrant Officer Henry Moser, of Johnstown, Pennsylvania, created a part for their milling machine that would do the job faster and better.

That one little improvisation may have saved fifty Americans' lives, may have cost the Germans a hundred men, may even have turned the tide of a battle.

And it's being done by a man forty-five years old wearing corporal stripes who doesn't have to be over here at all, and who could be making big money back home.

He too sleeps on the ground and works sixteen hours a day, and is happy to do it—for boys who are dying are not three thousand miles away and abstract; they are ten miles away and very, very real.

He sees them when they come back, pleading like children for another tank, another gun. He knows how terribly they need the things that are within his power to give.

Beachhead Breakout

in normandy, *August 5, 1944*—A few days after D-day you may remember we spoke in this column of five early phases of the continental invasion that would have to take place.

Phase Number Five was to be the breakout from our beachhead after we'd held it secure long enough to build up vast quantities of troops and supplies behind us. And once we'd broken out of the ring of Germans trying to hold us in and completed Phase Five, the real war in Western Europe would begin.

Well, we're in Phase Five now. At least we are while I'm writing this. Things are moving swiftly. You realize that several days elapse between the writing and the publication of this column. By the time you read this we may be out in the open and pushing into France.

Surely history will give a name to the battle that sent us boiling out of Normandy—some name comparable with Saint-Mihiel, or Meuse Argonne of the last war. But to us here on the spot at the time it was known simply as "the breakthrough."

*

We correspondents could sense that a big drive was coming. There are many little ways you can tell without actually being told, if you are experienced in war.

And then one evening Lt. Gen. Omar Bradley, commanding all American troops in France, came to our camp and briefed us on the coming operation. It would start, he said, on the first day we had three hours' good flying weather in the forenoon.

We were all glad to hear the news. There isn't a correspondent over here, or soldier, or officer I ever heard of who hasn't complete and utter faith in Gen. Bradley. If he felt we were ready for the push, that was good enough for us.

The general told us the attack would cover a segment of the German line west of Saint-Lô, about two-and-a-third miles wide. In that narrow segment we would have three infantry divisions, side by side. Right behind them would be another infantry and two armored divisions.

Once a hole was broken, the armored divisions would slam through several miles beyond, then turn right toward the sea behind the Germans in that sector in hope of cutting them off and trapping them.

The remainder of our line on both sides of the attack would keep the pressure on to hold the Germans in front of them so they couldn't send reinforcements against our big attack.

The attack was to open with a gigantic two-hour air bombardment by eighteen hundred planes—the biggest, I'm sure, ever attempted by air in direct support of ground troops.

It would start with dive bombers, then great four-motored heavies would come, and then mediums, then dive bombers again, and then the ground troops would kick off, with air fighters continuing to work ahead of them.

It was a thrilling plan to listen to. Gen. Bradley didn't tell us the big thing—that this was Phase Five. But other officers gave us the word. They said, "This is no limited-objective drive. This is it. This is the big breakthrough."

*

In war everybody contributes something, no matter how small or how far removed he may be. But on the front line, this breakthrough was accomplished by four fighting branches of the services and I don't see truly how one could be given credit above another.

None of the four could have done the job without the other three. The way they worked together was beautiful and precision-like, showering credit upon themselves and Gen. Bradley's planning. The four branches were the Air Corps, Tanks, Artillery and Infantry.

I went with the infantry because it is my love, and because I suspected the tanks, being spectacular, might smother the credit due the infantry. I teamed up with the 4th Infantry Division since it was in the middle of the forward three and spearheading the attack.

The first night behind the front lines I slept comfortably on a cot in a tent at the division command post, and met for the first time the 4th's commander—Maj. Gen. Raymond O. Barton, a fatherly, kindly, thoughtful, good soldier.

The second night I spent on the dirty floor of a rickety French farmhouse, far up in the lines, with the nauseating odor of dead cows keeping me awake half the night.

The third night I slept on the ground in an orchard even farther up, snugly dug in behind a hedgerow so the 88's couldn't get at me so easily. And on the next day the weather cleared, and the attack was on. It was July 25.

*

If you don't have July 25 pasted in your hat I would advise you to do so immediately. At least paste it in your mind. For I have a hunch that July 25 of the year 1944 will be one of the great historic pinnacles of this war.

It was the day we began a mighty surge out of our confined Normandy spaces, the day we stopped calling our area the beachhead, and knew we were fighting a war across the whole expanse of France.

From that day onward all dread possibilities and fears for disaster to our invasion were behind us. No longer was there any possibility of our getting kicked off. No longer could it be possible for fate, or weather, or enemy to wound us fatally; from that day onward the future could hold nothing for us but growing strength and eventual victory.

For five days and nights during that historic period I stayed at the front with our troops. And now, though it's slightly delayed, I want to tell you about it in detail from day to day, if you will be that patient.

Attack at Midday

IN NORMANDY, *August 7, 1944*—The great attack, when we broke out of the Normandy beachhead, began in the bright light of midday, not at the zero hour of a bleak and mysterious dawn as attacks are supposed to start in books.

The attack had been delayed from day to day because of poor flying weather, and on the final day we hadn't known for sure till after breakfast whether it was on or off again.

When the word came that it was on, the various battalion staffs of our regiment were called in from their command posts for a final review of the battle plan.

Each one was given a mimeographed sketch of the front-line area, showing exactly where and when each type bomber was to hammer the German lines ahead of them. Another mimeographed page was filled with specific orders for the grand attack to follow.

Officers stood or squatted in a circle in a little apple orchard behind a ramshackle stone farmhouse of a poor French family who had left before us. The stone wall in the front yard had been knocked down by shelling, and through the orchards there were shell craters and tree limbs knocked off and trunks sliced by bullets. Some enlisted men sleeping the night before in the attic of the house got the shock of their lives when the thin floor collapsed and they fell down into the cowshed below.

Chickens and tame rabbits still scampered around the farmyard. Dead cows lay all around in the fields.

The regimental colonel stood in the center of the officers and went over the orders in detail. Battalion commanders took down notes in little books.

The colonel said, "Ernie Pyle is with the regiment for this attack and will be with one of the battalions, so you'll be seeing him." The officers looked at me and smiled and I felt embarrassed.

Then Maj. Gen. Raymond O. Barton, 4th Division Commander, arrived. The colonel called, "Attention!" and everybody stood rigid until the general gave them, "Carry on."

An enlisted man ran to the mess truck and got a folding canvas stool for the general to sit on. He sat listening intently while the colonel wound up his instructions.

Then the General stepped into the center of the circle. He stood at a slouch on one foot with the other leg far out like a brace. He looked all around him as he talked. He didn't talk long. He said something like this:

"This is one of the finest regiments in the American Army. It was the last regiment out of France in the last war. It was the first regiment into France in this war. It has spearheaded every one of the division's attacks in Normandy. It will spearhead this one. For many years this was my regiment and I feel very close to you, and very proud."

The General's lined face was a study in emotion. Sincerity and deep sentiment were in every contour and they shone from his eyes. Gen. Barton is a man of deep affections. The tragedy of war, both personal and impersonal, hurts him. At the end his voice almost broke, and I for one had a lump in my throat. He ended: "That's all. God bless you and good luck."

Then we broke up and I went with one of the battalion commanders. Word was passed down by field phone, radio and liaison men to the very smallest unit troops that the attack was on.

There was still an hour before the bombers, and three hours before the infantry were to move. There was nothing for the infantry to do but dig a little deeper and wait. A cessation of motion seemed to come over the countryside and all its brown-clad inhabitants—a sense of last-minute sitting in silence before the holocaust.

The first planes of the mass onslaught came over a little before ten A.M. They were the fighters and dive bombers. The main road running crosswise in front of us was their bomb line. They were to bomb only on the far side of the road.

Our kick-off infantry had been pulled back a few hundred yards this side of the road. Everyone in the area had been given the strictest orders to be in foxholes, for high-level bombers can, and do quite excusably, make mistakes.

We were still in country so level and with hedgerows so tall there simply was no high spot—either hill or building—from where you could get a grandstand view of the bombing as we used to in Sicily and Italy. So one place was as good as another unless you went right up and sat on the bomb line.

Having been caught too close to these things before, I compromised and picked a farmyard about eight hundred yards back of the kick-off line.

And before the next two hours had passed I would have given every penny, every desire, every hope I've ever had to have been just another eight hundred yards further back.

A Surge of Doom-Like Sound

IN NORMANDY, *August 8, 1944*—Our front lines were marked by long strips of colored cloth laid on the ground, and with colored smoke to guide our airmen during the mass bombing that preceded our breakout from the German ring that held us to the Normandy beachhead.

Dive bombers hit it just right. We stood in the barnyard of a French farm and watched them barrel nearly straight down out of the sky. They were bombing about half a mile ahead of where we stood.

They came in groups, diving from every direction, perfectly timed, one right after another. Everywhere you looked separate groups of planes were on the way down, or on the way back up, or slanting over for a dive, or circling, circling, circling over our heads, waiting for their turn.

The air was full of sharp and distinct sounds of cracking bombs and the heavy rip of the planes' machine guns and the splitting screams of diving wings. It was all fast and furious, but yet distinct, as in a musical show in which you could distinguish throaty tunes and words.

*

And then a new sound gradually droned into our ears, a sound deep and all-encompassing with no notes in it—just a gigantic faraway surge of doomlike sound. It was the heavies. They came from directly behind us. At first they were the merest dots in the sky. You could see clots of them against the far heavens, too tiny to count individually. They came on with a terrible slowness.

They came in flights of twelve, three flights to a group and in groups stretched out across the sky. They came in "families" of about seventy planes each.

Maybe these gigantic waves were two miles apart; maybe they were ten miles, I don't know. But I do know they came in a constant procession and I thought it would never end. What the Germans must have thought is beyond comprehension.

Their march across the sky was slow and studied. I've never known a storm, or a machine, or any resolve of man that had about it the aura of such a ghastly relentlessness. You had the feeling that even had God appeared beseechingly before them in the sky with palms outward to persuade them back they would not have had within them the power to turn from their irresistible course.

I stood with a little group of men, ranging from colonels to privates, back of the stone farmhouse. Slit trenches were all around the edges of the farmyard and a dugout with a tin roof was nearby. But we were so fascinated by the spectacle overhead that it never occurred to us that we might need the foxholes.

The first huge flight passed directly over our farmyard and others followed. We spread our feet and leaned far back trying to look straight up, until our steel helmets fell off. We'd cup our fingers around our eyes like field glasses for a clearer view.

And then the bombs came. They began up ahead as the crackle of popcorn and almost instantly swelled into a monstrous fury of noise that seemed surely to destroy all the world ahead of us.

From then on for an hour and a half that had in it the agonies of centuries, the bombs came down. A wall of smoke and dust erected by them grew high in the sky. It filtered along the ground back through our own orchards. It sifted around us and into our noses. The bright day grew slowly dark from it.

By now everything was an indescribable cauldron of sounds. Individual noises did not exist. The thundering of the motors in the sky and the roar of bombs ahead filled all the space for noise on earth. Our own heavy artillery was crashing all around us, yet we could hardly hear it.

*

The Germans began to shoot heavy, high ack-ack. Great black puffs of it by the score speckled the sky until it was hard to distinguish smoke puffs from planes.

And then someone shouted that one of the planes was smoking. Yes, we could all see it. A long faint line of black smoke stretched straight for a mile behind one of them.

And as we watched there was a gigantic sweep of flame over the plane. From nose to tail it disappeared in flame, and it slanted slowly down and banked around the sky in great wide curves, this way and that way, as rhythmically and gracefully as in a slow-motion waltz.

Then suddenly it seemed to change its mind and it swept upward, steeper and steeper and ever slower until finally it seemed poised motionless on its own black pillar of smoke. And then just as slowly it turned over and dived for the earth—a golden spearhead on the straight black shaft of its own creation—and it disappeared behind the treetops.

But before it was done there were more cries of "There's another one smoking and there's a third one now."

Chutes came out of some of the planes. Out of some came no chutes at all. One of white silk caught on the tail of a plane. Men with binoculars could see him fighting to get loose until flames swept over him, and then a tiny black dot fell through space, all alone.

And all that time the great flat ceiling of the sky was roofed by all the others that didn't go down, plowing their way forward as if there were no turmoil in the world.

Nothing deviated them by the slightest. They stalked on, slowly and with a dreadful pall of sound, as though they were seeing only some thing at a great distance and nothing existed in between. God, how you admired those men up there and were sickened for the ones who fell.

An Inhuman Tenseness

IN NORMANDY, *August 9, 1944*—It is possible to become so enthralled by some of the spectacles of war that you are momentarily captivated away from your own danger.

That's what happened to our little group of soldiers as we stood in a French farmyard, watching the mighty bombing of the German lines just before our breakthrough.

But that benign state didn't last long. As we watched, there crept into our consciousness a realization that windrows of exploding bombs were easing back toward us, flight by flight, instead of gradually forward, as the plan called for.

Then we were horrified by the suspicion that those machines, high in the sky and completely detached from us, were aiming their bombs at the smokeline on the ground—and a gentle breeze was drifting the smokeline back over us!

An indescribable kind of panic comes over you at such times. We stood tensed in muscle and frozen in intellect, watching each flight approach and pass over us, feeling trapped and completely helpless.

And then all of an instant the universe became filled with a gigantic rattling as of huge, dry seeds in a mammoth dry gourd. I doubt that any of us had ever heard that sound before, but instinct told us what it was. It was bombs by the hundred, hurtling down through the air above us.

Many times I've heard bombs whistle or swish or rustle, but never before had I heard bombs rattle. I still don't know the explanation of it. But it is an awful sound.

We dived. Some got in a dugout. Others made foxholes and ditches and some got behind a garden wall—although which side would be "behind" was anybody's guess.

*

I was too late for the dugout. The nearest place was a wagon-shed which formed one end of the stone house. The rattle was right down upon us. I remember hitting the ground flat, all spread out like the cartoons of people flattened by steam rollers, and then squirming like an eel to get under one of the heavy wagons in the shed.

An officer whom I didn't know was wriggling beside me. We stopped at the same time, simultaneously feeling it was hopeless to move farther. The bombs were already crashing around us.

We lay with our heads slightly up—like two snakes—staring at each other. I know it was in both our minds and in our eyes, asking each other what to do. Neither of us knew. We said nothing.

We just lay sprawled, gaping at each other in a futile appeal, our faces about a foot apart, until it was over.

There is no description of the sound and fury of those bombs except to say it was chaos, and a waiting for darkness. The feeling of the blast was sensational. The air struck you in hundreds of continuing flutters. Your ears drummed and rang. You could feel quick little waves of concussions on your chest and in your eyes.

At last the sound died down and we looked at each other in disbelief. Gradually we left the foxholes and sprawling places, and came out to see what the sky had in store for us. As far as we could see, other waves were approaching from behind.

When a wave would pass a little to the side of us we were garrulously grateful, for most of them flew directly overhead. Time and again the rattle came down over us. Bombs struck in the orchard to our left. They struck in orchards ahead of us. They struck as far as half a mile behind us. Everything about us was shaken, but our group came through unhurt.

*

I can't record what any of us actually felt or thought during those horrible climaxes. I believe a person's feelings at such times are kaleidoscopic and uncatalogable. You just wait, that's all. You do remember an inhuman tenseness of muscle and nerves.

An hour or so later I began to get sore all over, and by mid-afternoon my back and shoulders ached as though I'd been beaten with a club. It was simply the result of muscles tensing themselves too tight for too long against anticipated shock. And I remember worrying about war correspondent Ken Crawford, a friend from back in the old Washington days, who I knew was several yards ahead of me.

As far as I knew, he and I were the only two correspondents with the 4th Division. I didn't know who might be with the divisions on either side—which also were being hit, as we could see.

Three days later, back at camp, I learned that Associated Press photographer Bede Irvin had been killed in the bombing and that Ken was safe.

We came out of our ignominious sprawling and stood up again to watch. We could sense that by now the error had been caught and checked. The bombs again were falling where they were intended, a mile or so ahead.

Even at a mile away a thousand bombs hitting within a few seconds can shake the earth and shatter the air where you are standing. There was still a dread in our hearts, but it gradually eased as the tumult and destruction moved slowly forward.

IN NORMANDY, *August 10, 1944*—With our own personal danger past, our historic air bombardment of the German lines holding us in the Normandy beachhead again became a captivating spectacle to watch.

By now it was definite that the great waves of four-motored planes were dropping their deadly loads exactly in the right place.

And by now two Mustang fighters, flying like a pair of doves, patrolled back and forth, back and forth, just in front of each oncoming wave of bombers, as if to shout to them by their mere presence that here was not the place to drop—wait a few seconds, wait a few more seconds.

And then we could see a flare come out of the belly of one plane in each flight, just after they had passed over our heads.

The flare shot forward, leaving smoke behind it in a vivid line, and then began a graceful, downward curve that was one of the most beautiful things I've ever seen.

It was like an invisible crayon drawing a rapid line across the canvas of the sky, saying in a gesture for all to see: "Here! Here is where to drop. Follow me."

And each succeeding flight of oncoming bombers obeyed, and in turn dropped its own hurtling marker across the illimitable heaven to guide those behind.

Long before now the German ack-ack guns had gone out of existence. We had counted three of our big planes down in spectacular flames, and I believe that was all. The German ack-ack gunners either took to their holes or were annihilated.

How many waves of heavy bombers we put over I have no idea. I had counted well beyond four hundred planes when my personal distraction obliterated any capacity or desire to count.

I only know that four hundred was just the beginning. There were supposed to be eighteen hundred planes that day, and I believe it was announced later that there were more than three thousand.

It seemed incredible to me that any German could come out of that bombardment with his sanity. When it was over even I was grateful in a chastened way I had never experienced before, for just being alive.

*

I thought an attack by our troops was impossible now, for it is an unnerving thing to be bombed by your own planes.

During the bad part a colonel I had known a long time was walking up and down behind the farmhouse, snapping his fingers and saying over and over to himself, "Goddamit, goddamit!"

As he passed me once he stopped and stared and said, "Goddamit!"

And I said, "There can't be any attack now, can there?" And he said "No," and began walking again, snapping his fingers and tossing his arm as though he was throwing rocks at the ground.

The leading company of our battalion was to spearhead the attack forty minutes after our heavy bombing ceased. The company had been hit directly by our bombs. Their casualties, including casualties in shock, were heavy. Men went to pieces and had to be sent back. The company was shattered and shaken.

And yet Company B attacked—and on time, to the minute! They attacked, and within an hour they sent word back that they had advanced eight hundred yards through German territory and were still going. Around our farmyard men with stars on their shoulders almost wept when the word came over the portable radio. The American soldier can be majestic when he needs to be.

*

There is one more thing I want to say before we follow the ground troops on deeper into France in the great push you've been reading about now for days.

I'm sure that back in England that night other men—bomber crews—almost wept, and maybe they did really, in the awful knowledge that they had killed our own American troops. But I want to say this to them. The chaos and the bitterness there in the orchards and between the hedgerows that afternoon have passed. After the bitterness came the sober remembrance that the Air Corps is the strong right arm in front of us. Not only at the beginning, but ceaselessly and everlastingly, every moment of the faintest daylight, the Air Corps is up there banging away ahead of us.

Anybody makes mistakes. The enemy makes them just the same as we do. The smoke and confusion of battle bewilder us all on the ground as well as in the air. And in this case the percentage of error was really very small compared with the colossal storm of bombs that fell upon the enemy.

The Air Corps has been wonderful throughout this invasion, and the men on the ground appreciate it.

A Slow, Cautious Business

ON THE WESTERN FRONT, *August 11, 1944*—I know that all of us correspondents have tried time and again to describe to you what this weird hedgerow fighting in northwestern France has been like.

But I'm going to go over it once more, for we've been in it two months and some of us feel that this is the two months that broke the German Army in the west.

This type of fighting is always in small groups, so let's take as an example one company of men. Let's say they are working forward on both sides of a country lane, and this company is responsible for clearing the two fields on either side of the road as it advances.

That means you have only about one platoon to a field. And with the company's understrength from casualties, you might have no more than twenty-five or thirty men in a field.

Over here the fields are usually not more than fifty yards across and a couple of hundred yards long. They may have grain in them, or apple trees, but mostly they are just pastures of green grass, full of beautiful cows.

The fields are surrounded on all sides by immense hedgerows which consist of an ancient earthen bank, waist-high, all matted with roots, and out of which grow weeds, bushes, and trees up to twenty feet high.

The Germans have used these barriers well. They put snipers in the trees. They dig deep trenches behind the hedgerows and cover them with timber, so that it is almost impossible for artillery to get at them.

Sometimes they will prop up machine guns with strings attached, so they can fire over the hedge without getting out of their holes. They even cut out a section of the hedgerow and hide a big gun or a tank in it, covering it with brush.

Also they tunnel under the hedgerows from the back and make the opening on the forward side just large enough to stick a machine gun through.

But mostly the hedgerow pattern is this: a heavy machine gun hidden at each end of the field and infantrymen hidden all along the hedgerow with rifles and machine pistols.

*

Now it's up to us to dig them out of there. It's a slow and cautious business, and there is nothing very dashing about it. Our men don't go across the open fields in dramatic charges such as you see in the movies. They did at first, but they learned better.

They go in tiny groups, a squad or less, moving yards apart and sticking close to the hedgerows on either side of the field. They creep a few yards, squat, wait, then creep again.

If you could be right up there between the Germans and the Americans you wouldn't see very many men at any one time—just a few here and there, always trying to keep hidden. But you would hear an awful lot of noise.

Our men were taught in training not to fire until they saw something to fire at. But that hasn't worked in this country, because you see so little. So the alternative is to keep shooting constantly at the hedgerows. That pins the Germans in their holes while we sneak up on them.

The attacking squads sneak up the sides of the hedgerows while the rest of the platoon stay back in their own hedgerow and keep the forward hedge saturated with bullets. They shoot rifle grenades too, and a mortar squad a little farther back keeps lobbing mortar shells over onto the Germans.

The little advance groups get up to the far ends of the hedgerows at the corners of the field. They first try to knock out the machine guns at each corner. They do this with hand grenades, rifle grenades and machine guns.

*

Usually, when the pressure gets on, the German defenders of the hedgerow start pulling back. They'll take their heavier guns and most of the men back a couple of fields and start digging in for a new line.

They leave about two machine guns and a few riflemen scattered through the hedge, to do a lot of shooting and hold up the Americans as long as they can.

Our men now sneak along the front side of the hedgerow, throwing grenades over onto the other side and spraying the hedges with their guns. The fighting is very close—only a few yards apart—but it is seldom actual hand-to-hand stuff.

Sometimes the remaining Germans come out of their holes with their hands up. Sometimes they try to run for it and are mowed down. Sometimes they won't come out at all, and a hand grenade, thrown into their hole, finishes them off.

And so we've taken another hedgerow and are ready to start on the one beyond.

This hedgerow business is a series of little skirmishes like that clear across the front, thousands and thousands of little skirmishes. No single one of them is very big. But add them all up over the days and weeks and you've got a man-sized war, with thousands on both sides being killed.

Everything is Confused

ON THE WESTERN FRONT, *August 12, 1944*—What we gave you yesterday in trying to describe hedgerow fighting was the general pattern.

If you were to come over here and pick out some hedge-enclosed field at random, the fighting there probably wouldn't be following the general pattern at all. For each one is a little separate war, fought under different circumstances.

For instance, you'll come to a woods instead of an open field. The Germans will be dug in all over the woods, in little groups, and it's really tough to get them out. Often in cases like that we will just go around the woods and keep going, and let later units take care of those surrounded and doomed fellows.

Or we'll go through the woods and clean it out, and another

company, coming through a couple of hours later, will find it full of Germans again. In a war like this one everything is in such confusion I don't see how either side ever gets anywhere.

Sometimes you don't know where the enemy is and don't know where your own troops are. As somebody said the other day, no battalion commander can give you the exact location of his various units five minutes after they've jumped off.

We will by-pass whole pockets of Germans, and they will be there fighting our following waves when our attacking companies are a couple of miles on beyond. Gradually the front gets all mixed up. There will be Germans behind you and at the side. They'll be shooting at you from behind and from your flank.

Sometimes a unit will get so far out ahead of those on either side that it has to swing around and fight to its rear. Sometimes we fire on our own troops, thinking we are in German territory. You can't see anything, and you can't even tell from the sounds, for each side uses some of the other's captured weapons.

*

The tanks and the infantry had to work in the closest cooperation in breaking through the German ring that tried to pin us down in the beachhead area. Neither could have done it alone.

The troops are of two minds about having tanks around them. If you're a foot soldier you hate to be near a tank, for it always draws fire. On the other hand, if the going gets tough you pray for a tank to come up and start blasting with its guns.

In our breakthrough each infantry unit had tanks attached to it. It was the tanks and the infantry that broke through that ring and punched a hole for the armored divisions to go through.

The armored divisions practically ran amuck, racing long distances and playing hob, once they got behind the German lines, but it was the infantry and their attached tanks that opened the gate for them.

Tanks shuttled back and forth, from one field to another, throughout our breakthrough battle, receiving their orders by radio. Bulldozers punched holes through the hedgerows for them, and then the tanks would come up and blast out the bad spots of the opposition.

It has been necessary for us to wreck almost every farmhouse and little village in our path. The Germans used them for strong points, or put artillery observers in them, and they just had to be blasted out.

Most of the French farmers evacuate ahead of the fighting and filter back after it has passed. It is pitiful to see them come back to their demolished homes and towns. Yet it's wonderful to see the grand way they take it.

*

In a long drive an infantry company may go for a couple of days without letting up. Ammunition is carried up to it by hand, and occasionally by jeep. The soldiers sometimes eat only one K-ration a day. They may run clear out of water. Their strength is gradually whittled down by wounds, exhaustion cases and straggling.

Finally they will get an order to sit where they are and dig in. Then another company will pass through, or around them, and go on with the fighting. The relieved company may get to rest as much as a day or two. But in a big push such as the one that broke us out of the beachhead, a few hours is all they can expect.

The company I was with got its orders to rest about five one afternoon. They dug foxholes along the hedgerows, or commandeered German ones already dug. Regardless of how tired you may be, you always dig in the first thing.

Then they sent some men with cans looking for water. They got more K-rations up by jeep, and sat on the ground eating them.

They hoped they would stay there all night, but they weren't counting on it too much. Shortly after supper a lieutenant came out of a farmhouse and told the sergeants to pass the word to be ready to move in ten minutes. They bundled on their packs and started just before dark.

Within half an hour they had run into a new fight that lasted all night. They had had less then four hours' rest in three solid days of fighting. That's the way life is in the infantry.

August 17, 1944—The commander of the particular regiment of the 4th Infantry Division that we have been with is one of my favorites.

That's partly because he flatters me by calling me "General," partly because just looking at him makes me chuckle to myself, and partly because I think he's a very fine soldier. (Security forbids my giving his name.) He is a Regular Army colonel and he was overseas in the last war. His division commander says the only trouble with him is that he's too bold, and if he isn't careful he's liable to get clipped one of these days.

He is rather unusual looking. There is something almost Mongolian about his face. When cleaned up he could be a Cossack. When tired and dirty he could be a movie gangster. But either way, his eyes always twinkle.

He has a facility for direct thought that is unusual. He is impatient of thinking that gets off onto byways.

He has a little habit of good-naturedly reprimanding people by cocking his head over to one side, getting his face below yours and saying something sharp, and then looking up at you with a quizzical smirk like a laughing cat.

One day I heard him ask a battalion commander what his position was. The battalion commander started going into details of why his troops hadn't got as far as he had hoped. The colonel cocked his head over, squinted up at the battalion commander, and said: "I didn't ask you that. I asked you where you were."

The colonel goes constantly from one battalion to another during battle, from early light till darkness. He wears a new-type field jacket that fits him like a sack, and he carries a long stick that Teddy Roosevelt gave him. He keeps constantly prodding his commanders to push hard, not to let up, to keep driving and driving.

He is impatient with commanders who lose the main point of the war by getting involved in details—the main point, of course, being to kill Germans. His philosophy of war is expressed in the simple formula of "shoot the sonsabitches."

Once I was at a battalion command post when we got word that sixty Germans were coming down the road in a counterattack. Everybody got excited. They called the colonel on the field phone, gave him the details and asked him what to do. He had the solution in a nutshell.

He just said, "Shoot the sonsabitches," and hung up. . . .

Pfc. Tommy Clayton

ON THE WESTERN FRONT, *August 18, 1944*—Soldiers are made out of the strangest people.

I've recently made a new friend—just a plain old Hoosier—who is so quiet and humble you would hardly know he was around. Yet in our few weeks of invasion he has killed four of the enemy, and he has learned war's wise little ways of destroying life and preserving your own.

He hasn't become the "killer" type that war makes of some soldiers; he has merely become adjusted to an obligatory new profession.

His name is George Thomas Clayton. Back home he is known as Tommy. In the Army he is sometimes called George, but usually just Clayton. He is from Evansville, where he lived with his sister.

He is a front-line infantryman of a rifle company in the 29th Division.

By the time this is printed he will be back in the lines. Right now he is out of combat for a brief rest. He spent a few days in an "Exhaustion Camp," then was assigned briefly to the camp where I work from—a camp for correspondents. That's how we got acquainted.

*

Clayton is a private first class. He operates a Browning automatic rifle [B.A.R.]. He has turned down two chances to become a buck sergeant and squad leader, simply because he would rather keep his powerful B.A.R. than have stripes and less personal protection.

He landed in Normandy on D-day, on the toughest of the beaches, and was in the line for thirty-seven days without rest. He has had innumerable narrow escapes.

Twice, 88's hit within a couple of arms' lengths of him. But both times the funnel of the concussion was away from him and he didn't get a scratch, though the explosions covered him and his rifle with dirt.

Then a third one hit about ten feet away, and made him deaf in his right ear. He had always had trouble with that ear anyway—earaches and things as a child. Even in the Army back in America he had to beg the doctors to waive the ear defect in order to come overseas. He is still a little hard of hearing in that ear from the shell burst, but it's gradually coming back.

When Tommy finally left the lines he was pretty well done up and his sergeant wanted to send him to a hospital, but he begged not to go for fear he wouldn't get back to his old company, so they let him go to a rest camp instead.

And now after a couple of weeks with us (provided the correspondents don't drive him frantic), he will return to the lines with his old outfit.

Clayton has worked at all kinds of things back in that other world of civilian life. He has been a farm hand, a cook and a bartender. Just before he joined the Army he was a gauge-honer in the Chrysler Ordnance Plant at Evansville.

When the war is over he wants to go into business for himself for the first time in his life. He'll probably set up a small restaurant in Evansville. He said his brother-in-law would back him.

*

Tommy was shipped overseas after only two months in the Army, and now has been out of America for eighteen months.

He is medium-sized, dark-haired, has a little mustache and the funniest-looking head of hair you ever saw this side of Buffalo Bill's show.

While his division was killing time in the last few days before leaving England, he and three others decided to have their hair cut Indian fashion. They had their heads clipped down to the skin, all except a two-inch ridge starting at the forehead and running clear to the back of the neck. It makes them look more comical than ferocious, as they had intended. Two of the four have been wounded and evacuated to England.

I chatted off and on with Clayton for several days before he told me how old he was. I was amazed; so much so that I asked several other people to guess at his age and they all guessed about the same as I did—about twenty-six.

Actually he is thirty-seven, and that's pretty well along in years to be a front-line infantryman. It's harder on a man at that age.

As Clayton himself says, "When you pass that thirty mark you begin to slow up a little."

It's harder for you to take the hard ground and the rain and the sleeplessness and the unending wracking of it all. And yet at thirty-seven he elected to go back.

ON THE WESTERN FRONT, *August 19, 1944*—The ways of an invasion turned out to be all very new to Pfc. Tommy Clayton.

It was new to thousands of others also, for they hadn't been trained in hedgerow fighting. So they had to learn it the way a dog learns to swim. They learned.

This Tommy Clayton, the mildest of men, has killed four of the enemy for sure, and probably dozens of unseen ones. He wears an Expert Rifleman's badge and soon will have the proud badge of Combat Infantryman, worn only by those who have been through the mill.

Three of his four victims he got in one long blast of his Browning automatic rifle. He was stationed in the bushes at a bend in a gravel road, covering a crossroads about eighty yards ahead of him.

Suddenly three German soldiers came out a side road and foolishly stopped to talk right in the middle of the crossroads. The B.A.R. has twenty bullets in a clip. Clayton held her down for the whole clip. The three Germans went down, never to get up.

His fourth one he thought was a Jap when he killed him. In the early days of the invasion lots of soldiers thought they were fighting Japs, scattered in with the German troops. They were actually

Mongolian Russians, with strong Oriental features, who resembled Japs to the untraveled Americans.

On this fourth killing, Clayton was covering an infantry squad as it worked forward along a hedgerow. There were snipers in the trees in front. Clayton spotted one and sprayed the tree with his automatic rifle, and out tumbled this man he thought was a Jap.

*

To show how little anyone who hasn't been through war can know about it—do you want to know how Clayton located his sniper?

Here's how:

When a bullet passes smack over your head it doesn't zing; it pops the same as a rifle when it goes off. That's because the bullet's rapid passage creates a vacuum behind it, and the air rushes back with such force to fill this vacuum that it collides with itself, and makes a resounding "pop."

Clayton didn't know what caused this, and I tried to explain.

"You know what a vacuum is," I said. "We learned that in high school."

And Tommy said, "Ernie, I never went past the third grade."

But Tommy is intelligent and his sensitivities are fine. You don't have to know the reasons in war; you only have to know what things indicate when they happen.

Well, Clayton had learned that the "pop" of a bullet over his head preceded the actual rifle report by a fraction of a second, because the sound of the rifle explosion had to travel some distance before hitting his ear. So the "pop" became his warning signal to listen for the crack of a sniper's rifle a moment later.

Through much practice he had learned to gauge the direction of the sound almost exactly. And so out of this animal-like system of hunting, he had the knowledge to shoot into the right tree—and out tumbled his "Jap" sniper.

*

Clayton's weirdest experience would be funny if it weren't so flooded with pathos. He was returning with a patrol one moonlit night when the enemy opened up on them. Tommy leaped right through a hedge and, spotting a foxhole, plunged into it.

To his amazement and fright, there was a German in the foxhole, sitting pretty, holding a machine pistol in his hands.

Clayton shot him three times in the chest before you could say scat.

The German hardly moved. And then Tommy realized the

man had been killed earlier. He had been shooting a corpse.

All these experiences seem to have left no effect on this mild soldier from Indiana, unless to make him even quieter than before.

The worst experience of all is just the accumulated blur, and the hurting vagueness of too long in the lines, the everlasting alertness, the noise and fear, the cell-by-cell exhaustion, the thinning of the ranks around you as day follows nameless day. And the constant march into eternity of your own small quota of chances for survival.

Those are the things that hurt and destroy. And soldiers like Tommy Clayton go back to them, because they are good soldiers and they have a duty they cannot define.*

Debris, Sunshine and Utter Silence

ON THE WESTERN FRONT, *August 21, 1944*—When you're wandering around our very far-flung front lines—the lines that in our present rapid war are known as "fluid"—you can always tell how recently the battle has swept on ahead of you.

You can sense it from the little things even more than the big things—

From the scattered green leaves and the fresh branches of trees still lying in the middle of the road.

From the wisps and coils of telephone wire, hanging brokenly from high poles and entwining across the roads.

From the gray, burned-powder rims of the shell craters in the gravel roads, their edges not yet smoothed by the pounding of military traffic.

From the little pools of blood on the roadside, blood that has only begun to congeal and turn black, and the punctured steel helmets lying nearby.

From the square blocks of building stone still scattered in the village street, and from the sharp-edged rocks in the roads, still uncrushed by traffic.

From the burned-out tanks and broken carts still unremoved from the road. From the cows in the fields, lying grotesquely with their feet to the sky, so newly dead they have not begun to bloat or smell.

From the scattered heaps of personal debris around a gun. (I don't know why it is, but the Germans always seem to take off their coats before they flee or die.)

*Clayton was killed three weeks after he returned to the lines. "It saddened me terribly, for I felt very close to him," Pyle said.

From all these things you can tell that the battle has been recent —from these and from the men dead so recently that they seem to be merely asleep.

And also from the inhuman quiet. Usually battles are noisy for miles around. But in this recent fast warfare a battle sometimes leaves a complete vacuum behind it.

The Germans will stand and fight it out until they see there is no hope. Then some give up, and the rest pull and run for miles. Shooting stops. Our fighters move on after the enemy, and those who do not fight, but move in the wake of the battles, will not catch up for hours.

There is nothing left behind but the remains—the lifeless debris, the sunshine and the flowers, and utter silence.

An amateur who wanders in this vacuum at the rear of a battle has a terrible sense of loneliness. Everything is dead—the men, the machines, the animals—and you alone are left alive.

*

One afternoon we drove in our jeep into a country like that. The little rural villages of gray stone were demolished—heart-breaking heaps of still-smoking rubble.

We drove into the tiny town of La Ditinais, a sweet old stone village at the "T" of two gravel roads, a rural village in rolling country, a village of not more than fifty buildings. There was not a whole building left.

Rubble and broken wires still littered the streets. Blackish gray-stone walls with no roofs still smoldered inside. Dead men still lay in the street, helmets and broken rifles askew around them. There was not a soul nor sound in town; the village was lifeless.

We stopped and pondered our way, and with trepidation we drove on out of town. We drove for a quarter of a mile or so. The ditches were full of dead men. We drove around one without a head or arms or legs. We stared, and couldn't say anything about it to each other. We asked the driver to go very slowly, for there was an uncertainty in all the silence. There was no live human, no sign of movement anywhere.

Seeing no one, hearing nothing, I became fearful of going into the unknown. So we stopped. Just a few feet ahead of us was a brick-red American tank, still smoking, and with its turret knocked off. Near it was a German horse-drawn ammunition cart, upside down. In the road beside them was a shell crater.

To our left lay two smashed airplanes in adjoining fields. Neither of them was more than thirty yards from the road. The hedge was low and we could see over. They were both British fighter planes. One lay right side up, the other lay on its back.

We were just ready to turn around and go back when I spied a lone soldier at the far side of the field. He was standing there looking across the field at us like an Indian in a picture. I waved and he waved back. We walked toward each other.

He turned out to be a second lieutenant—Ed Sasson, of Los Angeles. He is graves-registration officer for his armored division, and he was out scouring the fields, locating the bodies of dead Americans.

He was glad to see somebody, for it is a lonely job catering to the dead.

As we stood there talking in the lonely field, a soldier in coveralls, with a rifle slung over his shoulder, ran up breathlessly, and almost shouted: "Hey, there's a man alive in one of those planes across the road! He's been trapped there for days!"

We stopped right in the middle of a sentence and began to run. We hopped the hedgerow, and ducked under the wing of the upside-down plane. And there, in the next hour, came the climax to what certainly was one of the really great demonstrations of courage in this war.

ON THE WESTERN FRONT, *August 22, 1944*—We ran to the wrecked British plane, lying there upside down, and dropped on our hands and knees and peeked through a tiny hole in the side.

A man lay on his back in the small space of the upside-down cockpit. His feet disappeared somewhere in the jumble of dials and rubber pedals above him. His shirt was open and his chest was bare to the waist. He was smoking a cigaret.

He turned his eyes toward me when I peeked in, and he said in a typical British manner of offhand friendliness, "Oh, hello."

"Are you all right," I asked, stupidly.

He answered, "Yes, quite. Now that you chaps are here."

I asked him how long he had been trapped in the wrecked plane. He said he didn't know for sure as he had got mixed up about the passage of time. But he did know the date of the month he was shot down. He told me the date. And I said out loud, "Good God!"

For, wounded and trapped, he had been lying there for eight days!

His left leg was broken and punctured by an ack-ack burst. His back was terribly burned by raw gasoline that had spilled. The foot of his injured leg was pinned rigidly under the rudder bar.

His space was so small he couldn't squirm around to relieve his own weight from his paining back. He couldn't straighten out his legs, which were bent above him. He couldn't see out of his little prison. He had not had a bite to eat or a drop of water. All this for eight days and nights.

Yet when we found him his physical condition was strong, and his mind was as calm and rational as though he were sitting in a London club. He was in agony, yet in his correct Oxford accent he even apologized for taking up our time to get him out.

The American soldiers of our rescue party cussed as they worked, cussed with open admiration for this British flier's greatness of heart which had kept him alive and sane through his lonely and gradually hope-dimming ordeal.

One of them said, "God, but these Limeys have got guts!"

*

It took us almost an hour to get him out. We don't know whether he will live or not, but he has a chance. During the hour we were ripping the plane open to make a hole, he talked to us. And here, in the best nutshell I can devise from the conversation of a brave man whom you didn't want to badger with trivial questions, is what happened:

He was an RAF flight lieutenant, piloting a night fighter. Over a certain area the Germans began letting him have it from the ground with machine-gun fire.

The first hit knocked out his motor. He was too low to jump, so —foolishly, he said—he turned on his lights to try a crash landing. Then they really poured it on him. The second hit got him in the leg. And a third bullet cut right across the balls of his right-hand forefingers, clipping every one of them to the bone.

He left his wheels up, and the plane's belly hit the ground going uphill on a slight slope. We could see the groove it had dug for about fifty yards. Then it flopped, tail over nose, onto its back. The pilot was absolutely sealed into the upside-down cockpit.

"That's all I remember for a while," he told us. "When I came to, they were shelling all around me."

*

Thus began the eight days. He had crashed right between the Germans and Americans in a sort of pastoral No-Man's Land.

For days afterwards the field in which he lay surged back and forth between German hands and ours.

His pasture was pocked with hundreds of shell craters. Many of them were only yards away. One was right at the end of his wing.

The metal sides of the plane were speckled with hundreds of shrapnel holes.

He lay there, trapped in the midst of this inferno of explosions. The fields around him gradually became littered with dead. At last American strength pushed the Germans back, and silence came. But no help. Because, you see, it was in that vacuum behind the battle, and only a few people were left.

The days passed. He thirsted terribly. He slept some. Part of the time he was unconscious; part of the time he undoubtedly was delirious. But he never gave up hope.

After we finally got him out, he said as he lay on the stretcher, "Is it possible that I've been out of this plane since I crashed?"

Everybody chuckled. The doctor who had arrived said, "Not the remotest possibility. You were sealed in there and it took men with tools half an hour to make an opening. And your leg was broken and your foot was pinned there. No, you haven't been out."

"I didn't think it was possible," the pilot said, "and yet it seems in my mind that I was out once and back in again."

That little memory of delirium was the only word said by that remarkable man in the whole hour of his rescue that wasn't as dispassionate and matter-of-fact as though he had been sitting comfortably at the end of the day in front of his own fireplace.*

Pyle entered Paris with the French 2nd Armored Division on August 25. He moved into the Hotel Scribe with other correspondents, many of whom had entered the city in advance of Allied troops and "liberated" the hotel.

Liberating the City of Light

PARIS, *August 28, 1944*—I had thought that for me there could never again be any elation in war. But I had reckoned without the liberation of Paris—I had reckoned without remembering that I might be a part of this richly historic day.

We are in Paris—on the first day—one of the great days of all time. This is being written, as other correspondents are writing their pieces, under an emotional tension, a pent-up semi-delirium.

Our approach to Paris was hectic. We had waited for three days in a nearby town while hourly our reports on what was going on in Paris changed and contradicted themselves. Of a morning it

*The pilot's name was Flight Lieutenant Robert Gordon Follis Lee. He survived his injuries.

would look as though we were about to break through the German ring around Paris and come to the aid of the brave French Forces of the Interior* who were holding parts of the city. By afternoon it would seem the enemy had reinforced until another Stalingrad was developing. We could not bear to think of the destruction of Paris, and yet at times it seemed desperately inevitable.

That was the situation this morning when we left Rambouillet and decided to feel our way timidly toward the very outskirts of Paris. And then, when we were within about eight miles, rumors began to circulate that the French 2nd Armored Division was in the city. We argued for half an hour at a crossroads with a French captain who was holding us up, and finally he freed us and waved us on.

For fifteen minutes we drove through a flat gardenlike country under a magnificent bright sun and amidst greenery, with distant banks of smoke pillaring the horizon ahead and to our left. And then we came gradually into the suburbs, and soon into Paris itself and a pandemonium of surely the greatest mass joy that has ever happened.

*

The streets were lined as by Fourth of July parade crowds at home, only this crowd was almost hysterical. The streets of Paris are very wide, and they were packed on each side. The women were all brightly dressed in white or red blouses and colorful peasant skirts, with flowers in their hair and big flashy earrings. Everybody was throwing flowers, and even serpentine.

As our jeep eased through the crowds, thousands of people crowded up, leaving only a narrow corridor, and frantic men, women and children grabbed us and kissed us and shook our hands and beat on our shoulders and slapped our backs and shouted their joy as we passed.

I was in a jeep with Henry Gorrell of the United Press, Capt. Carl Pergler of Washington, D.C., and Corp. Alexander Belon of Amherst, Massachusetts. We all got kissed until we were literally red in face, and I must say we enjoyed it.

Once when the jeep was simply swamped in human traffic and had to stop, we were swarmed over and hugged and kissed and torn at. Everybody, even beautiful girls, insisted on kissing you on both

*An amalgam of underground resistance groups recognized by the Allies as a regular army. The FFI participated in the liberation of the country, often working in advance of Allied troops.

cheeks.* Somehow I got started kissing babies that were held up by their parents, and for a while I looked like a baby-kissing politician going down the street. The fact that I hadn't shaved for days, and was gray-bearded as well as bald-headed, made no difference. Once when we came to a stop, some Frenchman told us there were still snipers shooting, so we put our steel helmets back on.

The people certainly looked well fed and well dressed. The streets were lined with green trees and modern buildings. All the stores were closed in holiday. Bicycles were so thick I have an idea there have been plenty of accidents today, with tanks and jeeps overrunning the populace.

We entered Paris via Rue Aristide Briand and Rue d'Orléans. We were slightly apprehensive, but decided it was all right to keep going as long as there were crowds. But finally we were stymied by the people in the streets, and then above the din we heard some not-too-distant explosions—the Germans trying to destroy bridges across the Seine. And then the rattling of machine guns up the street, and that old battlefield whine of high-velocity shells just overhead. Some of us veterans ducked, but the Parisians just laughed and continued to carry on.

There came running over to our jeep a tall, thin, happy woman in a light brown dress, who spoke perfect American.

She was Mrs. Helen Cardon, who lived in Paris for twenty-one years and has not been home to America since 1935. Her husband is an officer in French Army headquarters and home now after two and a half years as a German prisoner. He was with her, in civilian clothes.

Mrs. Cardon has a sister, Mrs. George Swikart, of New York, and I can say here to her relatives in America that she is well and happy. Incidentally, her two children, Edgar and Peter, are the only two American children, she says, who have been in Paris throughout the entire war.

*

We entered Paris from due south and the Germans were still battling in the heart of the city along the Seine when we arrived, but they were doomed. There was a full French armored division in the city, plus American troops entering constantly.

The farthest we got in our first hour in Paris was near the Senate building, where some Germans were holed up and firing desper-

*Pyle commented to a correspondent friend: "Anybody who doesn't sleep with a woman tonight is just an exhibitionist."

ately. So we took a hotel room nearby and decided to write while the others fought. By the time you read this I'm sure Paris will once again be free for Frenchmen, and I'll be out all over town getting my bald head kissed. Of all the days of national joy I've ever witnessed this is the biggest.

August 29, 1944— . . . Paris seems to have all the beautiful girls we have always heard it had. The women have an art of getting themselves up fascinatingly. Their hair is done crazily, their clothes are worn imaginatively. They dress in riotous colors in this lovely warm season, and when the flag-draped holiday streets are packed with Parisians the color makes everything else in the world seem gray.

As one soldier remarked, the biggest thrill in getting to Paris is to see people in bright summer clothes again.

Like any city, Paris has its quota of dirty and ugly people. But dirty and ugly people have emotions too, and Hank Gorrell got roundly kissed by one of the dirtiest and ugliest women I have ever seen. I must add that since he's a handsome creature he also got more than his share of embraces from the beautiful young things.

There was one funny little old woman, so short she couldn't reach up to kiss men in military vehicles, who appeared on the second day carrying a stepladder. Whenever a car stopped she would climb her stepladder and let the boys have it with hugs, laughs and kisses.

The second day was a little different from the first. You could sense that during those first few hours of liberation the people were almost animal-like in their panic of joy and relief and gratitude. They were actually crying as they kissed you and screamed, "Thank you, oh thank you, for coming!"

But on the second day it was a deliberate holiday. It was a festival prepared for and gone into on purpose. You could tell that the women had prettied up especially. The old men had on their old medals, and the children were scrubbed and Sunday-dressed until they hurt.

And then everybody came downtown. By two in the afternoon the kissing and shouting and autographing and applauding were almost deafening. The pandemonium of a free and lovable Paris reigned again. It was wonderful to be here.

August 30, 1944— . . . You never saw so many bicycles in your life as in Paris. And they rig up the funniest contraptions on them, such as little two-wheeled carts which they tow behind. And we saw a wagon rigged up so it could be pulled by two bicyclists riding side by side, like a team of horses.

For twenty-four hours tanks were parked on the sidewalks all over downtown Paris. They were all manned by French soldiers, and each tank immediately became a sort of social center.

Kids were all over the tanks like flies. Women in white dresses climbed up to kiss men with grimy faces. And early the next morning we saw a girl climbing sleepily out of a tank turret.

French soldiers of the armored division were all in American uniforms and they had American equipment. Consequently most people at first thought we few Americans were French. Then, puzzled, they would say, "English?" and we would say, "No, American." And then we would get a little scream and a couple more kisses.

Every place you stopped somebody in the crowd could speak English. They apologized for not inviting us to their homes for a drink, saying they didn't have any. Time and again they would say, "We've waited so long for you!" It almost got to be a refrain.

One elderly gentleman said that although we were long in reaching France we had come swiftly since then. He said the people hadn't expected us to be in Paris for six months after invasion day. . . .

August 31, 1944—Eating has been skimpy in Paris through the four years of German occupation, but reports that people were on the verge of starvation apparently were untrue.

The country people of Normandy all seemed so healthy and well fed that we said all along: "Well, country people always fare best, but just wait till we get to Paris. We'll see real suffering there."

Of course the people of Paris have suffered during these four years of darkness. But I don't believe they have suffered as much physically as we had thought.

Certainly they don't look bedraggled and gaunt and pitiful, as the people of Italy did. In fact they look to me just the way you would expect them to look in normal times.

However, the last three weeks before the liberation really were rough. For the Germans, sensing that their withdrawal was inevitable, began taking everything for themselves.

There is very little food in Paris right now. The restaurants either are closed or serve only the barest meals—coffee and sandwiches. And the "national coffee," as they call it, is made from barley and is about the vilest stuff you ever tasted. France has had nothing else for four years.

If you were to take a poll on what the average Parisian most wants in the way of little things, you would probably find that he wants real coffee, soap, gasoline and cigarets. . . .

*

Although it appears that the Germans did conduct themselves fairly properly up until the last few weeks, the French really detest them. One woman told me that for the first three weeks of the occupation the Germans were fine but that then they turned arrogant. The people of Paris simply tolerated them and nothing more.

The Germans did perpetrate medieval barbarities against leaders of the resistance movement as their plight became more and more desperate. But what I'm driving at is that the bulk of the population of Paris—the average guy who just gets along no matter who is here—didn't really fare too badly from day to day. It was just the things they heard about and the fact of being under a bullheaded and arrogant thumb that created the smoldering hatred for the Germans in the average Parisian's heart.

You can get an idea how they feel from a little incident that occurred the first night we were here.

We put up at a little family sort of hotel in Montparnasse. The landlady took us up to show us our rooms. A cute little French maid came along with her.

As we were looking around the room the landlady opened a wardrobe door, and there on a shelf lay a German soldier's cap that he had forgotten to take.

The landlady picked it up with the tips of her fingers, held it out at arm's length, made a face, and dropped it on a chair.

Whereupon the little maid reached up with her pretty foot and gave it a huge kick that sent it sailing across the room.

September 2, 1944—We left Paris after a few days and went again with the armies in the field. In Paris we had slept in beds and walked on carpeted floors for the first time in three months.

It was a beautiful experience, and yet for some perverse reason a great inner feeling of calm and relief came over us when we once again set up our cots in a tent, with apple trees for our draperies and only the green grass for a rug.

Hank Gorrell of the United Press was with me, and he said:

"This is ironic, that we should have to go back with the armies to get some peace."

The gaiety and charm and big-cityness of Paris somehow had got a little on our nerves after so much of the opposite. I guess it indicates that all of us will have to make our return to normal life gradually and in small doses. . . .

*

As usual, those Americans most deserving of seeing Paris will be the last ones to see it, if they ever do. By that I mean the fighting soldiers.

Only one infantry regiment and one reconnaissance outfit of Americans actually came into Paris, and they passed on through the city quickly and went on with their war.

The first ones in the city to stay were such nonfighters as the psychological-warfare and civil-affairs people, public-relations men and correspondents.

I heard more than one rear-echelon soldier say he felt a little ashamed to be getting all the grateful cheers and kisses for the liberation of Paris when the guys who broke the German Army and opened the way for Paris to be free were still out there fighting without the benefit of kisses or applause.

But that's the way things are in this world.

"For six weeks," Pyle wrote a friend, "I've been dragging lower and lower, from mental exhaustion and just a sort of unendurable blue of too much war." He decided to go home for a rest.

Farewell to Europe

PARIS, *September 5, 1944*—This is the last of these columns from Europe. By the time you read this, the old man will be on his way back to America. After that will come a long, long rest. And after the rest—well, you never can tell.

Undoubtedly this seems to you to be a funny time for a fellow to be quitting the war. It *is* a funny time. But I'm not leaving because of a whim, or even especially because I'm homesick.

I'm leaving for one reason only—because I have just got to stop. "I've had it," as they say in the Army. I have had all I can take for a while.

I've been twenty-nine months overseas since this war started; have written around seven hundred thousand words about it; have totaled nearly a year in the front lines.

I do hate terribly to leave right now, but I have given out. I've been immersed in it too long. My spirit is wobbly and my mind is confused. The hurt has finally become too great.

All of a sudden it seemed to me that if I heard one more shot or saw one more dead man, I would go off my nut. And if I had to write one more column I'd collapse. So I'm on my way.

It may be that a few months of peace will restore some vim to my spirit, and I can go war-horsing off to the Pacific. We'll see what a little New Mexico sunshine does along that line.

*

Even after two and a half years of war writing there still is a lot I would like to tell. I wish right now that I could tell you about our gigantic and staggering supply system that keeps these great armies moving.

I'm sorry I haven't been able to get around to many branches of service that so often are neglected. I would like to have written about the Transportation Corps and the airport engineers and the wirestringers and the chemical mortars and the port battalions. To all of those that I have missed, my apologies. But the Army over here is just too big to cover it all.

*

I know the first question everyone will ask when I get home is: "When will the war be over?"

So I'll answer even before you ask me, and the answer is: "I don't know."

We all hope and most of us think it won't be too long now. And yet there's a possibility of it going on and on, even after we are deep in Germany. The Germans are desperate and their leaders have nothing to quit for.

Every day the war continues is another hideous black mark against the German nation. They are beaten and yet they haven't quit. Every life lost from here on is a life lost to no purpose.

If Germany does deliberately drag this war on and on she will so infuriate the world by her inhuman bullheadedness that she is apt to be committing national suicide.

In our other campaigns we felt we were fighting, on the whole, a pretty good people. But we don't feel that way now. A change has occurred. On the western front the Germans have shown their real cruelty of mind. We didn't used to hate them, but we do now.

The outstanding figure on this western front is Lt. Gen. Omar Nelson Bradley. He is so modest and sincere that he probably will not get his proper credit, except in military textbooks.

But he has proved himself a great general in every sense of the word. And as a human being, he is just as great. Having him in command has been a blessed good fortune for America.

*

I cannot help but feel bad about leaving. Even hating the whole business as much as I do, you come to be a part of it. And you leave some of yourself here when you depart. Being with the American soldier has been a rich experience.

To the thousands of them whom I know personally and the other hundreds of thousands for whom I have had the humble privilege of being a sort of mouthpiece, this then is to say goodbye—and good luck.

Before he left France, Pyle wrote a last chapter for Brave Men, *a collection of his European columns, in which he speculated about what it would be like for the war's survivors after the last shot was fired. "It will be odd to drive down an unknown road without that little knot of fear in your stomach; odd not to listen with animal-like alertness for the meaning of every distant sound; odd to have your spirit released from the perpetual weight that is compounded of fear and death and dirt and noise and anguish."*

He and many others had seen too much of battle. "Our feelings have been wrung and drained; they cringe from the effort of coming alive again." For Pyle, war had "become a flat, black depression without highlights, a revulsion of the mind and an exhaustion of the spirit." He had no doubt about the outcome—the Allies would be victorious—but he hoped that "in victory we are more grateful than we are proud." When the war is finally over, "all of us together will have to learn how to reassemble our broken world into a pattern so firm and so fair that another great war cannot soon be possible. . . . Submersion in war does not necessarily qualify a man to be the master of peace. All we can do is fumble and try once more—try out of the memory of our anguish—and be as tolerant with each other as we can."

THE PACIFIC:

January 1945—April 1945

FROM *AN ERNIE PYLE ALBUM*

Shortly before Pyle left France, General Omar Bradley urged him to go home and stay home; his chances, the general suggested, were about used up. Pyle's wife, Jerry, virtually begged him to abandon war correspondence. But the armed forces in the Pacific badly wanted Pyle to join them. It was apparent to them what a morale booster he had been in Europe, how he had made the war there so vivid to stateside readers, and they exerted considerable pressure on him to cover the Pacific Theater. Although he was emotionally not up to the job, Pyle acquiesced. After a too-short vacation, he set off to war again, beginning his Pacific columns with a piece on his reaction to the home front and another on his own popularity.

*February 7, 1945**— . . . People are always asking what I think of the home front, expecting me of course to raise hell about it.

Well, I don't know. In the first place it's so wonderful to be home that I find myself reluctant to criticize or even admit any flaws in the home front.

It is true that a great many people don't know there's a war on, or don't seem to care. And yet I realize that I could very easily let myself sit down and take it easy and never think of war again, except in an academic way.

I've had no bad incidents during these few months at home. But I have learned from experience that it's almost impossible—sometimes infuriating in a helpless sort of way—to talk to most civilians feelingly about the war.

On trains and in public places I find myself drifting automatically to boys in uniform with overseas ribbons or service stripes, for we can talk the same language.

As an example of what I mean, one man said to me one day in complete good faith, "Tell me now, just exactly what is it you don't like about war?"

I think I must have turned a little white, and all I could do was look at him in shock and say "Good God, if you don't know, then I could never tell you." It's little things like that which make returning soldiers feel their misery has all been in vain.

I don't think America at home is neither unwilling nor incapable of getting fully into the war. We need only to be told more what

*Pyle arrived in the Pacific Theater during mid-January, but his first pieces were delayed to give him time to begin steady production.

to do, and to have scarcities and grimness applied clear across the board.

Personally I'm glad for the President's proposal for a national service act. I think it will stiffen up the whole American nation, and through touching almost every family, make people buckle down. That, and the casualties that lie ahead of us.

I believe the worst of our war is still to come, and that before it is over everybody in America will really feel it. I hope so, because then the boys overseas won't feel so lonesome.

Hardly a Vacation

SAN FRANCISCO, *February 8, 1945*—These four months of furlough in America, away from the war, have gone like the wind. They have been full to overflowing. So full, in fact, that hardly anything has happened that I had hoped would happen.

There has been no rest. There has been no time for composure. No day has been long enough to finish the things required in that day.

I've had the one magnificent privilege of being away from the war, but aside from that I've had more duties and worked harder here at home on "vacation" than most of the time at the front.

Normal life for me has disappeared. The bulk of my time is now given to other people. It's almost impossible to count on a single hour alone. To get half a day uninterrupted with my own family I have to plan it days ahead and then bar the gates.

If the intrusions were by mere publicity-seekers, then I could be tough. But the pressure upon me is not from publicity-seekers or the curious.

Ninety percent of the people who phone, write, visit or stop me in public places have legitimate reasons for doing so. They are people who have done kind little things for me. They are people who just want to tell me, in complete sincerity, that they think I've done a good job—and a fellow never gets tired of hearing that.

They are people whose sons I've known overseas; they are people who wrote to tell me their sons are dead; they are people who want help in something they're doing for the war, people who have a part in this pattern of war that has grown up around me.

Yes, ninety percent of the destruction of my private life is from pure goodness and sincerity in people, and from unavoidable duties that have become as much a part of my job as the job itself.

I have never aspired to be famous. If I had, then I could say to myself, "All right, brother, you made your own bed, so now lie in it."

But this thing just happened. It came without planning or aspiration. I guess it comes in the category of an Act of God, like a blizzard or slipping on a banana peel.

You have to adjust yourself to this new condition, or else you're lost. You can't fight it, you can't ignore it, you can't run away from it. You've got to accept it. I do accept it as graciously as I can, but I feel sad about it.

I feel sad because it has given me the big things of life, and taken away the precious little things.

It has given me money, yet I dread to hear the telephone ring.

It has brought me a measure of renown, yet made me afraid to go into a restaurant because people whisper and stare, and I feel self-conscious.

It has put my book [*Brave Men*] at the top of the best-seller list, but robbed me of the time to read other people's books.

It has put me on easy terms with the great, but forbidden me the privilege of sitting alone with my old true friends.

It has made my homely face familiar throughout America, but taken away that saving gift of serenity of mind and soul. My life now, day and night, is a frenzy. There is no mental leisure in it; never the freedom to sit down and let your mind go blank.

I like people. I always have and I still do. And so it hurts me to have to shut off phone calls in a hotel. It hurts to turn letters over to a secretary. It hurts to tell old friends that I can't see them today —maybe tomorrow. It hurts to have to hide and cower like a criminal to get just an hour or two to myself.

But that's the way it is. I don't resent it, and I don't blame anybody. I'm grateful for the respect of such a great portion of America. I'm trying to take the bad things with the good, and get along the best I can.

Sometimes I feel like sitting down and crying because my old life is gone. But most of the time I see what is behind it, and realize that a man is blessed who is publicly obsessed by the goodness in people, instead of the bad.

When Pyle arrived in the Hawaiian Islands during mid-January 1945, most of the Allies' Pacific island-hopping campaigns were over; the Philippines had recently been taken after two-and-a-half years of Japanese occupation. Only Iwo Jima and Okinawa remained before the Allies could mount an invasion on the Japanese mainland itself. With this column, Pyle began to establish for his readers the differences between the war in the Pacific and the war in Europe. In subsequent weeks, he returned to this theme, much to the irritation of servicemen in the Pacific, who felt their war had long been misunderstood by the public and under-reported by the press.

Europe This is Not

HONOLULU, *February 16, 1945*—Covering this Pacific war is, for me, going to be like learning to live in a new city.

The methods of war, the attitude toward it, the homesickness, the distances, the climate—everything is different from what we have known in the European war.

Here in the beginning, I can't seem to get my mind around it, or get my fingers on it. I suspect it will take months to get adjusted and get the "feel" of this war.

Distance is the main thing. I don't mean distance from America so much, for our war in Europe is a long way from home too. I mean distances after you get right on the battlefield.

For the whole Western Pacific is our battlefield now, and whereas distances in Europe are hundreds of miles at most, out there they are thousands. And there's nothing in between but water.

You can be on an island battlefield, and the next thing behind you is a thousand miles away. One soldier told me the worst sinking feeling he ever had was when they had landed on an island and were fighting, and on the morning of D-day plus three he looked out to sea and it was completely empty. Our entire convoy had unloaded and left for more, and, boy, did it leave you with a lonesome and deserted feeling.

As one admiral said, directing this war is like watching a slow-motion picture. You plan something for months, and then finally the great day comes when you launch your plans, and then it is days or weeks before the attack happens, because it takes that long to get there.

As an example of how they feel, the Navy gives you a slick sheet of paper as you go through here, entitled "Airline Distances in Pacific." And at the bottom of it is printed "Our Enemy, Geography." Logistics out here is more than a word; it's a nightmare.

Here's another example of their attitude toward distances in the Pacific:

At Anzio in Italy just a year ago, the 3rd Division set up a rest camp for its exhausted infantrymen. The rest camp was less than five miles from the front line, within constant enemy artillery range.

But in the Pacific, they bring men clear back from the western islands to Pearl Harbor to rest camps—the equivalent of bringing an Anzio beachhead fighter all the way back to Kansas City for his two-weeks' rest.

It's thirty-five hundred miles from Pearl Harbor to the Marianas, all over water, yet hundreds of people travel it daily by air as casually as you'd go to work in the morning.

*

And there is another enemy out here that we did not know so well in Europe—and that is monotony. Oh sure, war everywhere is monotonous in its dreadfulness. But out here even the niceness of life gets monotonous.

The days are warm and on our established island bases the food is good and the mail service is fast and there's little danger from the enemy and the days go by in their endless sameness and they drive you nuts. They sometimes call it going "pineapple crazy."

Our high rate of returning mental cases is discussed frankly in the island and service newspapers. A man doesn't have to be under fire in the front lines finally to have more than he can take without breaking.

He can, when isolated and homesick, have more than he can take of nothing but warmth and sunshine and good food and safety—when there's nothing else to go with it, and no prospect of anything else.

*

And another adjustment I'll have to make is the attitude toward the enemy. In Europe we felt our enemies, horrible and deadly as they were, were still people.

But out here I've already gathered the feeling that the Japanese are looked upon as something inhuman and squirmy—like some people feel about cockroaches or mice.

I've seen one group of Japanese prisoners in a wire-fenced courtyard, and they were wrestling and laughing and talking just as humanly as anybody. And yet they gave me a creepy feeling and I felt in need of a mental bath after looking at them.

I've not yet got to the front, or anywhere near it, to find out how the average soldier or sailor or Marine feels about the thing he's fighting. But I'll bet he doesn't feel the same way our men in Europe feel.

Pyle flew to the Marianas Islands, first to Guam, where his celebrity thwarted his writing, then to nearby Saipan, from which B-29 Superfortresses were bombing mainland Japan.

February 17, 1945—Now we are far, far away from everything that was home or seemed like home. Five thousand miles from America, and twelve thousand miles from my friends fighting on the German border.

Twelve thousand miles from Sidi-Bou-Zid and Venafro and Troina and Sainte-Mère-Eglise—names as unheard of on this side of the world as are Kwajalein and Chichi Jima and Ulithi on the other side.

The Pacific names are all new to me too, all except the outstanding ones. For those fighting one war do not pay much attention to the other war. Each one thinks his war is the worst and the most important war. And unquestionably it is. . . .

February 21, 1945—It is tropical where we are now, wonderfully tropical.

It looks tropical, and best of all, it feels tropical. Just now is the good season, and it is like the pleasantest part of summer at home.

But it is hotter than you think, and you change your whole approach to the weather here.

You get from the Navy a long-billed "baseball" cap to shield your eyes from the sun. Your clothes closet has an electric light burning constantly in it, to keep it dry so your clothes won't mold. You change your leather wristwatch strap to a canvas one, for a leather one would mold on your arm.

You put on heavy high-topped shoes again, for it still rains some and the red mud is sloppy. And instead of light socks for coolness as you'd think, you put on heavy socks to help cushion your feet in the big shoes, and to absorb the moisture.

Officers wear their sunglass cases hooked to their belts. Ties are unknown. There is no glass in the windows. Wide slanting eaves jut out far beyond the windows in all the permanent barracks buildings, for when it rains here it really pours.

And as someone said, it rains "horizontally" down here. In the few showers since we arrived, I've seen that the rain does come at quite an angle.

Actually the rainy season is supposed to be over. Consequently, every time it showers during the day, the Californians in camp point out that the weather is "unusual."

*

Lt. Comdr. Max Miller* and I are staying briefly in a room of a Bachelor Officers' Quarters—or BOQ. Our famous Seabees† have put them up all over these various islands since we took over from the Japanese last summer.

They are in the curved form of immense Quonset huts, made of corrugated metal and with concrete floors. Some of them are even two-storied. They have a wide hall down the center, and individual rooms on each side. The walls are cream-colored.

The outside wall is almost all window, to let lots of air in. The spaces are screened but have no glass, for it never gets so cold you'd want to shut the window. But it is pleasantly cool at night, and we sleep under one blanket.

Each room has a clothes closet and a washstand and a chest of drawers. And also two beds. These beds are the talk of the Marianas.

They are American beds, with double mattresses, soft and wonderful. As everybody says, they're finer beds than you'd have at home. I ran into one Army officer who had served in Europe, and he laughed and said, "After the way we roughed it there, I feel self-conscious about sleeping like this over here. But if the Navy wants to send over these beds, I'm sure as hell going to sleep in them."

Naturally everybody on these islands doesn't live like that, for these quarters are only for transient visitors like myself, and staff officers.

The great working camps of the Seabees and the troops are largely of tents, with ordinary cots in them. But on the whole, now that we have been improving the islands for several months, everybody lives pretty comfortably. . . .

A Finger on the Wide Web of the War

IN THE MARIANAS ISLANDS, *February 22, 1945*—You may wonder why we have American troops at all here in the Marianas Islands, since we are fifteen hundred miles away from the Philippines, China or Japan itself.

Well, it's because in this Pacific war of vast water distances, we have to make gigantic bases of each group of islands we take, in

*Miller, a well-known West Coast author, and Pyle had met during Pyle's travel days. The Navy had assigned Miller to be Pyle's guide.
†The Navy's construction arm.

order to build up supplies and preparations for future invasions farther on.

The Marianas happen to be a sort of crossroads in the Western Pacific. Stuff can go either west or north from here. Whoever sits in the Marianas can have his finger on the whole wide web of the war.

Thus the Marianas are becoming a heart of the Pacific war. Our naval and military leaders make no bones about it, for the Japs know it anyhow, but they're too far away to do anything about it.

The Marianas are both thrilling and engaging right now. Scores of thousands of troops of all kinds are here. Furious building is going on. Planes arrive on schedule from all directions as though this were Chicago Airport—only they've come thousands of miles over water. Convoys unload unbelievable tonnage.

These islands will hum throughout the war and they will never return to their former placid life, for we are building on almost every inch of usable land.

Supplies in staggering quantities are being stacked up here for future use. You can take your pick of K-rations or lumber or bombs, and you'd find enough of each to feed a city, build one, or blow it up.

Fleets can base here between engagements. Combat troops train here. Other troops come back to rest. Great hospitals are set up for our future wounded. Pipelines crisscross the islands. Trucks bumper to bumper dash forward as though they were on the Western Front. Oxcart trails turn almost overnight into four-lane macadam highways for military traffic.

There is no blackout in the islands. If raiders come the lights are turned off, but they seldom come anymore. The Marianas are a pretty safe place now.

Great long macadam airstrips are in operation and others are being laid. The Marianas are the seat of some of our B-29 bomber fleets which will grow and grow and grow.

Thousands of square tents, thousands of curved-steel Quonset huts, thousands of huge, permanent warehouses and office buildings dot the islands.

Lights burn all night and the roar of planes, the clank of bulldozers and the clatter of hammers is constant. It is a strange contrast to the stillness that dwelt amidst this greenery for so many centuries.

There are fifteen islands in this chain, running due north and south. They string out a total distance of more than four hundred miles. We are on the southern end.

We hold only three islands, but they are the biggest and the only three that count. The other islands are completely "neutralized" by our occupancy of these three.

There are a few Japs living on some of the others, but there's nothing they can do to harm us. The islands we haven't bothered with are small and worthless. Most of them have no inhabitants at all.

The islands we took are Guam, Tinian and Saipan. Guam had been ours for many years before Japan took it away from us just after Pearl Harbor. Tinian and Saipan had been Japanese since the last war. We took the whole batch last sumer.

Guam is the biggest, and southernmost. Tinian and Saipan are right together, one hundred twenty miles north of Guam. You can fly up there in less than an hour, and our transport planes shuttle back and forth several times daily on a regular schedule. They have to make a "dog-leg" around the island of Rota, about halfway up, for there are still Japs on it with 50-caliber machine guns, and they'll shoot at you.

I've been on all three of our islands, and I must admit two things —that I like it here, and that you can't help but be thrilled by what the Americans are doing.

And from all I've picked up so far, I think it can be said that most Americans like the Marianas Islands, assuming they have to be away from home at all.

The savage heat and the dread diseases and the awful jungles of the more southern Pacific islands do not exist here. The climate is good, the islands are pretty, and the native Chamorros are nice people.

Health conditions among our men are excellent. They work in shorts or without shirts and are deeply tanned. The mosquito and fly problem has been licked. There is almost no venereal disease. Food is good. The weather is always warm but not cruelly hot. Almost always a breeze is blowing. Anywhere you look, you have a pretty view.

Yes, the islands are a paradise and life here is fine—except it's empty and there is no diversion and the monotony eventually gnaws at you.

Japs Do the Silliest Things

IN THE MARIANAS ISLANDS, *February 23, 1945*—There are still Japs on the three islands of the Marianas chain that we have occupied for more than six months now.

The estimate runs into several hundred. They hide in the hills and in caves, and come out at night to forage for food. Actually many of their caves were so well-stocked that they could go for months without getting too hungry.

Our men don't do anything about the Japs anymore. Oh, troops in training for combat will go out on a Jap-hunt now and then just for practice, and bring in a few. But they are no menace to us, and by and large we just ignore them. A half dozen or so give up every day.

The Japs don't try to practice any sabotage on our stuff. It would take another Jap to figure out why. The Japanese are thoroughly inconsistent in what they do, and very often illogical. They do the silliest things.

Here are a few examples. One night some of our Seabees left a bulldozer and an earth-mover sitting alongside the road up in the hills.

During the night, the Japs came down. They couldn't hurt anybody, but they could have put that machinery out of commission for a while. Even with only a rock they could have smashed the spark plugs and ruined the carburetor.

They didn't do any of these things. They merely spent the night cutting palm fronds off nearby trees and laying them over the big machinery. Next morning when the Seabees arrived they found their precious equipment completely "hidden." Isn't that cute?

*

On another island, there were many acts of sabotage the Japs could have committed. But all they ever did was to come down at night and move the wooden stakes the engineers had lined up for the next day's construction of buildings!

*

There is another story of a Jap who didn't take to the hills like the rest, but who stayed for weeks right in the most thickly American-populated section of the island, right down by the seashore.

He hid in the bushes just a few feet from a path where hundreds of Americans walked daily. They found out later that he even used the officers' outdoor shower bath after they got through, and raided their kitchens at night.

There was a Jap prison enclosure nearby, and for weeks, peering out of the bushes, he studied the treatment his fellow soldiers were getting, watched how they were, watched to see if they were dwindling away from malnutrition.

And then one day he came out and gave himself up. He said he had convinced himself they were being treated all right, so he was ready to surrender.

And here's another one. An American officer was idly sitting on an outdoor box-toilet one evening after work, philosophically studying the ground, as men will do.

Suddenly he was startled. Startled is a mild word for it. For here he was, caught with his pants down, so to speak, and in front of him stood a Jap with a rifle.

But before anything could happen the Jap laid the rifle on the ground in front of him, and began salaaming up and down like a worshiper before an idol.

The Jap later said that he had been hunting for weeks for somebody without a rifle to give himself up to, and had finally figured out that the surest way to find an unarmed prospective captor was to catch one on the toilet!

*

But don't let these little aftermath stories mislead you into thinking the Japs are easy after all. For they are a very nasty people while the shooting's going on.

IN THE MARIANAS ISLANDS, *February 24, 1945*—Soldiers and Marines have told me stories by the dozen about how tough the Japs are, yet how dumb they are; how illogical and yet how uncannily smart at times; how easy to rout when disorganized, yet how brave.

I've become more confused with each story. At the end of one evening, I said, "I can't make head nor tail out of what you've told me. I'm trying to learn about the Jap soldiers, but everything you say about them seems to be inconsistent."

"That's the answer," my friends said. "They are inconsistent. They do the damndest things. But they're dangerous fighters just the same."

*

They tell one story about a Jap officer and six men who were surrounded on a beach by a small bunch of Marines.

As the Marines approached, they could see the Jap giving emphatic orders to his men, and then all six bent over and the officer went along the line and chopped off their heads with his sword.

Then as the Marines closed in, he stood knee-deep in the surf and beat his bloody sword against the water in a fierce gesture of defiance, just before they shot him.

What code led the officer to kill his own men rather than let them fight to the death is something only another Jap would know.

*

Another little story: a Marine sentry walking up and down before a command post on top of a steep bluff one night heard a noise in the brush on the hillside below.

He called a couple of times, got no answer, then fired an exploratory shot down into the darkness. In a moment there was a loud explosion from below. A solitary Jap hiding down there had put a hand grenade to his chest.

Why he did that, instead of tossing it up over the bluff and getting himself a half dozen Americans, is beyond an American's comprehension.

*

On Saipan, they tell of a Jap plane that appeared overhead one bright noonday, all alone. He obviously wasn't a photographic plane, and they couldn't figure out what he was doing.

Then something came out of the plane, and fluttered down. It was a little paper wreath, with a long streamer to it. He had flown it all the way from Japan, and dropped it "In Honor of Japan's Glorious Dead" on Saipan.

We shot him down into the sea a few minutes later, as he undoubtedly knew we would before he ever left Japan. The gesture was touching—but so what?

*

As I've talked with Marines, I've begun to get over that creepy feeling that fighting Japs is like fighting snakes or ghosts.

They are indeed queer, but they are people with certain tactics and now by much experience our men have learned how to fight them.

As far as I can see, our men are no more afraid of the Japs than they are of the Germans. They are afraid of them as any modern soldier is afraid of his foe, not because they are slippery or rat-like, but simply because they have weapons and fire them like good tough soldiers. And the Japs are human enough to be afraid of us in exactly the same way.

Some of our people over here think that, in the long run, the Japs won't take the beating the Germans have. Others think they will, and even more.

I've not been here long enough really to learn anything of the Jap psychology. But the Pacific war is gradually getting condensed, and consequently tougher and tougher. The closer we go to Japan itself, the harder it will be.

The Japs are dangerous people and they aren't funny when they've got guns in their hands. It would be tragic for us to underestimate their power to do us damage, or their will to do it. To me it looks like soul-trying days for us in the years ahead.

Pyle wrote a series on the B-29 crews of the 73rd Bombardment Wing, based on Saipan. Serving with the 73rd was Lt. Jack Bales, step-grandson of Pyle's Aunt Mary Bales, who kept house for Pyle's father in Indiana. Pyle called Jack his "nephew."

A Long, Tough Bombing Program

IN THE MARIANAS ISLANDS, *February 27, 1945*—When you see a headline saying "Superforts Blast Japan Again," I hope you don't get the idea that Japan is being blown sky-high and that she'll be bombed out of the war within another week or two.

Because that isn't the case. We are just barely starting on a program of bombing that will be long and tough. Even with heavy and constant bombings it would take years to reduce Japan by bombing alone. And our bombings are not yet heavy.

Too, we have lots of things to contend with. Distance is the main thing, and Jap fighters and ack-ack and foul weather are other things. The weather over Japan is their best defense. As one pilot jokingly suggested, "The Nips should broadcast us the weather every night, and save both themselves and us lots of trouble."

Almost the first thing the B-29 boys asked me was, "Do the people at home think the B-29's are going to win the war?"

I told them the papers played up the raids, and that many wishful-thinking people felt the bombings might turn the trick. And the boys said: "That's what we were afraid of. Naturally we want what credit we deserve, but our raids certainly aren't going to win the war."

The B-29 raids are important, just as every island taken and every ship sunk is important. But in their present strength it would be putting them clear out of proportion if you think they are a dominant factor in our Pacific war.

I say this not to belittle the B-29 boys, because they are wonderful. I say it because they themselves want it understood by the folks at home.

*

Their lot is a tough one. The worst part is that they're over water every inch of the way to Japan, every inch of the way back. And brother, it's a lot of water. The average time for one of their missions is more than fourteen hours.

The flak and fighters over Japan are bad enough, but that tense period is fairly short. They are over the Empire only from twenty minutes to an hour, depending on their target. Jap fighters follow them only about fifteen minutes off the coast.

What gives the boys the woolies is "sweating out" those six or seven hours of ocean beneath them on the way back. To make it worse, it's usually at night.

Some of them are bound to be shot up, and just staggering along. There's always the danger of running out of gas, from many forms of overconsumption. If you've got one engine gone, others are liable to quit.

If anything happens, you go into the ocean. That is known as "ditching." I suppose around a B-29 base you hear the word "ditching" almost more than any other word.

"Ditching" out here isn't like "ditching" in the English Channel, where your chances of being picked up are awfully good. "Ditching" out here is usually fatal.

We have set up a search-and-rescue system for these "ditched" fliers but still the ocean is awfully big, and it's mighty hard to find a couple of little rubber boats. The fact that we do rescue about a fifth of our "ditched" fliers is amazing to me.

Yes, that long drag back home after the bombing is a definite mental hazard, and is what eventually makes the boys sit and stare.

*

Maybe you've heard of the "buddy system" in the infantry. They use it in the B-29's, too. For instance, if a plane is in distress on the way back and has to fall behind, somebody drops back with him to keep him company.

They've known planes to come clear home accompanied by a "buddy," and you could go so far as to say some might not have made it were it not for the extra courage given them by having company.

But the big point of the "buddy system" is that if a plane does have to ditch, the "buddy" can fix his exact position and get surface rescuers on the way.

The other morning after a mission, my friend Maj. Gerald Robinson was lying on his cot resting and reminiscing, and he said:

"You feel so damn helpless when the others get in trouble. The air will be full of radio calls from those guys saying they've only got two engines or they're running short on gas.

"I've been lucky and there I'll be sitting with four engines and a thousand gallons extra of gas. I could spare any of them one engine and five hundred gallons of gas if I could just get it to them. It makes you feel so damn helpless."

Inside a Super Fortress

IN THE MARIANAS ISLANDS, *March 1, 1945*—The B-29 is unquestionably a wonderful airplane. Outside of the famous old Douglas DC-3 workhorse, I've never heard pilots so unanimous in their praise of an airplane.

I took my first ride in one the other day. No, I didn't go on a mission to Japan. We've been through all that before. I don't believe in people going on missions unless they have to. And as before, the pilots here all agreed with me.

But I went along on a little practice bombing trip of an hour and a half. The pilot was Maj. Gerald Robinson, who lives in our hut. His wife, incidentally, lives in Albuquerque, New Mexico, on the very same street as our white house.

I sat on a box between the pilots, both on the takeoff and for the landing, and as much as I've flown, that was still a thrill. These islands are all relatively small, and you're no sooner off the ground than you're out over water, and that feels funny.

If the air is a little rough, it gives you a very odd sensation sitting way up there in the nose. For the B-29 is so big that, instead of bumping or dropping, the nose has a "willowy" motion, sort of like sitting out on the end of a green limb when it's swaying around.

The B-29 carries a crew of eleven. Some of them sit up in the cockpit and the compartment just behind it. Some others sit in a compartment near the tail. The tail gunner sits all alone, way back there in the lonely tail turret.

The body of the B-29 is so taken up with gas tanks and bomb racks that there's normally no way to get from front to rear compartments. So the manufacturers solved that by building a tunnel into the plane, right along the rooftop.

The tunnel is round, just big enough to crawl in on your hands and knees, and is padded with blue cloth. It's more than thirty feet long, and the crew members crawl back and forth through it all the time. Maj. Russ Cheever reported that he accomplished the impossible the other day by turning around in the tunnel.

On missions, some of the crew get back in this tunnel and sleep for an hour or so. But a lot of them can't stand to do that. I've heard combat crewmen bring up the subject a half dozen times. They say they get claustrophobia in the tunnel.

There used to be some sleeping bunks on the B-29, but they've been taken out, and now there's hardly even room to lie down on the floor.

A fellow does get sleepy on a fourteen-hour mission. Most of the pilots take naps in their seats. One pilot I know turned the plane over to his copilot and went back to the tunnel for "a little nap," and didn't return for six hours, just before they hit the coast of Japan. They laughingly say he goes to sleep before he gets his wheels up.

The B-29 is a very stable plane and hardly anybody ever gets sick, even in rough weather. The boys smoke in the plane, and the mess hall gives them a small lunch of sandwiches and oranges and cookies to eat on the way.

On mission days all flying crewmen, even those not going on the mission, get all the fried eggs they want for breakfast. That's the only day they have eggs.

The crewmen wear their regular clothes on missions, usually coveralls. They don't have to wear heavy fleece-lined clothes and all that bulky gear, because the cabin is heated. They do slip on their heavy steel "flak vests" as they approach the target.

They don't have to wear oxygen masks except when they're over the target, for the cabin is sealed and "pressurized"—simulating a constant altitude of eight thousand feet.

Once in a great while one of the Plexiglas "blisters" where the gunners sit will blow out from the strong pressure inside, and then everybody better grab his oxygen mask in an awful hurry. The crew always wears the oxygen mask over the target, for a shell through the plane "depressurizes" the cabin instantly, and they'd pass out.

The boys speak frequently of the unbelievably high winds they hit at high altitudes over Japan. It's nothing unusual to have a one-hundred-fifty-mile-an-hour wind, and my nephew, Jack Bales, said that one day his plane hit a wind of two hundred fifty miles an hour.

Another thing that puzzles and amuses the boys is that often they'll pick up news on their radios, when still only halfway home, that their bombing mission has been announced in Washington. Thus all the world knows about it, but they've still got a thousand miles of ocean to cross before it's finished. Science, she is wonderful.

Watching and Waiting

IN THE MARIANAS ISLANDS, *March 3, 1945*—No sooner have the B-29 formations disappeared to the north on their long flight to Japan than single planes begin coming back in.

These are called "aborts," which is short for "abortives." It is a much-used word around a bomber base.

The "aborts" come straggling back all day, hours apart. They are planes that had something happen to them which forbade them continuing on the long dangerous trip. Sometimes it happens immediately after takeoff. Sometimes it doesn't happen until they are almost there.

The first "abort" had a bomb-bay door come open, and couldn't get it closed. The second had part of the cowl flap come unfastened, and a mechanic undoubtedly caught hell for that. A third had a prop run away when he lost an engine.

My friend Maj. Walter Todd of Ogden, Utah, "aborted" on the mission I watched take off. He blew a cylinder head clear off.

He was within sight of Japan when it happened, and he beat the others back home by only half an hour. He flew thirteen-and-a-half hours that day, and didn't even get credit for a mission. That's the way it goes.

*

Those left on the field will idly look at their watches as the long day wears on, mentally clocking the progress of their comrades.

"They're about sighting the mainland now," you'll hear somebody say.

"They should be over the target by now. I'll bet they're catching hell," comes a little later from somebody.

By late afternoon you look at your watch and know that by now, for good or bad, it is over with. You know they're far enough off the coast that the last Jap fighter has turned for home, and left our men alone with the night and the awful returning distance, and their troubles.

Our planes bomb in formation, and stick together until they've left the Japanese coast, and then they break up and each man comes home on his own.

It's almost spooky the way they can fly through the dark night, up there above all that ocean, for more than six hours, and all arrive here at these little islands almost within a few minutes of each other.

By late afternoon we've begun to get radio messages from the returning planes. A flight leader will radio how the weather was, and if anybody went down over the target. It isn't a complete picture, but we begin to patch together a general idea.

We lost planes that day. Some went down over the target. Some just disappeared, and the other boys never knew where they went. Some fought as long as they could to keep crippled planes going, and then had to "ditch" in the ocean.

*

And one tenacious planeload miraculously got back when it wasn't in the cards for them at all. They had been hit over the target, had to drop down and back alone, and the Jap fighters went for him, as they do for any cripple.

Five fighters just butchered him, and there was nothing our boys could do about it. And yet he kept coming. How, nobody knows. Two of the crew were badly wounded. The horizontal stabilizers were shot away. The plane was riddled with holes. The pilot could control his plane only by using the motors.

Every half hour or so he would radio his fellow-planes, "Am in right spiral and going out of control." But he would get control again, and fly for an hour or so, and then radio again that he was spiraling out of control.

But somehow he made it home. He had to land without controls. He did wonderfully, but he didn't quite pull it off.

The plane hit at the end of the runway. The engines came hurtling out, on fire. The wings flew off and the great fuselage broke in two and went careening across the ground. And yet every man came out of it alive, even the wounded ones.

Two other crippled planes cracked up that night too, on landing. It was not until late at night that the final tally was made, of the known lost, and of missing.

But hardly was the last returning bomber down until a lone plane took off into the night and headed northward, to be in the area by dawn where the "ditchings" were reported. And the others, after their exciting stories were told, fell wearily into bed.

March 5, 1945—There are five officers and six enlisted men on the crew of a B-29. All the enlisted men of a crew stay in the same hut, because that's the way the boys want it. Thus there are usually three crews of six men each in a Quonset hut.

The enlisted men's huts are more crowded than the officers'. Outside of that there is no difference. They have a few more duties than the officers when not on missions, but they still have plenty of spare time.

"My" crew is a grand bunch of boys, as I suppose most of them are. They have trouble sleeping the night before a mission, and they're tense before the takeoff. As one of them laughingly said at the plane just before takeoff one morning, "How do you get rid of that empty feeling in your chest?"

But they relax and expand and practically float away with good feeling once they get back and have another one safely under their belts.

The six enlisted men of "my" crew are Sgts. Joe Corcoran of Woodhaven, Long Island; Fauad Smith of Des Moines, Iowa; Joe McQuade of Gallup, New Mexico; John Devaney of Columbus, Ohio; Norbert Springman of Wilmont, Minnesota; and Eugene Florio of Chicago.

Springman and Florio are radio men, and all the others are gunners. . . .

March 6, 1945— . . . One of the most vital members of a bomber's family is the ground-crew chief, even though he doesn't fly. But he's the guy who sees that the airplane does fly.

A good crew chief is worth his weight in gold. Maj. Robinson says he has the finest crew chief in the Marianas. I could believe it after seeing him.

He is Sgt. Jack Orr of Dallas, Texas. He's a married man, tall and good-looking and modest. He is so conscientious it hurts, and he takes a mission harder than the crew members do themselves.

Maj. Robinson said that on one trip they had some trouble, and were the last ones in, long after the others had landed. It did look kind of bad for a while.

Sgt. Orr was waiting for them at the "hard-stand." Maj. Robinson said that when they got out of the plane he was all over them, jumping up and down like a puppy dog, shouting and hugging them, and they could hardly get him stopped, he was so happy.

Maj. Robinson says he was sort of embarrassed, but I've heard him tell it two or three times, so I know how touched he was. There is indeed a fraternalism in war that is hard for people at home to comprehend.

"Sack Time"

IN THE MARIANAS ISLANDS, *March 9, 1945*—"Sack time" is one of the most-used expressions in the B-29 outfits. It means simply lying on your cot doing nothing.

Combat fliers everywhere have lots of spare time, because they are under a terrific nervous strain when they work, and they need much recuperative rest.

But out here there is a double, even a triple incentive for spending practically all your time, both waking and sleeping, in "the sack." These are:

1) A fourteen-hour mission is an exhausting thing. The boys say the reaction is a delayed one, and they really don't feel it so keenly until the afternoon of the next day. Then they're just plumb worn-out. It takes some of them two or three days to get to feeling normal after a mission.

2) The climate, warm and enervating, seems to make you sleepy all the time. I've found it doubly hard to write my columns out here, because I just can't stay awake.

3) There's really nothing else to do except lie on your cot. Combat crews have few duties between missions. And since there's no amusement or diversion out on these islands, except homemade ones, they just lie and talk and lie some more.

The result of it all is that you just get lazier than sin. As one pilot said, "I've got so lazy I'll never be worth a damn the rest of my life."

*

It's one of the phases of isolation. It's what leads to "island neurosis," or to going "pineapple crazy." Troop commanders know the importance of keeping their men busy to overcome this, but it's difficult to do that with combat crewmen.

But new classes have been organized, and the fliers have to go to school part of each day. Those who are especially good are getting further intensive training as "lead crews" and they go to school from morning till night.

Endless talk and arguments go on in every tent and Quonset hut. They can argue about the damndest things. One afternoon several pilots got into an argument over whether or not you do everything in reverse when you're flying upside down. They were all veteran fliers, and yet they split about fifty-fifty on whether you do or not.

Another day they got to arguing about what causes planes to leave vapor trails behind them at high altitudes. I had always thought it was the heat from the exhaust stacks condensing the moisture at certain temperatures. But one pilot said no, it was moisture being whirled off the tips of the propellers. That started a long discussion in which nobody won.

They argue about God, and they recount funny stories of escapades during training, and they wonder why the Japs don't do this or that.

Some play solitaire. Some write letters all the time. One flier told me he had written to people he hadn't thought of in years, not because he wanted letters back, but just to have something to do. Others, with nothing but time on their hands, can't make themselves write at all.

They read magazines, but very few books. At first they spent weeks making furniture for themselves out of packing crates. But that's all finished now.

Some of them swim daily, and they all take daily showers. The camps are dotted with concrete-floored baths, which are roofless. Water comes from a tank set on high stilts nearby. It is not heated, and although the weather is always warm, a cold bath in the morning is pretty nippy. The best time is around two in the afternoon when the sun has made the water good and warm.

The fliers send some of their laundry to the Army laundry unit, but it takes about ten days, so most of them do their own washing.

Every bath unit has a white-porcelained Thor washing machine and wringer in it. The fliers build a bonfire of discarded lumber and heat water in big cans, carry it in to the washing machine, and turn her on. Between every Quonset hut there is always a clothesline full of wash flying in the wind.

Some days they play volleyball, some days they take setting-up exercises, and some days they swim. My friend Capt. Bill Gifford spurns all these things, and just lies in bed. Every day they ask if he isn't going to "P.T.," which means physical training, and he says "Hell no, I'm too old to get out there and jump up and down like a goddamned Russian ballet dancer."

Keeping "Island Complex" at Bay

IN THE MARIANAS ISLANDS, *March 13, 1945*—One thing that might help you visualize what life is like out here is to realize that even a little island is lots bigger than you think.

There are many, many thousands of Americans scattered in camps and at airfields and in training centers and harbors over the three islands which we occupy here.

Rarely does a man know many people outside his own special unit. Even though the islands are small by our standards, they're big enough that the individual doesn't encompass them by any means. It would be as impossible for one man to see or know everybody on one of these islands as it would to know everybody in Indianapolis.

You could live and work in your section, and never visit another section for weeks or months at a time. And that's exactly what does happen.

For one thing, transportation is short. We are still building furiously here, such fast and fantastic building as you never dreamed of. Everything that runs is being used, and there's little left over just to run around in for fun.

And anyhow, there's no place to go. What towns there were have been destroyed. There is nothing even resembling a town or city on these islands now. The natives have been set up in improvised camps, but they offer no "city-life" attractions.

As we drove around one of the islands on my first day here, we went through one of the Marianas towns that had been destroyed by bombing and shelling. It had been a good-sized place, quite modern too in a tropical way. It had a city plaza and municipal buildings and paved streets, and many of the buildings were of stone or mortar.

In destruction, it looked exactly as destroyed cities all over Europe look. The same jagged half-standing walls, the stacks of rubble, the empty houses you could see through, the roofless homes, the deep craters in the gardens.

There was just one difference. Out here tropical vegetation is lush. And Nature thrusts up her greenery so swiftly through rubble and destruction that the ruins now are festooned with vines and green leaves, and it gives them the look of very old and time-worn ruins, instead of fresh modern ones, which they are.

*

An American soldier in Europe, even though the towns may be "off-limits" to him or destroyed completely, still has a sense of being near civilization that is like his own.

But out here there is nothing like that. You are on an island, the natives are strange people, there's no city and no place to go. If you had a three-day pass you'd probably spend it lying on your cot. Eventually, boredom and the "island complex" starts to take hold.

For that reason the diversions supplied by the Army are even more important out here than in Europe. Before I left America I heard that one island out here had more than two hundred outdoor movies on it. I thought whoever told that must be crazy, for in Europe the average soldier didn't get a chance to see a movie very often.

But the guy wasn't crazy. These three Marianas islands have a total of two hundred thirty-three outdoor movies on them. And they show every night. Even if it isn't a good movie, it kills the time between supper and bedtime.

The theaters are usually on the slope of a hill, forming a natural amphitheater. The men sit on the ground, or bring their own boxes, or sometimes they use the ends of metal bomb crates for chairs.

You can drive along and sometimes you'll pass three movies not more than three hundred yards apart. That's mainly because there is not enough transportation to haul the men any distance, so the movie has to come to them.

There is lots of other stuff provided besides movies, too. On one island there are sixty-five theater stages, where soldiers themselves put on "live" shows, or where USO troupes can perform. Forty pianos have been scattered around at these places.

In Europe it was a lucky bunch of soldiers who got their hands on a radio. Over here in these small islands, the Army has distributed thirty-five hundred radios, and they have a regular station broadcasting all the time, with music, news, shows and everything.

The sports program is big. On one island there are ninety-five softball diamonds, thirty-five regular diamonds, two hundred twenty-five volleyball courts and thirty basketball courts. Also there are forty-five boxing arenas. Boxing is very popular. They've had as high as eighteen thousand men watching a boxing match.

In addition to all this program, which is deliberate and supervised, the boys do a lot to amuse themselves. The American is adept at fixing up any old place in the world to look like home, with little picket fences and all kinds of Rube Goldberg contraptions inside to make it more livable. All this uses up time.

Just as an example, the coral sea bottom inside the reef around these islands abounds with fantastic miniature marine life, weird and colorful. Soldiers make glass-bottomed boxes for themselves, and wade out and just look at the beautiful sea bottom.

I've seen them out there like that for hours, just staring at the sea bottom. At home they wouldn't have gone to an aquarium if you'd built one in their backyard. . . .

Pyle flew to the island of Ulithi, several hundred miles from the Marianas, and boarded the aircraft carrier USS Cabot. *The carrier, and the huge fleet it sailed in, were part of a task force carrying planes that would bomb Tokyo and firepower to support the landings on Iwo Jima.*

"We'll start right at the beginning," Pyle wrote, "and within the limits of Naval security, I'll try to tell you what living on an aircraft carrier is like, and how a big task force works when it goes out after the enemy." He explained his choice of the Cabot*: "I had asked to be put on a small carrier, rather than a big one. The reasons were many. For one thing, the large ones are so immense and carry such a huge crew that it would be like living in Grand Central Station. I felt I could get the 'feel' of a carrier more quickly, could become more intimately a member of the family, if I were to go on a smaller one."*

Aboard a Fighting Ship

IN THE WESTERN PACIFIC, *March 15, 1945*—An aircraft carrier is a noble thing. It lacks almost everything that seems to denote nobility, yet deep nobility is there.

A carrier has no poise. It has no grace. It is top-heavy and lop-sided. It has the lines of a well-fed cow.

It doesn't cut through the water like a cruiser, knifing romantically along. It doesn't dance and cavort like a destroyer. It just plows. You feel it should be carrying a hod, rather than wearing a red sash.

Yet a carrier is a ferocious thing, and out of its heritage of action has grown its nobility. I believe that today every Navy in the world has as its No. 1 priority the destruction of enemy carriers. That's a precarious honor, but it's a proud one.

*

My carrier is a proud one. She's small, and you have never heard of her unless you have a son or husband on her, but still she's proud, and deservedly so.

She has been at sea, without returning home, longer than any other carrier in the Pacific, with one exception. She left home in November 1943.

She is a little thing, yet her planes have shot two hundred thirty-eight of the enemy out of the sky in air battles, and her guns have knocked down five Jap planes in defending herself.

She is too proud to keep track of little ships she destroys, but she has sent to the bottom twenty-nine big Japanese ships. Her bombs and aerial torpedoes have smashed into everything from the greatest Jap battleships to the tiniest coastal schooners.

She has weathered five typhoons. Her men have not set foot on any soil bigger than a farm-sized uninhabited atoll for a solid year. They have not seen a woman, white or otherwise, for nearly ten months. In a year and a quarter out of America, she has steamed a total of one hundred forty-nine thousand miles!

Four different air squadrons have used her as their flying field, flown their allotted missions, and returned to America. But the ship's crew stays on—and on, and on.

She is known in the fleet as "The Iron Woman," because she has fought in every battle in the Pacific in the years 1944 and 1945.

Her battle record sounds like a train-caller on the Lackawanna Railroad. Listen—Kwajalein, Eniwetok, Truk, Palau, Hollandia, Saipan, Chichi Jima, Mindanao, Luzon, Formosa, Nansei Shoto [Ryukyu Islands], Hong Kong, Iwo Jima, Tokyo . . . and many others.

She has known disaster. Her fliers who have perished could not be counted on both hands, yet the ratio is about as it always is—about one American lost for every ten of the Exalted Race sent to the Exalted Heaven.

She has been hit twice by Jap bombs. She has had mass burials at sea . . . with her dry-eyed crew sewing 40-mm shells to the corpses of their friends, as weights to take them to the bottom of the sea.

Yet she has never even returned to Pearl Harbor to patch her wounds. She slaps on some patches on the run, and is ready for the next battle. The crew in semi-jocularity cuss her chief engineer for keeping her in such good shape they have no excuse to go back to Honolulu or America for overhaul.

*

My carrier, even though classed as "light," is still a very large ship. More than a thousand men dwell upon her. She is more than seven hundred feet long.

She has all the facilities of a small city. And all the gossip and small talk too. Latest news and rumors have reached the farthest cranny of the ship a few minutes after the captain himself knows about them. All she lacks is a hitching rack and a town pump with a handle.

She has five barbers, a laundry, a general store. Deep in her belly she carries tons of bombs. She has a daily newspaper. She carries fire-fighting equipment that a city of fifty thousand back in America would be proud of.

She has a preacher, she has three doctors and two dentists, she has two libraries, and movies every night, except when they're in battle. And still she is a tiny thing, as the big carriers go. She is a "baby flat-top." She is little. And she is proud.

She has been out so long that her men put their ship above their captain. They have seen captains come and go, but they and the ship stay on forever.

They aren't romantic about their long stay out here. They hate it, and their gripes are long and loud. They yearn pathetically to go home. But down beneath, they are proud—proud of their ship and proud of themselves. And you would be too.

March 16, 1945—There was nothing dramatic about our start for Japan.

We simply pulled anchor about eight o'clock one morning and got underway. The whole thing seemed peacetime and routine.

Our ships were so spread out they didn't seem as they actually were. It wasn't like the swarming, pulsing mass of ships that literally blanketed the water when we started to Sicily and to Normandy.

Once at sea our force broke up into several prearranged units and each put some distance between itself and the next.

Each was self-sufficient. Each could protect itself. Each had battleships, carriers, cruisers and destroyers. Each was complete unto itself.

The eye could easily encompass the entire formation in which you were sailing. And very dimly, far off on the horizon, you could see the silhouettes of the bigger ships on each side of you, although they seemed remote, and not like neighbors.

The rest of the fleet was out of sight, far over the horizon. Altogether, the ships must have covered a hundred miles of ocean. . . .

*

We had a long way to go from our starting point, and our route was a devious one to boot. We steamed for several days before we were at our destination off Japan. We sailed long enough to have crossed the Atlantic Ocean—if we had been in the Atlantic.

But those days were busy ones. Our planes began operating as soon as we were under way. Three fighters that had been based on the island flew out and landed aboard an hour after we started, to fill our complement of planes.

We were up before dawn every morning, and our planes were in the air before sunup. We kept a constant aerial patrol over our ships. Some flew at great height, completely out of sight. Others took the medium altitude. And still others roamed in great circles only a few hundred feet above us.

And out on the perimeter our little destroyers plowed the ocean, always alert for subs or airplanes. You really couldn't help but feel safe with such a guard around you.

*

Living was very comfortable aboard our carrier. I shared a cabin with Lt. Comdr. Al Masters from Terre Haute, Indiana, just a few miles from where I was born and raised.

In our cabin we had metal closets and writing desks and a lavatory with hot and cold water. We had a telephone, and a colored boy to clean up the room. Our bunks were double-decked, with good mattresses. I was in the upper one.

Our food was wonderful, and you could buy a whole carton of cigarets a day if you wanted to (doesn't that make you jealous?). We saw a movie every night except when in battle. The first four nights our movies were *New York Town*, *The Major and the Minor*, *Swing Fever*, and *Claudia*. I don't know enough about movies to know whether they were old or not, but it doesn't make any difference to a sailor who hasn't been home.

I came aboard with a lot of dirty clothes, for I'd had nothing washed since leaving San Francisco about a month before.

Our cabin boy took my clothes to the laundry about nine-thirty one morning. When I came back to the cabin about an hour and a half later, here was my washing all clean and dry and ironed, lying on the bed. What a ship!

Their Lives are Pretty Good

IN THE WESTERN PACIFIC, *March 17, 1945*—It's easy to get acquainted aboard a Naval vessel.

The sailors are just as friendly as the soldiers I'd known on the other side. Furthermore, they're so delighted to see a stranger and to have somebody new to talk to that they aren't a bit standoffish.

They're all sick to death of the isolation and monotony of the vast Pacific. I believe they talk more about wanting to go home than even the soldiers in Europe.

Their lives really are empty lives. They have their work, and their movies, and their mail, and that's just about all they do have. And nothing to look forward to.

They never see anybody but themselves, and that gets mighty old. They sail and sail, and never arrive anywhere. They've not even seen a native village for a year.

Three times they've been to remote, lifeless sandbars in the Pacific, and have been allowed to go ashore for a few hours and sit under palm trees and drink three cans of beer. That's all.

*

Yet they do live well. Their food is the best I've run onto in this war. They take baths daily, and the laundry washes their clothes. Their quarters are crowded, but each man has a bunk with a mattress and sheets, and a private locker to keep his stuff in. They work hard, but their hours are regular.

The boys ask you a thousand times how this compares with the other side. I can only answer that this is much better. They seem to expect you to say that, but they are a little disappointed too.

They say, "But it's tough to be away from home for more than a year, and never see anything but water and an occasional atoll." And I say yes, I know it is, but there are boys who have been in Europe more than three years, and have slept on the ground a good part of that time. And they say yes, they guess in contrast their lives are pretty good.

Seaman Paul Begley looks at his wartime life philosophically. He is a farm boy from Rogersville, Tennessee. He talks a lot in a soft voice that is Southern clear through. He's one of the plane pushers on the flight deck.

"I can stand this monotony all right," he says. "The point with us is that we've got a pretty good chance of living through this. Think of the Marines who have to take the beaches, and the infantry in Germany. I can stand a lot of monotony if I know my chances are pretty good for coming out of it alive."

But others yell their heads off about their lot, and feel they're being persecuted by being kept out of America a year. I've heard some boys say, "I'd trade this for a foxhole any day." You just have to keep your mouth shut to a remark like that.

At least fifty percent of the sailors' conversation, when talking to a newcomer like myself, is about three things: the terrible typhoon they went through off the Philippines; the times they were hit by Jap bombs; and their desire to get back to America.

The typhoon was awful. Many thought they would go the same way as the three destroyers that capsized. This ship is inclined to roll badly anyhow. Today she still has immense dents in her smokestacks where they smacked the water when she rolled that far over. A lot of experienced people were seasick during that storm.

Very few of the boys have developed any real love for the sea—the kind that will draw them back to it for a lifetime. Some of course will come back if things get tough after the war. But mostly they are temporary sailors, and the sea is not in their blood.

Taking it all in all, they're good boys who do what is asked of them, and do it well. They are very sincere and genuine, and they are almost unanimously proud of their ship.

I think I've been asked a hundred times how I happened to come on this ship, with so many to choose from. It is always said in that hopeful tone of wondering if I chose it because it has such a noble reputation.

So I tell them that I asked to be put on a light carrier like this, rather than a big one. But that being a newcomer to the Pacific I didn't know one ship from another, so this was the ship the Navy put me on.

But that satisfies them just as well, for then they assume that Navy itself considers their ship a superior one—which I'm sure it does.

March 19, 1945—The men aboard an aircraft carrier could be divided, for purposes of clarity, into three groups.

There are the fliers, both officer-pilots and enlisted radiomen and gunners, who actually fly in combat. They do nothing but fly, and study, and prepare to fly.

Then there are the men who maintain the fliers. The air officers, and the mechanics and the myriad plane-handlers who shift and push and manhandle the planes a dozen times a day around the deck.

These men are ordinarily known as "Airedales," but the term isn't much used on our ship. Usually they just call themselves "plane-pushers."

And third is the ship's crew—the deckhands, engineers, signalmen, cooks, plumbers and barbers. They run the ship, just as though it were any ship in the Navy.

*

The fliers aren't looked upon as gods by the rest of the crew, but they are respected. Hardly a man on the crew would trade places with them. They've seen enough crash-landings on deck to know what the fliers go through.

But there is a feeling—a slight one—between the ship's regular crew and the air-maintenance crew. The feeling is on the part of the ship's crew. They feel that the plane-handlers think they're prima donnas. . . .

*

It is these "plane-pushers" who make the flight deck of an aircraft carrier look as gay and wildly colorful as a Walt Disney cartoon. For they dress in bright colors.

They wear cloth helmets and sweaters that are blue, green, red, yellow, white or brown. They make the flight deck look like a flower garden in June.

This colorful gear isn't just a whim. Each color identifies a special type of workman, so they can be picked out quickly and sent on hurried tasks.

Red is the gasoline and fire-fighting detail. Blue is for the guys who just push the planes around. Brown is for plane captains and mechanics. White stands for radiomen and the engineering bosses. Yellow is for the plane directors.

Yellow is what a pilot looks for the moment he gets on deck. For the plane directors guide him as though they were leading a blind man. They use a sign language with their hands that is the same all over the Navy, and by obeying their signs explicitly, the pilot can taxi his plane within two inches of another one without ever looking at it.

*

All the pilots and ship's officers live in "officers' country" in the forward part of the ship. They live in comfortable cabins, housing from one to four men.

The crew lives in compartments. They are of all shapes and sizes. Some hold as few as half a dozen men. Others are big and house a hundred men.

The Navy doesn't use hammocks anymore. Every man has a bed. It is called a "rack." It's merely a tubular framework, with wire springs stretched across it. It is attached to the wall by hinges, and is folded up against the wall in the daytime.

The "racks" aren't let down till about seven in the evening (except for men standing regular watch who must sleep in the daytime). Hence a sailor has no regular place to sit or lie down during the day if he does nab a few spare minutes. . . .

Over the Side

IN THE WESTERN PACIFIC, *March 20, 1945*—We were launching our midmorning patrol flight. The sun was out bright, and the day warmly magnificent. Everything was serene.

I had already become acquainted with some of the pilots, and before each flight I would go to the "ready room" and find out from the blackboard the number of the planes my friends were flying, so I could identify them as they went past.

Lt. Jimmy Van Fleet is one of the pilots I know best. We got acquainted because we have a mutual friend—war correspondent

Chris Cunningham, with whom I shared a tent and sometimes worse through Tunisia and Sicily and Italy. Jimmy and Chris are from the same hometown—Findlay, Ohio.

*

We knew the very moment he started that Jimmy was in trouble. His plane veered sharply to the right, and a big puff of white smoke spurted from his right brake band. Then slowly the plane turned and angled to the left as it gained speed.

The air officer up in the "island" sensed catastrophe, and put his hand on the warning squawker. All the sailors standing on the catwalk, with their heads sticking up over the edge of the flight deck, quickly ducked down. Yet such is the rigidity of excitement, I never even heard the squawker.

It was obvious Jimmy couldn't stop his plane from going to the left. He had his right wheel locked, and the tire was leaving burned rubber on the deck, yet it wouldn't turn the plane. And it was too late for him to stop now.

It had to happen. About midway of the flight deck, exactly opposite from where I was standing, he went over the side at full tilt, with his engine roaring.

His wheels raked the anti-aircraft guns as he went over, his propeller missed men's heads by inches, his left wing dropped, and in a flash he disappeared over the side.

It all happened in probably no more than six seconds. I had stood frozen while it went on, unable to move or make a sound, eyes just glued to the inevitable. We all thought it was the end for Jimmy. But it wasn't. We got him back three days later.

*

When the plane again came into view, only the tail was sticking out of the water. And then Jimmy bobbed up beside it. He had gotten out in a few seconds.

"Get your smoke bombs over," the air officer boomed to the crew over the loudspeaker. Those were to mark his position for any ship that would pick him up.

When he got back to us, Jimmy told me what happened from there on. He said that when the plane went in the water, it went so deep that it got dark in the cockpit. Jimmy wasn't hurt by the crash, outside of a small cut on his forehead.

He pulled his various buckles, opening his hatch cover and releasing himself from his seat harness. But as he did so he fell forward (the plane was riding nose down in the water, of course) and in a moment was standing on his head, under water, and in a hell of a fix.

But somehow he got himself upright, and then he couldn't get out because his radio cord, attached to his helmet, was still plugged into its socket in back of his seat.

So he took his big sheath knife out of its holder, cut the radio cord, and then carefully put the knife back. He says he doesn't know why he put it back. All this happened under water, and in mere seconds.

Some part of Jimmy's clothing caught as he was getting out, and he gave a big yank to free himself. Thus he tore his Mae West wide open, both compartments of it, and he had no buoyancy at all. But he is an excellent swimmer, so he stayed up.

*

When Jimmy went over the side, a destroyer was running about a mile to our left. Here Jimmy was lucky again. For that wasn't the destroyer's normal position; it just happened to be cutting across the convoy to deliver some mail on the other side.

Jimmy had hardly hit the water when we saw the destroyer heel over in a swath-cutting turn. They had been watching the takeoffs through their glasses, and had seen him go over. Our own ship, of course, had to keep right on going straight ahead. And our next plane took off without the slightest wait, as though nothing had happened.

The destroyer had Jimmy aboard in just seven minutes. They didn't put over a boat for him, but instead sent a swimmer out after him, with a line tied around his waist.

He got to Jimmy just in time. Jimmy passed out in his arms. With no lifebelt, he had taken too much salt-water aboard.

In the meantime the destroyer had let down a metal stretcher, and another swimmer was there to help get Jimmy into it. It took a while for them to get him on, for he was dead weight, and the stretcher kept going up and down with the waves.

But finally they managed it. Jimmy was safe and alive, although a very water-laden and passed-out young man from Ohio.

March 24, 1945—The first time you see a plane land on a carrier you almost die. At the end of the first day my muscles were sore just from being all tensed up while watching the planes come in.

It is all so fast, timing is so split-second, space is so small—well, somebody said that carrier pilots were the best in the world, and they must be or there wouldn't be any of them left alive.

Planes don't approach a carrier as they would on land—from way back and in a long glide. Instead, they almost seem to be sneaking up as if to surprise it. They're in such an awkward position and flying at such a crazy angle you don't see how they can ever land on anything.

But it's been worked out by years of experience, and it's the best way. Everything is straightened out in the last few seconds of flying. That is—if it works.

Anything can happen in those last few seconds. Once in a great while the plane loses its speed and spins into the water just behind the ship. And planes have been known to ram right into the stern of the ship.

The air currents are always bad. The ship's "island" distorts the currents, and makes the air rough. Even the wake of the ship—the waters churned up by the propellers—have an effect on the air through which the planes must pass.

If half a dozen planes come in successively without one getting a "wave-off" from the signalman, you're doing pretty well. For landing on the deck of a small carrier in a rough sea is just about like landing on half a block of Main Street while a combined hurricane and earthquake is going on.

*

You would call it a perfect landing if a plane came in and hit on both wheels at the same time, in the center of the deck headed straight forward, and caught about the third one of the cables stretched across the deck.

But very few of them are perfect. They come in a thousand different ways. If their approach is too bad, the signalman waves them around again.

They'll sometimes come in too fast and hit the deck so hard a tire blows. They'll come in half-sideways, and the cable will jerk them around in a tire-screeching circle.

They'll come in too close to the edge of the deck, and sometimes go right on over into the catwalk. They'll come in so high they'll miss all the arresting gear and slam into the high cables stretched across mid-decks, called "the barrier."

Sometimes they do a somersault over the barrier, and land on their backs. Sometimes they bounce all around and hit the "island." Sometimes they bounce fifty feet in the air and still get down all right. Sometimes they catch fire.

During the Tokyo strike, one of the big carriers running near us lost three planes in ten minutes. One was shot up and had to "ditch" in the water alongside the ship.

The next one slammed into the "island," and was so wrecked they just heaved the wreckage over the side. The next one to come in crashed the "barrier" and burned up.

And on the other hand, you'll land planes for weeks without a bad crackup. We wrecked three planes our first three days out in crashes —and not a single one after that. . . .

No Rest Tomorrow

IN THE WESTERN PACIFIC, *March 26, 1945*—There are moments when a voyage to war has much of the calm and repose of a pleasure cruise in peacetime.

For day after day we sailed in seas that were smooth and warm, under benign skies. There was no air of urgency about us. True, we kept air patrols in the sky, but it was really a practice gesture, for we were far away from any enemy.

Sailors at work wore no shirts. Little bunches of flying fish skimmed the blue water. You needed dark glasses on deck. Pilots took sun baths on the forecastle.

Up on the broad flight deck, clad only in shorts, the chaplain and executive officer were playing deck tennis. And in the afternoon the forward elevator was let down, and officers and men played basketball.

Every night we had movies after supper. It was hard to keep it in your mind that we were a ship of war, headed for war.

*

Then ever so gradually the weather changed, as we plowed northward. Yesterday and all the days behind it had been tropically hot. Today was surprisingly and comfortably cool. Tomorrow would be cold. We were nearing the Great Hunting Grounds off Japan.

On the last day you could sense the imminence of it all over the ship. Not by anything big, but by the little things. Our weeks of monotony and waiting were at an end.

The daily briefings of the pilots became more detailed. There was less playboyishness among the crew. Ordinary ship's rules were changed to battle rules.

What is known as the "extended action bill" went into effect. Sailors could let down their racks in the daytime, and get a little extra rest.

Meal hours, instead of being at noon and six o'clock sharp, were changed to run from eleven till one, and from four-thirty to six-thirty, so that men on watch could trade off and dash in for a bit. The captain never left the bridge, neither to eat nor sleep.

When you came into your cabin, you found your bunk had been made up with a "flash sheet" around it. That is a black rubberized sheet, to protect you from bomb burns.

Everybody was issued "flash gear." That consists of several items —a thin gray hood that covers your head and hangs down over your shoulders; a white cloth on an elastic band to cover your nose and mouth; isinglass goggles for your eyes; and long gray cloth gloves with a high gauntlet.

All of this to save your hands and face from the searing, flame-throwing blast of a big shell or bomb when it explodes. On some ships the men paint their faces with an anti-flash grease, making them look like circus clowns, but we didn't on our ship.

On the lower decks, every compartment door was closed. This was done so that if a torpedo should hit, it would flood only the compartment where it struck. All the rest of the ship would be sealed off from it.

The ship's hospital was shut off, and the medics set up business in the many prearranged aid stations scattered on higher decks about the ship. They could even perform operations at any one of a dozen temporary spots set up in mess halls or cabins.

*

Also we broke out cold-weather gear for the bone-chilling days ahead. An extra blanket was put on our bunks. Blue Navy sweaters came out for the first time. And blue stocking caps, and several kinds of rain capes with a parka to pull over your head, and you even saw a few pea jackets.

And yes, believe it or not, we even had long underwear too. It had never been used before, and goodness knows how long it had been baled up in shipboard stockrooms.

Some of it was moldy. In fact, the suit they got out for the captain —well, they had to wash and dry it hurriedly before giving it to him, because it smelled so bad from mold.

*

After supper on the night before our strike, we saw the movie *The Magnificent Dope.* I guess it's old, but it was good and awfully funny.

At least we thought so, for everybody laughed hilariously. When tension builds up in a man before a period of great danger, the tension is usually inner, and not often visible. That's the way it was at the movie that night.

Except I noticed there were only half as many people at the movie as usual. And not long after it was over, everybody had gone to bed. For they knew there would be no rest tomorrow.

March 27, 1945— . . . The fighter pilots were given their last briefing. In the "ready room" the squadron commander and intelligence officer showed them on maps and by drawings on the blackboard just where they would strike.

The squadron commander asked how many of the pilots had no wrist watches. Six held up their hands. The funny part was that the ship had no extra wrist watches, so I don't know why he asked the question in the first place.

Then he told what our approximate total of planes over Japan would be, and how many it was probable the Japs would put up against us. And then he said: "So you see, each one of us will only have to take care of three Jap planes!"

The pilots all laughed and looked at each other sheepishly. (Days later, when the final scores were in, we found our force had destroyed Japs at nine-to-one.)

And at the end of his briefing, the squadron commander gave strict orders for the pilots not to shoot at Japs coming down in parachutes.

"They're supposed to do it to us," he said, "but it isn't the thing for us to do."

*

The bomber pilots and their enlisted gunners and radiomen were briefed the same way. After the intelligence officer had finished, the squadron commander said: "We're going to dive low on the target before releasing our bombs. Since we're risking our necks anyhow, there's no point in going at all unless we can do some damage, so go down low."

*

All through the various strikes on Japan, our task force kept enough planes back to fly a constant blanket of protection in the sky above us.

I remember the funny sign chalked on the blackboard of the "ready room" first day, urging our patrol pilots to extra vigilance for Jap planes that might sneak out from the mainland to attack us. The sign said: "Keep alert—remember your poor scared pals on the ship!"

*

We didn't know whether our first planes over the mainland would surprise the Japs or not. It didn't seem possible, yet there were no indications that they knew.

For two days on our approach we had been knocking off Jap reconnaissance planes and picket boats. We hoped we had got these scattered planes and boats before they had time to radio back home the news of our presence. One of our destroyers had even sat all day on top of a Jap submarine to keep him from coming to the top and sending a warning.

But still we didn't know for sure, so there was tenseness that first morning. We knew almost exactly what time our first planes would be over the Tokyo area.

We went to the radio room to listen. The usual Japanese programs were on the air. We watched the clock. Suddenly—at just the right time—the Jap stations all went off the air.

There was silence for a few minutes. And then the most Donald Duck-like screaming and jabbering you ever heard. The announcer was so excited you had to laugh.

We knew our boys were there. After that, for us on the ship, it was just a matter of waiting, and hoping. And as the blackboard sign said, of being poor scared pals.

Rescue

IN THE WESTERN PACIFIC, *March 28, 1945*—All but six of our planes were back from their strike on Tokyo and safely landed.

The six formed a separate flight, and we couldn't believe that all of them had been lost, and for that reason our officers didn't feel too concerned.

And then came a radio message from the flight leader. It said that one of the six was down in the ocean, and that the other five were hanging around to try to direct some surface vessel to his rescue. That's all we knew for hours. When we finally got the story, this was it:

Ens. Robert Buchanan of Clementon, New Jersey, was hit by flak as they were diving on their target some twenty miles west of Tokyo. Buchanan himself was not hurt.

He kept his plane up till he got over water, but it was still very much Japanese water. In fact, it was in Tokyo's outer bay—the bigger one of the two bays you see on the map leading into Tokyo.

Ens. Buchanan is an ace, with five Jap planes to his credit. He ditched his plane successfully, and got out in his rubber boat. He was only eight miles from shore, and five miles from the big island that stands at the bay entrance.

Then the flight leader took charge. He is Lt. John Fecke of Duxbury, Massachusetts. He is also an ace, and an old hand at the game. He has downed seven Jap planes.

Fecke took the remaining four of the flight, and started out looking for an American rescue ship. They found one about thirty miles off the bay entrance.

They talked to him on the radio, told him of the circumstances, and he sent back word he was willing to try. But he asked them to stick with him and give air support.

So Lt. Fecke ordered the other four to stay and circle above the ship, while he went back to pick up Buchanan's location and guard him.

But when he got there, he couldn't find Buchanan. He flew for twenty-five minutes around Tokyo Bay and was about to despair, when he began getting sun flashes in his eyes.

He flew over about three miles and there was Buchanan. He had used his signal mirror, just like it says in the book.

In the meantime, the ship's progress was slow. It took almost two hours to get there. And one by one the aerial escort began getting in trouble, and one by one Fecke ordered them home to our ship, which was getting farther away all the time.

Lt. Irl Sonner of Petaluma, California, lost the use of his radio, and had to leave.

Lt. Max Barnes of Olympia, Washington, got dangerously low on gas, and Fecke sent him home. Gas shortage also sent back Lt. Bob Murray of Muncie, Indiana.

That left only Lt. Fecke circling above the man in the boat, and Lt. Arnold Berner of Springdale, Arkansas, flying lone aerial escort for the rescue ship.

Finally the ship was past the bay entrance. The skipper began to have his doubts. He had to go within three miles of the gun-dotted island. He was within five minutes' flying distance of land, and Jap planes could butcher him.

Furthermore he looked at his chart, and saw that he was in "restricted waters," meaning they were probably mined. It was certainly no place for a ship to be.

The skipper radioed Fecke and said he couldn't go any farther. Fecke radioed back and said, "It's only two miles more. Please try."

The skipper answered and said, "Okay, we'll try."

And they pulled it off. They went right into the lion's mouth, pulled out our pilot, and got safely away. Then, and then only, did Fecke and Berner start home.

They came back to us three hours after all the rest had returned. They had flown six hours on a three-hour mission. But they helped save an American life by doing so.

*

That night I lay in my bunk reading a copy of *Flying* magazine. It was the issue of last October, nearly six months old. It was the annual Naval Aviation issue.

And in an article entitled "Life on a Carrier" on page 248, was this paragraph:

"It's a mighty good feeling to know that even if you were shot down in Tokyo harbor, the Navy would be in to get you."

It had never happened when that piece was written. But it has happened now.

*

The rescue ship radioed us the next day that Buchanan was feeling fine, and that just to be impartial, they had also rescued another Navy pilot, a disgruntled Jap pilot, and a lone bedraggled survivor of a Jap picket boat!*

Pyle spent three weeks aboard the Cabot, *then transferred to a destroyer escort en route back to Guam, where he wrote the preceding series. Operation Iceberg, the invasion of Okinawa, was imminent. Just four hundred miles from Japan, Okinawa was heavily fortified; routing the Japanese would be a costly business, but having airfields so close to Japan was vital to what strategists saw as the certainty of a mainland invasion.*

Badly frightened by the prospect of yet another invasion, Pyle was nonetheless convinced that doing so would spice up his copy, which of late he found "uninspired and dull." He decided to go, sending word to his wife through a friend that this would be his last landing. On Ulithi, he boarded an assault transport with units of the 1st Marine Division. The invasion was to begin on Easter Sunday, April 1, 1945.

*Pyle's column for March 29 provided this background on Buchanan and Fecke: "Remember the boys we wrote about yesterday—Ens. Robert Buchanan, who was shot down into Tokyo Bay, and Lt. John Fecke, who directed the rescue? Well, it wasn't the first time those two had seen exciting times together. Last fall, off Formosa, a flight of seventy Jap planes pounced on two of our cruisers that were crippled. Fecke was leading a flight of eight of which Buchanan was one. Those eight took on the seventy Japs. They shot down twenty-nine of them, lost only one plane, broke up the attack and saved the cruisers. Fecke and Buchanan each got five Jap planes in that one foray. And each got the Navy Cross for the job. So this little Tokyo Bay incident didn't rattle them."

Waiting for Tomorrow

OFF THE OKINAWA BEACHHEAD, *April 3, 1945*—This is the last column before the invasion. It is written aboard a troop transport the evening before we storm onto Okinawa.

We are nervous. Anybody with any sense is nervous on the night before D-day. You feel weak and you try to think of things, but your mind stubbornly drifts back to the awful image of tomorrow. It drags on your soul and you have nightmares.

But those fears do not mean any lack of confidence. We will take Okinawa. Nobody has any doubt about that. But we know we will have to pay for it. Some on this ship will not be alive twenty-four hours from now.

*

We are in convoy. Many, many big ships are lined up in columns with our warships escort on the outsides. We are an impressive sight —yet we are only one of many similar convoys.

We left from many different places. We have been on our way many days. We are the biggest, strongest force ever to sail in the Pacific. We are going into what we expect to be the biggest battle so far in the Pacific.

Our ship is an APA, or assault transport. The ship itself is a war veteran. She wears five stars on her service ribbon—Africa, Sicily, Italy, Normandy and southern France. She wears the Purple Heart, Bronze Star and Legion of Merit Silver Star. She has fared well on the other side. We hope her luck holds out in the Pacific.

We are carrying Marines. Some of them are going into combat for the first time. Others are veterans from as far back as Guadalcanal.* They are a rough, unshaven, competent bunch of Americans. I am landing with them. I feel I am in good hands.

*

I've shared a cabin with Marine Maj. Reed Taylor of Kensington, Maryland. He is a Guadal vet and he jokingly belittles newcomers who weren't through "Green Hell." The major and I are sort of two of a stripe and we get along fine.

We have the nicest cabin either of us ever had at sea. And we've taken advantage of it by sleeping away almost the whole trip. We've slept day and night. So have many others.

*Guadalcanal, in the Solomon Islands, was the scene of a series of land and naval battles in 1942 in which the Allies defeated the Japanese.

There is a daily argument on ship whether or not you can store up sleep and energy for the ordeal ahead. The doctor says it's nonsense—that you can't store up sleep.

Between naps I've read two books. They are Bob Hope's *I Never Left Home* (how I wish I never had!) and Bob Casey's *Such Interesting People.* Only I wish I could hear Bob Casey tell all those stores in person, lying on his cot in France and roaring and shaking with his own laughter. Bob's laughter would be good for us now. A Marine officer said, "I haven't laughed for three days."

Our trip has been fairly smooth and not many of the troops were seasick. Down in the holds the Marines sleep on racks four tiers high. It isn't a nice way to travel. But I've never heard anybody complain. They come up on the deck on nice days to sun and to rest and to wash clothes, or lie and read or play cards.

We don't have movies. The ship is darkened at sunset and after that there are only dim lights. The food is good. We get news every morning in a mimeographed paper, and once or twice a day the ship's officers broadcast the latest news over the loudspeaker.

They've kept us informed daily of the progress of the Okinawa bombardment that preceded our landing. Every little bit of good news cheers us. The ship, of course, is full of rumors, good and bad, but nobody believes any of them.

Meetings are held daily among the officers to iron out last-minute details of the landing. Day by day, the Marine troops are fully briefed on what they are to do.

Everything we read about Okinawa stresses that the place is lousy with snakes. It's amazing the number of people who are afraid of snakes. Okinawa "snake-talk" crops into every conversation.

On the last day we changed our money into newly manufactured "invasion yen," drew two days K-rations, took a last bath, and packed our kits before supper. We had a huge turkey dinner.

"Fattening us up for the kill," the boys laughingly say.

At three o'clock on the last afternoon there was a celebration of the Lord's Supper. It was the afternoon before Easter Sunday. A lot of us could not help but feel the tragic irony of it, knowing about tomorrow's battle.

After a ham-and-egg breakfast at four-thirty Easter Sunday morning, Pyle boarded a landing craft for the slow trip to the Okinawan shore. "I felt miserable and that awful weight was still on my heart. There's nothing romantic whatever in knowing that an hour from now you may be dead."

An Easter Sunday Surprise

WITH THE MARINES ON OKINAWA BEACHHEAD, *April 4, 1945*—You wouldn't believe it. And we don't either. It just can't be true. And yet it is true.

The regiment of Marines that I am with landed this morning on the beaches of Okinawa and were absolutely unopposed, which is indeed an odd experience for a Marine.

Nobody among us had dreamed of such a thing. We all thought there would be slaughter on the beaches. There was some opposition to the right and to the left of us, but on our beach, nothing, absolutely nothing.

We don't expect this to continue, of course. A Marine doesn't fool himself like that. Certainly there will be hard fighting ahead and we all have our fingers crossed. But to get the firm foothold we have, with most of our men ashore and our supplies rolling in, is a gift for which we are grateful.

*

This is Easter Sunday morning [April 1, 1945]. It is a beautiful one. One of the Marines, after spending months in the tropics, remarked a while ago, "This weather feels more like American weather than anything since I left home."

It is sunshiny and very warm. We had heard it would be cold and many of the boys wore heavy underwear. Now we are sweating and regretting. I wore two pairs of pants, but I am about to take off one of them.

We are dressed in green herringbone combat uniforms. Everybody made the trip in khaki and changed this morning aboard ship. The men left their old khaki lying on their bunks and they'll be collected by the Navy, cleaned and used to clothe prisoners and our own casualties who have lost their clothes.

On our ship we were up at four A.M. We had done our final packing of gear last night. We brought ashore only what we could carry on our backs. When we put on our new green fatigues, one Marine remarked, "The latest Easter style—herringbone twill."

*

My schedule for landing was an early one. I was ashore a short time after the first wave. Correspondents were forbidden to go before the fifth wave. I was on the seventh.

I had dreaded the sight of the beach littered with mangled bodies. My first look up and down the beach was a reluctant one. And then like a man in the movies who looks and looks away and then suddenly looks back unbelieving, I realized there were no bodies anywhere—and no wounded. What a wonderful feeling!

In fact, our entire regiment came ashore with only two casualties. One was a Marine who hurt his foot getting out of an amphibious truck. And the other was, of all things, a case of heat prostration!

And to fulfill the picnic atmosphere, listen to this:

Aboard ship we had turkey dinner last night. So this morning they fixed me up with a big sack of turkey wings, bread, oranges and apples. So instead of grabbing a hasty bite of K-rations our first meal ashore, we sat and lunched on turkey wings and oranges.

*

There are low chalky cliffs on this island. In these cliffs are caves. In the caves are brick-colored urns a couple of feet high. And in these urns are the ashes of many honorable ancestors.

Our bombardment had shattered many of these burial vaults. What our big guns missed, the soldiers and Marines took a precautionary look into by prying off the stone slabs at the entrances.

In front, looking out to sea, stands our mighty fleet with scores of little black lines extending to shore—our thousands and thousands of landing craft bringing more men and big guns and supplies.

And behind me, not two feet away, is a cave full of ex-Japanese. Which is just the way it should be. What a nice Easter Sunday after all.

Pyle had decided to cover the Marines, a service branch he had never written about. "Marine Corps blitzes [in the Pacific] have all been so bitter and the Marines have performed so magnificently that I had conjured up a mental picture of a Marine that bore a close resemblance to a man from Mars." Pyle was relieved to find them to be just "good, human Americans."

A Bloodless Beach

OKINAWA, *April 9, 1945*—Never before had I seen an invasion beach like Okinawa.

There wasn't a dead or wounded man in our sector of it. Medical corpsmen were sitting among their sacks of bandages and plasma and stretchers, with nothing to do.

There wasn't a single burning vehicle. Nor a single boat lying wrecked on the reef or shoreline. The carnage that is almost inevitable in an invasion was wonderfully and beautifully not there.

There was hardly anybody at all on the beach when we landed. The few assault waves ahead of us had pushed on inland. And all that vast welter of people and machines that make a beach hum with work were still many waves behind us.

The bulldozers and the jeeps had not yet arrived. There was no activity and hardly any sound. It was almost as though we were the original explorers.

Our little party, which was the regimental staff, moved to the foot of a bluff about a hundred yards back of the beach. It was full of caves and our naval gunfire had made a rubble at the foot of the bluff. But several cave mouths still gaped open.

We decided to set up there until the colonel could get the picture in his mind, through information brought by runners, of just what was going on.

There were about a hundred men with us in addition to the officers. The men were under 1st Sgt. Andy Anderson from Washington State. The first thing Andy had them do was to make sure there were no Japs hiding in the caves to snipe on us, for the first waves had gone through too fast to clean everybody out—if anybody had been there.

So they would sneak up on a hole, with rifles ready. Then Andy would take out a hand grenade and throw it into the hole. But the first one hit the edge of the hole and rolled down outside.

Andy threw himself on the sand and all the rest of us lay flat. The grenade went off with a bang, but nobody got hurt. From then on we kidded Andy about the fine display of Marine marksmanship he had given us.

*

In addition to being great fighters, I believe the Marines are the friendliest bunch I've ever been with. I've never had any trouble with people being unfriendly, but these Marines seem to have it bred into them to be pleasant and to make you feel at home.

Nothing like Okinawa had ever happened to them before. They're accustomed to butchery on the beaches. They'd keep saying to me, "If you could just have been with us before, we'd have shown you some excitement."

And I would reply, "Brother, I've had all the excitement I need for a lifetime. This kind of invasion suits me fine."

*

I started wandering up and down the beach. One boy was carrying a little vase in his hand, saying, "Here's the first souvenir of Okinawa!"

He was James Cosby, pharmacist first class, of Cereal Spring, Illinois. (All medical corpsmen with the Marines are actually in the Navy, you know.) He had found the vase lying outside one of the burial vaults. It had blue Japanese characters on it.

Then I noticed a tall and heavily laden Marine, carrying a big roll of telephone wire on his shoulders and leading a white nanny goat, tied to a string. I stopped him and said, "Would you like to have you and your goat in the newspapers?"

He grinned and said, "Sure, why not?"

He was Pfc. Ben Glover of Baird, Texas. He was a telephone lineman at home, and that's what he is here. Linemen are always among the first ashore.

By evening of Love Day,* scores of Marines had baby goats for pets and were leading them around. There are lots of goats on Okinawa and the little ones were so white and so cute that we animal-loving Americans couldn't resist adopting them.

I saw one Marine who had commandeered a horse and had it carrying his pack. Another had a bicycle. By Love Day plus three, I'm sure they'll be carrying little Japanese babies on their backs. Americans are the damndest people! Why can't everybody be like them?

It Looks Like America

OKINAWA, *April 10, 1945*—Since this island is the closest to Japan we've landed on and since we seem to feel this really is Japan, rather than just some far outpost, I'll try to describe to you what it looks like.

Actually it doesn't look a great deal different from most of America. In fact it looks much more like America than anything the Marines have seen for the last three years.

The climate is temperate rather than tropical, and so is the vegetation. There are tropical-like trees on and near the beaches—I think they're pandanus bushes. But there are also many trees of the fir family with horizontal limbs.

*D-day on Okinawa.

The country over which my regiment passed during the first two days was cultivated. It rose gradually from the sea and was all formed into small fields.

It didn't look at all unlike Indiana in late summer when things have started to turn dry and brown, except that the fields were much smaller.

The wheat, which looks just like ours, is dead ripe in the fields now. The Marines are cutting it with little sickles. In other fields are cane and sweet potatoes.

Each field has a ditch around its edge, and dividing the fields are little ridges about two feet wide. On top of the ridges are paths where the people walk. All through the country are narrow dirt lanes and now and then a fairly decent gravel road.

As you get inland, the country becomes rougher. In the hills there is less cultivation and more trees. It is really a pretty country. We had read about what a worthless place Okinawa was, but I think most of us have been surprised about how pretty it is.

*

Okinawan civilians we bring in are pitiful. The only ones left seem to be real old or real young. And they all are very, very poor.

They're not very clean. And their homes are utterly filthy. Over and over you hear Marines say, "This could be a nice country if the people weren't so dirty."

Obviously their living standard is low. Yet I've never understood why poverty and filth need to be synonymous. A person doesn't have to be well-off to get clean. But apparently he has to be well-off to want to keep clean. We've found it that way clear around the world.

The people here dress as we see Japanese dressed in pictures: women in kimonos and old men in skin-tight pants. Some wear a loose, knee-length garment that shows their skinny legs.

The kids are cute as kids are all over the world. I've noticed Marines reaching out and tousling their hair as they marched past them. We're rounding up all the civilians and putting them in camps. They are puzzled by it all.

Most of the farm families must have got out when our heavy bombardments started. Lots of farmhouses have either been demolished or burned to the ground before we came. Often, in passing a wrecked farmhouse, you smell the sickening odor of death inside.

But there are always people who won't leave no matter what. We couldn't help feeling sorry for the Okinawans we picked up in the first few days. We found two who spoke a little English. They had once lived in Hawaii. One was an old man who had a son (Hawaii-an-Japanese) somewhere in the American Army!

They were all shocked from the bombardment and yet I think rather stupid too, so that when they talked they didn't make much sense.

I don't believe they had any idea of what it was all about. As one Marine officer said, "The poor devils. I'll bet they think this is the end of the world."

They were obviously scared to death. On Love Day the Marines found many of them hiding from us in caves. They found two old women, seventy-five years old or more, in a cave caring for a paralyzed girl. She wasn't wounded, just paralyzed from natural causes. One of the old ladies had a small dirty sack with some money in it. When the Marines found her she cried and tried to give them the money—hoping I suppose that she could buy herself off from being executed.

After all the propaganda they've been fed about our tortures, it's going to be a befuddled bunch of Okinawans when they discover we brought right along with us, as part of the intricate invasion plan, enough supplies to feed them, too!

War Sounds

OKINAWA, *April 12, 1945*—Our first night on Okinawa was uncanny and full of old familiar sounds—the exciting, sad, weary little sounds of war.

It had been six months since I'd slept on the ground, or heard a rifle shot. With the Marines it was about the same.

I was tagging along with a headquarters company of a regiment. We were on a pretty, grassy slope out in the country. The front lines were about a thousand yards ahead. Other troops were bivouacked all around us.

There were still a few snipers hiding around. An officer was brought in just before dark, shot through the arm. So we were on our toes.

Just at dusk three planes flew slowly overhead in the direction of the beach. We paid no attention, for we thought they were ours. But they weren't.

In a moment all hell cut loose from the beach. Our entire fleet and the guns ashore started throwing stuff into the sky. I've never seen a thicker batch of ack-ack.

As one of the Marines said, there were more bullets than there was sky. Those Jap pilots must have thought the world was coming to an end to fly into a lead storm like that only ten hours after we had landed on Okinawa. All three were shot down.

*

As deep darkness came on we got into our foxholes and settled down for the night. The countryside became as silent as a graveyard —silent, that is, between shots. The only sounds were war sounds. There were no country sounds at all. The sky was a riot of stars.

Capt. Tom Brown was in the foxhole next to me. As we lay there on our backs, looking up into the starry sky, he said: "There's the Big Dipper. That's the first time I've seen that since I've been in the Pacific." For, you see, Marines of this division have done all their fighting under the Southern Cross, where our Big Dipper doesn't show.

As full darkness came, flares began lighting the country ahead of us over the front lines. They were shot in shells from our battleships, timed to burst above our lines, and float down on parachutes. That was to keep the country lighted up so we could see the Japs if they tried to infiltrate, which is one of their favorite tricks.

The flares were shot up several per minute from dusk until the moon came out full. It was very bright after that and the flares were not needed.

But all night long two or three ships kept up a slow shelling of the far hills where the Japs were supposed to be. It wasn't a bombardment, just two or three shells per minute. They passed right over us and I found that passing shells have the same ghostly "window-shade rustle" on this side of the world as on the other.

My foxhole was only about twenty feet from where two field telephones and two field radios were lying on the ground. All night, officers sat on the ground at these and directed our troops.

As I lay there listening in the dark, the conversation was startlingly familiar—the words and the thoughts and actions exactly as I'd known them for so long in the infantry.

All night I could hear these low voices over the phones—voices in the darkness, voices of men running the war at the front.

*

Not long after dark the rifle shots started. There would be a little flurry far ahead, maybe a dozen shots. Then silence for many minutes.

Then there would be another flurry, way to the left. Then silence.

Then the blurt of a machine gun closer, and a few scattered single shots sort of framing it. Then a long silence. Spooky.

All night it went like that. Flares in the sky ahead, the crack of big guns behind us, then of passing shells, a few dark figures coming and going in the night, muted voices at the telephones, the rifle shots, the mosquitoes, the stars, the feel of the damp night air under the wide sky—back again at the kind of life I had known so long.

The old familiar pattern, unchanged by distance or time from war on the other side of the world. A pattern so imbedded in my soul that, coming back into it again, it seemed to me as I lay there that I'd never known anything else in my life. And there are millions of us.

April 16, 1945—We camped one night on a little hillside that led up to a bluff overlooking a small river. The bluff dropped straight down for a long way. Up there on top of the bluff it was just like a little park.

The bluff was terraced, although it wasn't farmed. The grass on it was soft and green. And those small, straight-limbed pine trees were dotted all over it.

Looking down from the bluff, the river made a turn and across it was an old stone bridge. At the end of the bridge was a village—or what had been a village.

It was now just a jumble of ashes and sagging thatched roofs from our bombardment. In every direction little valleys led away from the turn in the river.

It was as pretty and gentle a sight as you ever saw. It had the softness of antiquity about it and the miniature charm and daintiness that we see in Japanese prints. And the sad, uncanny silence that follows the bedlam of war.

A bright sun made the morning hot and a refreshing little breeze sang through the pine trees. There wasn't a shot nor a warlike sound within hearing. I sat on the bluff for a long time, just looking. It all seemed so quiet and peaceful. I noticed a lot of the Marines sitting and just looking too. . . .

These and subsequent columns were released for publication after Pyle's death (April 18th) on Ie Shima, a small island west of Okinawa. An editor's note supplied by United Feature said: "We believe he would have wanted us to. As a great reporter, a great newspaperman and a great person, he would have wanted his stories to go through, despite his tragic death."

They Just Lay There, Blinking

OKINAWA, *April 21, 1945*—Now I've seen my first Jap soldiers in their native state—that is, before capture. But not for long, because the boys of my company* captured them quicker than a wink.

It was mid-forenoon and we had just reached our new bivouac area after a march of an hour and a half. The boys threw off their packs, sat down on the ground, and took off their helmets to mop their perspiring foreheads.

We were in a small grassy spot at the foot of a hill. Most of these hillsides have caves with household stuff hidden in them. They are a rich field for souvenir hunters. And all Marines are souvenir hunters.

So immediately two of our boys, instead of resting, started up through the brush, looking for caves and souvenirs. They had gone about fifty yards when one of them yelled:

"There's a Jap soldier under this bush."

We didn't get too excited for most of us figured he meant a dead Jap. But three or four of the boys got up and went up the hill. A few moments later somebody yelled again:

"Hey, here's another one. They're alive and they've got rifles."

So the boys went at them in earnest. The Japs were lying under two bushes. They had their hands up over their ears and were pretending to be asleep.

The Marines surrounded the bushes and, with guns pointing, they ordered the Japs out. But the Japs were too scared to move. They just lay there, blinking.

The average Jap soldier would have come out shooting. But, thank goodness, these were of a different stripe. They were so petrified the Marines had to go into the bushes, lift them by the shoulders, and throw them out in the open.

My contribution to the capture consisted of standing to one side and looking as mean as I could.

One Jap was small, and about thirty years old. The other was just a kid of sixteen or seventeen, but good-sized and well-built. The kid had the rank of superior private and the other was a corporal. They were real Japanese from Japan, not the Okinawan home guard.

They were both trembling all over. The kid's face turned a sickly white. Their hands shook. The muscles in the corporal's jaw were

*Pyle had moved to a company of the 1st Marine Division. The company commander was Capt. Julian Dusenbury of Claussen, South Carolina.

twitching. The kid was so paralyzed he couldn't even understand sign language.

We don't know why those two Japs didn't fight. They had good rifles and potato-masher hand grenades. They could have stood behind their bushes and heaved grenades into our tightly packed group and got themselves two dozen casualties, easily.

The Marines took their arms. One Marine tried to direct the corporal in handbook Japanese, but the fellow couldn't understand.

The scared kid just stood there, sweating like an ox. I guess he thought he was dead. Finally we sent them back to the regiment.

*

The two Marines who flushed these Japs were Corp. Jack Ossege of Silver Grove, Kentucky, across the river from Cincinnati, and Pfc. Lawrence Bennett of Port Huron, Michigan.

Okinawa was the first blitz for Bennett and this was the first Jap soldier he'd ever seen. He is thirty years old, married, and has a baby girl. Back home he was a freight dispatcher.

The Jap corporal had a metal photo holder like a cigaret case. In it were photos which we took to be of three Japanese movie stars. They were good-looking, and everybody had to have a look.

Ossege had been through one Pacific blitz, but this was the first Jap he ever took alive. As an old hand at souvenir hunting he made sure to get the Jap's rifle.

That rifle was the envy of everybody. Later when we were sitting around, discussing the capture, the other boys tried to buy or trade him out of it. "Pop" Taylor, the black-whiskered corporal from Jackson, Michigan, offered Ossege a hundred dollars for the rifle.

The answer was no. Then Taylor offered four quarts of whiskey. The answer still was no. Then he offered eight quarts. Ossege weakened a little. He said, "Where would you get eight quarts of whiskey?" Pop said he had no idea. So Ossege kept the rifle.

So there you have my first two Japs. And I hope my future Japs will all be as tame as these two. But I doubt it.

Settling In

OKINAWA, *April 23, 1945*—It's marvelous to see a bunch of American troops go about making themselves at home wherever they get a chance to settle down for a few days.

My company of 1st Division Marines dug in at the edge of a bomb-shattered village. The village was quaint and not without charm. I was astonished at the similarity with the villages of Sicily and Italy.

The town didn't really seem Oriental. The houses were wooden one-story buildings, surrounded by little vegetable gardens. Instead of fences each lot was divided by rows of shrubs or trees. The cobblestoned streets were just wide enough for a jeep. They were winding and walled on both sides by head-high stone walls.

A good part of the town lay shattered. Scores of the houses had burned and only ashes and red roofing tile were left. Wandering around, I counted the bodies of four Okinawans still in the streets. Otherwise the town was deserted.

The people had fled to their caves in the hillsides, taking most of their personal belongings with them. There is almost no furniture in Japanese houses, so they didn't have to worry about that.

After a few days the grapevine carried the word to them that we were treating them well so they began to come out in droves and give themselves up. I heard one story about a hundred Okinawa civilians who had a Jap soldier among them, and when they realized the atrocity stories he had told them about the Americans were untrue, our M.P.'s had to step in to keep them from beating him.

*

Our commander picked out a nice little house on a rise at the edge of town for his command post.

The house was very light, fairly clean, and the floors were covered with woven straw mats. A couple of officers and a dozen men moved into the house and slept on the floor and we cooked our rations over an open stone cookstove in the rear.

Then the word went around for the men of the company to dig in for several days. Two platoons were assigned to dig in along the outer sides of the nearby hills for perimeter defense.

The boys were told they could keep the houses they had commandeered, that they could carry wooden panels out of the houses to make little doghouses for themselves, but not to take anything else, and that they could have fires, except during air alerts.

They weren't to start their daily mop-up patrols in the brush until the next day, so they had the afternoon off to clean themselves up and fix up their little houses.

Different men did different things. Some built elaborate houses about the size of chicken houses, with floor mats and chairs and even kerosene lanterns hanging from the roof.

One Mexican boy dug a hole, covered it with boards, and then camouflaged it so perfectly with brush you really couldn't see it.

Some spent the afternoon taking baths and washing clothes in the river. Some rode bicycles around town. Some rode their horses up and down. Some foraged around town through the deserted houses. Some went looking for chickens to cook. Some sat in groups and talked. Some just slept.

*

An order went out against wearing Jap clothing or eating any of the local vegetables, pork, goat, beef or fowl. But this was before the order came out.

The Marines had dug up lots of Japanese kimonos out of the smashed houses and put them on while washing their one set of clothes. If you ever want to see a funny sight, just take a look at a few dozen dirty and unshaven Marines walking around in pink-and-blue women's kimonos.

A typical example was Pvt. Raymond Adams of Fleason, Tennessee. He had fixed himself a dugout right on the edge of a bluff above the river. He had a grand view and a nice little grassy front yard. Out there he had driven stakes and built a fire. He hung his helmet over the fire like a kettle and was stewing a chicken. He had taken off his clothes and put on a beautiful pink-and-white kimono.

Later a friend came along with a Jap bicycle with one pedal off, and Adams tried without much success to ride it up and down a nearby lane.

If there ever is a war play about Marines I hope they include one tough-looking private in a pink-and-white kimono, stewing chicken and trying to ride a one-pedaled bicycle through a shattered Japanese village.

Pvt. Adams is married and has a boy eight months old he has never seen. If the baby could have seen his father that day he would probably have got the colic from laughing so much.

April 25, 1945— . . . One morning I wandered down to our mortar platoon and ran onto a young fellow with whom I have a great deal in common. We are both from Albuquerque and we both have mosquito trouble.

This New Mexico lad was Pfc. Dick Trauth. Both his eyes were swollen almost shut from mosquito bites. At least one of mine is swollen shut every morning. We both look very funny.

Dick still is just a boy. He's seen nineteen months in the Marines and a year overseas. He's a veteran of combat and still he's only seventeen years old. He has one brother in the Marines and another in the army in Germany.

Dick writes letters to movie stars and not long ago he got back a picture of Shirley Temple, autographed to his company just as he had asked her to do. Dick is very shy and quiet and I had a feeling he must be terribly lonesome. But the other boys say he isn't and that he gets along fine. . . .

April 27, 1945— . . . Marines may be killers, but they're also just as sentimental as anybody else.

There is one pleasant boy in our company whom I had talked with but didn't have any little incident to write about him, so didn't put his name down. The morning I left the company and was saying goodbye all around, I could sense that he wanted to tell me something, so I hung around until it came out. It was about his daughter.

This Marine was Corp. Robert Kingan of Cuyahoga Falls, Ohio. He has been a Marine for thirteen months and over here eleven months. His daughter was born about six weeks ago. Naturally he has never seen her, but he's had a letter from her!

It was a V-letter written in a childish scrawl and said: "Hello, Daddy, I am Karen Louise. I was born Feb. 25 at four minutes after nine. I weight five pounds and eight ounces. Your Daughter, Karen."

And then there was a P.S. on the bottom which said: "Postmaster —Please rush. My Daddy doesn't know I am here."

Bob didn't know whether it was actually his wife or his mother-in-law who wrote the letter. He thinks maybe it was his mother-in-law—Mrs. A. H. Morgan—since it had her return address on it.

So I put that down and then asked Bob what his mother-in-law's first name was. He looked off into space for a moment, and then started laughing.

"I don't know what her first name is," he said. "I always just called her Mrs. Morgan!"

This was Pyle's last published column.

Fred Painton: A Tribute

OKINAWA, *April 28, 1945*—This is a column about Fred Painton, the war correspondent who dropped dead on Guam a short time ago.

Fred wrote war articles for *Reader's Digest* and many other magazines. He even gambled his future once writing a piece for the *Saturday Evening Post* about me.

Fred was one of the little group of real old-timers in the European war. He was past forty-nine and an overseas veteran of the last war. His son is grown and in the Army. Fred had seen a great deal of war for a man his age.

He was just about to start back to America when he died. He had grown pretty weary of war. He was anxious to get home to have some time with his family.

But I'm sure he had no inkling of death, for he told me in Guam of his postwar plans to take his family and start on an ideal and easy life of six months in Europe, six in America. He had reached the point where life was nice.

*

Fred Painton was one of the modest people; I mean real down-deep modest. He had no side whatever, no ax to grind, no coy ambition.

He loved to talk and his words bore the authority of sound common sense. He had no intellectualisms. His philosophy was the practical kind. He was too old and experienced and too wise in the ways of human nature to belittle his fellow man for the failures that go with trying hard.

Fred didn't pretend to literary genius but he did pride himself on a facility for production. He could get a thousand dollars apiece for his articles and he wrote a score of them a year. And his pieces, like himself, were always honest. I've known him to decline to do an assignment when he felt the subject prohibited his doing it with complete honesty.

Fred's balding head and crooked nose, his loud and friendly nasal voice, his British Army trousers and short leggings were familiar in every campaign in Europe.

He took rough life as it came and complained about nothing, except for an occasional bout with the censors. And even there he made no enemies for he was always sincere.

There were a lot of people Fred didn't like, and being no introvert everybody within earshot knew whom he didn't like and why. And I have never known him to dislike anyone who wasn't a phony.

*

Fred and I have traveled through lots of war together. We did those bitter cold days, early in Tunisia, and we were the last stragglers out of Sicily.

We both came home for short furloughs after Sicily. The Army provided me with a powerful Number Two air priority, while Fred had only the routine Number Three.

We left the airport at Algiers within four hours of each other on the same morning. I promised Fred I would call his wife and tell her he would be home within a week.

When I got to New York I called the Painton home at Westport, Connecticut. Fred answered the phone himself. He had beat me home by three days on his measly little priority! He never got over kidding me about that.

*

As the war years rolled by we have become so indoctrinated into sudden and artificially imposed death that natural death in a combat zone seems incongruous, and almost as though the one who died had been cheated.

Fred had been through the mill. His ship was torpedoed out from under him in the Mediterranean. Anti-aircraft fire killed a man beside him in a plane over Morocco.

He had gone on many invasions. He was in Cassino. He was ashore at Iwo Jima. He was certainly living on borrowed time. To many it seems unfair for him to die prosaically. And yet . . .

The wear and the weariness of war is cumulative. To many a man in the line today fear is not so much of death itself, but fear of the terror and anguish and utter horror that precedes death in battle.

I have no idea how Fred Painton would have liked to die. But somehow I'm glad he didn't have to go through the unnatural terror of dying on the battlefield. For he was one of my dear friends and I know that he, like myself, had come to feel that terror.

The following is a rough draft of a column Pyle had been preparing for release upon the end of the war in Europe. It was found on his body the day he was killed on Ie Shima, twenty days before the Germans surrendered.

On Victory in Europe

And so it is over. The catastrophe on one side of the world has run its course. The day that it had so long seemed would never come has come at last.

I suppose emotions here in the Pacific are the same as they were among the Allies all over the world. First a shouting of the good news with such joyous surprise that you would think the shouter himself had brought it about.

And then an unspoken sense of gigantic relief—and then a hope that the collapse in Europe would hasten the end in the Pacific.

It has been seven months since I heard my last shot in the European war. Now I am as far away from it as it is possible to get on this globe.

This is written on a little ship lying off the coast of the Island of Okinawa, just south of Japan, on the other side of the world from Ardennes.

But my heart is still in Europe, and that's why I am writing this column.

It is to the boys who were my friends for so long. My one regret of the war is that I was not with them when it ended.

For the companionship of two-and-a-half years of death and misery is a spouse that tolerates no divorce. Such companionship finally becomes a part of one's soul, and it cannot be obliterated.

True, I am with American boys in the other war not yet ended, but I am old-fashioned and my sentiment runs to old things.

To me the European war is old, and the Pacific war is new.

Last summer I wrote that I hoped the end of the war could be a gigantic relief, but not an elation. In the joyousness of high spirits it is easy for us to forget the dead. Those who are gone would not wish themselves to be a millstone of gloom around our necks.

But there are many of the living who have had burned into their brains forever the unnatural sight of cold dead men scattered over the hillsides and in the ditches along the high rows of hedge throughout the world.

Dead men by mass production—in one country after another—month after month and year after year. Dead men in winter and dead men in summer.

Dead men in such familiar promiscuity that they become monotonous.

Dead men in such monstrous infinity that you come almost to hate them.

These are the things that you at home need not even try to understand. To you at home they are columns of figures, or he is a near one who went away and just didn't come back. You didn't see him lying so grotesque and pasty beside the gravel road in France.

We saw him, saw him by the multiple thousands. That's the difference. . . .

NOTES

During Pyle's war-reporting years, many people sent newspaper clippings pertaining to him and his work to the journalism school at Indiana University in Bloomington. Often as not, they neglected to record the name of the publication in which the item appeared, the page number, and the date. I have provided here all such information available and marked these entries with an asterisk.

Page

FRONT QUOTES

v "We have to remember": Eleanor Roosevelt, "My Day," syndicated column, 5 June 1945, *Indianapolis Times.** "We felt most": Randall Jarrell, "Ernie Pyle," *The Nation*, 19 May 1945, p. 570.

INTRODUCTION

xiv "the psychological transition": Pyle column, 22 April 1943.

xv "sense of surging accomplishment": Joseph Kraft, syndicated column, 30 January 1983, Los Angeles Times Syndicate.

xv "That which is most unendurable": Jean Larteguy, *The Face of War: Reflections on Men and Combat,* translated by Beth de Bilio (Indianapolis: Bobbs-Merrill, 1979), p. 17.

BIOGRAPHY

5 "He thought the war": Interview with Paige Cavanaugh by David Nichols, Orange, California, March 1982.

6 "The Ideal Girl": quoted in Lee G. Miller, *The Story of Ernie Pyle* (New York: Viking, 1950), p. 18.

6 "the type who is willing": quoted in *ibid.*,, p. 18.

6 Pyle wedding date: supplied by city clerk's office, Alexandria, Virginia.

6 "for years they made": Miller, p. 35.

7 Pyle's unemployment fears: interview with Paige Cavanaugh.

8 "I will go where I please": quoted in Miller, p. 53.

8 "Many times on this trip": letter to Paige Cavanaugh, 24 February 1940, Manuscripts Department, Lilly Library, Indiana University, Bloomington.

9 Pyle's impotence: Miller referred to this as a "functional incapacity" (p. 69), but Pyle in his correspondence was far less euphemistic. Miller stated the problem was "eventually redressed," though the Pyle letters I read indicate otherwise.

10 "Personally, I'm just about to bust": letter to Paige Cavanaugh, 11 September 1939, Lilly Library.

10 "For the last two weeks": *ibid.*

Page

10 "But to pretend": quoted in Miller, p. 137.

10 "stabbed with great fires": Pyle column, 30 December 1940.

11 "drinking collossally": letter to Paige Cavanaugh, 4 September 1941, Lilly Library.

11 "will stay here": *ibid.*

11 "psychopathic case": quoted in Miller, p. 196.

11 "Because of her futility complex": quoted in *ibid.*, p. 196.

12 Pyle's love affair: letters to Paige Cavanaugh, 27 December 1941, 5 February 1942, 8 August 1942, Lilly Library.

12 "doping and drinking": quoted in Miller, p. 179.

12 "I *can't* give you a child": quoted in *ibid.*, p. 185.

12 "into a realization": quoted in *ibid.*, p. 191.

12 "get to work": quoted in *ibid.*, p. 191.

12 "I'm coming back": quoted in *ibid.*, p. 200.

13 "Stability cloaks you": Ernie Pyle, *Home Country* (New York: William Sloane, 1947), p. 245.

13 "I am all alone": quoted in Miller, p. 200.

14 "regular little boxed-up": letter to Paige Cavanaugh, 29 October 1940, Lilly Library.

14 "As much as I": letter to Jerry Pyle, 26 September 1942, Lilly Library.

14 "My future without you": letter to Jerry Pyle, 29 October 1941, Lilly Library.

14 "something I don't love": letter to Jerry Pyle, 3 November 1941, Lilly Library.

15 "like firecrackers": Pyle column, 9 February 1943.

15 "couldn't help having": *ibid.*

16 "It was just dusk": letter to Jerry Pyle, 21 February 1943, Lilly Library.

16 "I've been at the front": letter to Paige Cavanaugh, 28 February 1943, Lilly Library.

17 "If anybody had ever told me": letter to Jerry Pyle, 21 February 1943, Lilly Library.

17 "some peace with the world": quoted in Miller, p. 244.

17 "tragedy and insanity": letter to Jerry Pyle, 13 March 1943, Lilly Library.

17 "I know I can't escape": *ibid.*

17 "Somehow I can look": Pyle column, 22 April 1943.

17 "at last the enormity": *ibid.*

18 "with a clear conscience": quoted in Miller, p. 259.

18 "older and a little apart": Ernie Pyle, *Here Is Your War* (New York: Henry Holt, 1943), p. 297.

Page

18 "The stress of war": *ibid.*, p. 299.

19 "I'm getting": letter to Jerry Pyle, 11 July 1943, Lilly Library.

19 "death rattle": Pyle column, 9 August 1943.

19 "I find myself": letter to Jerry Pyle, 15 August 1943, Lilly Library.

19 "the war gets so complicated": *ibid.*

19 "I had come to despise": Pyle column, 11 September 1943.

20 "horrible anguish": quoted in Miller, p. 284.

20 "my normal feeling": quoted in *ibid.*, p. 284.

20 "she is the only thing": quoted in *ibid.*, p. 284.

20 "But what can a guy do?": Pyle column, 6 September 1943.

21 "boyish curiosity": Miller, p. 280.

21 Pyle's taxes: letter to Jerry Pyle, 8 November 1943, Lilly Library.

21 "this semi-barbarian life": quoted in *ibid.*, p. 302.

21 "ability to weigh and describe": Pyle column, 11 September 1943.

22 "was probably the most": Frederick C. Painton, "The Hoosier Letter Writer," *The Saturday Evening Post*, 2 October 1943, p. 17.

22 "haven't had anything yet": Pyle column, 6 November 1943.

22 "all the war of the world": Pyle column, 18 January 1944.

23 "a senior partner": Pyle column, 22 February 1944.

23 "I know it ain't": *ibid.*

23 "right": quoted in Miller, p. 317.

23 "in the clasp of": Pyle column, 29 April 1944.

23 "distinguished war correspondence": *The Pulitzer Prize Story*, John Hohenberg, ed. (New York: Columbia University Press, 1959) p. 345.

23 "of course I am": letter to Jerry Pyle, 27 April 1944, Lilly Library.

24 "I'm going to be": letter to Jerry Pyle, 16 May 1944, Lilly Library.

24 "beginning to feel": quoted in Miller, p. 325.

24 "know and appreciate": Pyle column, 12 July 1944.

24 "a large personal impress": A. J. Liebling, "Pyle Set the Style," *New Yorker*, 2 September 1950, p. 69.

25 "some of it": letter to Jerry Pyle, 22 July 1944, Lilly Library.

25 "admit his fear": "Ernie Pyle's War," *Time*, 17 July 1944, p. 65.

25 "without any dignity": letter to Jerry Pyle, 22 July 1944, Lilly Library.

25 "have any premonition": *ibid.*

25 "In fact I": *ibid.*

25 "created a legend": quoted in Miller, p. 347.

25 "all of an instant": Pyle column, 9 August 1944.

Page

25 "an inhuman tenseness": *ibid.*

25 "grateful in a chastened way": Pyle column, 10 August 1944.

25 "chaos and bitterness": *ibid.*

26 "I have had all": Pyle column, 3 September 1944.

26 "humbly—and numbly": quoted in Miller, p. 365.

26 "if you linger": quoted in *ibid.*, p. 366.

26 "real terror": quoted in *ibid.*, p. 147.

26 "wrung and drained": Ernie Pyle, *Brave Men* (New York: Henry Holt, 1944), p. 464.

26 "cringe from the effort": *ibid.*

27 "on the right side": letter to Paige Cavanaugh, 31 October 1944, Lilly Library.

28 "that her indirect threats": quoted in Miller, p. 378.

28 income-tax figure: Miller, p. 383.

28 "Despite all the frenzy": Pyle column, 7 February 1945.

28 "That Girl": Pyle column, 9 February 1945.

29 "I want you bastards": interview with Paige Cavanaugh.

29 "Well, you begin": Robert C. Elliott, Scripps-Howard dispatch, San Francisco, 24 January, 1945.*

29 "I'm sorry, darling": letter to Jerry Pyle, 10 January 1945, Lilly Library.

29 "I'm a long way": quoted in Miller, p. 386.

29 "That has to be up to you": letter to Jerry Pyle, 10 January 1945, Lilly Library.

29 "mystic device": *ibid.*

30 "I think it's the lack": *ibid.*

30 "Ernie is a bit dubious": Robert C. Elliott, Scripps-Howard dispatch, San Francisco, 24 January, 1945.*

30 "go overboard on sympathy": quoted in Miller, p. 392.

30 "island complex": quoted in *ibid.*, p. 392.

30 "Now we are far": Pyle column, 17 February 1945.

31 "just as friendly": Pyle column, 17 March 1945.

31 "The boys ask you": *ibid.*

31 "There's nothing romantic": Pyle column, 6 April 1945.

32 "pitiful": Pyle column, 10 April 1945.

32 "not very clean": *ibid.*

32 "why poverty and filth": *ibid.*

32 "were all shocked": *ibid.*

32 "old familiar pattern": Pyle column, 12 April 1945.

Page

32 "so imbedded in my soul": *ibid.*

32 "faulty": quoted in Miller, p. 408.

32 "fit in with the honor": quoted in *ibid.*, p. 409.

32 "My love reaches": quoted in *ibid.*, p. 409.

33 "the unnatural sight": Pyle column draft, Lilly Library.

33 "the nation is saddened": United Press dispatch, Washington, D.C., 18 April 1945.*

33 "great distress": *ibid.**

33 "unending gratitude": *ibid.**

33 "I have known": *ibid.*

34 "The only difference": United Press dispatch, Rome, 18 April 1945.*

34 " 'That Girl' ": Elizabeth Shaffer, " 'That Girl' Takes News Bravely," Scripps-Howard dispatch, *Rocky Mountain News*, Denver, Colorado, 19 April 1945, p. 16.*

34 "no vice president": Editorial in the *La Porte Herald-Argus*, La Porte, Indiana, 19 April 1945.*

34 "There are many men": Randall Jarrell, "Ernie Pyle," *The Nation*, 19 May 1945, p. 576.

34 "A brave man": *Congressional Record*, 24 May 1945, p. A2652.

35 "certain lines of dialogue": "G.I. Dialogue Banned," *New York Times*, 19 May 1945, p. 15.

35 "such deep feeling": *ibid.*

35 "his own pencilled corrections": "Highest Bidder to Receive Pyle Manuscript at Movie," *Indianapolis Times*, 25 June 1945.*

35 "landscaped, lake-studded": "Protests Pyle Memorial," *New York Times*, 22 August 1945, p. 25.*

35 "honored dead": newspaper editorial; newspaper and date unknown.*

35 footnote: "I hope to God": letter to Paige Cavanaugh, 30 June 1944, Lilly Library.

36 "horrified and indignant": "Protests Pyle Memorial," *New York Times*, 22 August 1945, p. 25.*

36 "entirely out of keeping": Associated Press dispatch, Albuquerque, New Mexico, 21 August 1945.*

36 "consent to having": *ibid.**

36 "Ernie is lying where": *ibid.**

36 "magnificent blast": "Strictly Personal," Sydney J. Harris, newspaper and date unknown.*

36 "vulgar": *ibid.**

36 "living memorials": *ibid.**

36 "reams and reams": Paige Cavanaugh interview.

Page

37 "the foothills of martyrdom": *Home Country*, p. 245.

37 "a kind of unrighteousness": *ibid.*, p. 245.

37 "in real life": *ibid.*, p. 245.

GREAT BRITAIN

41 "a crater in a suburban street": Pyle column, 24 December 1940.

41 "The only thing is": *ibid.*

41 "like something mysterious": Pyle column, 26 December 1940.

NORTH AFRICA

57 "feeling self-conscious": Pyle column, 16 December 1942.

57–58 "finally broke down": Pyle column, 19 December 1942.

58 "The night by its": Pyle column, 21 December 1942.

58 "like twine": Pyle column, 23 December 1942.

133 "It may be": Pyle, p. 303.

133 "worm's-eye view": *ibid.*, p. 304.

133 "tired and dirty soldiers": *ibid.*, p. 304.

133 "It has to be": *ibid.*, p. 303.

133 "those whose final": *ibid.*, p. 302.

133 "they died and other lived": *ibid.*, p. 304.

SICILY

137 "soft underbelly": Louis L. Snyder, *Louis L. Snyder's Historical Guide to World War II* (Westport, Connecticut: Greenwood Press, 1982), p. 123.

137 "unconditional surrender": *ibid.*, p. 124.

137 "somewhat surreptitiously": Pyle column, 12 July 1943.

137 "into the blessedness": *ibid.*

141 "resembled a distant city": Pyle column, 19 July 1943.

141 "youngsters of scant experience": Pyle column, 20 July 1943.

141 "young man who": Pyle column, 22 July 1943.

142 "carrying across this ageless": *ibid.*

142 "pinioned us": Pyle column, 26 July 1943.

142 "alone in the blessed darkness": *ibid.*

144 editor's note: "you ache all over": Pyle column, 7 August 1943.

165 footnote: "HELP WANTED": Pyle column, 6 September 1943.

166 footnote: "I'm grateful": Pyle column, 14 September 1943.

ITALY

171 "the most sincere plaudits": Pyle column, 8 November 1943.

171 "like a deserter": Pyle column, 6 November 1943.

Page
171 "It is one of our": *ibid.*

171 "I've never hated to do": *ibid.*

171 "With us so big": *ibid.*

171 "Materially, it seems": *ibid.*

171 "We haven't had": *ibid.*

172 "The long winter misery": quoted in Miller, p. 294.

183 footnote: Coca-Cola's contribution: E. J. Kahn, Jr., "The Universal Drink," in *Far-flung and Footloose: Pieces from The New Yorker, 1937–1978* (New York: Putnam, 1979), p. 298.

198 footnote: reaction to Willie and Joe's appearance: Miller, p. 310.

199 editor's note: "colorless and anticlimactic": quoted in *ibid.*, p. 306.

233–234 "a great big thing": Pyle column, 21 March 1944.

236 "couldn't help but": Pyle column, 24 March 1944.

France

275 "Being so close": quoted in Miller, p. 321.

275 "nerves": quoted in *ibid.*, p. 328.

275 "I'm sick of living in misery": quoted in *ibid.*, p. 336.

284 editor's note: "Sometimes planes would": Pyle column, 20 June 1944.

304 editor's note: "kept tenaciously": Pyle column, 11 July 1944.

347 footnote: "It saddened me": quoted in Miller, p. 380.

353 footnote: "Anybody who doesn't": quoted in *ibid.*, p. 362.

357 editor's note: "For six weeks": quoted in *ibid.*, p. 362.

359 "It will be odd": Pyle, *Brave Men*, p. 464.

359 "Our feelings have": *ibid.*, p. 464.

359 "become a flat, black depression": *ibid.*, p. 465.

359 "in victory": *ibid.*, p. 465.

359 "all of us together": *ibid.*, p. 466.

The Pacific

386 "We'll start": Pyle column, 14 March 1945.

386 "I had asked": *ibid.*

401 "uninspired and dull": quoted in Miller, p. 403.

403 editor's note: "I felt miserable": Pyle column, 6 April 1945.

405 editor's note: "Marine Corps blitzes": Pyle column, 14 April 1945.

405 "good, human Americans": *ibid.*

418–419 Pyle's victory-in-Europe column: Lilly Library.

BIBLIOGRAPHY

I am indebted to the following books, or sections thereof, for much useful background information.

Allen, Frederick Lewis. *The Big Change: America Transforms Itself, 1900–1950.* New York, 1952.

Blum, John Morton. *V Was for Victory: Politics and American Culture During World War II.* New York, 1976.

Fussel, Paul. *The Boy Scout Handbook and Other Observations.* New York, 1982.

Goodman, Jack (editor). *While You Were Gone: A Report on Wartime Life in the United States.* New York, 1946.

Hodgson, Godfrey. *America in Our Time.* Garden City, New York, 1976.

Karl, Frederick P. *American Fictions: 1940–1980.* New York, 1983.

Keegan, John. *The Face of Battle,* New York, 1976.

Knightley, Phillip. *The First Casualty. From Crimea to Vietnam: The War Correspondent as Hero, Propagandist, and Myth Maker.* New York, 1975.

Larteguy, Jean. *The Face of War: Reflections on Men and Combat.* Indianapolis, 1979.

Lingeman, Richard R. *Don't You Know There's a War On? The American Home Front, 1941–1945.* New York, 1970.

Manchester, William. *The Glory and the Dream: A Narrative History of America, 1932–1972* (two volumes). Boston, 1973.

Perrett, Geoffrey. *Days of Sadness, Years of Triumph: The American People 1939–1945.* New York, 1973.

Robertson, James Oliver. *American Myth, American Reality.* New York, 1980.

Snyder, Louis L. *Louis L. Snyder's Historical Guide to World War II.* Westport, Connecticut, 1982.

Stott, William. *Documentary Expression and Thirties America.* New York, 1973.

INDEX